Communicating in the Workplace

Thomas Cheesebro
Waukesha County Technical College

Linda O'Connor
Waukesha County Technical College

Francisco Rios
University of Wyoming

Prentice Hall
Upper Saddle River, New Jersey
Columbus, Ohio

Library of Congress Cataloging-in-Publication Data

Cheesebro, Thomas
   Communicating in the workplace / Thomas Cheesebro, Linda O'Connor, Francisco Rios.
      p. cm.
   Includes bibliographical references and index.
   ISBN 978-0-13-613691-0 (alk. paper)
1. Business communication. 2. Communication. I. O'Connor, Linda, 1950- II. Rios, Francisco,
1956- III. Title.
HF5718.C452 2010
658.4'5—dc22

Editor in Chief: Vernon Anthony
Acquisitions Editor: Gary Bauer
Editorial Assistant: Megan Heintz
Production Coordination: Carla Kipper/S4Carlisle Publish
Project Manager: Christina Taylor
AV Project Manager: Janet Portisch
Operations Specialist: Pat Tonneman
Art Director: Diane L. Ernsberger
Cover Designer: Ali Mohrman
Cover Images: Jupiter, Banana Stock
Manager, Image Resource Center, Rights and Permissions:
Image Permission Coordinator: Jan Marc Quisumbing
Director of Marketing: David Gesell
Marketing Manager: Leigh Ann Sims
Marketing Assistant: Les Roberts

This book was set in Sabon and was printed and bound by C.J. Krehbiel. The cover was printed by
Lehigh-Phoenix Color Corporation.

Pearson Prentice Hall™ is a trademark of Pearson Education, Inc.
Pearson® is a registered trademark of Pearson plc
Prentice Hall® is a registered trademark of Pearson Education, Inc.

Pearson Education Ltd., London
Pearson Education Singapore Pte. Ltd.
Pearson Education Canada, Inc.
Pearson Education—Japan

Pearson Education Australia Pty. Limited
Pearson Education North Asia Ltd., Hong Kong
Pearson Educación de Mexico, S.A. de C.V.
Pearson Education Malaysia Pte. Ltd.

Prentice Hall
is an imprint of

www.pearsonhighered.com

10 9 8 7 6 5 4 3

ISBN 13: 978-0-13-613691-0
ISBN 10:   0-13-613691-5

To all of our colleagues, friends, and families who continue to teach us how to apply what we know about communication to the complexity and wonder of human relations.

Brief Contents

Contents

Preface

WELCOME TO *COMMUNICATING IN THE WORKPLACE*

Our goal in writing *Communicating in the Workplace* was to create a text suited to the needs of students in technical and career-oriented college programs. The primary focus for these students is to develop communication skills that will ensure their success on the job. This student-friendly text is designed to provide students with a solid working understanding of communication concepts, develop communication skills, and allow students to practice creative applications. *Communicating in the Workplace* accomplishes these three tasks in an engaging manner and with a warm, understandable tone.

Students majoring in career and technology programs, such as business, allied health, nursing, criminal justice, hospitality, graphic design, and various technology programs are generally required to complete an oral communication course. They are preparing for employment in a wide range of occupations and will most often take this course in a diverse classroom setting. Consequently, this text is designed to address the needs of a heterogeneous student body. Though concepts and skills presented in *Communicating in the Workplace* are often presented in a workplace context, they will also be readily applicable to the challenges students will face in school and throughout their career.

ORGANIZATION

Fifteen chapters introduce topics essential to a comprehensive study of oral communication. Each chapter includes learning objectives, readable text, skill-building assignments, discussion questions, self-assessments, and practical applications. In addition, chapters will incorporate a variety of the following: introductory stories, visual summaries, case studies, and web activities.

Chapter 1 highlights the importance of effective communication as a foundation for personal and professional success. It includes a definition of effective communication and explains a process model that introduces the reader to basic terminology. We present communication principles that point to the complexity of human interaction, reminding students that communication occurs in a variety of contexts and at different levels. We also explore common communication barriers that include noise and gaps. Finally, we focus on the role that technology plays in communicating with others.

Chapter 2 explores the role perception plays in everyday communication at school and in the workplace. Special attention is paid to factors that influence one's view of reality. Students will sharpen their awareness of how perception develops and impacts their interpersonal relationships. In addition, students will develop skills to perceive the world around them with greater clarity. These skills include learning the differences between facts and opinions, checking perceptions for accuracy, and stating opinions clearly. Learning conversations provide a strategy for students to share their perceptions and create greater empathy with others. The chapter concludes with a discussion of technology's role in perception and guidelines for becoming effective consumers of the media.

Chapter 3 helps students develop cross-cultural competence. Success at both school and work often depends on communicating effectively with those who have different customs, values, and orientations. Chapter 3 addresses the richness of diversity in its many facets. In this chapter, students will learn principles of and barriers to cross-cultural communication. Furthermore, students will develop a series of skills to increase their competence when communicating with diverse groups of individuals. Finally, students recognize the challenges and opportunities that technology offers in creating a global community.

Chapter 4 begins by examining the power of the spoken word. Students are introduced to the principles that govern effective verbal communication and are provided guidelines needed to achieve clarity, accuracy, and conciseness. Equally important, students will become more sensitive to the role of nonverbal messages in creating shared understanding. Body language, vocal intonation, time, and space are presented with an emphasis on cross-cultural dimensions.

Chapter 5 focuses on receiving verbal and nonverbal messages. The importance of listening is emphasized, along with the types of listening used most frequently. A unique feature of this chapter is the discussion of specific listening skills used at school, at work, and at home. A comprehensive explanation of response styles completes the chapter.

In Chapter 6, students learn about the importance interpersonal relationships. Supportive and defensive relationships are contrasted, with an emphasis on developing an assertive style. Students are introduced to assertive sharing techniques that help them clearly communicate observations, feelings, consequences, and requests to others.

Chapter 7 examines the values and risks of conflict, as well as the types of conflicts students encounter. This chapter explains several conflict management styles including avoiding, accommodating, compromising, forcing, and collaborating. Further, students are introduced to coping skills that will help them deal with criticism.

In Chapter 8, students will discover the principles of small-group communication and engage in teamwork and collaboration activities that develop their skills as team members and leaders. This chapter discusses the importance and benefits of teamwork, analyzes the characteristics of effective teams, outlines the stages of team development, and identifies positive participation skills. Also, students learn about a problem-solving approach called reflective thinking.

Chapter 9 introduces the informative speech preparation process. Students learn to choose a topic, determine a specific purpose, and state a central idea. In addition, they learn four categories from which informative topics can be chosen: tools/mechanisms, processes and procedures, incidents, and ideas. Audience analysis helps students prepare effective and confident presentations.

In Chapter 10, students continue the informative speech preparation process by developing their central ideas with main points. The chapter discusses chronological, spatial, and topical patterns of organization, enabling students to create effective outlines.

Chapter 11 allows students to develop their main points with verbal and visual supports. Students use explanations, examples, statistics, stories, testimonies, and comparisons to expand their outlines. In addition, students review various types of visual supports including objects and models, charts and graphs, lists and tables, and photographs and diagrams. Guidelines are offered for using visuals effectively.

Chapter 12 gives students both direction and confidence to do the research needed for effective presentations. Students explore print and electronic sources for their research. Students also learn to document their sources using APA and MLA styles. Special emphasis is placed on avoiding plagiarism.

In Chapter 13, students make their hard work pay off by reviewing the elements of an effective delivery. Various delivery styles are discussed, such as manuscript, memorized, extemporaneous, and impromptu. Attention is given to nonverbal elements of delivery as well. Finally, students learn strategies for coping with speaker anxiety.

In Chapter 14, students develop persuasive speaking abilities by recognizing the importance of persuasion and the variety of forms that persuasion takes. Elements of persuasion, organizational strategies, and ethical considerations are examined to enhance persuasive appeal. Finally, students make emotional appeals, cite convincing evidence, and increase their credibility with an audience.

Chapter 15 introduces the all important employment interview. Students learn to prepare for, participate in, and follow up after the interview. The chapter includes commonly asked job interview questions including behavior-based and illegal questions. Sample follow-up letters are provided along with a special section on phone interviews.

KEY FEATURES

INSPIRING REAL-LIFE STORIES

Inspiring real-life stories used throughout the text will generate reader interest and reinforce the importance of communication skill development. Students will read about the following:

- William D. Green, chairman and CEO of a $20-billion-dollar company, credits the start of his education at a two-year community college.

- Heidi Golbach, Madison, Wisconsin, police officer, tells how listening accounts for one of her chief law-enforcement skills.

- Nissa Stenz, motorcycle accident survivor, discovered the critical role of teamwork among health care professionals when she was involved in a serious motorcycle accident.

- John Francis, author of *Planetwalker: 22 Years of Walking, 17 Years of Silence*, shares his remarkable communication journey while maintaining seventeen years of self-imposed silence.

- Eric Peterson, U.S. Army Captain, describes his brave attempt to use conflict resolution skills in Iraq between Sunni and Shiite factions.

SELF-ASSESSMENT EXERCISES

In addition, a variety of self-assessments in the text enable students to identify their strengths and areas for improvement in communication. In Chapter 6, Interpersonal Relationship Skills, for example, students identify how assertive they are.

CASE STUDIES

Case studies, a number of which address timely ethical questions, appear at the end of each chapter and challenge students to reflect on communication concepts addressed in the text.

In the Chapter 1 Case Study, students will have an opportunity to discuss their reaction to the tragic story of Megan Meier.

The Chapter 14 Case Study will offer students a chance to persuasively present their own viewpoint on the controversial issue of conceal and carry legislation, particularly as it relates to recent surges of campus violence.

BUILDING COMMUNICATION SKILLS

Skill-building assignments at the end of each chapter are designed to help students strengthen skills and increase self-confidence in using those skills in both personal and occupational settings. Chapters are structured to provide clear, step-by-step explanations, and realistic scenarios that illustrate how and when to use the various skills that are addressed.

Students then take that information and demonstrate their abilities to apply what they have learned in a wide variety of skill-based applications. For example, in Chapter 6, Assignment 6.6, students explore the components of Four-Part Assertion Messages and then construct their own assertive messages.

ONLINE RESOURCES FOR STUDENTS

- **Companion Website.** Go to **www.pearsonhighered.com/cheesebro** to find additional study aids. The companion website includes links to helpful online resources, self-grading chapter quizzes to check your knowledge of chapter topics, chapter learning objectives and summaries, and PowerPoint Chapter Reviews.

RESOURCES FOR INSTRUCTORS

INSTRUCTOR'S MANUAL

- The Instructor's Manual includes a sample course outline, teaching notes, test bank, and answer keys to exercises in the book.

COMPUTERIZED TEST GENERATOR
POWERPOINT LECTURE PRESENTATION PACKAGE

- These supplements are available to download from the Instructor's Resource Center. To access supplementary materials online, instructors need to request an instructor access code. Go to **www.pearsonhighered .com/irc**, where you can register for an instructor access code. Within 48 hours of registering, you will receive a confirming e-mail including an instructor access code. Once you have received your code, locate your text in the online catalog and click on the Instructor Resources button on the left side of the catalog product page. Select a supplement and a login page will appear. Once you have logged in, you can access instructor material for all Prentice Hall textbooks.

COMMUNICATION VIDEOS

- JWA Videos on human relations and interpersonal communication topics are available to qualified adopters. Contact your local representative for details.

ONLINE COURSE SOLUTIONS

- Ready-made **WebCT** and **Blackboard** online courses! If you adopt an online course, student access cards will be packaged with the text, at no extra charge to the student. Online courses include **Research Navigator,** a premium online research tool.

ACKNOWLEDGMENTS

Special thanks to Lisa Pearson for proofreading and editing the manuscript and Lisa Baker for securing permissions, developing the test bank, and designing chapter PowerPoint slides.

We would also like to thank the people who reviewed the manuscript during development and provided insight and guidance to help us refine and complete this textbook:

Carolyn Clark
Salt Lake Community College

Matt Dietsche
Wisconsin Indianhead Technical College–Superior

Dale Dittmer
Chippewa Valley Technical College

Tresha Dutton, Ph.D.
Whatcom Community College

Cindy Ellenbecker
Lakeshore Technical College

Denise Elmer
Southeast Community College Beatrice

Connie Haack-Hurlbut
Mid State Technical Insitute

Deborah Holder
Piedmont Technical College

Alma Martinez-Egger
Tarrant County Junior College NE

Randy Mueller
Gateway Technical College

Beverly Neville
Central New Mexico Community College

Nan Peck
Northern Virginia Community College

Jeff Pomeroy
Southwest Texas Junior College

Larry Richesin
University of Alaska, Fairbanks, Bristol Bay Campus

Christine Saxild
Wisconsin Indianhead Technical College–Ashland

Katherine Taylor
University of Louisville

Robert Zetocha
Southeast Community College-Lincoln

Charles Zimmerman
University of Louisville

We hope that you find this book both useful and interesting to read.

Thomas Cheesebro
Linda O'Connor
Francisco Rios

Credits

Chapter 1

p. 1 © Justin Pumfrey/Getty Images; p. 4 © Villareal; p. 9 Ruth Jenkinson © Dorling Kindersley; p. 15 James Estrin/The New York Times

Chapter 2

p. 29 Peter Chen © Dorling Kindersley; p. 30 Chris Stowers © Dorling Kindersley; p. 32 Andy Crawford © Dorling Kindersley; p. 32 Bill le Fever © Dorling Kindersley; p. 33 Eddie Lawrence © Dorling Kindersley; p. 34 Andrew McKinney © Dorling Kindersley; p. 44 Gary Ombler © Dorling Kindersley; p. 44 Andy Crawford © Dorling Kindersley; p. 47 © Dorling Kindersley

Chapter 3

p. 59 © Dorling Kindersley; p. 64 Neil Setchfield © Dorling Kindersley; p. 66 Andy Crawford/Dorling Kindersley © Imperial War Museum, London; p. 69 Steve Gorton © Dorling Kindersley

Chapter 4

p. 85 Nigel Hicks © Dorling Kindersley; p. 89 © Dorling Kindersley; p. 91 © Dorling Kindersley; p. 92 Justin Slide © Dorling Kindersley; p. 94 © Dorling Kindersley

Chapter 5

p. 104 Andy Crawford © Dorling Kindersley; p. 117 Andy Crawford © Dorling Kindersley

Chapter 6

p. 153 Photodisc/Getty Images

Chapter 7

p. 160 © Dorling Kindersley

Chapter 9

p. 205 Thomas E. Franklin/The Bergen Record/Corbis SABA

Chapter 10

p. 220 Steve Gorton © Dorling Kindersley; p. 221 Tony Souter © Dorling Kindersley

Chapter 12

p. 244 Getty Images; p. 246 Tony Souter © Dorling Kindersley; p. 248 Tony Souter © Dorling Kindersley

Chapter 13

p. 256 Roger Dixon © Dorling Kindersley; p. 269 © Dorling Kindersley; p. 269 © Dorling Kindersley; p. 269 © image100/Alamy

Chapter 14

p. 275 www.smokingisugly.com. Reprinted by permission of Christy Turlington; p. 285 Mark Hamilton © Dorling Kindersley

Communicating in the Workplace

Chapter 1

Communication Concepts

Learning Objectives

At the end of this chapter, you should be able to meet the following objectives:

1. Understand the importance of communication.
2. Explain the elements that make up the communication process.
3. Describe how the five communication principles influence interpersonal relationships.
4. Explain how barriers can interfere with effective communication.
5. Recognize the impact of technology on communication.

"Once a human being has arrived on this earth, communication is the largest single factor determining what kinds of relationships he makes with others and what happens to him in the world about him."

Virginia Satir

Communication Is Important

Congratulations! You have made an excellent choice by enrolling in a community college program that will profoundly affect your future. William D. Green, chairman and CEO of Accenture, made a similar choice back in 1971 (figure 1.1). Green comments in the following excerpt from *Newsweek* (2006):

> If you had told me back in 1971—the year I graduated high school—that I'd be going off to college soon, I would have assured you that you were sorely mistaken. I was the son of a plumber living in western Massachusetts, and we had all assumed that in the end I'd be a plumber too.
>
> I spent the year after high school working in construction. Then one day I went to visit some friends who were students at Dean College, a two-year residential college 45 minutes outside of Boston, and my mind-set began to change. As I walked around campus and listened to my friends talk about their experiences, I realized this was an opportunity to change my path that might not come again—an opportunity to take another shot at learning. So I enrolled at Dean, and I can honestly say it was a life-altering experience. (Green, 2006, p. 22)

FIGURE 1.1 ■ William D. Green, chairman and CEO of Accenture

Today Green is running a global management consulting, technology services and outsourcing company that employs 180,000 workers with $20 billion in revenue. He comments in the article that "there is no doubt that my two years at Dean College not only prepared me for advancing my education and gearing up for a career, but also transformed me as a person. And that's not a bad start no matter where life takes you" (Green, 2006, p. 22).

Whenever Green has the opportunity, he talks to young people, urging them to consider other options than four-year schools. He states, "Junior and community colleges can help them [students] become better equipped to continue their education and to face real-world challenges. These colleges can smooth their transition from high school to work life, provide them with core decision-making skills and teach them how to think and learn" (Green, 2006, p. 22).

Whether you are preparing for a career in nursing, accounting, the culinary arts, or child care at your community college, you will have the opportunity to develop the technical skills needed to excel in your field. However, these technical skills alone are not sufficient. The cultivation of effective communication skills will largely determine the career success and personal satisfaction you experience.

In the spring of 2006, the Conference Board, Corporate Voices for Working Families, the Partnership for 21st Century Skills, and the Society for Human Resource Management surveyed human resource professionals to determine what skills are necessary for two-year college graduates to meet the needs of tomorrow's workforce (figure 1.2). The report noted, "For two-year college graduates, the five most frequently reported applied skills considered 'very important' are *Professionalism/Work Ethic* (83.4 percent),

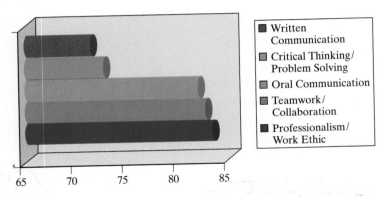

65   70   75   80   85

FIGURE 1.2 ■ Very
Important Skills
*Source: Are They Really
Ready to Work?
Employers' Perspectives on
the Basic Knowledge and
Applied Skills of New
Entrants to the 21st
Century U.S. Workforce,*
by J. Casner-Lotto and
L. Barrington (2006,
October).

Teamwork/Collaboration (82.7 percent), *Oral Communication* (82.0 percent), *Critical Thinking/ Problem Solving* (72.7 percent), and *Written Communication* (71.5 percent)" (Casner-Lotto & Barrington, 2006, p. 20).

We can also explore specific careers, such as law enforcement, to discover the importance of effective communication skills.

According to the National Coalition Building Institute (NCBI), an international and nonprofit leadership training organization based in Washington, DC, "Most situations in protective services are resolved with voluntary compliance. Communication skills are one of the officer's most important weapons on the street. While many hours of instruction are provided on firearms, most officers will use their firearms infrequently throughout their careers. In contrast, effective communication skills are essential on a daily basis, yet very little emphasis is placed on this important skill in most academy training" (NCBI, n.d., p. 2).

Nursing is another field that places emphasis on the importance of effective communication. An article published by the Commonwealth Department of Education, Science, and Training claims that communication skills are essential for a nurse's success. As a social activity, nursing requires excellent interpersonal interactions with patients. Equally important, poor communication skills can lead to tragic consequences for patients and result in costly litigation (Francis, Bowman, & Redgrave, 2001, p. 1).

The article asserts that the communication skills most necessary for nurses are as follows: listening, relationship building, instructing, motivating, exchanging routine information, and giving feedback (figure 1.3).

It is safe to assume that these skills required in nursing and law enforcement are also demanded in other occupational areas. The significance of these skills is discussed in an article titled "Behavior Matters: Communication Research on Human Connections." The article states that communication "is what needs improvement when relationships go poorly, when organizations struggle, or when nations are at an impasse. It is suspect when bad decisions are made, whether communication processes are faulty or not" (National Communication Association, p. 3). On the other hand, the ability to communicate enhances our development, strengthens our self-concept, and increases our ability to influence others. Effective communication makes employment possible, builds stronger relationships with co-workers from diverse backgrounds, and enhances our problem-solving skills.

Development of the skills required for effective communication is what this text is all about. As you read the material that follows, both in this chapter and in upcoming chapters, you will discover information and strategies that will enhance your communication with others. These skills will offer you opportunities for enjoying greater career satisfaction and rewarding personal relationships.

FIGURE 1.3 ■ Necessary Communication Skills

Communication Defined

What is communication? This is the first question to consider before you undertake the study of it. Obviously, communication means different things to different people. To a student in class, it is a means of learning new concepts and skills. To an employee, it is a way of making sure that the job gets done. To those who love us, it is a way of maintaining those relationships. To friends and co-workers, it is the tool that helps us to get along.

Communication is sometimes defined as the process of sending and receiving messages. When a customer explains a problem to you about the exhaust system of a car, a message has been sent, and you have, supposedly, received it. What if the language used, however, is not clear? For example, if the customer says, "Every time I'm driving, my car makes funny noises, and smoke comes from that thing in the back and from that little jobber over yonder." A message has been sent, and you have received it. Communication, as previously defined, has taken place. However, you still do not know what is wrong with the car or how the customer wants the problem fixed.

This situation suggests that more needs to happen for communication to be effective. For one thing, the customer needs to be more specific in describing the problem. You need to listen carefully and ask clarifying questions. The key to effective communication is *shared understanding* of the information. Consequently, a more accurate definition of communication is a shared understanding between the sender and the receiver of the message sent.

In addition, effective communication involves more than just understanding the information. It involves the shared understanding of the feelings, thoughts, wants, needs, and intentions of the communicators, which may not be openly expressed in words. Note that shared understanding and receiving the message are different. For example, you may "get the message" that your boss wants customer accounts filed a particular way, but you may not share her understanding of why or how important this procedure is in the office. When you share her understanding of the message, you sense her meaning and the feelings she has about the message.

Communication Process Model

One way to see how communication works is to examine a process model. A process model for communication is much like an assembly drawing for a mechanism. They both show the internal workings of a complex process in a simplified way. A communication process model breaks down communication into its separate parts and puts it onto a two-dimensional surface for inspection. An interpersonal model of effective communication might look like figure 1.4. Elements of the communication process model are described as follows and are shown in figure 1.5.

SENDER/RECEIVER

The first component of communication is the sender/receiver. It is important to keep in mind that you send and receive messages simultaneously. For example, while you are speaking to someone, you also are receiving nonverbal feedback, enabling you to act as a "transceiver," both sending and receiving messages.

ENCODING

More specifically, senders originate a communication message. An idea comes into mind, and an attempt is made to put this thought into symbols

FIGURE 1.4 ■ Communication Process Model

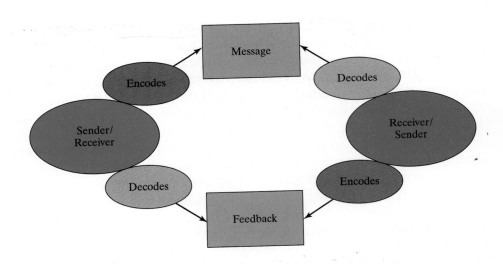

FIGURE 1.5 ■ Communication Process Elements

Communication Process Elements	Definitions
Sender/Receiver	You act as a "transceiver."
Encoding	The process of changing thoughts and feelings into symbols.
Decoding	The process of assigning meaning to symbols.
Message	The idea, thought, feeling, or opinion to be communicated.
Channel	The medium through which the message travels.
Feedback	The receiver's response to the sender's message.

(gestures or words) that the receiver will understand. This process of changing thought into symbols is called encoding.

DECODING

The receiver, who is the destination of the communication message, must assign meaning to the symbols in order to understand the message. This process of assigning meaning to symbols is called decoding. Like encoding, decoding happens so fast, you rarely are aware of its occurrence. As you read and listen, you simply assume you understand what the symbols mean. Each person, sender and receiver, is a product of experiences, feelings, gender, occupation, religion, values, mood, etc. As a result, encoding and decoding are unique for each person. For instance, you could tell a co-worker that your new secretarial job has great benefits and mean you are satisfied because you get a three-week paid vacation. Your co-worker may think that you mean you have family insurance coverage.

MESSAGE

The message is the idea, thought, feeling, or opinion to be communicated. Sometimes the message is clear and direct, such as, "Please help me log onto this computer." Other times the message is unclear, as when a job interviewer says, "We'll keep your application on file." Does this comment mean you will be called for the next vacancy, or is this remark a polite way of saying you are not qualified, and you will never hear from the employer again? In addition, at all times, you are sending several messages simultaneously. Along with the actual content of a message, you may nonverbally be sharing a feeling or defining how you see your relationship with the other person.

CHANNEL

The channel is the medium through which the message travels from sender to receiver. In face-to-face communication, messages are carried by sound and light waves. Though you use sound and light primarily, people can and do use any sensory channel. How a person smells communicates, as does how firmly a person shakes hands. In addition, communication technology is requiring you to communicate in new and different ways. Whether you are using email or voice mail, teleconferencing or audio-conferencing, you need to know how and when to use the proper technology.

FEEDBACK

Feedback is the receiver's response to the message and indicates how the message is seen, heard, and understood, and often how the receiver feels about the message and/or the sender. In the case of oral communication, effective feedback comes after careful listening. Most students and employees spend more time listening than reading, writing, or speaking. Communication experts, in general, estimate that you spend close to 50 percent of your day listening. Part of a listener's responsibility is to provide feedback, making communication a two-person affair, and as important, senders must seek out and attend to the feedback that is offered by their receivers. In interpersonal relationships where understanding is the goal, you will want to stimulate and use as much feedback as possible. In short, feedback is the primary means of increasing personal awareness and establishing a shared understanding. You should give and get as much feedback as possible.

Communication Principles

If you think about the career for which you are preparing, you will probably agree that most careers operate on the basis of certain fundamental principles. Accountants, for instance, balance books, prepare tax documents, and compute payroll by following established accounting principles. Engineers design products and processes, troubleshoot systems, and test new materials using scientific principles. Nurses adhere to ethical principles by treating patients with dignity and respect, being honest and trustworthy in their professional relationships, and maintaining patient confidentiality.

Since communication skills are an integral part of your career, these skills are based upon a set of principles as well. Let's examine some of them.

COMMUNICATION OCCURS WITHIN A CONTEXT

Stop and think for a moment about when, where, why, and with whom you communicate. These factors form the context of your communication with others. Picture this scenario: It is eight o'clock in the morning, and you've had barely four hours of sleep due to a second-shift job (**when**). You're sitting in a hot, stuffy classroom (**where**) listening to an economics lecture on supply and demand (**why**) delivered by an instructor (**whom**) with a monotone delivery that makes it difficult for you to keep your eyes open. Your experience in this instance is likely to be much different than if it were lunchtime (**when**) in the campus cafeteria (**where**), and you were having a lively discussion about an upcoming Super Bowl (**why**) with a group of close friends (**whom**).

Based upon this comparison, you can see how the time of day, the location and purpose of the interaction, and the nature of the relationship all influence the kind of communication that occurs. Being tired, uncomfortable, and bored in the economics classroom, you may not feel inclined to be an active participant. Talking with your friends, on the other hand, in a laid-back setting about a favorite topic will probably stimulate an engaging conversation.

These two examples reveal that your communication with others is influenced by the following contexts:

Physical Context
Influences
Communication

Chronological Context This context represents the time at which communication occurs. The previous examples referred to time of day, but other chronological frameworks can be just as significant. Consider the days of the week, the seasons of the year, and the sequence of events. These factors can also exert a powerful influence on your interaction with others.

Physical Context This context refers to the location or setting of your communication. In addition, the location influences the way you send and receive messages. For example, your communication will be different if you are in a classroom, an office cubicle, a posh restaurant, or a neighborhood bar.

Functional Context This context reflects the purpose of the communication. You communicate to fulfill **practical** needs such as securing a job, renting an apartment, and maintaining your health and safety. You also communicate to satisfy **social** needs. As a human being, you desire to establish connections with others. Building these ties contributes to your sense of belonging and well-being. Finally, you communicate to facilitate **decision making**. Generally, the more information you receive, the better decisions you make. These decisions can range from deciding how to dress for the weather to what job to take, where to live, and whom to marry.

Relational Context This context is determined by the person or persons with whom you are communicating and the type of relationship you have with these individuals. Obviously, what you say and how you say it will change depending upon whether you are talking to your spouse, a total stranger, your boss, or a prospective date.

Cultural Context Finally, this context reflects diversity factors that impact interpersonal relationships. They include race, ethnicity, gender, age, sexual orientation, disabilities, and so on. As an example, imagine that you are

Relational Context Influences Communication

Cultural Context Influences Communication

communicating with someone from a different culture. This individual may prefer to stand closer and establish more eye contact than you find comfortable. Maybe your co-worker is more relaxed about time, a perspective that you find annoying when there is work to be done. In addition, cultural context can include **corporate culture**—the way employees view their place of employment. In some companies, for instance, employees may feel comfortable approaching their supervisor who has an open door policy. These employees may also be encouraged to contribute new ideas, participate in decision making, and further their education. In contrast, other companies may discourage involvement, preferring that employees punch in, do their jobs, and punch out. Obviously corporate culture is a significant influence in determining productivity, morale, and personal satisfaction.

COMMUNICATION IS UNAVOIDABLE

Try to stop communicating. What would you do? Leave? Sleep? Go into a corner with your iPod? If nothing else, you would communicate a desire *not* to communicate. Although you may associate communication with the spoken word, nonverbal cues can be just as powerful when it comes to sending and receiving information.

John Francis, Ph.D., and author of the book *Planetwalker: 22 Years of Walking, 17 Years of Silence,* is a testimony to the vital nature of nonverbal communication in human interaction (figure 1.6). A social activist, particularly concerned about the environment, Francis gave up the use of motor vehicles in 1971 after seeing a massive oil spill in San Francisco Bay. Many looked upon his decision as crazy and told him that one person alone couldn't make a difference. He decided that he didn't want to spend the rest of his life arguing, so on his birthday, he gave up speaking for one day. That day, he

FIGURE 1.6 ■ John Francis, Ph.D., A Social Activist Who Used Silence as a Form of Communication

realized he hadn't been listening, so he decided to be quiet for another day. Those two days eventually turned into 17 years of silence, during which he founded a nonprofit organization (Planetwalk.org) and started walking across the country. Even more amazing is the fact that Francis earned a master's degree and Ph.D. in environmental studies at the University of Wisconsin without speaking (Francis, 2006).

Francis' primary means of communication included improvised sign language, notes, and his ever-present banjo. "For the first time, he found he was able to truly listen to other people and the larger world around him, transforming his approach to both personal communication and environmental activism" (Hertsgaard, 2005, p. 1).

Francis' experience also illustrates the **intrapersonal** dimension that makes communication unavoidable. Whether or not you are in the presence of others, you engage in a continual internal monologue that judges, comments, worries, dreams, and analyzes. Silencing that inner voice would be almost as impossible as trying to live without breathing. Francis comments, "As I entered into the silence, I discovered lots of things about myself—some painful; all illuminating. It became a journey of self-discovery" (Francis, 2006, p. 78).

COMMUNICATION OCCURS AT DIFFERENT LEVELS

Stop and think for a moment about the ways you talk to those with whom you live, work, and socialize. A bit of reflection will probably convince you that the nature and depth of your communication occurs on a variety of levels. The intimate sharing of feelings, hopes, and fears that you may do with family members and close friends is likely to be very different than the conversations you have with fellow employees or casual acquaintances.

It is important to remember that because no two of your relationships with others is exactly alike, the levels at which you communicate are going to be different as well. Author John Powell in his book, *Why am I Afraid to Tell You Who I Am?* (1969), explained that people reveal themselves on different levels. Following are four levels that you may have experienced in your communication.

Small Talk This level of conversation enables you to establish contact with others and build rapport. Greeting a fellow classmate in the hall, talking with an acquaintance about the weather, or introducing yourself to someone you don't know at a party can all be considered small talk. The content is not as important as the interpersonal contact this type of conversation provides. In some cases, your communication with others will never go beyond this level. In other instances, small talk serves as an icebreaker, leading to more substantive content as the relationship develops.

Information Talk This level of conversation occurs after you have gotten to know someone and feel more comfortable sharing information. The type of information shared can include hobbies and interests, likes and dislikes, personal preferences, and so on. In a workplace setting, co-workers use information to get their jobs done. Whether an automotive service writer explains to a technician what repairs need to be performed on a vehicle or a team of marketing assistants strategize an ad campaign, both are using information to accomplish their objective.

Opinion Talk   This level of communication is somewhat riskier than the other two levels already described. At this point, you are willing to let others know what you think about various subjects. Co-workers voicing political viewpoints over lunch, classmates telling each other the perspectives they have on the school grading policies, and friends critiquing the latest release of a new interactive video game are all engaging in opinion talk. Whenever you share your opinions, you open yourself to criticism from others. In addition, the disagreement that arises from differences of opinion can escalate into conflicts. Quite often the basis of those conflicts involves attempts to convince someone that your viewpoint is the "right" one. If you recognize that opinions simply represent personal perspectives, all of which are subject to error, you may be less inclined to engage in pointless argumentation.

An ancient parable from India called *The Blind Men and the Elephant* illustrates the limitations of personal perspectives or viewpoints (figure 1.7).

Feelings Talk   This level of communication is frequently the most challenging of all because when you share feelings with others, you expose parts of your innermost selves. Such exposure can make you feel vulnerable or subject to hurt, criticism, and ridicule. Think of the difficulty you may experience when you risk expressing any of the following: "I'm angry about that"; "I love

American poet John Godfrey Saxe (1816–1887) based this poem, *The Blind Men and the Elephant,* on a fable that was told in India many years ago. It is a good warning about how our sensory perceptions can lead to misinterpretations.

(Continued)

It was six men of Indostan
   To learning much inclined,
Who went to see the Elephant
   (Though all of them were blind),
That each by observation
   Might satisfy his mind.

The First approached the Elephant,
   And happening to fall
Against his broad and sturdy side,
   At once began to bawl:
"God bless me! but the Elephant
   Is very like a wall!"

The Second, feeling of the tusk,
   Cried, "Ho! what have we here
So very round and smooth and sharp?
   To me 'tis mighty clear
This wonder of an Elephant
   Is very like a spear!"

The Third approached the animal,
   And happening to take
The squirming trunk within his hands,
   Thus boldly up and spake:
"I see," quoth he, "the Elephant
   Is very like a snake!"

The Fourth reached out an eager hand,
   And felt about the knee.
"What most this wondrous beast is like
   Is mighty plain," quoth he;
"'Tis clear enough the Elephant
   Is very like a tree!"

The Fifth, who chanced to touch the ear,
   Said: "E'en the blindest man
Can tell what this resembles most;
   Deny the fact who can
This marvel of an Elephant
   Is very like a fan!"

(Continued)

The Sixth no sooner had begun
   About the beast to grope,
Than, seizing on the swinging tail
   That fell within his scope,
"I see," quoth he, "the Elephant
   Is very like a rope!"

And so these men of Indostan
   Disputed loud and long,
Each in his own opinion
   Exceeding stiff and strong,
Though each was partly in the right,
   And all were in the wrong!

Moral:
So oft in theologic wars,
The disputants, I ween,
Rail on in utter ignorance
Of what each other mean,
And prate about an Elephant
Not one of them has seen!

FIGURE 1.7 ■ *The Blind Men and the Elephant* Highlights How Our Sensory Perceptions Can Lead to Incorrect Conclusions
Source: Used with permission from www.wordinfo.info.

you"; "I'm feeling afraid." However, taking the risk to share your feelings has some significant benefits as well. Sharing feelings with family promotes intimacy. Researchers are also finding that sharing feelings has a positive effect on surviving serious illnesses. According to a Reuters Health article, one study indicates that sharing thoughts, feelings, and fears of breast cancer survivors can reduce the "effect that negative thoughts can have on quality of life" (Reuters Health, 2000–2005, p. 1). The article goes on to point out that "survivors who disclosed their hopes, fears and concerns with people who were close to them had a better mental and physical quality of life than those who did not share their feelings, regardless of their cancer treatment" (Reuters Health, 2000–2005, p. 1).

"The results of this study suggest that social support may be an important buffer to long-term negative effects of cancer and its treatment on the lives of long-term survivors," Julie A. Lewis of Children's National Medical Center in Washington, DC, and colleagues write in the *Journal of Behavioral Medicine* (Reuters Health, 2000–2005, p. 1).

COMMUNICATION REQUIRES ETHICAL CHOICES

Of all of the freedoms you possess as Americans, perhaps one that you value most is the right to free speech. You only need to turn on the radio or television, at any time of the day or night, to discover an endless variety of talk shows ranging from the latest Hollywood gossip to projections about the state of the economy. However, from an ethical standpoint, freedom of speech does not mean that you have the right to say anything you please. Certainly, what you say can nurture others, resolve misunderstandings, and create intimacy. On the other hand, your words can strain relationships, destroy trust, or land you in jail. In other words, your communication choices carry with them a certain responsibility.

Consider, for example, the Enron Corporation scandal, representing one of the most notorious bankruptcy cases in U.S. history. Enron had been the nation's seventh largest publicly traded company with a market value exceeding $77 billion ("Enron Scandal Mushrooms," 2002, p. 1). However, this highly successful company essentially collapsed when it was discovered that its apparent financial status was the result of internal accounting fraud. Unfortunately, investors and employees lost life savings because of the unethical practices of the company.

In addition, you need only read the daily newspaper or listen to the nightly news to learn about political figures who lose credibility with their constituents all because of a thoughtless remark. Even formal apologies fail to repair the damage that has already been done.

On a smaller scale, you can find incidents of plagiarism on college campuses when students neglect to give credit to authoritative sources used for class assignments. Penalties for such careless use of speech can range from failing a course to being expelled from school.

In the workplace, unethical communication can occur when employees falsify records, make inaccurate claims about products or services, withhold information that jeopardizes safety, or engage in some form of harassment.

Unethical Choices in Communication Can Have Far-reaching Ramifications

COMMUNICATION HAS ITS LIMITATIONS

This final principle acknowledges that communication cannot solve all of your interpersonal problems. Although becoming an effective communicator can greatly enhance your relationships with family, friends, and co-workers, the complexity of human nature demands many other skills to make relationships work. These skills require you to be committed, flexible, open to change, willing to adjust, forgiving, and the list could go on and on.

In addition, factors such as day-to-day stresses, psychological problems, substance abuse, or financial strains can threaten the stability of your relationships at home, work, or school. Many times these problems cannot be resolved only by "talking them out." They may call for major behavioral and attitudinal shifts, along with professional intervention.

A *Time Magazine* article by Amy Dickinson underscores the point that your most intimate connections with others, as in marriage, also require hard work and commitment. She refers to Natalie Low, Ph.D., a clinical psychologist and instructor at Harvard.

> Low comments that the couples she sees "are trying to nurture their relationships along with raising perfect kids and maintaining careers, but in this compartmentalized era, they are without the benefit of support systems of extended families and communities." But "the facts of life are very grinding, so the reality of marriage is grinding," says Low, who has been married for 51 years. "Marriage is now, as it has been, hard work. Marriage is not a static event that can be measured, but a series of developments—those triumphs and setbacks—that make up life. There is no obvious course to follow, so couples just have to keep working. A person sees dramatic changes during a marriage," Low says, "so a couple has to be committed to a way of life." (1999, p. 112)

Apart from your personal life, relationships in the workplace can be just as demanding. Working with a difficult boss, co-worker, or customer can create stresses that require you to develop a host of coping skills that do not solely include communication. For example, you may work with individuals who have argumentative personalities, critical natures, or unpleasant dispositions. Although you can use your most effective communication skills, you may also need to accept these individuals just as they are. In addition, you may opt to avoid contact with those you find difficult, if that is possible, or change your own attitudes when you are with those persons.

On a larger scale, you need only look at the problems faced by nations who are attempting to live in harmony with one another in the global community. Peace summits, cease-fire talks, and international accords seem never ending, and yet unrest and hostility still exist among nations. Communication alone is not likely to resolve deeply ingrained differences that are the result of religion, values, or ideological views.

Communication Barriers

On the surface, the communication process may seem pretty simple and straightforward. You need a sender, a message, a channel, and a receiver. However, this process can be affected by a number of factors that make understanding difficult, if not seemingly impossible. These barriers can be grouped under two major headings: noise and gaps.

NOISE

Three types of noise contribute to communication breakdowns. These types include internal, external, and semantic noise.

Internal Noise   Although you may think of noise as an environmental distraction, it can also occur inside of both the sender and the receiver. Stop and think for a moment about your own personal barriers. The beliefs you hold, the values you cherish, and the assumptions you make influence how you send and receive messages (figure 1.8). Let's say, for example, that you believe in gender equality in the workplace and that your supervisor has a different point of view. Chances are you may have a hard time convincing this supervisor that both genders are equally capable of performing their tasks well. It may even be that one gender or the other is denied advancement opportunities because of the supervisor's position.

Beliefs	Assumptions
Values	Defensiveness

FIGURE 1.8 ▪ Sources of Internal Noise

Consider a conversation over lunch in which a co-worker expresses his or her values about gay rights. If your values are unlike the co-worker's, you could have a hard time even hearing the co-worker out. Faulty assumptions can also be the basis for misunderstandings. An abrupt comment from your boss might be interpreted to mean he or she is upset with you. A significant other who breaks a date at the last minute might have you wondering if the relationship is in trouble. Although making these assumptions is perfectly normal, believing them to be true can result in unnecessary concern or anxiety.

In addition, when your beliefs and values are in conflict with those of others or when you make faulty assumptions, emotions can surface and present another form of internal noise. When listening to a powerful motivational speaker or a skillful persuader, for example, audience members may become overly enthusiastic. Such reactions can short-circuit reasoning and prevent the listeners from receiving the information objectively. On the other hand, hostile or defensive responses can occur when speakers present disagreeable or offensive topics. As a result, listeners may mentally block out incoming messages, plan a response to the attack, or distort what is being said. In addition, "trigger" words or "hot buttons" can evoke strong emotional responses in the listener, although reactions to these words vary from person to person. Emotional words for some may include political labels, profanities, ethnic slurs, or stereotypes. Being aware of terms, phrases, or topics that create an emotional response in both you and the people with whom you interact is a necessary first step in overcoming this barrier. Recognize that people have different views of the world and that these differences can enrich relationships. Adopting a curiosity about other viewpoints and why they exist will also be helpful.

Another type of internal noise can occur in the form of defensiveness. The tendency to misinterpret another's comments as a personal attack when that was not the intention is typical of defensiveness. For example, to make conversation, you might ask if a co-worker has heard about the missing equipment in the storage room; the co-worker might assume that you are making an accusation of theft and react defensively. As another example, an employer might mention that certain employees are not working to their full capacity. Some of the employees may assume that the employer is talking about them. Defensiveness can be minimized by developing an accurate self-concept, by checking possible interpretations with the speaker, and by sharing thoughts and feelings honestly.

External Noise External noise occurs outside of both sender and receiver. Maybe you work in a busy retail setting where background music and talkative customers compete for your attention while you're answering the phone. Sitting in a classroom lecture when construction work is taking place right outside the window could make it hard for you to hear. Trying to talk to your date at a wedding reception where a few hundred people are conversing at nearby tables might make it difficult to understand one another. Unlike internal noise, external noise may be easier to control by moving to a quieter location or closing a window. However, in other instances, you may be required to speak and listen as best you can in spite of the distractions. Technology also gives rise to various forms of external noise. When the battery is running low on your cell phone, for instance, you may experience difficulty completing a conversation with a friend; network problems might bring a halt to a video conference; a mechanical error in your car's CD player could make it impossible for you to listen to the review lecture you downloaded for one of your classes. Examples such as these often require professional assistance and patience on your part while you wait for the problems to be resolved.

Semantic Noise Semantic noise, the third type of noise, occurs when the receiver of a message doesn't understand a word or gesture used by the sender or has a different meaning for the word or gesture. This type of barrier can be particularly apparent when you converse with people from diverse cultures. When an East Indian co-worker, for example, talks about "garden eggs" and "blowers," would you have any clue that this worker was referring to eggplants and windbreaker jackets? Also be careful with the gestures you choose when communicating in a cross-cultural setting. To you, the V sign may signal "victory," but someone from a different culture may see it as a symbol of profanity.

Semantic noise is also evident when technicians use jargon with laypersons. Information systems personnel may use acronyms like OLAP (online analytical processing) or NTFS (new technology file system) that leave unfamiliar listeners totally clueless.

In addition, when a supervisor tells you to complete the semi-annual inventory report ASAP, does the supervisor mean drop whatever you're doing or make this report next in line?

Describing the kinds of noise that interrupt communication is one thing; figuring out what to do about these noises is more difficult. One strategy for reducing internal noise is to stay focused on the message by increasing your concentration. In addition, being aware of the topics and words that arouse strong emotions is another important step. With external noise, you need to eliminate distractions by tuning them out, asking others to speak up, or changing locations. Finally, to reduce semantic noise, you must be aware that people often have different meanings for the same words. Ask questions and paraphrase to clarify meanings and confirm understanding.

GAPS

Gaps represent another barrier to effective communication because people are different. These gaps can result from a variety of differences including gender, age, ethnicity, race, status, and sexual orientation. Consider, for example, the gender gap.

Author Deborah Tannen, in her book *Talking from Nine to Five*, explores the communication gaps that can result when men and women in the workplace communicate with one another. Although each person has his or her unique style of communicating, Tannen observes that a number of these styles do, in fact, seem to be gender based. For instance, in general, women give orders indirectly, offer praise and compliments more often, and establish more eye contact when conversing. Men, in general, give orders directly, offer praise and compliments less often, and use less eye contact when conversing. Certainly these traits are not true for all men and women. However, recognizing the existence of common patterns can help us to better understand those of the opposite gender (Tannen, 1994).

Generation gaps provide another illustration of potential communication barriers. In recent years, categories have emerged in an attempt to classify groups of individuals on the basis of when they were born.

The Generation Mirage (Hudson, 2005) groups these individuals as shown in figure 1.9.

Information abounds about the characteristics of individuals who fall within these groupings. For instance, the Silent Generation is depicted as hard working, economically conservative, and possessing strong moral values. Further on the spectrum, Generation Y is described as materialistic, self-centered, and technologically savvy. While research seems to indicate that these patterns reflect generational stereotypes, it is reasonable to conclude that those born during the Great Depression of the 1920s and '30s, for example, are likely to have a different worldview than those born in the 1980s and '90s, a period of greater economic prosperity.

Generation Category	Year of Birth
Silent Generation	1929–1945
Baby Boomers	1946–1964
Generation X	1965–1977
Generation Y	1978–1994
Generation Z	1995–2005

FIGURE 1.9 ■ The Generations by Category

COMMUNICATION AND TECHNOLOGY

When Play Station 3, Sony's seventh-generation–era video game console, hit the market, consumers lined up outside retail stores nationwide days in advance of the sale. A Milwaukee-area Best Buy provided turf for eager gamers to set up tents and lawn chairs, making themselves as cozy as possible as they braved the brisk November temperatures. News articles even told of prospective buyers trying to sell their place in line for $500. Such incidents indicate that computer technology is here to stay.

The popularity of computer technology is by no means limited to gaming alone. In fact, education is capitalizing on this popularity by making instruction more appealing to computer-savvy students.

An article by Sandy Cullen in the *Madison State Journal* (2006) discussed how University of Wisconsin-Madison students are using iPods. To help students absorb the material presented in lectures, "some instructors have begun making their lectures and supplemental material available as podcasts—audio and video files that students can access online, download to their personal computers and put on their iPods" (p. 1).

The result of this technology is that students can replay important information at their convenience. Working out at the gym, taking a long bike ride, or making the commute to school provide opportunities for reviewing course content before a major exam. UW-Madison student Kelly Egan comments that her life has been made easier now that she can listen to her lectures again and hone in on the information her professor has emphasized (Cullen, p. 1).

Some additional facts of interest come from a 2006 survey conducted by UW-Madison's Division of Information Technology:

Nearly 70 percent of students have used an online course-management system.
Laptop computer ownership surpassed desktop ownership for the first time:
Almost two-thirds of students own a laptop, compared to 46 percent of students who own a desktop computer.
More than half of laptop owners use wireless Internet in their homes.
Seventy-nine percent of students own a cell phone.
More than half of students own a portable music or video player.
Students use the Internet an average of 19 hours per week. (Cullen, p. 3)

Given these trends, we might well ask how technology will impact communication. Certainly, students and workers alike need to become computer literate. Gone are the days when computer skills were relegated to information systems personnel. Nowadays, students are expected to word process assignments, email instructors, and access course materials over the Internet. Workers need to email customers and clients, enter information into databases, and take part in videoconferencing.

Apart from technical "know-how," we all need to acknowledge how technology demands adjustments in our communication styles. For example, an article on videoconferencing entitled "Seven Steps to a Vital Videoconference" (2004) offered the following suggestions for participants (figure 1.10):

Even though technology offers seemingly endless potential for communicating with others, some claim that this potential does not come

Prepare. Preparation requires participants to familiarize themselves with the technology before showing up to speak.

Pause and Listen. Time delays may occur, so participants need to wait for a response before making their next comments.

Use Small Gestures. Because movements are amplified during videoconferencing, expansive gestures can result in "distorted, fuzzy images."

Appoint a Moderator. Moderators can facilitate the meeting as well as operate the technology, thereby freeing participants to focus on their message.

Dress for TV. Distracting jewelry, shiny outfits, and bold prints should be avoided.

Create a Connection. Start off with hellos. Waves are also standard forms of greeting in videoconferencing.

Minimize Distractions. Keep noise down, turn off beepers and cell phones, and consider posting a "Do Not Enter" sign on the door.

FIGURE 1.10 ■ Seven Steps to a Vital Videoconference
Source: DiResta, D. (2004, pp. 1–2).

without a price. Syndicated columnist Ellen Goodman raises such concerns in her editorial "Technology Has Weakened Our Connections."

She indicates that the swiftness and efficiency of communication technology also contributes to a more hectic, stressful lifestyle. Along with the desire for innovative ways to stay in touch with one another, we actually have become less connected to those around us, including colleagues, friends, and family (Goodman, 2005, B9). In other words, email and text-messages are "short and sweet," but what about the comfort and support we can give each other when we just sit and talk about what matters most to us over a cup of coffee? Internet chat rooms may offer exciting opportunities to meet new acquaintances, but what about the time many spend in front of a computer screen instead of looking into the eyes of a spouse, child, or close friend?

Maybe what we can take away from Goodman's editorial is the need to find balance in our communication with others. Although technology offers us speed and convenience, face-to-face contact nurtures the connections that transform encounters into relationships.

"Cell phone...must...have... cell...phone."

Source: www.CartoonStock.com.

Review Questions

1. Briefly explain three specific situations where communication skills will be important in your future occupation.

2. Your text states that the goal of effective communication is to achieve "shared understanding." Explain what shared understanding means. Provide three suggestions that you think would make this goal more likely to occur between senders and receivers.

3. The section "Communication Process Model" mentions that when communicating, you function as a "transceiver." Describe two situations where you were a transceiver, both sending and receiving messages simultaneously.

4. Communication occurs within a context. Describe the physical, functional, relational, and cultural context of an interaction you recently had with someone else.

5. Give some recent examples of messages you have sent to others at each of the following levels:
   a. Small talk
   b. Information talk
   c. Opinions talk
   d. Feelings talk

6. Find a short article from a magazine, newspaper, or Internet site that illustrates the relationship between communication and ethics. Provide a brief summary of the article.

7. Describe one of the barriers discussed in chapter 1 with which you have some difficulty. What makes this barrier especially troublesome for you? List two steps you think you could take to minimize this barrier.

8. Brainstorm a list of at least three advantages and three disadvantages of communication technology.

Key Terms and Concepts

Channel 7

Chronological Context 9

Cultural Context 10

Decoding 7

Effective Communication 4

Encoding 6

External Noise 18

Feedback 7

Feelings Talk 12

Functional Context 9

Gaps 19

Information Talk 11

Internal Noise 17

Message 7

Opinion Talk 12

Physical Context 9

Receiver 6

Relational Context 9

Semantic Noise 18

Sender 6

Small Talk 11

Web Activities

- For an interesting view of future trends in communication and technology check out "Did You Know; Shift Happens–Globalization; Information Age" on You Tube at http://youtube.com/watch?v=ljbI-363A2Q.

- A mini tutorial of the communication process and other aspects of communication is provided by Happy Fun Communication Land at http://www.rdillman.com/HFCL/TUTOR/ComProcess/ComProc1.html.

- An interactive PowerPoint presentation presents "Noise in the Communication Process" at http://www.wisc-online.com/objects/index_tj.asp?objID=OIC2501.

Assignments

ASSIGNMENT 1.1: COMMUNICATION PROCESS MODEL

Directions: Think of a misunderstanding you experienced when communicating with someone else at work, home, or school. Then fill in the blanks of the chart below.

Who was the sender?	
Who was the receiver?	
What was the message?	
What channel was used to send the message?	
What was the misunderstanding that occurred?	
How could the misunderstanding have been avoided?	

Bring your completed chart to class for sharing in small groups. After each group member has shared his or her example with other group members, answer the following questions:

1. What did you learn about the communication process from this activity?
2. What seemed to be the main causes of the misunderstandings?
3. What tips can you suggest for preventing misunderstandings in communication?

Each group will report its responses to the rest of the class.

ASSIGNMENT 1.2: FEEDBACK EXERCISE

This exercise will help you discover the importance of feedback as it relates to creating a shared understanding. Read the following instructions before you begin.

1. To complete this assignment, work with another student.
2. Each of you will have five 3x5 cards on a table or desk in front of you.

3. Sit so that the two of you are back to back, facing away from one another.
4. The student who is the sender will place one set of 3x5 cards in an arrangement.
5. The sender will then give directions to the receiver explaining how to arrange the other set of cards so that the receiver's arrangement matches the sender's.
6. The receiver may not provide any verbal or nonverbal feedback to the sender.
7. In the table below, note the following information under Arrangement 1:
   a. Accuracy: How many of the receiver's cards were in the same positions as the sender's cards?
   b. Confidence: How sure were both of you that your cards matched the sender's cards?
   c. Time: How much time was needed to arrange the cards?

	Arrangement 1 Without Feedback	Arrangement 2 With Feedback
Accuracy		
Confidence		
Time		

8. After this exchange, have the sender rearrange the cards and give directions for the revised arrangement.
9. This time have the receiver provide as much feedback as needed to create a shared understanding of the sender's directions.
10. In the previous table, under Arrangement 2, note information as you did with item 7.

Answer the following questions after completing this feedback assignment.

1. Which arrangement took longer explaining? Why?
2. Which arrangement was more frustrating to listen to?
3. Which arrangement had the higher degree of accuracy?
4. Which arrangement had the higher level of confidence?
5. What conclusions can you draw from this assignment about the role of feedback in communication?

ASSIGNMENT 1.3: COMMUNICATION TIPS PRESENTATION

Find a two- to three-page article that provides helpful suggestions for overcoming barriers or improving workplace communication. You can find articles online or in the periodical section of your school or local library.

Make a photocopy of the article and prepare a typed summary of the key information contained in the article.

You will turn in the photocopy and typed summary to your instructor and present a two- to three-minute presentation to your class, sharing with them what you learned.

ASSIGNMENT 1.4: PERSONAL EXPERIENCE TALK

The goal is to increase your confidence in speaking before groups. You are asked to share a personal experience from your life and explain the lesson you learned from that experience.

The guidelines for this speech experience are as follows:

1. Choose a personal experience that was meaningful and true. The talk may be serious or humorous. The experience you share should also be one you feel will be of interest to the class.
2. Be sure to share all the necessary details of the experience by including answers to the questions of who, what, where, when, and why. Create a storytelling atmosphere by using specific and vivid language.
3. Finish your talk with a short and clear statement of what you learned from the experience.
4. The amount of time suggested for this presentation is between two and three minutes.
5. Practice the speech several times before the actual classroom presentation. Practice in front of a friend and ask for improvement suggestions.
6. Include *who, where, when, what,* and *why* in your talk. You are encouraged, however, to speak extemporaneously—carefully prepared but delivered without notes.

ASSIGNMENT 1.5: COMMUNICATION SELF-ASSESSMENT

This survey is intended to give you an opportunity to see your strengths and weaknesses as they relate to your communication abilities. This survey is not going to be used by any person other than yourself, so you should be honest in answering the questions. When completed, this survey will give you some idea of which areas you may want to pay particular attention to as you proceed through the course.

Scoring should be based on the following scale:

3 points = a definite strength
2 points = an area needing improvement
1 point = a definite weakness

____ 1. Able to define effective communication.
____ 2. Give and receive feedback.
____ 3. Communicate with sensitivity to ethical considerations.
____ 4. Seek to minimize communication barriers.
____ 5. Use communication technology appropriately.
____ 6. Recognize the limitations of first impressions.
____ 7. Understand the origins of your perceptions.
____ 8. Believe that not everyone views the world in the same way.
____ 9. Separate facts from opinions.
____ 10. Check the accuracy of perceptions you have.
____ 11. Value diverse traditions and customs.
____ 12. Recognize intercultural communication styles.
____ 13. Communicate with sensitivity to cultural differences.
____ 14. Recognize stereotyped treatment of others.
____ 15. Work to overcome personal biases.
____ 16. Understand that words can have multiple meanings.
____ 17. Use specific language to communicate ideas.
____ 18. Seek clarification of ambiguous nonverbal cues.
____ 19. Use nonverbal cues to enhance the verbal messages.

_____ 20. Appreciate the role of nonverbal communication in human interaction.

_____ 21. Listen attentively without distraction.

_____ 22. Respond to others in a way that shows you are listening.

_____ 23. Detect main ideas and supporting facts.

_____ 24. Use clarifying questions to promote understanding.

_____ 25. Summarize information and feelings you receive from others.

_____ 26. Build satisfying relationships.

_____ 27. Maintain satisfying relationships.

_____ 28. Repair troubled relationships.

_____ 29. Treat others with respect.

_____ 30. Share feelings, opinions, and wants confidently.

_____ 31. Recognize different types of conflicts.

_____ 32. Choose appropriate styles of conflict management.

_____ 33. Identify the benefits of conflict.

_____ 34. Avoid destructive behaviors in conflict.

_____ 35. Respond appropriately to criticism.

_____ 36. Identify benefits of teamwork.

_____ 37. Recognize characteristics of effective teams.

_____ 38. Participate skillfully as a team member.

_____ 39. Demonstrate team leadership responsibilities.

_____ 40. Employ successful problem-solving techniques.

_____ 41. Develop central ideas with main points.

_____ 42. Support main points with verbal and visual information.

_____ 43. Organize outlines for oral presentations.

_____ 44. Research information for a speech using a variety of resources.

_____ 45. Deliver a speech confidently with minimal notes.

_____ 46. Influence others with emotional appeals.

_____ 47. Recognize logical fallacies.

_____ 48. Present a message with maximum credibility.

_____ 49. Use persuasive strategies to convince others.

_____ 50. Organize a message to persuade others.

Communication Self-Assessment Scoring Key

Use the following scoring key to assess your perceived ability to communicate. Total your points for items 1–5, 6–10, 11–15, etc. When finished scoring, check your rating and answer the questions which follow.

Communication Concepts (1–5)	Perception Skills (6–10)	Diversity Skills (11–15)	Language Skills (16–20)	Listening Skills (21–25)
_____	_____	_____	_____	_____
Interpersonal Skills (26–30)	Conflict Skills (31–35)	Teamwork Skills (36–40)	Speaking Skills (41–45)	Persuasive Skills (46–50)
_____	_____	_____	_____	_____

Rating Scale for Communication Survey

11–15 points	No perceived problem with these communication skills.
6–10 points	Need work to improve these skills.
5 points	Need maximum efforts to develop communication strengths.

Answer the following questions:

1. What do the results of this survey tell you about your ability to communicate?
2. How closely do these results compare with your own personal assessment of your communication ability?
3. In what areas do you need special improvement? How might you go about improving your ability in these areas?

ASSIGNMENT 1.6: CASE STUDY: ETHICAL DILEMMA

In October 2006, 13-year-old Missouri girl, Megan Meier, took her life, and her parents believe her suicide was the result of harassment she experienced on MySpace.com, a social networking site.

The news media alleged that the mother of Megan's former friend created the fictitious profile of "Josh Evans," a supposed 16-year-old boy who befriended Megan online.

Unfortunately, what began as a potential friendship resulted in a devastating outcome when comments made by "Josh" became cruel and insulting.

Megan, who reportedly suffered from low self-esteem and depression, apparently found the personal attacks too much to bear and tragically ended her young life.

The mother supposedly claimed she created "Josh" as a way of finding out what Megan was saying online about her daughter, Megan's former friend.

Sometime after the incident, Missouri changed its laws against harassment to include "cyberbullying."

Questions:

1. Do you think whoever created "Josh" should face criminal charges? Why or why not?
2. Should users of web sites like MySpace.com be allowed to say whatever they want as a form of free speech? Why or why not?
3. What standards should web sites meet in order to prevent online bullying and harassment?

References

Casner-Lotto, J., & Barrington, L. (2006, October). Are they really ready to work? Employers' perspectives on the basic knowledge and applied skills of new entrants to the 21st Century U.S. workforce. The Conference Board, Corporate Voices for Working Families, Partnership for 21st Century Skills, and the Society for Human Resource Management. Retrieved October 4, 2006, from http://www.cvworkingfamilies. org/downloads/FINAL_PDF_9_29_06.pdf?CFID= 9383895&CFTOKEN=49915062

Cullen, S. (2006, November 10). Professor in an iPod. *Wisconsin State Journal*, A1.

Dickinson, A. (1999, September 27). Positive illusions. *Time Magazine*, vol. 154, issue 13, 112.

DiResta, D. (2004). Seven steps to a vital videoconference. *Ezine Articles*. Retrieved November 16, 2006, from http://www.ezinearticles.com/?Seven-Steps-to-a-Vital-Videoconference&id=956

Enron scandal mushrooms. (2002, January 7). *San Diego Union Tribune*. Retrieved December 7, 2007, from https://resourcea.wctc.edu/Ancillaries/temp/ 63998tempe00231.asp

Francis, J. (2006, October). The sound of silence. *Deliciousliving*, 78.

Francis, K., Bowman, S., & Redgrave, M. (2001, December 4). Rural nurses: Knowledge and skills required to meet the challenges of a changing work environment in the 21st Century: A review of the literature.

Commonwealth Department of Education, Science, and Training. Retrieved November 10, 2006, from http://www.dest.gov.au/archive/highered/nursing/pubs/ rural_nurses/9.htm

Goodman, E. (2005, August 13). Technology has weakened our connections. *Boston Globe*, p. B9.

Green, W. D. (2006, May 1). We've overlooked one of our greatest assets. *Newsweek*, 22.

Hertsgaard, M. (2005, May 10). Ped dispenser. *Grist*. Retrieved October 17, 2006, from http://www.grist.org/news/maindish/2005/05/10/ hertsgaard-francis/

Hudson. (2005). *The generation mirage*. Hudson Highland Group, Inc. Retrieved December 22, 2006, from http:// nz.hudson.com/documents/emp_au_ whitepaper_ generation_mirage.pdf

International Listening Association. (2005, June 12). *Listening factoids*. Retrieved November 10, 2007, from http://www.listen.org/Templates/factoids.htm

National Coalition Building Institute. (n.d.). About NCBI. Retrieved November 10, 2006, from http://www.ncbi .org/what_we_offer/customized_programs/ law_enforcement___protective_services/

National Communication Association. (n.d.). Behavior matters: Communication research on human connections. Decade of Behavior. Retrieved September 22, 2006, from http://www.decadeofbehavior.org/ NCA_pamphlet.2.pdf

Powell, J, (1969). *Why am I afraid to tell you who I am?* Niles, IL: Argus Communications.

Reuters Health. (2000–2005). Sharing feelings can help breast cancer survivors. *Ad Council/Cancerpage.Com.* Retrieved October 25, 2006, from http://www.cancerpage.com/news/article.asp?id=3007

Saxe, J. G. (n.d.). Blind men and the elephant. Retrieved October 24, 2006, from http://www.wordinfo.info/words/index/info/view_unit/1/?letter=B&spage=3

Tannen, D. (1994). *Talking from nine to five.* New York: HarperCollins.

Chapter 2

Perception

Learning **Objectives**

At the end of this chapter, you should be able to meet the following objectives:

1. Illustrate the importance of perception in your life and the lives of others.
2. Explain how perception influences and is influenced by communication.
3. Describe how prior knowledge, psychological variables, and emotional variables impact perception.
4. Clarify how selective attention, self-fulfilling prophecy, halo effect, attribution error, and projection impact perception and communication.
5. Develop skills to sharpen communication of your perceptions.
6. Ask questions when critically viewing materials from the media.

"No man has the right to dictate what other men should perceive, create or produce, but all should be encouraged to reveal themselves, their perceptions and emotions, and to build confidence in the creative spirit."

Ansel Adams

Perception Is Important

In twelfth-century Japan, a samurai was murdered after his wife was raped. A notorious bandit was put on trial for the murder. He recounted his version of the events that transpired. The bandit, the more skillful of the two warriors, killed the samurai in a spirited duel. The woman, who survived the attack, testified that after the rape, her husband, the samurai, rejected her. Despondent, she murdered her husband. A psychic was brought into the courts. The psychic recounted the story to the court from the perspective of the dead samurai. The man killed himself after learning that the woman was actually in a relationship with the bandit. A woodcutter, who testified that he had witnessed the event, told the court that both the samurai and the bandit had rejected the woman. She implored them to duel, which they did, neither with skill nor with ferocity. The samurai died more by bad luck than by the skilled sword of the bandit.

Picture of Tiger in Forest

More recently, a former commander during the Gulf War was asked to investigate the events that led to the death of a helicopter pilot to determine whether the pilot should be awarded a Medal of Honor. While interviewing one member of the company, the commander heard that the helicopter pilot was brave in the face of battle after the helicopter had been shot down. She acted honorably in an attempt to protect those in the company. However, while interviewing a second soldier, the commander was told that the helicopter pilot was a coward who was attempting to surrender to the enemy; rather than permit the surrender, the second soldier killed the pilot. At the end of his investigation, the commander learned that the pilot had been wounded and not killed as the second soldier had led people to believe. Believing the pilot was dead, another aircraft dropped a bomb on the helicopter wreckage to keep it from being used by the enemy, unknowingly killing the pilot.

What unites these two seemingly diverse stories? First, both are movies that attempt to explain the death of a key character. The former is the 1950s film from Japan titled *Roshomon* (Jingo & Kurosawa, 1950). The latter is the 1996 film *Courage Under Fire* (Carracciolo, Chase, & Zwick). More importantly, these two movies are dramatic illustrations of the differences in perceptions held by key characters in the films. Like these characters, you tend to perceive the world from your own point of view. Powerful yet invisible filters or lenses through which you view the world influence you, no matter how good your eyesight.

Of course, any number of other illustrations could be used to demonstrate the power of differences in perception. Consider the following examples. Social science researcher Richard Nisbett (2005) has shown that

Chinese and American students, when presented with a picture of a tiger in a forest, looked at different parts of the picture. The Chinese students focused more on the forest in the background, whereas the American students focused more on the tiger in the foreground. This contrast gives some credence to the belief that Easterners are more holistic in their thinking, paying more attention to the "big picture" in which an event is happening than are Westerners, who are more analytical, paying more attention to specific details.

Viewing people out of context involves a similar process. You may, for instance, focus on one particular characteristic of a person to the exclusion of other important traits. Elaine Pomerantz, who uses a motorized wheelchair, recounts waiting for a friend in front of a store when a person came up to her and tried to put money into her hands (Eglash, 2007). The perception, Pomerantz asserts, is that persons with disabilities are unable to care for themselves and, therefore, must be charity cases. Pomerantz, who has her master's degree and works as a rehabilitation counselor, is hoping that the general public will begin to move away from the stereotypes about people with disabilities and recognize the important contributions they have made to society.

Perceptional differences are also evident in the world of business. Vasconcellos (2005) described the challenges of a merger for two companies from different countries, the United States and Sweden. The U.S. pharmaceutical company Upjohn and the Swedish company Pharmacia ran into trouble when addressing different perceptions of the work environment. The American company didn't understand why workers should have so much vacation time. The Swedes couldn't understand why alcohol was not permitted

A Visible Disability Does Not Mean a Person Is Not Self-sufficient

as a lunchtime beverage. These small disagreements were just the beginning. The Swedes were accustomed to a more collaborative, problem-solving approach to work, which favored attending to the process of how decisions are made. By contrast, the U.S. company was driven more by top-down decision making with the intent to maximize efficiency and results.

Although international differences might be expected, even within our own borders differences in perception abound. Differences are evident in how people think about politics, leading some to suggest that you avoid discussing political viewpoints in public. Differences were evident in highly visible court cases like the O.J. Simpson trial, signifying how black and white Americans viewed this case differently. Also consider the differences in perception regarding what is considered "good" or "bad" art or theatre or music. Even professional critics disagree when rating a movie or live performance.

Even closer to home, you probably can recall your own differences of perception with others. Maybe you had trouble agreeing how to spend an "enjoyable" Saturday night with your significant other. You might welcome the chance to go to a concert whereas your partner prefers to go to the ballpark. At school, you may have a disagreement with an instructor about the C grade you received on a paper that you believed was worthy of an A grade. At work, your expectation for a bonus or a promotion may not match your boss's expectations.

As you become more aware, you will probably observe that differences in perception are widespread. However, not all differences are of equal importance. Clearly the difference in perception with a friend over whether a movie was "thumbs up" or "thumbs down" is of fairly little consequence. On the other hand, your friend's belief that it is appropriate to lie to you so as not to hurt your feelings can provoke a major challenge to your relationship if you value openness and honesty. At work, a difference in perception over whether to write a report using 12-point Times New Roman font or New Century Schoolbook may not be particularly important. However, interpreting "as soon as possible" to mean "after you complete the project you are currently working on" might conflict with your boss's meaning to "drop what you are doing and attend to this at once."

This latter example also sheds light on another key difference in perception. Not everyone's perceptions are of equal status. For example, although you may disagree with a teacher about the workload in a particular class, the teacher has the authority to make decisions about curriculum. Alternately, as a volunteer of a community organization, your point of view about a fundraising activity might be dismissed by the director who has a different vision in her mind about how the fundraising event should proceed.

A question you might be asking right now is this: What does perception have to do with communication? First, you communicate your perceptions of the world through the language you use. For example, suppose you have just been offered a promotion at your place of employment. You might tell a colleague that your boss, whom you admire as a manager, has just made a great decision to promote you. On the other hand, your co-worker, who doesn't get along with your boss and was passed over for a promotion, may speak in less favorable terms about the boss.

a. Motorcycle

b. Swine

FIGURE 2.1 ■ A Hog?

A second connection relates to how you listen to the messages of others. That is, you interpret the words and body language of others through your own perceptual filters. When your motorcycle-riding friend, Barbara, mentions that she has a new "hog," chances are that your farmer friend, Roberto, might have a different image in his mind of what Barbara has recently purchased (figure 2.1).

A final connection comes by understanding how communication shapes perception. On one level, the communication you engage in shapes your perceptions of the people with whom you are interacting. Consider meeting a new co-worker who comes from the Appalachian region of the United States, a region with a distinct spoken dialect. As the person speaks, you develop a perception about that person, rightly or wrongly, simply based on the dialect. On another level, consider how your perceptions are influenced by another person's communications. For example, suppose a co-worker mentions that a new employee is unqualified but was offered a job due to a friendship with the owner of the company. You might be looking for and finding indications of the person's faults in an effort to confirm what you heard about the person being unqualified. Keep in mind too that although you have perceptions of others, they have perceptions of you that likewise influence their interaction with you.

One interesting example of the connection between communication and perception deals with disabilities. Prior to 1997, the Education for all Handicapped Children Act was the national law governing services and accommodations for handicapped children in schools. In 1997, the law was revised. Along with important revisions was a decision to rename the law the Individuals with Disabilities Education Act (IDEA). Members of the disability community, as well as their advocates, were successful in switching the language from "handicapped children," implying that a handicap was a child's primary characteristic, to "individual with disabilities" to imply that the defining characteristic is the individual, the person, and not the disability. Those responsible for these changes hoped the new language would shape the way people feel about a person with a disability.

This chapter will provide a definition of perception, describe a model that explains how perception works, and then identify four essential concepts related to perception. The chapter then will examine three skills related to sharpening your perception. The chapter ends by describing the impact of technology on perception.

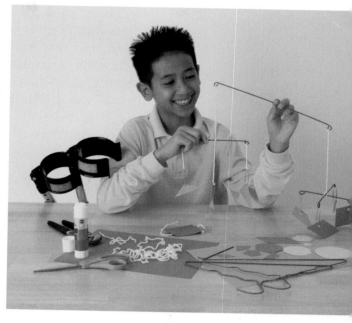

The Use of Crutches Does Not Necessarily Imply Limited Activities

Perception Defined

Perception can be defined as "the way in which an individual gives meaning" to an object, a message, or an event (Rogers & Steinfatt, 1999, p. 145).

This definition implies that perception is a process. The actual object, message, or event is objective reality. To give meaning to objective reality, you "filter" this reality through your past experiences, your prior knowledge, and even your own psychological state. The result of this filtering is your subjective reality.

Consider the following example. You hear a baby crying (objective reality). You attach meaning to this event based on your past experiences with babies, your prior knowledge of what a baby's cry signifies, and your psychological state at the time. Thus, your perception of the baby's crying as an annoyance (subjective reality) might lead you to close the baby's door. On the other hand, your perception might be that babies cry because they want attention, leading you to pick up the baby.

Because each person is different in terms of experiences, knowledge, and psychological states, everyone interprets reality differently. To be sure, the more you and another person are alike in these dimensions, the more likely that the differences in perception will be slight. However, the more different you are from another person, the more likely that each of your perceptions of reality will be different as well.

A key idea then that comes from this definition is recognition that people process "reality" in different ways. In other words, no two people will experience the exact same reality. Equally important, even though people have their own subjective realities, they often live in ways and act upon these subjective realities as if they were "real." Therefore, you might often try to convince others that the reality you see and describe is the only "right, true, and accurate" perspective.

The Sound of a Baby Crying Can Evoke Nurturing Responses in Some, and Annoyance in Others

These ideas should help you to recognize the special importance communication plays in your life. That is, you have to be able to communicate your reality to another person in a way that helps that person to understand the reality you are describing. You also have to be open to listening, really listening, to those people in your life who share their reality with you. In doing so, you might achieve the shared understanding with them that is desired. Even if the two realities shared are different, you are well on your way to building or maintaining strong relationships built on effective communication.

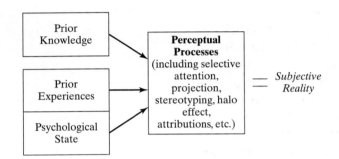

FIGURE 2.2 ■ Factors Affecting Perception

A Perception Model

You can see that perception is the process of translating objective reality into subjective reality. To explore more fully how this process works, you will find the model and explanation in figure 2.2 helpful.

Prior Knowledge The knowledge base that you have developed over years of schooling impacts your perceptions. However, you have learned a whole host of things from experiences outside of school as well. This knowledge base is critical to make sense of what you see and hear around you. Listening to a lecture about advanced astrophysics when you have very little background in the field would be like listening to a lecture in a foreign language that you didn't speak. Likewise, an auto mechanic, when opening the hood of a car, sees far more than "just an engine." The mechanic will see the various parts of the engine and may begin to diagnose apparent problems that you would not observe. In short, you use your prior knowledge to help you make sense of the world around you.

Prior Experiences A second factor is your prior experiences. Much like your knowledge base, you use your prior experiences to help you make sense of your world. Your prior experiences help you to focus on things you wouldn't otherwise. For example, imagine you are searching the Internet, and you see a picture of Angel Island in California (figure 2.3). For some who view this Internet picture,

FIGURE 2.3 ■ Angel Island

the photo might be "just a picture of an island." However, suppose you have visited Angel Island, picnicked, biked, and hiked there. Suppose that while you were there, you listened to an elderly Japanese American discuss how Angel Island served as an immigration station—much like Ellis Island in New York—for Japanese and Chinese immigrants in the early 1900s. Suppose you also met a former military soldier who was stationed there during the 1940s when the island was used as a military outpost in case of an attack on San Francisco. Angel Island has become, for you, more than just a picture of an island in a book.

Identity
Personality Traits
Values/Worldview
Self-Concept
Emotional State
Physical Condition

FIGURE 2.4 ■ Psychological State Factors Affecting Perception

Psychological State　A third factor impacting your perceptions is a combination of psychological and emotional variables (figure 2.4).

One such psychological variable is your sense of identity. Your identity is your sense of self as a unique individual. You tend to interact with the world in relationship to the way you define yourself. For example, if one central part of your identity is your marital status, and you are single, noting whether an attractive person of the opposite gender is wearing a wedding ring may be important to you. If a central aspect of your identity is your career, you may gravitate to others who share your occupation.

Many such identity characteristics could be discussed. Men and women, for instance, don't see the world in the same way, partly because of the experiences they have had as men or women, partly because of the ways in which they have been raised, and partly because of the genetic and biological differences that distinguish them. In addition, a young person's view of the world is different than that of an elderly person. You also may imagine that a person who has been born into wealth views money differently than a person who has been born poor. People who are Muslim or Hindu or Christian or atheist have different perceptions on the afterlife. The marketing major may not have the same subjective reality of customer service that the auto mechanic does.

Identity Affects Perception—A Place to Sleep May Look Different to Someone Rich Versus Poor

Personality traits might be another aspect of identity. If you see yourself as being sociable and comfortable around others, you might easily approach someone at a party. If you see yourself as quiet, shy, and introverted, making such contact might be difficult and uncomfortable.

In addition, these identity factors can influence your values and worldviews. Values reflect what you see as good or bad, right or wrong. Worldviews are group-related value orientations that influence the group members' perceptions of the world. For example, Native Americans are often seen as valuing nature and placing their priorities on living in harmony with their surroundings. In contrast, many mainstream Americans value mastery over nature and support technical advances to control their environment.

Another factor that influences perception is your self-concept. First, you will want to understand how self-concept differs from identity. Identity, you may recall, centers on how you define yourself in relationship to the world. Identity is primarily based on external traits such as marital status, race, ethnicity, occupation, socioeconomic status, and so on. Self-concept, on the other hand, has more to do with how you view yourself. You may see yourself as intelligent, compassionate, honest, and so forth. When you perceive yourself in positive ways, you are more likely to see the world around you in a positive light as well.

A third variable is your emotional state. It would seem obvious that your emotional state is a filter that colors your perceptions. Consider, for example, a person on your work team who did not perform well on an assigned project. As a result, the company lost an important account. You are angry that the person did not do the job adequately, did not apologize, nor even acknowledge responsibility for the loss of business. Now the person is asking you to go out after work to socialize and cannot understand why you responded with a blunt "no."

Anxiety is a particularly interesting emotional state. When you have a mild to moderate degree of anxiety, your senses are heightened, and you are more engaged with the task at hand. For instance, you may feel some anxiety before a major presentation, an athletic event, or a blind date. This type of anxiety can actually help you perform more effectively, since you view the anxiety as excitement. In contrast, if your anxiety is too intense, you might engage in avoidance behavior and resist opportunities to experience life's challenges.

Finally, a whole set of physical variables needs to be considered. You know about the role of alcohol in traffic accidents, given the way it slows reaction times and diminishes sensory acuity. Your physical health is also a factor affecting your perceptions. For example, your enthusiasm for a new work project might be dampened if you are battling a cold. A physical location that limits your angle of vision also is important. Imagine the thousands of fans sitting in a stadium at a baseball game booing an umpire's call despite the fact that the umpire has a unique advantage to make the call. Another variable to consider is the actual weaknesses in your senses: vision, hearing, smell, touch, and taste. Someone who is color-blind, for instance, or has a hearing impairment may not see or hear the world in the same way as you do. Finally, imagine the impact of hunger, fatigue, and daily cycles, those times in the day when you are more alert than other times in the day, as they might affect perception.

Collectively, some combination of these variables is at play when you experience events, objects, or interactions in the objective world. These variables filter what you see. Of course, you can probably list many more of these variables. However, the most important point to make is that everything about who you are or who you think you are serves as a filter, leading to the subjective reality that you create.

Physical Variables, Such as Fatigue, May Affect Perception

Perception Processes and Concepts

This next section will discuss several processes that help to explain how the factors described in the preceding section work to shape your perceptions. Specifically, this section will discuss the role of selective attention, self-fulfilling prophecy, the halo effect, attribution error, and projection.

Selective Attention   One of the processes that affects your perceptions is selective attention. You are bombarded by so many visual, auditory, tactile, and olfactory messages that you can't possibly pay attention to them all. Consequently, you usually make decisions to pay attention to some messages more than others. For instance, you often pay attention to those things that are novel or new. It would be hard not to note your little brother's Mohawk haircut when you came home after a long day of work. A building that looks like it has been picked up and placed upside down, like the WonderWorks children's science museums in Orlando, Florida, and Pigeon Forge, Tennessee, would also be certain to catch your attention as you drive by (figure 2.5).

FIGURE 2.5 ■
WonderWorks
Children's Science
Museum
Source: http://www
.aravisarwen.com/
wonderworks.jpg.

In addition, you pay attention to those things that are thrust upon you such as loud noises, dazzling colors, and pungent smells. It would be difficult, for instance, to ignore a cherry-red hot rod with loud mufflers spewing exhaust as it comes down the street of a quiet neighborhood. In fact, the police purposefully use loud sound and bright lights on their cars to catch the attention of drivers as the officers make their way to an accident or a crime scene.

You also pay more attention to what interests you. Consider watching a couple walking down the street. A sociologist who studies how people interact might focus on the relationship behaviors of the couple. An architect might not focus on the couple at all but rather attend to the buildings and landscape around which the couple walks. A fashion designer might pay attention to the clothes being worn by the couple. A pickpocket might be attending to the location of a purse or wallet. You also attend to those stimuli that relate to you specifically. You might be able to recall a time when you were able to quickly scan lists of names to find your own name, for instance. In addition, consider how, despite the amount of background noise, you can hear someone call your name.

An important idea to think about is that while you are selectively attending to some stimuli, you are ignoring others. When at a party, you might be able to recall lots of details about a new person you met and "hit it off" with in the hopes of developing a stronger relationship. However, you might not be able to recall much detail about other persons at the party or the décor of the house where the party was held.

Denial is selective attention in the extreme. Sometimes, you just don't want to see or hear something, especially when it challenges your identity or sense of integrity. Hearing that a good co-worker of yours has been stealing from the company might lead you to reject such a charge as wrong and an outrage, even when the evidence mounts against the co-worker. Likewise, you might deny or explain away things that demonstrate that you might not be as competent as you believe yourself to be.

Self-fulfilling Prophecy   The second perceptual mechanism is the self-fulfilling prophecy. This relates to the role expectations play in your perceptions. Basically, the self-fulfilling prophecy states that you see what you want or expect to see.

Some of these self-fulfilling prophecies relate to expectations you have about yourself. Consider the example of a job that you believe you are highly unlikely to receive. As a result of this belief, you do not do much to prepare for the interview. In addition, you communicate your uncertainty and lack of excitement about the job both verbally and nonverbally to the interview team and do not follow up after the interview. The interview team notes that you knew little about the company, showed no real interest in the job, and never heard from you afterwards. Thus, they decide not to hire you. For your part, the company's response just confirmed your initial expectations.

Some of the self-fulfilling prophecies you have are about others. A classic study in the 1960s showed the power of these prophecies. A group of researchers told a group of teachers that 20 percent of the students assigned to their class showed unusual academic promise. The researchers, however, just chose 20 percent of the class members at random to describe as "bright." At the end of the year, those students who had been identified by the researchers as gifted had outperformed their peers during the school year. The teachers treated the students in ways that not only assumed the students were smart but also communicated to the students that they were indeed smart. The result was a positive school experience.

This research raises another aspect about the self-fulfilling prophecy, namely that people tend to live up to the expectations both positive or negative of significant others. Consider the effect of negative stereotypes people develop around race or ethnicity. Since 1995, Claude Steele and his colleagues have been investigating a concept called the **stereotype threat**. This concept proposes that negative cultural stereotypes about a group can create for its members a belief in the stereotype (Steele & Aronson, 1995). Thus, when African Americans and whites who believed that African Americans were not as smart as whites were told they were taking a test of intellectual ability, the African Americans performed poorly in comparison to the whites. When a similar group was told they were taking a test of verbal ability, the test scores for the African Americans and whites were similar. What made this experiment informative was that it was the same test used for intellectual ability and verbal ability!

Some Individuals Would Believe Certain Traits About Another Person Depending on That Person's Race or Ethnicity

The Halo Effect, Attribution Error, and Projection   The **halo effect** occurs when you make assumptions, either positive or negative, based upon limited information. For example, assume you meet a young person who tells you that she has just been accepted into Harvard. You might then assume the person is smart, self-motivated, wealthy, articulate, etc. The fact is that the person may possess all of those qualities, or the person may not possess any of those qualities. Perhaps the person is a good test taker and particularly good at writing letters for admission while having good but not great grades.

On the other hand, consider how you perceive a co-worker who may have lied to you. You may now tend to interpret whatever this co-worker says or does as being dishonest or insincere. In the case of someone you love, you may even take negative characteristics and attempt to see them in a positive light. Consequently, someone who is abusive may be perceived as an individual who is just under a lot of stress.

Related to the halo effect is **attribution error.** This error is an attempt to attribute causes of events to either personalities or external situations. As one basic example, if you think you are particularly smart and do well on a test, you might conclude that the good score was due to your intelligence. However, if you perform poorly on the test, you might blame the teacher, the test, or the bad day you were having. However, the opposite is true for your perceptions of others. If someone you do not like does well on a test, you more likely will attribute the success to situational variables such as an easy test. When the person does something poorly, you may tend to fault the individual personally.

Projection is the tendency to see your own faults, and sometimes your strengths, in others, calling these traits to the other person's attention. The phrase "the pot calling the kettle black" best describes this process. For example, if a project is not meeting the deadlines that have been provided, you might complain about a co-worker who is not putting in the time needed to help complete the project in a timely manner. It may be that you also have not put in the time either and that your decision to go on vacation during a critical phase of the project may have contributed to the delay. However, the focus of your criticism is entirely on your colleague. You might consistently interrupt a friend who is sharing concerns about your communication skills by telling him that he is not a good listener. On the other hand, you might compliment a friend for his or her thoughtfulness, seeing in this individual a trait you believe yourself to possess.

I DON'T KNOW, THERE'S SOMETHING ABOUT THE GUY IN THE MIDDLE I DON'T TRUST...HE JUST DOESN'T **LOOK** RIGHT!

We Tend to Like or Not Like the Traits of Others That We Like and Don't Like About Ourselves
Source: www.CartoonStock.com.

By now you *probably* have become more aware of the factors that influence your perception of reality. In order to minimize the communication breakdowns that result from perceptual differences, keep in mind the following four concepts.

Recognize the Distinction between Objective and Subjective Reality As discussed previously, it will be helpful for you to keep in mind the distinction between objective and subjective reality. Truth or reality is filtered through the lenses—based on points of view and experiences—that you bring to the world. Despite this fact, people often will argue long and loud to get others to see their point of view, to reach the same conclusions they have reached, and to do what they think needs to be done. This belief that their view of the world is right and that of others is wrong rarely leads to positive and healthy relationships.

Your Differences in Perception Are Rooted in Individual Differences   Remember that all personal differences including gender, age, race, ethnicity, social economic status, past experiences, education, religion, and so forth influence the way you experience the world. By recognizing the individual differences among those with whom you communicate, you are better able to understand how others perceive the world around them.

How You Look at Differences Matters   The mere existence of differences in perception is not a problem. How you think about and respond to these differences, however, can be a problem or an opportunity. It is a Western conception of the world that inconsistencies in worldview are to be avoided (Nisbett, 2005). On the other hand, an Eastern conception of the world suggests that differences are a natural part of life that bring with them many opportunities. For example, some individuals may find that variations in viewpoints allow for alternative perspectives when it comes to problem solving. Consequently, a problem is understood more completely. The result is a greater number and different kinds of solutions that respond more fully and accurately to the problem. In summary, differences in perception can be healthy, helpful, and positive. The varied perceptions that people hold are, in part, what make all individuals unique and interesting human beings.

Communication Is a Central Skill in the Perception Process   Connected with this last concept is the idea that these differences in perception can be positive if they are handled effectively. You have the choice when sharing your point of view that it must win out over another's or simply be regarded as a different point of view to be understood. You can assume that everyone sees the world exactly as you do, or you can check your perceptions of important events, experiences, and interactions to verify consistency in meaning. As a result, communication becomes a

© Mike Baldwin/Cornered

"No, please, go on. It's so refreshing to talk to someone with an entirely different point of view."

Seeing Differences in Point of View as Positive
Source: www.CartoonStock.com.

central skill in the perception process that can help you to deal with different viewpoints in a constructive way.

Sharpening Your Perceptions

Three skills can help you to sharpen your communication about perceptions. The first two, distinguishing facts from opinions and perception checking, are specific skills of value to you as you communicate your impressions to others. The third is an approach to sharing perceptions and listening to the perceptions of others by way of a learning conversation.

Fact/Opinion Confusion Communication barriers and misunderstandings between people occur for a variety of reasons. One of these reasons involves the failure to separate facts from opinions.

Suppose you firmly believe women should be given equal opportunity to pursue work in nontraditional occupations such as welding, automotive repair, or electronics. Your friend and co-worker, on the other hand, thinks a woman's place is in the home fulfilling the role of homemaker and mother, or at the very least, doing jobs "nature intended" for women, which include being a teacher, nurse, or secretary.

Now if both of you have forgotten that your opinions are just that—opinions—and subject to change and error, it is highly probable that neither of you will be able to discuss this topic calmly without trying to convince the other of the "facts." However, if you both recognize your opinions for what they are—nonfactual—you will be more willing to listen open-mindedly to conflicting views and respect the right of others to think as they do even if you do not personally agree.

Some of the characteristics that separate facts from opinions are listed.

Statements of Fact

1. Are based on observable sensory data—Observations report only what you can see, hear, taste, touch, or smell.
2. Are only about the past or the present, never the future—Statements about future events are purely opinion since the events have not yet occurred and are, therefore, not observable.
3. Are objective and devoid of any interpretations, conclusions, or assumptions about what has been observed—Observing someone eating alone in the cafeteria is a fact. Assuming this person is antisocial is an opinion.

Statements of Opinion

1. Go beyond what has been observed.
2. Are about the past, present, or future.
3. Include interpretations, conclusions, or assumptions about what has been observed and are, consequently, subjective.

Forming opinions is a natural and important process. Communicating your opinions in such a way as to acknowledge their subjective nature is essential. Thus, it is often a good idea to state your opinions to others in non-factual terms by including the use of an "I" message. For example, rather than saying, "Women should have the right to pursue work in nontraditional occupations," say instead, "I have come to believe women should have the right to pursue work in nontraditional occupations." Phrases such as "I think," "To me," and "From my point of view" work equally well.

CHECKING PERCEPTIONS

Perception checks, sometimes called impression checks, are responses to someone's verbal or nonverbal communication that share an impression of the person's message in an open-minded, non-evaluative way and that invite a response from the person. As a communication tool, perception checks help you verify assumptions or opinions that are formed in response to another's words or actions. Perception checks provide a way to confirm what you are thinking about without always having to ask a question.

Clear Perception Checks Should Be Phrased as Follows:

1. State your perception of another person's behavior. That is, state what you think that individual is wanting, needing, thinking, feeling, or going to do. For example, "I get the impression you want some time to yourself."
2. Present your perception in an open-minded or tentative way which suggests "I may be wrong" by using phrases such as "It seems" or "It looks as if . . ."
3. Express your perception in a non-evaluative manner. Not even the tone of your voice should imply that you are judging, belittling, or putting down the sender. "It looks like you really botched the computer program this time" makes an evaluation of the sender and should be avoided.
4. Invite a response by using either a rising inflection at the end of your statement or by a very short question. Questions like "Are you?", "Am I right?", or "Is that it?" invite a response without taking attention away from the perception check. These very brief questions should just invite a response to verify the accuracy of the perception. Avoid a longer, more involved question that will open a whole new area of concern.

Now that you know what perception checks are, let's examine when you might use these tools. Suppose someone has said or done something that you do not completely understand. You have some idea of what the sender might be feeling, wanting, needing, or thinking, but you are not sure. At this point, you may ask a question, or you may just pretend you know what is going on and not say anything. Sometimes questions will clear things up; at other times, you will get only a vague response.

Perception checks give you another tool to use at times like this. They help to start conversations when you want to show some empathy for the other person or when you need clarification of some assumption you have made. Perception checks have to be used with a curious, questioning tone of voice that communicates your interest and concern. Perception checks encourage the other person to confirm your assumptions or to show you where they are incorrect. Either way, this skill enables you to show that you are listening and care enough to try to understand the other person.

LEARNING CONVERSATIONS

A third skill aimed at sharpening communication of your perceptions is actually a process for learning about the perceptions of others when perceptual differences have led to some difficulty in your relationship or ability to complete a task. It was developed in the Program on Negotiation at Harvard Law School as the first in a long list of activities related to negotiations on the international or national level. However, as a first step, you can employ their method in your home, community, school, and workplace.

To begin, you have to distinguish between two kinds of conversations: **debates** and **dialogues**. In a debate, the attempt is to "win." That is, you want to convince the other person of the "rightness" of your point of view, your understanding of a situation, or your solution to a problem. In a debate, someone wins, and someone loses. In a dialogue, however, the goal is not to win but rather to understand. Instead of your coming into the conversation with a desire to force a viewpoint on someone, a dialogue requires you to express curiosity about others: How do they view the world, what sense do they make of what happened, how are they feeling, and how does their point of view represent their identity? When you realize that you and another person have a difference in point of view about an important matter, consider a dialogue via a learning conversation.[1]

Anytime there is an important conversation taking place, there are at least three elements being communicated. First are content messages about what happened. These messages are meant to describe the facts but often include assumptions about why something happened. Sometimes these messages include who is to blame or what must be done to resolve a difficulty. The second part of the conversation is feeling messages. This part includes messages about how someone

---

[1]Much of the information presented here on learning conversations came from Romney and Hardiman, 2007.

Debates Versus Dialogues

is feeling. The difficulty is that although these feeling messages are expressed, more likely they are not expressed except via body language. The third part of a conversation includes identity messages. These messages are about how people see themselves and how the issue under consideration affects how the people see themselves.

Thus a learning conversation is aimed at understanding another person's point of view, sharing with the person your point of view, understanding and sharing each other's feelings, and working together to figure out how to resolve a problem so that the two of you can move forward. This process recognizes that people have different viewpoints as a result of the different information that is available to them, resulting in different observations that lead to different interpretations as well as different conclusions.

The key attitudinal shift you must make to engage in an authentic learning conversation is from convincing the other person of your point of view to cultivating curiosity about the view of others. Curiosity is what makes this process a learning conversation rather than a winning conversation. Unless you and the other person make this attitudinal shift and show genuine curiosity, it will be difficult for either of you to really hear the story the other person wishes to convey. Equally important, it will be difficult for both of you to share your story. That is, if someone believes you are listening only to use what is shared to convince him or her that you are right, that person will be hesitant to share. In addition, your curiosity about the other's story should not imply that you must give up your point of view. You can accept another person's story without abandoning your own position.

In the first phase of a learning conversation, invite the person to share with you his or her *different* point of view. You will want to communicate to the person that you know you have a difference of opinion, that the relationship is important, and that you would like to find a time and place to give you both a chance to work out the differences. If and when the person is ready to discuss the difference with you, the second phase can begin.

In the second phase, share the differing points of view. Employing a curious mind-set, ask for specific information about the person's experience, the effect of the experience on him or her, and what the person believes the intentions might have been, what conclusions were reached, etc. Be sure to focus on the person's feelings. Ask about and listen to the influence this experience had on the person's identity. Paraphrase the speaker's message throughout to assure your understanding and to communicate that you are listening. When it is your turn, do the same sharing of experiences, effects, intentions, conclusions, feelings, and influences on identity.

Throughout the entire process, remember to keep the focus of the conversation away from winning and toward learning, away from finding truth and toward accepting multiple perceptions, away from placing blame and toward understanding differing contributions.

Sometimes, the sharing of different points of view is all that is required. Both you and the other person will feel better about communicating these differences and understanding one another more fully. However, sometimes the conflict requires some resolution. In this case, the final phase would be to begin problem solving. Look for or invent options that meet both your and the other person's needs. Look for those solutions that result in mutual caregiving—assuring that each person gets what he or she needs to be successful. End by setting up a plan to determine how things are going and to maintain openness in further communications.

One final note concerns the role of courage. You may prefer to avoid conflicts. They can be difficult, challenging, and often painful. In addition, conflicts usually come with high stress. However, consider the long-term mutual interests that the two of you share: an important work relationship, a concern for the health and well-being of the organization, or the need to be able to accomplish life and work tasks in a positive way. Keeping these long-term, mutual interests in mind might provide the courage needed to engage in learning conversations.

Perception and Technology

By now you are probably more aware of the complex factors that affect your perception of the world around you. One final factor you might want to examine is the influence of technology. Take a look at the three pictures in figure 2.6.

In all three photos, digital manipulation has been used to create images you wouldn't expect to see: a human eye with the pupil replaced by a dollar sign; a man with his interior skeletal structure superimposed over his face and body; and transparent brains floating in a clouded blue sky, creating a dreamlike illusion.

The use of art and technology to challenge your perceptions is not new. In the fifteenth, sixteenth, and seventeenth centuries, artists like Leonardo da Vinci and Jan van Eyck used the power of optical illusion to make a person see something that was not really there. In the early 1900s, one of the most

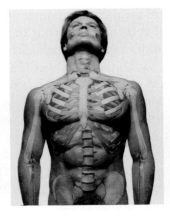

FIGURE 2.6 ■ Perception and Technology

a. M. C. Escher, *Relativity*, (c) 2009 The M. C. Escher Company-Holland. All rights reserved. www.mcescher.com.

FIGURE 2.7 ■ Optical Illusions as Art
Source: From Here Right Now, 2002, Toronto Transit Commission, by Panya Clark Espinal, image by Javier Espinal, DSCN1941.jpg

b. M. C. Escher's *Ascending and Descending*, 1960. Lithograph, 13.75 × 11.25" (c) 2009 The M. C. Escher Company-Holland. All rights reserved. www.mcescher.com.

famous of the optical illusion artists, M. C. Escher, was busy creating art that challenged people's sense of logic and perception. Two of his most famous works of ascending and descending staircases are presented in figures 2.7(a) and (b).

More recently, artists continue to challenge your perceptions with visual images that amaze and entertain. Consider this imaginary staircase painted by Canadian artist, Panya Clark Espinal, in Bayview Subway Station, Toronto, Canada, figure 2.7(c).

New technologies have allowed people with computers to change and shape your sense of reality even further. The question becomes, can you still embrace the old adage that seeing is believing, or must you now add a new element to the equation: Thinking critically about seeing is believing?

This equation includes not only considering images like those provided at the beginning of this section. It also means that you must be critical of what

5 Questions for Critical Media Viewing

- Who created this message?
- What creative techniques were used to attract my attention?
- How might other people understand this message differently than I?
- What values, lifestyles, and points of view are being represented in, or omitted from, this message?
- Why is this message being sent?

FIGURE 2.8 ■ Questions for Critical Viewing

you see and hear from television as well. For example, news companies may record multiple hours of an event but cut those hours down to only a few minutes worth of sound and video bites. In other words, you may see only what media executives wish you to see. As a result, you would be right to ask, "But what am I not being shown?"

This practice has led some to call for critical media literacy awareness (Center for Media Literacy, 2005). This awareness is based on five core ideas (figure 2.8). The first idea is that the media constructs messages to be broadcast. Second, these messages use a creative language with specific rules. Third, based on human differences, the same message from the media is understood differently by different people. Fourth, those who make decisions about the messages they wish to communicate have a particular value orientation and point of view that influences what is communicated. Finally, for most of the media, the goal is more money and/or more power.

Given these five core ideas, you would be wise to ask a series of questions related to what you are watching and/or hearing: Who created this message? What creative techniques are used to attract my attention? How might other people understand this message differently than I? What values, lifestyles, and points of view are represented in, or omitted from, this message? Why is this message being sent? (Center for Media Literacy, 2005).

Although there is much more required of you to think critically about the world you experience around you, asking these questions is a necessary first step that will put you heads above those more casual and uncritical observers.

After reading this chapter, you can see just how critical the role of perception is in human interaction. Your communication is influenced by a host of variables that reflect your prior knowledge and experiences, your emotional states, and your expectations. Although you bring your own unique background to the encounters you have with others, you can still bridge perceptional gaps by developing a variety of skills. Using perception checking, separating facts from opinions, and employing learning conversations all provide a way to bring your view of reality and those of others a little bit closer.

Review Questions

1. Provide at least two examples of different points of view you have had with someone else. What do you think caused these different viewpoints? How did you deal with them?

2. After reading this chapter, what does perception mean to you? How does perception affect your communication?

3. Explain, in your own words, the difference between objective and subjective reality. Why would this distinction be important for you to know?

4. Complete the following statement: The idea that every aspect of people's identities, including their gender, race, ethnicity, etc., influences their perceptions suggests that . . .

5. List and describe the elements of the perception model (figure 2.2).

6. List the three processes people use to make sense of the world around them.

7. Explain the differences between facts and opinions.

8. What is a perception check? When would you use perception checking? Why would it be an important skill to have?

9. Share a time when you had a learning conversation with someone. How did it go? What worked? What didn't work?

10. How would the five questions for thinking critically about what appears in the media benefit you?

Key Terms and Concepts

Attribution Error   39

Content Messages   43

Emotional State   36

Facts   41

Feeling Messages   43

Filters   32

Halo Effect   38

Identity   35

Identity Messages   44

Learning Conversations   43

Objective Reality   33

Opinions   42

Perception   33

Perception Checks   42

Perceptual Process   34

Physical Variables   36

Prior Experience   34

Prior Knowledge   34

Projection   39

Psychological State   35

Selective Attention   37

Self-fulfilling Prophecy   38

Stereotype Threat   38

Subjective Reality   33

Web Activities

- Check out the perception exercises at the following website: http://www3.shastacollege.edu/communication/rsaunders/Documents/SP10PEXS01.ppt

- Also check the illusions presented at this website: http://www.scientificpsychic.com/graphics/

- Discover an interesting application of the self-fulfilling prophecy at the following website: http://www. accel-team.com/pygmalion/index. html

Assignments

ASSIGNMENT 2.1: SELF-PERCEPTION EXERCISE

Directions: All people have a particular perception of themselves that guides much of what they do and how they see the world around them. In this assignment, use the following rating sheet to uncover your perception of yourself. Place an X along the rating scale for each item. All people also have a perception of who they'd like to be. On the second rating sheet, place an O along the rating scale based on how you would like to describe yourself ideally.

NOTE: Use column # 4 for those things you don't know, are uncertain about, or wish not to communicate.

OPTIONAL EXTENSIONS:

1. In a group of three or four persons, one at a time, have members introduce themselves by stating how they rated themselves on three of these characteristics and why they rated themselves that way.
2. After discussing how group members see themselves, have them share how they would like to be. Have them explain why.
3. Answer the following questions by yourself.
   a. When you looked at your "real" and "ideal" self, what was similar? What was different? What might explain these differences in perceptions about you?

Real Self

CHARACTERISTIC	1	2	3	4	5	6	7	CHARACTERISTIC
open-minded								closed-minded
dominating								submissive
kind								unkind
unsympathetic								sympathetic
active								passive
physically weak								physically strong
dull								bright
self-confident								timid
nervous								composed
thoughtful								thoughtless
simple								complex
introverted								extroverted
cooperative								uncooperative
unpredictable								predictable

Ideal Self

CHARACTERISTIC	1	2	3	4	5	6	7	CHARACTERISTIC
open-minded								closed-minded
dominating								submissive
kind								unkind
unsympathetic								sympathetic
active								passive
physically weak								physically strong
dull								bright
self-confident								timid
nervous								composed
thoughtful								thoughtless
simple								complex
introverted								extroverted
cooperative								uncooperative
unpredictable								predictable

b. How do you feel regarding what you wrote about yourself? How do you feel about how you would like to be?

c. What have you learned from this activity? What would you like to do differently?

ASSIGNMENT 2.2: OTHERS' PERCEPTION OF YOU

Directions: After completing Assignment 2.1, ask two to three people *whose opinions you value* to complete the following worksheet. Make as many copies of the worksheet as you need. You could ask family members, friends, or co-workers for their honest opinions. After they have completed the worksheet, have them discuss their responses with you. Recall that you do not have to accept their perceptions of you, but try to uncover how they arrived at their perceptions.

Instructions for others who will provide opinions: *Thanks for taking time to share your perceptions with me. I'm interested in knowing how people perceive me. Answer the following questions. Please do so honestly. If you and I wish, we can discuss your comments afterwards. Place an X in the space below that indicates how strong that feeling is. If you do not know, are undecided, or don't want to say, place the X in column # 4.*

REVIEW QUESTIONS:

1. In comparison to how you rated yourself, how did others perceive you similarly? Differently? Why?
2. How do you feel about the ratings you received? What surprised you? What worried you? What made you feel happy?
3. What did you learn about yourself as a result of doing this activity?

Your Perceptions of Me

CHARACTERISTIC	1	2	3	4	5	6	7	CHARACTERISTIC
open-minded								closed-minded
dominating								submissive
kind								unkind
unsympathetic								sympathetic
active								passive
physically weak								physically strong
dull								bright
self-confident								timid
nervous								composed
thoughtful								thoughtless
simple								complex
introverted								extroverted
cooperative								uncooperative
unpredictable								predictable

ASSIGNMENT 2.3: FACT–OPINION CONFUSION EXERCISES

The following exercises will help you to become more aware of the differences between facts and opinions and to realize how easy it is to confuse the two. From the following stories, determine whether the statements are factually true (T), factually false (F), or an opinion of any kind (?). Base your decision on the information in the story. True statements will be verified in the story, false statements will be contradicted in the story, and opinions will leave you guessing.

The owner of Webster's Auto Repair, who was getting ready to close shop for the evening, turned and noticed one of the mechanics stuffing impact and torque wrenches, sockets, and a micrometer into a knapsack. The owner called to the mechanic, but the mechanic picked up the knapsack, ran out of the garage, hopped into a waiting vehicle, and drove off. The garage owner immediately called the police.

T   F   ?   1. The garage owner was named Webster.

T   F   ?   2. The mechanic was seen stuffing tools in a knapsack.

T   F   ?   3. The man with the knapsack ran out of the garage and into a waiting vehicle.

T   F   ?   4. The car with the mechanic in it drove off.

T   F   ?   5. The mechanic stole the tools.

Terry, who was the first one to punch in on Friday, arrived at Department 325 and noticed the job that had been worked on Thursday afternoon had been moved to another machinery area. Another casting, with "RUSH" painted on its side, had been moved into Terry's machine. Friday's assignment called for Terry to work on the same machine as on Thursday. The supervisor for Department 325 was at a staff meeting all Friday morning.

T F ? 1. Terry's work assignment had changed for Friday.

T F ? 2. The supervisor forgot to tell Terry about a new rush job.

T F ? 3. Terry was the first person to arrive at Department 325 on Friday morning.

T F ? 4. The job Terry had been working on had not been moved.

T F ? 5. Terry has been reassigned to another machinery area.

Sandy and Pat, both data processors, are especially good at their jobs. Their combined experience totals some thirty years. They are reliable, hardworking, and very physically strong individuals. In fact, Sandy lifts weights for a hobby, and Pat plays basketball.

T F ? 1. This story concerns two men named Sandy and Pat.

T F ? 2. Sandy and Pat are both hard workers.

T F ? 3. Sandy is handicapped.

T F ? 4. Pat and Sandy are married to each other.

T F ? 5. Sandy never lifted weights.

ASSIGNMENT 2.4: PERCEPTION CHECKING SKILLS

As suggested earlier in this chapter, sometimes it is important for you to check your perceptions to see if they are correct. Checking perceptions also gives others the chance to offer additional information or explanations that might help you reconsider your point of view.

Directions: In part 1, place an X next to those statements that you see as effective perception checks. In part 2, use the scenario provided to write three perception checks of your own.

PART 1

1. _____ I have the impression that this was not a good day for you, Bob.

2. _____ You are just being rude.

3. _____ Despite what you say, I know you purposefully allowed me to win today; didn't you?

4. _____ It seems to me that we did this task incorrectly; is that right?

5. _____ When will you stop hassling the new co-worker?

6. _____ It is my opinion that the management is trying to drive a wedge between us; could that be?

7. _____ It is my perception that our relationship has moved to a new level.

8. _____ I am thinking that the people at this meeting are interested in developing a local community newsletter. Is that what I'm hearing?

9. _____ Wow, that new boss really does not like you; does he?

10. _____ Why are you trying to undermine my work?

PART II

A co-worker is talking on the phone. The co-worker is talking loudly and knows that people can hear. The co-worker mentions that he has just received a promotion. He mentions that although there were other people who applied, he was clearly the most qualified. He then begins to detail all the benefits that come with the new position. You were one of those who had applied. After he hangs up the phone, you want to share your perception with him in as skillful a way as you can.

1.
2.
3.

ASSIGNMENT 2.5: LEARNING CONVERSATION

Earlier in this chapter, you read about learning conversations. In this assignment, you are asked to try out the skills associated with this type of interaction.

Directions: Consider a situation that has happened in the recent past where you and another person had a disagreement over a particular point of view. It should be a situation in which you want to better understand the other person's views. Consider a disagreement that was minor to moderate so that you feel comfortable with the skills and mind-set required for a learning conversation.

The purpose of this conversation is to meet with the other person and engage in a dialogue aimed at creating a mutual understanding.

Keep in mind the following guidelines:

- Remember the goal is learning, not winning.
- Develop an attitude of curiosity.
- Be willing to share your point of view as well.
- Share facts/ideas as well as feelings and identity.
- Be sure to invite the person to have this conversation and hold it when the other person signals that he or she is ready.
- Explain the disagreement and invite the other to share; then share your perceptions.
- If a solution is called for, look for options that result in mutual caregiving.

After completing the conversation, answer the following questions:

1. What was the disagreement about? What happened the first time the two of you discussed it?
2. How did this learning conversation go? What was easy? Difficult?
3. What would an outside observer say about how well you employed the guidelines described here?
4. What did you learn about yourself? About the other? About the use of learning conversations?

ASSIGNMENT 2.6: CASE STUDY: CRITICAL MEDIA LITERACY

Directions: In pairs or trios, watch a video segment from *60 Minutes, Dateline NBC, 48 Hours,* or some other news journal show. The segment should be between fifteen and thirty minutes in length. After the segment, first write your own answers to the following critical viewing questions. When all members of the group have answered the questions on their own, share your answers with one another.

Title of Show: _____

Title of Segment: _____

Date/Time Aired: _____

Brief Synopsis of Segment: _____

1. Who created this message?
2. What creative techniques were used to attract my attention?
3. How might different people understand this message differently than I?
4. What values, lifestyles, and points of view were represented in, or omitted from, this message?
5. Why was this message being sent?

References

Carracciolo, J. M., Chase, D. M. (Producers), & Zwick, E. (1996). *Courage under fire* [Motion Picture]. United States: Fox Pictures.

Center for Media Literacy. (2005). *Media lit kit.* Retrieved August 28, 2007, from http://www.medialit.org/pdf/mlk/14A_CCKQposter.pdf

Eglash, R. (2007). Second class citizens? *The Jerusalem Post*, July 20, 2007, p. 20.

Jingo, M. (Producer), & Kurosawa, A. (Director). (1950). *Roshomon* [Motion Picture]. Japan: Daiei Studios.

Nisbett, R. E. (2005). *The geography of thought: How Asians and Westerners think differently—and why.* Nicholas Brealey.

Rogers, E. M., & Steinfatt, T. M. (1999). *Intercultural communication.* Prospect Heights, IL: Waveland Press.

Romney, P., & Hardiman, R. (2007, August). *Moving from difficult conversations to learning conversations.* Paper presented at the University of Wyoming, Laramie, WY.

Souza De Vasconcellos, J. A. (2005). *Strategy moves: 14 complete and attack defence strategies for competitive advantage.* FT Press.

Steele, C. M., & Aronson, J. (1995). Stereotype threat and the intellectual test performance of African Americans. *Journal of Personality and Social Psychology, 69,* 797–811.

Chapter **3**

Cultural Diversity

Learning **Objectives**

At the end of this chapter, you should be able to meet the following objectives:

1. Illustrate the influence of international and cross-cultural differences on your life and describe what is meant by global interdependence.
2. Share six key principles about communicating interculturally.
3. Identify the meaning of key terms related to bias and include descriptions of the various ways in which bias is communicated.
4. Clarify how culture affects your style of communication.
5. Construct a list of cross-cultural competencies you wish to pursue by identifying your strengths and areas for improvement in cross-cultural communication.
6. Conduct a cross-cultural communication interview with someone from a social group different from your own.

"We all should know that diversity makes for a rich tapestry, and we must understand that all the threads of the tapestry are equal in value no matter what their color."

Maya Angelou

Diversity Is Important

A middle-aged man spoke about his younger days when the group he affiliated with often told raunchy, sexist jokes. Years later, upon reflection, he recognized that even within this crowd, the jokes were inappropriate. He recalled a more formal dinner party where, feeling a bit uncomfortable, he tried to break the ice by telling one of those jokes. The response was not what he expected—a long awkward silence. The man reported feeling stupid for not apologizing, but at least he had the good sense to stop telling such jokes.

At a construction site, a supervisor pulled aside a Mexican American employee who had worked for the company for some time. In an attempt to offer a compliment, the supervisor said to the employee, "You're a good worker. You're not like the other Mexicans." The employee nodded politely and went back to work. Upon reflection, the employee wished that he had responded differently. He would have wanted to acknowledge the compliment of his work along with stating the message had a racist overtone.

An African American man, shopping in a retail establishment observed an employee being rude to a customer whose first language was not English. The man stepped up and asked the customer if he could help. The man then turned to the employee and said, "These people live in your community, they spend money in your store, and you have a responsibility to treat all customers with courtesy."

What do all of these three examples, as described in Willougby (2007), have in common? They demonstrate that diversity includes multiple characteristics such as gender, race, and language. However, you will discover as you read further in this chapter that diversity encompasses more than just these three characteristics. The first two examples demonstrate that people often have not developed the communication skills necessary to respond to diversity with respect and sensitivity. The last example, however, shows how a person can support those who are the targets of unfair treatment and provides a model of how to confront others in an attempt to lead them to more respectful acceptance and affirmation of diversity.

Today you are more likely to interact with people who are ethnically and linguistically different from you in your community, in your school, and in your workplace. Advances in transportation, the move toward a global economy, and the movement of people in search of increased living standards—as well as those who are forced to move due to war, famine, and poverty—all mean that diversity is part of the landscape in communities and places of work across the United States.

It is important to recognize that diversity is a hallmark of society in the United States. Historically, American culture was forged by European and Asian immigrants who came to this country and encountered a diverse group of native peoples. Noted sociologist Marcelo Suarez-Orozco (2007) explains that although immigration is the historical legacy of the United States, it also represents current and future trends. In addition, the country is diverse in terms of gender, sexual orientation, regional affiliations, religious beliefs, and so on.

Interactions Are Marked by Increasing Diversity

It is important to understand that you are not just interacting with people who are different from you, but you rely on them for your health, for your education, and for your food. People from diverse cultures are your customers, your neighbors, your employers, your fellow workers, your friends, and, possibly, your family.

Much has also been made of increasing *global interdependence*. When the eleven nations making up the Organization of Petroleum Exporting Countries (OPEC) raised the price of oil in the 1970s, people in the United States had to sit in long lines at gas stations and pay four to five times more for gas. When a nuclear reactor accident occurred in Chernobyl, Russia, nuclear emissions did not stop at the Russian border. Political borders did not stop the killer bees first introduced in Brazil as they made their way into the southern part of the United States. Viruses from the Hong Kong flu to AIDS did not stop at U.S. borders either. Drugs, some of which ravage communities, and others of which show the promise to heal, come from other countries too. On September 11, 2001, North Americans learned that terrorist organizations in other parts of the world recognize the United States as a target for violent attacks. The U.S. military response in both Afghanistan and Iraq should remind you of the global nature of political conflicts.

Your workplace is also influenced by the nation's global interdependence. Many of the jobs that you work at are dependent, either directly or indirectly, on foreign trade. Often, the products that you rely on to do your job and live the lifestyle you have become accustomed to have been manufactured abroad. Indeed, you might work for companies that will be owned by people who are not born in the United States. As the number of companies moving to other countries to manufacture products, and take advantage of lower wage requirements with less stringent safety protections for workers increases, your very employment is put at risk.

In considering these factors, you must not focus on the changes that come with increased "internationalization" alone. You also need to consider the increases in U.S.-born ethnic minority and language minority people. The 2000 U.S. Census data characterized 12.5 percent of the U.S. population as Latino, 12.3 percent as African Americans, and 10 percent as other (U.S. Department of Commerce, 2001). In addition, the number of people who classify themselves as "biracial" is 2.4 percent. Collectively, these numbers are describing more than 100 million of your fellow citizens. In short, more than 1 of every 3 North Americans can be classified as an ethnic minority (figure 3.1). You would also be remiss if you ignored the number of people born in the United States who speak languages other than English at home. Consider that the number of school-aged children for whom English is not a first language rose from 2.2 million in 1989 to 4.4 million in 2000—a 105 percent increase since 1989 (Kinder, 2002).

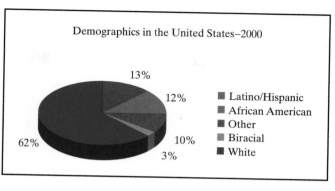

Importantly, these are not just numbers. They represent the people you know, care about, and depend upon. These people enrich your life because of their differences and help you to imagine new ways of thinking and behaving. They have helped you to understand what culture is and the profound influence it has had on your life.

People from diverse ethnic and linguistic backgrounds also have made many people more aware of variations in communication styles. You might observe, for example, that when some individuals communicate, they are more expressive, whereas others are more reserved; some are more relationship-oriented, whereas others are more task-oriented; and, some are more individual-focused, whereas others are more group-focused. Given the number of differences you are likely to encounter in school, at work, or in your personal relationships, you may find it helpful to examine a more in-depth explanation of intercultural communication.

FIGURE 3.1 ■ Demographics in the United States
Source: U.S. Department of Commerce

Picture Intercultural Communication

In chapter 1, you looked at how people in the United States typically think communication works. Mainstream U.S. culture tends to value sending messages directly and clearly, assuring that nonverbal messages are complementary. Taking turns between being either a speaker or a listener is commonplace. However, people from other cultures often view the communication process differently.

Consider the Enryo-Sasshi Japanese model of communication as described in Klopf (1997). To understand this model (figure 3.2), examine this extended example. You want to tell a customer that you can't fill an order as requested. To begin, the model represents all the possible information that you could potentially share with the customer. That information could include all of the following: "I can't complete this task because it's part of someone else's job." "I might create a conflict." "My job is already on the line." "I don't like you." "My boss is standing nearby listening to our conversation." You then carefully narrow the message (*enryo* means to be discreet, hesitant, restrained). Once the information

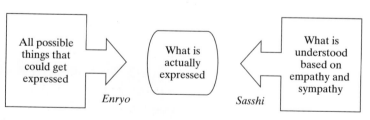

FIGURE 3.2 ■ Enryo-Sasshi Model
Source: Adapted from Satoshi Ishii's Communication Model, Klopf, 1997.

has been selected, you choose the verbal and nonverbal symbols to express your thoughts. You say to the customer, "Completing this order will be most difficult" while looking down at your feet.

The receiver, whose job is more important than the sender's in this model, must be wide open to receiving not only the verbal message but also the nonverbal message. As the information is decoded, the receiver expands upon all these messages (*sasshi* means to be sympathetic, surmise, guess). In addition, the receiver adds to the decoding his or her own experiences and reaches an understanding of what is being expressed. Thus, what goes on inside the receiver's head significantly influences the interpretation of the message.

This model works efficiently because the Japanese, in comparison to Americans, who are a very homogeneous people who find it easier to understand each other and can, therefore, guess about a person's real meanings more accurately. The closest that North Americans get to this model is in intimate relationships. In these relationships, you recognize certain cues as reflective of the sender's true thoughts and feelings. If you know, for instance, that your spouse goes out and works in the garage while banging things around when upset or angry, you'll likely know "something is up" the next time your spouse retreats to the garage and starts making noise. Indeed, the better people understand each other, the better they will be at making their own communication more efficient and effective.

Understanding these different perspectives about "how communication works" is a necessary first step in communicating effectively in cross-cultural situations.

Cross-Cultural Communication Principles

Just as certain principles govern communication in general, so do important principles control communicating cross-culturally. Keeping these principles in mind, as adapted from Sarbaugh (1993), will help you move toward effective communication, regardless of the specific differences you encounter while interacting with people from different ethnic and linguistic backgrounds.

The first principle states that the greater the cultural/linguistic difference between people, the greater the likelihood that there will be a communication breakdown. For example, communicating with customers from Iran will likely lead to more communication difficulties for you than would be true if you were communicating with customers from England. Differences in worldviews, values, and communication styles can all contribute to misunderstandings.

A second principle suggests that when communication breakdowns occur during cross-cultural encounters, the breakdowns are most often attributed to cultural differences. Although these differences may be the cause of breakdowns, effective communicators also think about other possible causes as well. Such breakdowns could be the result of a misunderstanding based on personal differences or any of the breakdowns described in Chapter 1 such as gaps or noise.

A third principle illustrates that communicating across cultures often leads people to be more conscious about their own communication. You may, as a result, choose your words more carefully, ask clarifying questions, and refrain from discussing "politically incorrect" topics. Also, you may be more conscious of how your nonverbal messages might be misinterpreted. You are more apt to be cautious about the gestures that you make when you realize that hand gestures signaling victory or "OK" among North Americans may mean something quite different to those from other cultures. Note too that this increased awareness can make you uncomfortable and more self-conscious about communicating with those from other cultures.

A fourth principle states that cultures vary with respect to the number and kind of "do's and taboos" that are required of its members. Some cultural groups, for example, have very formal rules that are rarely violated by its members or by anyone who desires to have strong relationships with members of that group. Other cultural groups have few formal rules for interaction. However, all groups have some do's and taboos. The effective cross-cultural communicator learns what they are and is respectful of them. Roger Axtell, former CEO of the Parker Pen Company, has written extensively about the do's and taboos of interacting cross-culturally. For example, Axtell (1990) recommends that you provide a small gift when meeting Japanese visitors. However, you would not wrap the gift in white paper since white is a sign of death, nor should the gift ever be a knife since it suggests the visitor commit suicide.

A fifth principle urges you to keep in mind that learning about the norms and variations in communication styles of a particular cultural group helps increase your understanding of that group. You may find it especially helpful to understand the worldview and/or value systems different groups of people hold since communication patterns reflect these orientations. You can learn about these groups by consulting books, by talking with people who have interacted with these groups, and from reflecting on your own experiences with cross-cultural communication. While pursuing this information, recognize these sources may fail to provide you with all you need to know about another culture. Variations within the same culture exist from community to community. Changes in cultures occur over time, and the biases of authors and people you meet may paint a less than complete or accurate picture of the cultural group.

Cooperative Cross-Cultural Communication Is Possible If the Communicators Are Sensitive to Each Other's Cultures

The sixth principle asserts that if you see others as friendly, cooperative, and trustworthy, barriers will be more easily overcome. When you sense these qualities in others, you are more likely to work together to achieve understanding despite differences in culture, language, and worldview.

In summary, diversity abounds in your society and in your communication with others. You can experience personal enrichment and interpersonal satisfaction by seeking out these differences, affirming these differences, and learning from these differences.

Cross-Cultural Communication Differences

Although every aspect of communication is influenced by culture, gender, religion, etc., it is helpful to think about how a particular social group's value orientations affect communication styles. Scholars have identified several of these differences in value orientations. This section will describe some of them.

One value orientation is related to being task-oriented versus relationship-oriented. One of the first questions some North Americans commonly ask others when they meet is, "What do you do?" The focus for many people in the United States is on what a person does and accomplishes. Often North Americans "get right down to business" when meeting with others. On the other hand, some people, such as East Indians, hold a relationship orientation, which seeks to focus more on the person rather than the accomplishments. For these people, "getting right down to business" may seem impersonal and aggressive. Building and strengthening relationships is necessary before any tasks can be accomplished.

A second value orientation is related to individualism versus collectivism. Individualist orientations, held by most in the United States, focus on "doing one's own thing," on self-improvement, and on personal achievement. When conflicts arise between the needs of the group and the needs of the individual, those with an individualist orientation will often choose to meet their own needs. Collectivist social groups, in contrast, focus on the importance of the group over the individual. For these social groups, considering how one's actions affect others is paramount in making decisions. The Japanese saying captures their collectivist orientation: "The nail that sticks up gets hammered down."

Another value orientation is related to power distance. Some groups seek a small power distance in relationships and ask that all be treated equally. It is not uncommon, for example, that your teachers, your bosses, and your elders ask that you call them by their first names. In some other cultures, a high power distance is formed, and relationships are not equal but are hierarchical with some people of higher status than others. India's caste system is one such example. Addressing people by their full titles and with formality is expected and required. In some instances, power distance also influences who people can and cannot interact with in meaningful ways.

Geert Hofstede (2001), in a comprehensive study of IBM employees in more than 74 countries, identified two additional value orientations (figure 3.3). These include masculinity versus femininity and uncertainty avoidance. To illustrate these value orientations, Hofstede examined IBM companies in Iran and Switzerland. Hofstede found in Iran that the two highest value orientations were power distance and high uncertainty avoidance, or a desire for clear rules and regulations. Thus, leaders in this IBM company had virtually unlimited power to do whatever they wanted and had very strict rules and regulations guiding employee performance and expectations. In contrast, Switzerland's two highest value orientations were masculinity, as opposed to femininity, and individualism. Thus both male and female workers valued assertiveness and competition (both masculine traits) as well as independence evidenced by a desire to take care of one's own self and immediate family above all. Imagine how working in either of these two companies would present a very different experience for its workers.

Remember that these value orientations are not absolute but represent degrees of orientation. For example, no one is completely individualist or completely relationship-oriented.

Another interesting issue arises when you observe what happens in transnational companies—companies that are global by design. The question raised is whether these transnational companies are shaped by local value orientations, as Hofstede suggests, or whether their global corporate culture shapes workers to fit into this new corporate culture, imposing the company's values on the workers from the local culture. Fleming and Søborg (2006) show that since both the corporate culture and the local culture are strong, transnational companies develop a "third culture," a local-corporate culture, which is a unique melding of both.

By now you should be able to see how these differing value orientations would result in very different styles of communication. Those who prefer more formal, assertive, task-oriented, and individualist value orientations will communicate differently than those who prefer more informal, nurturing, relationship-oriented, and collectivist value orientations. These orientations will impact just about every aspect of communications, including topics appropriate for conversations, approaches to greeting, uses of language, and meaning and purpose of nonverbal communication.

Task Versus Relationship Orientation

Individualism Versus Collectivism

High Versus Low Power Distance

Masculinity Versus Femininity

High Versus Low Uncertainty Avoidance

FIGURE 3.3 ■ Five Value Orientations

Masculinity Versus Femininity

Cross-Cultural Communication Barriers

By now it should be evident that variations in communication abound as a result of cultural differences. However, you also need to know how to identify specific barriers to effective intercultural communication (Barna, 1998). In the section that follows, you will read about four such barriers.

The first barrier to effective intercultural communication is called *walking on eggs*. Certain topics create tension for people who have been historically oppressed. This tension can make those communicating with these groups hesitant to approach these topics. Further, it is sometimes difficult to know exactly what these topics are or what comments spur this tension in communication. One particularly tension-producing form of communication is ethnic, racist, or sexist jokes. Other politically sensitive topics include affirmative action, bilingual education, race relations, same-sex marriage, and religion.

Several suggestions can help you deal with this barrier. First, if you think it is difficult walking on eggs, think about what it must feel like if you were the egg—that is, if you were the target of such jokes or topics! These topics are profoundly personal and can affect how people feel and think about themselves. Consequently, try to develop empathy for the person or group with whom you are communicating. In addition, remember that listening is a vital link in any constructive communication interaction. You communicate genuine interest in the receiver when you demonstrate active, attentive listening. You might also find ways to communicate your support for people who are different from you. For example, you could invite others into discussions and ask them to share their perceptions of the topic at hand. Finally, it is best to avoid sensitive topics of discussion until you have established a stronger relationship marked by trust.

Hot buttons are another barrier. Hot buttons are words that evoke an emotional response in another person. Calling someone an "affirmative action hire," for example, does little to produce positive working relations. Sometimes words used are simply misunderstood. Profanity can be a hot button, especially for those people who have a more formal view of the world. Other hot buttons are derogatory words used to describe people from different social groups. In 2007, radio disc jockey Don Imus created a controversy when he used inflammatory words to describe the women's basketball team from Rutgers. His remarks led to dismissal from his job.

It will help you to identify both the hot buttons for you and for those with whom you interact. Then learn to avoid these hot buttons. Equally important, when they are used by someone, work hard to control your emotional responses. At some other point, when tension is minimized, talk to the other person about your reactions to these hot buttons as well as why they produce that reaction.

A third barrier is *stereotyping* another group's culture. Stereotyping occurs when you take what you have learned about a group and apply that "learning" to all members of that group without considering variations within that group.

The Importance of Proper Language
Source: www.CartoonStock.com.

Although it is often helpful to learn as much as you can about a group from books, articles, the Internet, and listening to the experiences of others, it is important that you remain open to differences within a group. Some of the information received may describe the person quite well whereas other information may be outdated and based on limited contact. Keep in mind that social groups change and that individuals develop their own personalities within the bounds of their group's expectations. Also keep in mind that most individuals belong to multiple groups—such as ethnic, gender, sexual orientation, and religious groups—that may account for the variation of people within that group.

The fourth barrier is *language, vernacular, or accent bias*. Almost all people, including mainstream Americans in the United States, have a particular affinity for their language. With language comes identity, access to ideas, and a level of comfort. To suggest that one language is better than another does little to create constructive relations with those who speak other languages. All languages are capable of communicating every possible thought. Related to language bias is vernacular bias. Vernacular refers to the specific language used in particular communities, such as that spoken by people in the Appalachians, or by certain ethnic groups, such as Black English. The film *American Tongues* is excellent for its exploration of these vernacular variations. Finally, there are certain biases that come with a particular accent such as Valley girl, southern drawl, or midwesterner. It helps to identify your biases about language, vernaculars, or accents and to actively work to overcome these. In addition, you should recognize that there is power in learning a new language. The ability to speak a second language provides another opportunity to value diversity.

Cross-Cultural Communication Tools

The specific tools for effective communication across cultures are easy to list and describe but difficult to employ. This section will detail five such tools: overcoming personal biases, relating culture to communication, empathizing with those for whom English is not their first language, recognizing your own privileges, and developing cross-cultural competence.

OVERCOME PERSONAL BIASES

Racism, stereotypes, and discrimination negatively affect your communication with others. These are the source of hurt feelings and can result in miscommunication, damaged relationships, and loss of productivity. The history of ethnic relations in America makes it difficult to overcome current struggles with discrimination since the mentality that justified slavery and forced the removal of the first North Americans from their ancestral lands, for example, is still present in much of this country's consciousness. Relations become strained when Euro-Americans assert that these historical practices are over and that ethnic minority people should "just move on" or when feelings of guilt keep Euro-Americans from creating meaningful relationships with ethnic minorities. The concept of overcoming biases is so strong that it motivated the creation of the Museum of Tolerance in Los Angeles in 1993 (figure 3.4).

First, to overcome personal biases, you will find it useful to develop an understanding of some key terminology listed in Table 3.1. Second, recognize that racism, sexism, homophobia, and discrimination are still a powerful part

FIGURE 3.4 ■ Display in the Museum of Tolerance, Los Angeles

Prejudice	A set of rigid and unfavorable attitudes toward a particular group or groups that is formed in disregard of facts. It is, thus, an unsupported judgment usually accompanied by disapproval.
Stereotype	A preconceived or oversimplified generalization often involving negative beliefs about a particular group. Negative stereotypes are frequently at the base of prejudice. The danger of stereotyping is that it no longer considers people as individuals but rather categorizes them as members of a group who all think and behave in the same way.
Discrimination	Unequal treatment based on unfair categorization. When you act on your prejudices, you engage in discrimination. Discrimination often involves keeping people out of activities or places because of the group to which they belong.
Sexism	Assigning certain characteristics to people on the basis of their gender, with an assumption of superiority or inferiority, and resulting in unequal treatment.
Racism	Coupling the false assumption that race determines psychological and cultural traits with the belief that one race is superior to another. Based on the belief that certain groups are inferior, racists justify discriminating against, scapegoating, and/or segregating these groups. The term *racism* is being used here in a broad sense to include discrimination against both ethnic and racial minorities.

Homophobia	Literally, the fear of homosexuality is a prejudicial hatred of homosexuality, which often results in discriminatory practices and sometimes even violent attacks.
Ethnocentrism	The tendency to judge other groups by the norms, values, behaviors, and expectations of your own group; that is, your own group is at the "center" of all other groups. Ethnocentrism includes the tendency to elevate the value of your group.
Scapegoating	The deliberate policy of blaming an individual or group for things they did not really do. Prejudicial attitudes and discriminatory acts lead to scapegoating. Members of the disliked group are denied social privileges such as housing and employment. They are usually politically powerless to defend themselves. Scapegoating can lead to verbal and physical violence, including death.
Institutional Racism	Discrimination that is not individual in nature but is embedded in the policies and practices of particular institutions like schools, banks, governments, and so on. That is, the institution carries out its tasks in ways that some gain privileges, and others are denied access to those privileges. Thus, the decision to have higher interest rates for home loans in low-income neighborhoods is an example of institutional racism against poorer persons.

TABLE 3.1 ■ Definition of Terms

of the American landscape. Make a commitment not only to be sensitive to the possibility of your own biases, but also develop strategies to actively resist these if they occur in your workspace.

Third, be especially attuned to how people communicate their prejudices. In this regard, Brislin's (1988) description is helpful. His description moves from the most obvious and derogatory to the least. As these ways of communicating prejudices are described in the next paragraph, ask yourself if you have heard, or perhaps have made, comments like these in the recent past.

Overt racism occurs when you make a statement that would be considered by most people as racist. Such statements as "All . . . are lazy" or " . . . should go back where they came from" fall into this category. **Symbolic racism** is attacking some symbol of importance to a particular group of people. These symbols might be affirmative action, bilingual education, or reparations for land lost. By not attacking the people themselves, individuals fool themselves into believing that they are not racist. Symbolic racists reject these symbols without being fully informed about them; that is, the response is emotional and not based on fact. As one example, saying affirmative action requires companies to hire people who are not qualified is, in reality, a distortion of the actual policy. **Tokenism** is communicated by people who say, "I can't be racist; one of my best friends is . . . . " Believing that knowing one person is enough to prove that an individual is not racist is illogical at best. **Arm's-length racism** suggests that you don't mind ethnic minority people to work with or to socialize with but that you would oppose any closer relationship such as, for example, dating or marrying a person from a different group.

These forms of racism are frequently based upon fear. You might find yourself fearful, for example, of those with whom you are unfamiliar. However, only through genuine communication can you move beyond the unfamiliar and create cooperative relations with others who are different from you. As Martin Luther King suggested:

"People fail to get along because they fear each other; they fear each other because they don't know each other; they don't know each other because they have not properly communicated."

RELATE CULTURE TO COMMUNICATION

At this point in the chapter, you should understand the powerful connection between culture and communication. Culture is not simply a matter of the foods, fashions, or folklores of a particular group of people. For example, you cannot teach others about North American culture by simply having them wear jeans, eat hot dogs and apple pie, and listen to the legend of Johnny Appleseed.

Likewise, every aspect of communication is impacted by culture. Language and culture are intimately connected. In fact, it is hard to know a language without simultaneously learning the culture of that people. Nonverbal communication is influenced by culture-specific meanings that you would be remiss to ignore. Finally, the ways you communicate convey much about your values and worldview to the people with whom you interact.

The Yellow Star to Mark People as Jewish Is an Example of Discrimination

To make these ideas more real, think about the differences between the games boys and girls traditionally play and the influence these games have on resulting communication styles (Leaper, 1998). Traditionally, girls' games, like "house" or "school," are played by multiple children with a focus on interpersonal relationships where the objectives and rules of the game are not defined. To make these games work requires that the participants talk to each other to agree on the objectives and rules. From these games, girls learn three rules for communication: Be collaborative, don't criticize, and pay attention to others' feelings. In contrast, boys' games, such as baseball or football, have clear rules and goals where the individual tries to outshine the others while winning and where aggression is valued. From these experiences, boys learn three rules of communication: Assert yourself, pursue achievement and winning, and value competition. Note that since the rules and goals are set, less communication is needed in these male games than for the female games.

Childhood Games Reflect Gender Communication Styles

Keep in mind that culture is invisible, and most people are not aware of how culture affects them. Most people do not know, for example, the origin and purpose of throwing rice at a wedding, wearing a tie in a business meeting, or kissing a "boo-boo" on a child's skinned knee (Tejula, 1999). It is true that people often have very little clue about the purpose behind culturally appropriate behavior, even their own, beyond explaining that it is tradition.

Skillful intercultural communicators will seek to understand and affirm these cultural differences while recognizing that tremendous value results in the variation of human orientations. They will appreciate the interdependent nature of groups, as described in the beginning pages of this chapter. These communicators will desire to learn about the history, current social issues, and perspectives of diverse groups. They will especially note the culture-specific differences in communication that characterize intercultural interactions. Finally, skillful intercultural communicators will work to become an ally of people from diverse groups, committed to achieving social equality and justice for all.

EMPATHIZE WITH THOSE FOR WHOM ENGLISH IS NOT THEIR FIRST LANGUAGE

Speaking a language that is not the dominant language of the people with whom you work and live is difficult. Likewise, learning to speak a second language is a challenging activity for most. This difficulty involves many factors, including how you feel about the new language and yourself as a second language learner, the degree to which you experience anxiety in language learning situations, the number and quality of meaningful interactions you have with speakers of the language you wish to learn, and learning style differences when it comes to language learning.

The skillful intercultural communicator develops empathy for second language learners. One way to develop empathy is by learning a second language yourself. You will quickly come to appreciate the challenge facing someone for whom English is a second language. Additionally, you communicate that you value languages and appreciate the attempts by others to learn your language. Above all, keep in mind that a person's intelligence has nothing to do with his or her ability to speak English. Maintaining a respectful orientation will be critical in this regard.

The two primary things you want to do when communicating with those for whom English is a second language is to minimize the level of stress and to work to make the message as understandable as possible. Minimizing stress is important to enable the language learner to be open to messages presented in a language not fully understood and encourages risk taking in efforts to speak the new language. Make the message more understandable by providing as many clues as possible. Also, use visuals, gestures, pictures, and objects to enhance the likelihood that the message will be more fully understood.

RECOGNIZE YOUR OWN PRIVILEGES

While acknowledging how others are often the target of unfair treatment and expectations, you may find it easy to forget that members of certain social groups are privileged in your society. These individuals may also take their privileges for granted. Think for a moment about the privileges of being Caucasian.

- If you ask to speak to the supervisor, you're likely to talk with someone who looks like you.

- You can see many examples of people from your race who are wealthy and powerful in this society.

- If someone offers you a position, you don't have to wonder if your race had anything to do with the offer.

- If a family moves from your neighborhood just as you move in, you don't have to ask yourself if they are moving out because you are Caucasian.

- You can find "flesh-colored" band-aids that are the color of your flesh.

- You are never asked to explain why Caucasian people act or feel or believe a certain way or to speak on behalf of all those of your race.

It could be argued that one reason for the persistence of prejudice in our society is the majority's lack of interest in jeopardizing these privileges. Indeed, it takes much for you to take a stand in favor of others in a way that might result in fewer benefits for you.

Use Gestures to Enhance Understanding

It is not being privileged that is a problem but what you do with those privileges. For example, do you use your privileges to speak up against sexism, racism, and homophobia when it plays out in the work setting? Do you use your privileges to challenge friends who make racist, sexist, or homophobic statements? Finally, do you recognize and acknowledge your privileges?

DEVELOP CROSS-CULTURAL COMPETENCE

Although the previous suggestions are critical to cross-cultural effectiveness, it is also important for you to develop a full range of other cross-cultural competencies (Spitzburg, 1999). The kind of competence meant here is an ability to accomplish goals while also reducing misunderstandings and building strong interpersonal, cross-cultural relationships. This is a lifelong process and must be engaged in purposefully; that is, it will not just happen. These competencies will enhance the overall quality of your life as well as your relationships.

Here is a brief list of these skills. Think about these and assess where you stand with respect to them. Identify a couple that you want to work on and then move toward effectiveness in those areas. Cross-cultural competencies include the following:

- An ability to acknowledge your own prejudices and biases and the lifelong work needed to overcome them.

- An ability to work toward equal status relationships with people who are different from you.

- An ability to challenge your own personal assumptions about the skills and competencies of employees who are different.

- An ability to learn as much as possible about how your own culture is different from others and how that difference contributes to a particular way of viewing yourself and others.

- An ability to take risks in an effort to communicate with people from other cultures.

- An ability to learn about how individuals and groups of people like to be treated and accommodate them as much as possible.

Developing Competence in Cross-Cultural Communication Requires That You Explore Your Own Attitudes and Abilities

One additional skill involves knowing how to handle instances where someone makes remarks that can be considered racist, sexist, homophobic, etc. First, it is important to acknowledge that responding to these remarks requires courage. It would, no doubt, be easier to let someone else deal with the remarks, to just ignore them, or to justify no response at all since the remarks do not affect you personally. It is even more difficult when those making these insensitive remarks are your family, friends, or co-workers.

Second, you also need skills in responding to these remarks. Fortunately, there are some excellent resources that provide specific guidelines for confronting intolerance. One such guidebook is titled *Speak Up! Responding to Everyday Bigotry* (Willoughby, 2005). It provides specific guidelines for interrupting biases among family and friends at work, at school, and in public.

Perhaps you can take heart in knowing the tremendous risk and creative spirit evident in people who have taken a stand against bias and hate. One example from history involved Quaker families who moved their homes toward the underground railroad—a network of houses that provided safety for African Americans fleeing slavery in the south—for the purpose of supporting them in their quest for freedom. Perhaps you can find additional encouragement from those who belong to the Southern Poverty Law Center, including its director Morris Dees. Their webpage, Tolerance.org, provides a comprehensive resource for any and all who are committed to combating bias and promoting equity and justice.

Diversity and Technology

Media scholar Marshall McLuhan coined the term *global village* to describe the influence that television would have on your life. That is, television would shrink the globe into one tiny village where what happened at one end of the village would be quickly noticed at the other end. People were witness, via television, to the fall of the Berlin wall, the confrontation between a lone Chinese dissident and a Chinese Army tank, and the devastating effects of the tsunami in Indonesia that killed nearly 220,000 people.

Today, you can add the computer and especially email to the list of technologies that serve to bring you ever closer to others who are different from you. You can send an email message to friends who may be in any part of the world as well as answer your own email messages from remote locations on the globe. Via webpages, you can learn more about a company, an organization, or a person than what was available before. Many service centers have outsourced technical service assistance to places beyond the U.S. borders.

Another new opportunity involves people taking control of Internet material in ways not even imaginable just ten years ago. With YouTube, you can place your own videos and images online as well as be exposed to those of others who are very different from you. With Facebook, you can create your own personal webpage to communicate with both strangers and friends in ways that reveal your personal and cultural identities.

All of these technologies have important implications for communicating across differences. Many companies, called multinational organizations, have company offices and work facilities in multiple locations across the

Technology and
Communication

globe. These may require you to make phone calls to Bangkok, send emails to Iceland, and order parts from India or Honduras. Sometimes, after many encounters, you may even have the opportunity to establish meaningful relationships with specific employees, culminating in overseas visits or exchanges. These opportunities are in addition to the diversity of persons with whom you might be speaking via telephone or writing via email even if those persons are here in the United States.

Finally, a few basic guidelines will help you in assuring effective cross-cultural communication while using technology. First, don't assume anything about the person's gender or race simply by seeing a name. Second, continue to apply all the guidelines described earlier in this chapter. Third, recognize and appreciate the effort others are making to communicate with you, usually in English, which may not be their first language. Fourth, refuse to send or pass on emails with jokes that might be perceived, even by the most sensitive person, as offensive. In fact, it is best to send emails related *only* to business. At all times recognize that your communication via technology represents not only you, but also your company and your country.

Review Questions

1. What are some important cross-cultural communication experiences you have had? What did you learn from these?

2. Marshall McLuhan described the world as a global village. Explain how events and activities in other parts of the world affect you.

3. Describe the importance of cross-cultural communication to you.

4. Explain the concept that your intercultural communication might involve "walking on eggs."

5. Explain the meaning of "arm's-length" racism.

6. List three strategies for communicating with people for whom English is not their first language.

7. Identify three privileges that you have experienced because of your race, ethnicity, gender, religion, or sexual orientation.

8. Which cross-cultural communication competencies would you like to develop?

9. Describe some of your own "hot buttons" and the ways you deal with these in an interpersonal communication setting.

Key Terms and Concepts

Arm's-Length Racism   66
Collectivism   60
Discrimination   64
Enryo-Sasshi   57
Ethnocentrism   65
Global Interdependence   56
Homophobia   65
Hot Buttons   62
Individualism   60

Institutional Racism   65
Masculine-Feminism Value
   Orientation   61
Overt Racism   66
Power Distance   60
Prejudice   64
Racism   64
Relationship Orientation   60
Scapegoating   65

Sexism   64
Stereotyping   62
Symbolic Racism   66
Task Orientation   61
Tokenism   66
Uncertainty Avoidance   61
Walking On Eggs   62

Web Activities

- Windows of the World contains images from around the world at this website: http://woow .phil-sllvn.co.uk/windows/

- Guidelines for international travelers who are doing business can be found here: http://www .executiveplanet.com/index.php?title=Main_Page

- Business professionals promoting international relations learn how at this website: http://www .businessfordiplomaticaction.org/who/

Assignments

ASSIGNMENT 3.1: INTERCULTURAL PERSONALITY PROFILE

Directions: To assess how easy it is for you to interact with people from a different culture, complete the following questionnaire. Use a scale of 1 to 5 to indicate how strongly you agree with each statement.

Low Agreement   1   2   3   4   5   High Agreement

1. I am constantly trying to understand myself better.
2. I respect the opinions of others, though I may not always agree.
3. I interact well with people who are very different from me in age, race, economic status, gender, and sexual orientation.
4. I can usually apply what I learn to real-life situations.
5. I can function well even though I don't understand everything going on around me.
6. I am able to change my plans or expectations to fit new situations.
7. I often find humor in difficult situations.
8. When I have to wait, I am patient.
9. I constantly seek new experiences, new people, and new places.
10. I am resourceful when I find myself in unfamiliar circumstances.
11. I tackle problems confidently without needing the help of others.
12. When things go badly, I am able to maintain a positive attitude as I attempt to resolve problems.
13. I realize that my culture is not better than other cultures.
14. In an unfamiliar situation, I watch and listen before acting.
15. I am able to put myself in another's place.
16. When I am lost, I ask for directions.
17. When I work with others, building a good relationship is just as important as completing our task.
18. I can accept people as they are.
19. I am sensitive to the feelings of others.
20. I like to try new ways of doing things.

Total Score _____

Based upon your total score, respond to the following:

1. List two specific strengths you have when communicating with people from a different culture.
2. List two specific cross-cultural competencies you would like to develop.

ASSIGNMENT 3.2: MAKING INTERCULTURAL CONTACT: SHOW AND TELL

Although you may think of diversity in terms of other people who are different from you, all people are unique in some way. For example, maybe a close friend of yours is a vegetarian. Perhaps one of your co-workers is a member of a female rock band. Maybe a next-door neighbor is involved with Habitat for Humanity or volunteers at a community food pantry.

The purpose of this interaction is for you to identify what makes you different in some way and to share that difference with classmates. Below are the steps you will follow to complete this interaction.

Steps:

1. Identify a unique personal quality you would be comfortable sharing with others in class. If you can, speak to a quality about your age, your race or ethnicity, your gender, physical disability, religion, or sexual orientation. Again, be sure the quality is something you feel comfortable sharing with others.
2. Bring to class some object or article that could symbolize that quality. The vegetarian might bring in an apple, the female rocker a piece of sheet music, the Latino a poncho from his or her hometown.
3. Join together with four or five other classmates and take turns displaying the objects or articles brought to class.
4. As each member takes a turn, the other members must try to guess what the object or article symbolizes. For example, group members might guess that the vegetarian who brought in the apple is a gardener.
5. If the group members incorrectly guess what the object or article means, the individual sharing must inform the group about what the item truly represents.
6. Once these steps have been completed, each member must describe to the group specific ways in which his or her uniqueness enriches life and also poses challenges. The vegetarian, for instance, might explain how a meatless diet benefits the environment but also causes problems when dining out.

Once these six steps have been completed, group members should discuss and respond to the following questions.

1. Identify ways in which your perceptions of those in the group changed as a result of this sharing.
2. List advantages you think can occur when individuals talk about their differences with one another.
3. Formulate a statement to reflect the role and value of personal diversity in your interactions with others.

When finished, each group should share its responses to these questions with the entire class.

Note: People doing this activity are sharing something that is important to them, something that represents a core of who they are as people, their very identity. It is important that people in the group refrain from laughing, criticizing, or belittling what the person brings or says. This is a prime opportunity to practice all the skills associated with cross-cultural competence!

ASSIGNMENT 3.3: MAKING INTERCULTURAL CONTACT: ARTICLE SEARCH

Directions: For this assignment, you will expand your awareness of diversity and cultural competence by learning about a culture different from yours. Your assignment is to research a culture using at least three Internet sites or printed articles. Describe what you have learned about that particular cultural group in a three- to five-minute presentation to your class.

Internet/Article Search

Your Internet research can begin at the following website: http://www.executiveplanet.com/index.php?title=Main_Page.

Consider also the description of a country/culture by looking at Hofstede's website at: http://www.geert-hofstede.com/.

Other websites to access include *Culture Grams, CIA: The World Fact Book*, and *Globe Trekker*.

Articles can be found at your local library, or you can ask the reference librarian for assistance if you are having difficulty.

As you begin your research, select a country or culture of interest, focusing on the people, meetings/greetings, body language, corporate culture, etc. Conclude your research by noting what you have learned about that particular culture. It is best if you can also find advice for communicating with that particular group.

Presentation

In a small group setting (three to five persons), introduce the culture you researched. Respond to the following questions:

1. What are some of the key values of this group?
2. What has this group's experience been with or within the United States?
3. What are some notable achievements of this group?
4. What are some of the "do's and taboos" for this group?
5. What are some of the most important communication patterns of this group?
6. What's the most important thing someone needs to know when communicating with this group?

ASSIGNMENT 3.4: MAKING INTERCULTURAL CONTACT: INTERVIEW

Directions: It is believed that experience is the best teacher. For this assignment, you need to interview someone in your community, someone in your school, or someone from your place of employment who is part of a cultural group different from your own. It might be best if you choose someone from a cultural group that you investigated for Assignment 3.3. In particular, you might want to see if your school has a program for English language learners and connect with students from those classes. Make notes and explain to your class what you have learned about cross-cultural communication.

Consider the following guidelines for conducting the interview:

1. Get the person's permission to conduct an interview. Tell her/him that you will not identify her/him in your class report. Explaining that this is a school assignment and explaining the purpose of the assignment might be helpful in getting the person's assistance.
2. Adopt a genuine curiosity about the other culture. Don't argue with anything said. Listen and be open.
3. Begin by trying to build a relationship of trust before asking the questions that make up this assignment. Remember that some cultures are more relationship-oriented than they are task-oriented.
4. As you ask a question, consider follow-up questions that ask for clarifications, examples, or extensions of what the person just said. These follow-ups are often the best source of specific information.

5. At the end of the interview, thank the person for participating and for helping you to learn.

Several questions for your interview follow:

1. How is your culture similar to mainstream American culture?
2. How is your culture different from mainstream American culture?
3. What differences do you notice in gender relations within your culture?
4. What is one thing you wished people understood about your culture or people from your culture?
5. Explain a time when you and another person miscommunicated, and you believed that the misunderstanding was the result of cross-cultural communication differences.
6. What piece of advice can you offer others to be more effective communicators when interacting with people from your culture?

Presentation

In a small group setting, take three to five minutes to describe the person you interviewed.

Respond to the following questions:

1. Who was the person and why did you choose her/him?
2. What did you learn about that cultural group from this person?
3. What did you notice or learn about differing styles of communication?
4. What have been the most important insights you have gained as a result of this cross-cultural communication experience?
5. What's the most important thing someone needs to know when communicating with this group?

ASSIGNMENT 3.5: CASE STUDY: CONFRONTING BIAS AND DISCRIMINATION

As mentioned earlier in this chapter, it is difficult to confront comments and behaviors that you might consider biased and discriminatory. Such confrontation takes both courage and skill. One way to develop both is through role-playing.

Directions: Download the guidebook *Speak Up! Responding to Everyday Bigotry* from http://www.tolerance.org/speakup/index.html. Under the Speak Up! section on the left side of the screen, select "At Work." Within this section is information for what you can do about casual comments, workplace humor, sexist remarks, meeting missteps, the boss bias, and your own bias. In a small group, select one of the above categories and do the following:

1. Read the information on the page that comes up.
2. Discuss the suggestions provided.
3. Add any other ideas based on your group members' experiences with this form of bias.
4. Develop a role play showing an instance of that form of bias. There are real-life examples within the section you read to help you think of an incident to dramatize. Perform the role play in front of the class showing both the instance but also someone or a group confronting the bias.
5. Discuss with the class their reactions to your role play.

At the conclusion of all the role plays, discuss what the class learned about discouraging bias but especially about developing courage and skill.

References

Axtell, R. (1990). *Do's and taboos of hosting international visitors*. New York: Wiley.

Axtell, R. (1993). *Do's and taboos around the world*. New York: Wiley.

Axtell, R. (1998). *Gestures: The do's and taboos of body language around the world*. New York: Wiley.

Barna, L. (1998). Stumbling blocks in intercultural communication. In M. J. Bennett (Ed.), *Basic readings in intercultural communication: Selected readings* (pp. 173–190). Yarmouth, ME: Intercultural Press.

Brislin, R. W. (1988). Prejudice in intercultural communication. In L. A. Samovar and R. E. Porter (Eds.), *Intercultural communication: A reader* (5th ed., pp. 339–343). Belmont, CA: Wadsworth.

Chinese Cultural Connection. (1987). Chinese values and the search for culture-free dimensions of culture. *Journal of Cross-Cultural Psychology, 18*, 143–164.

Fleming, D., & Søborg, H. (2006). *Human resource policy and Danish multinational companies: A study of Danish multinational companies' human resource policy in their subsidiaries in Malaysia and Singapore* (Working paper/International Development Studies, Roskilde University; 37). Roskilde: International Development Studies, Roskilde University.

Gray, J. (1993). *Men are from Mars, women are from Venus.* New York: HarperCollins.

Hofstede, G. (2001). *Culture's consequences: Comparing values, behaviors, institutions and organizations across nations.* Thousand Oaks, CA: Sage.

Kinder, A. L. (2002). *Survey of the states' limited English proficient students and available programs and services, 1999–2000 summary report.* Washington, DC: National Clearinghouse for English Language Acquisition.

Klopf, D. W. (1997). *Intercultural encounters: The fundamentals of intercultural communication* (4th ed.). Englewood, CO: Morton.

Leaper, C. (1998). The relationship of play activity and gender to parent and child sex-typed communication. *International Journal of Behavioral Development, 19,* 689–703.

McIntosh, P. (1998, Winter). White privileges: Unpacking the invisible knapsack. *Independent Schools, 49* (2), 31–36.

Sarbaugh, L. E. (1993). *Intercultural communication* (2nd ed.). New Brunswick, NJ: Transaction Books.

Spitzburg, B. H. (1999). Communicating interculturally: Becoming competent. In L. A. Samovar & R. E. Porter (Eds.), *Intercultural communication: A reader* (pp. 373–387). Boston, MA: Wadsworth.

Suarez-Orozco, M. (2007). *Immigration and education in global perspective.* Paper presented at the Annual Meeting of the American Educational Research Association, Chicago.

Tejula, T. (1999). *Curious customs.* New York: Galahad Books.

Willoughby, B. (2005). *Speak Up! Responding to everyday bigotry* (Available at http://www.tolerance.org/speakup/index.html). Montgomery, AL: Southern Poverty Law Center.

U.S. Department of Commerce (2001). *Overview of race and Hispanic origin: Census 2000 brief.* (U.S. Census Publication No. C2KBR/01-1). Washington, DC: U.S. Government Printing Office.

Chapter 4

Language

"We should have a great fewer disputes in the world if words were taken for what they are, the signs of our ideas only, and not for things themselves."

John Locke

Learning Objectives

At the end of this chapter, you should be able to meet the following objectives:

1. Define language in your own words and describe four key components of language.
2. Discuss five key principles related to verbal communication and share the implications of these principles.
3. List and explain the five key principles related to nonverbal communication.
4. Identify and provide an example of each of the seven types of nonverbal communication: chronemics, proxemics, oculesics, kinesics, haptics, vocalics, and personal style.
5. Employ key guidelines related to effective verbal and nonverbal communication.
6. Illustrate the impact of gender and culture on your verbal and nonverbal communication.

Language Is Important

Hector Verdugo was a man on the verge of life in prison. Born to parents who were both drug addicts, he too became involved in drug dealing at an early age. By the age of eighteen, he was arrested and sent to prison for two years. Vowing to change his life, he accepted low-skilled jobs but also enrolled in a local community college in his East Los Angeles neighborhood.

Freddy Jacinto was just ten years old and living with his single mother, who did her best to steer him toward healthy decisions. However, Freddy ended up getting into "tagging"—a form of graffiti using spray paint—and became involved in gang life. In the gang, Freddy found the "family" that he felt was missing in his life. After Freddy was arrested for tagging one night, the police warned his mom that her son was headed for a life in crime.

As reported by *Los Angeles Times* correspondent Erika Hayasaki (2007), both Hector and Freddy met novelist Leslie Schwartz. As part of Homeboy Industries, an antigang program, Schwartz sought to help those in the program to understand the power of words to hurt and to heal. Schwartz stated, "There are people all over the world in prison because of the things they've said and the things they've written. Poetry has put people in prison. Why is that? Because words are way more powerful than a gun or a bomb or a knife will ever be" (p. 1). Indeed, American poet Ezra Pound was imprisoned for his antiwar poetry during World War II. Death threats to writer Salman Rushdie and the murder of songwriter Victor Jara in Chile are two more examples that demonstrate the power of words.

Both Hector and Freddy entered the antigang program with skepticism. Little by little, both began to open up. They used language to share their experiences, emotions, and perceptions with Schwartz. Seeing Schwartz's passion for language, Hector came to see the power in words and that he had a story to share. He is currently fiction editor for Homeboy Press. While Freddy continued to struggle in and out of school, he did eventually leave his gang members behind. To Schwartz's dismay, he also disappeared from the antigang program.

Language is powerful indeed. Imprisonment, threats of death, and the actual murder of poets, writers, and songwriters resulted from individuals' use of language. In contrast, language can also change a person's life from one of desperation to one of hope, as was true for Hector Verdugo. With these examples as a backdrop, you might begin thinking about the importance of language in your own life.

What would your life be like without language or nonverbal actions to communicate? As you can imagine, it would be most difficult to get anything accomplished. You would not be able to communicate thoughts, ideas, hopes, feelings, and reactions. It would be difficult to attain the shared understanding that was described as the goal of communication in Chapter 1.

Fortunately, an inability to communicate is a challenge that only a few people experience. However, many individuals face limitations that make communication difficult. Consider those with hearing, speaking, or sight

Language Has Been Used
to Help Gang Members

disabilities; a child with autism or a senior citizen with Alzheimer's. Although the inability to communicate verbally or nonverbally is a serious problem, a more common concern rests with how much of the language you use lacks clarity and purposefulness.

History provides two significant examples. With respect to clarity, examine how the multiple meanings of words can lead to misunderstanding and, in this example, the loss of thousands of lives. Close to the end of World War II, Allied forces sent a message to the Japanese: Surrender or be crushed. For their part, the Japanese issued a response with the word "mokusatsu," which means both "ignore" and "withhold comment." According to the Japanese, they were seeking more time to consider the ultimatum and, therefore, were seeking to "withhold comment" for right now. The Allied forces, however, interpreted the response as "ignore." As you probably know, several days later, the United States dropped atomic bombs on Hiroshima and Nagasaki resulting in the loss of thousands of lives.

With respect to purposefulness, people often act in ways that demonstrate carelessness in their language choice; a person can use different words to describe the same event but with different effects. During World War II, an order from the president, Executive Order 9066, led to the forced relocation of 120,000 people of Japanese American ancestry. Some called the locations where these American citizens of Japanese heritage were sent "country clubs." To others, they were popularly known as "internment camps." To many of the Japanese who resided there under harsh conditions, these "camps" could have been better described as "prisons." In reality, these words were used to describe the same place but were used for much different reasons. The words minimized the event in the "county club" case and highlighted the traumatic experience in the "prison" case. Being purposeful in your language choice requires you to think deeply about the kind of impact you want to make with your language—and then to be purposeful in its use.

With respect to nonverbal communication, you also need to be clear and purposeful in your use of gestures, posture, vocal inflections, and eye contact. Regarding clarity, some gestures, for example, have different meanings especially as you move across cultural lines. The "A-OK" gesture—thumb and index finger form a circle while the other fingers are held straight—is not "A-OK" in many Latin American countries. With respect to purposefulness, even minor variations in your vocal inflection can actually change the meaning of your message. Note how meaning changes based on word emphasis in the following statements:

"Of course, *I* want you to do this job."

"*Of course*, I want you to do this job."

"Of course, I *want* you to do this job."

"Of course, I want *you* to do this job."

"Of course, I want you to *do* this job."

"Of course, I want you to do *this* job."

Adolescent Youth Are Pictured at Heart Mountain Internment Camp, Wyoming, Where More Than 10,000 Japanese Americans Lived from August 12, 1942, to November 10, 1943

As one final example of the importance of language, let's examine the political discussion around "official" languages. Some would like to make English the official language of the United States. For others, doing so would violate the human and democratic rights of U.S. society. Realize that language is connected to culture and a person's very identity. Knowing this might help you to understand why this topic is so emotionally charged. Whatever side you are on in this political debate, you have probably seen how heated the discussion can quickly become.

In summary, language is important. Central to its importance is a strong need to assure that your language and nonverbal communication are both clear and purposeful.

The focus of this chapter will examine the principles of language and guidelines for effective verbal communication. The chapter will then turn attention to nonverbal communication. It will include principles of nonverbal communication, types of nonverbal communication, and guidelines for effective nonverbal communication. You will note that there will be many cross-cultural examples to extend what you have learned from reading Chapter 3. As well as being interesting, these cross-cultural examples will provide a more vivid demonstration of the importance of language and nonverbal communication.

| |
Phonemes — The sounds of the language

Syntax — The grammatical structure of the language

Semantics — The meanings of words

Pragmatics — The appropriateness of your language for the places and people with whom you interact

FIGURE 4.1 ■ Components of Language

Language Defined

You might be thinking: What is language? One definition of language is that it is "the use of vocalized sounds, or written symbols representing these sounds or ideas, in patterns organized by grammatical rules in order to express thoughts and feelings" (Rogers & Steinfatt, 1999, p. 126).

More specifically, it is helpful to understand some of the various components of language: phonemes, syntax, semantics, and pragmatics (figure 4.1). Phonemes represent the sound system of a language and often the smallest level at which language is understood. Linguists have identified 200 vowel sounds and 600 consonant sounds used around the world. However, most languages make use of between only fifteen and eighty-five different sounds. In English, for example, people use about forty-five sounds, depending upon the dialect. Note that most languages of the world are "tonal," which means that changes in pitch change the meaning of a word. Although English is not a tonal language, you can get some sense of this concept by considering the change in meaning via pronunciation for these two words:

How *does* he do that?

Those *does* (several female deer) near the building sure are friendly.

She tied the documents together in a *bow*.

The Japanese often *bow* as their form of greeting.

In addition, for each language, certain letters or sounds are just not used together. For example, in English, you would not know how to pronounce a word that starts with "ng" or "ts." However, those same letters can be used together if they appear at the end of a word such as in "moving" or "cats." In Spanish, words do not begin with "sp," but words often begin with "es." Consequently, you will often hear a Spanish-speaker pronounce "speech" as "espeech."

A second component of language is **syntax.** Syntax focuses on the pattern or structure of a language and the rules for that structure. The definition of language you read earlier emphasizes syntax. Speakers of English usually put the subject first, the verb second, and the object third. "Marcela hit the ball" is an example of this structure. However, the most common pattern for languages across the world is subject-object-verb: "Marcela the ball hit." As one other example, the rules of syntax in English dictate that you place descriptive words close to the words that they modify. Not doing so results in "dangling modifiers," and, in some cases, embarrassment. Here are two examples:

For those of you who have children and don't know it, there's a nursery downstairs. (Implies you don't know that you have children.)

New choir robes are needed due to the addition of new members to the choir and the deterioration of the old ones. (Implies that some members of the choir, not their robes, have deteriorated.)

"Chair" Can Have
Different Meanings

A third element of language is **semantics**. Semantics focuses on the meaning of words. The meanings of words are shaped by what the words stand for, your experiences, and your purpose for communication. Essentially, four classes of meaning have been identified:

- **Denotative.** People might focus on the object(s) to which the word refers. The word *chair* refers to the wood, plastic, or metal structure you sit on but also to a leadership role a person plays within a business or school such as a chair of a committee or department. Keep in mind that the most common 500 words have 10,000 different definitions, an average of 20 meanings each for the 500 most common words.

- **Connotative.** Sometimes people focus on the emotional meanings of words. Being *bony, skinny,* or *thin* may be used to describe the same person's body shape but will garner different emotional responses—especially from the person being described.

- **Contextual Meaning.** Word meanings are shaped by the places where they are spoken and by the people speaking them. You can imagine that the meaning of the statement, "Please take off your clothes" changes if spoken in a doctor's office versus in a hotel room. Do the words change when spoken by a doctor versus by your spouse? You should assume that they do.

- **Figurative Language.** The beauty of the spoken word lies in the use of figurative language. You might *give the shirt off your back* to a person you care about, fall *head over heels in love,* and then feel like you're *walking on cloud nine.* Sometimes, however, it could be *raining cats and dogs,* and you're tired of your boss *pulling your leg* when it comes to a favored work assignment, so you just want to leave work *like a bat out of hell.* Imagine how those who speak English as a foreign language and interpret these phrases literally might misunderstand what you mean.

The last component of language is **pragmatics**. Pragmatics focuses on identifying the appropriate use of language for the setting and the relationship between

CENTRAL SUB-COMMITTEE STEERING GROUP FOR THE FACILITATION OF BREVITY & CLARITY OF LANGUAGE USAGE IN THE USER/PROVIDER COMMUNICATION INTERFACE (Formerly the plain English group)

"Plain English" Group
Source: www.CartoonStock .com.

the two speakers. Shirley Brice Heath (1983) argued that knowing how and when to use a language is as important as knowing the language itself. Pragmatics often guides what can be talked about, when it can be discussed, and by whom it can be communicated. As some examples, consider that in the United States, people often think it inappropriate to ask about a person's age, income level, or sexual orientation unless the relationship is a close one. As another example, people in the United States have an unspoken rule about taking turns when it comes to talking. That is, most communicators will talk until they are finished, and then it is the other person's turn to talk. What would you make, then, of your Hawaiian co-worker who consistently violates the clear turn-taking rule to which you have become accustomed? Instead, this person consistently talks while you are talking in what has been termed "talk-story" in Hawaiian culture. You might also get frustrated when requesting advice from your elderly Native American neighbor who responds by telling a story that, at first glance, is completely irrelevant to the topic. Both are examples of the importance of attending to pragmatics when you are thinking about language in communication.

Principles of Verbal Communication

In addition to understanding how language can be defined, you will find it helpful to review some principles of verbal communication.

The first principle is to recognize that all languages have value. No language is better than any other in complexity, logic, or ability to convey thought. All languages are important because they are connected to people whose very cultural identity is tied to that language. Gloria Anzaldúa (1987) wrote about this connection:

> So if you want to really hurt me, talk badly about my language. Ethnic identity is twin skin to linguistic identity—I am my language. Until I can take pride in my language, I cannot take pride in myself (p. 207).

A second principle is to understand that everyone speaks a dialect. Dialects are regional variations of language with unique pronunciation, vocabulary, and grammar. The United States has several distinct dialect regions including the western, midwestern, eastern, and southern. Some dialects are specific within certain regions such as New England on the East Coast, Appalachian folk talk within the South, or Valley girl talk on the West Coast. The key is to recognize that even with these dialect differences, you can still understand what is being said. It is also important to stop yourself from being negatively influenced by those stereotypes that often are attached to people who speak a particular dialect. More positively, dialects offer a unique richness to any language.

A third principle is to understand that words do not mean the same thing to all people. Sometimes the word is simply misunderstood. A teacher mentioned to students that "foul" language was not allowed in class. A concerned student from Turkey came to the office to ask why students could not talk about chickens and birds ("fowl") in class. At other times, the same word can have different meanings, especially as you cross cultural borders. In England, asking for a wake-up call in a small, family-owned residence is sometimes referred to as being "knocked up," a phrase which has very different meanings in the United States.

In addition, you would also be wise to a stay away from jargon, the specialized language of an occupation, unless you are certain the receiver is familiar with the jargon. This is especially true of acronyms, letters put together to make up a phrase. Don't be surprised if you are not understood when telling a new person in your work department to "Complete the DRF for the new CNC PDQ but after finishing the CWA for the last project" (translation: Complete the *Department Request for Funds form* for the new *computer numerical control, pretty darn quick* but after finishing the *Completion of Work Assignment form* for the last project). When using language that might be misunderstood, consider the following statement: "We describe it as . . . ; how would you say this?"

A fourth principle is to recognize variations in how spoken language is used across cultures. In the United States, for instance, people generally value the power of the spoken word. The numerous talk shows on radio and television, the popularity of motivational speakers, and the acclaim that is given to performing celebrities are just a few examples. The emphasis placed on the spoken message is so powerful that many speakers of English often feel uncomfortable in silence and quickly talk to fill the voids. A recent study by James Pennebaker, reported in *U.S. News & World Report* (Shute, 2007), found that both women and men speak about 16,000 words per day. One person in the study spoke only 700 words for the low, whereas another person spoke 47,000 words for the high. Although the quantity of language was about the same for both sexes, Pennebaker found that women spoke about "people" more often than men, and men spoke about "things" more often.

In contrast, other cultures are skeptical of language. They believe language can never reveal the truth, and so "chitchat" is to be avoided. Consequently, individuals from these cultures are more comfortable with silence. Raymond Tong in *Language of the Buddha* (1975), for example, says that ". . . the Buddha values restraint of words, knowing that silence is often more expressive than the finished poem" (p. 75).

Examine this extended example. A salesperson from the United States is pitching a new computer program for customers at a trade show in Japan. After the salesperson highlights the features of the new computer, the Japanese

Statue of Buddha, in Hawaii, Is a Reminder That Silence Can Be an Important Part of Communication

customers are silent. Assuming that this silence signals that the customers are unimpressed, the salesperson offers to include free packing and shipping. When the Japanese buyers still are quiet, the salesperson adds a complete maintenance and upgrade of the computer at the computer company's expense in the third year. Thus, when the Japanese buyers finally agree, the profit for the company is significantly reduced because the salesperson didn't understand the meaning of the customers' silence.

The final principle is to follow suggestions for effective verbal communication as one way to move closer to "shared understanding." In turn, these suggestions can assist you in garnering advancement on the job as well as helping you to build stronger relationships. If you wish to be rated positively by managers, certain kinds of communication should be avoided. These include using "teen speak," cursing, using strong dialects, halting or hesitating while talking, and speaking in ways that are grammatically incorrect (Lublin, 2004). Lublin reports that some companies even hire speech coaches to assist promising employees to sharpen their communication as part of a professional skill. At minimum, asking for feedback about your communication skills from employers during employee evaluation discussions would be worthwhile (Lublin, 2004). With respect to the kinds of communication that promote stronger relationships, *Psychology Today* (1999) reports that expressing what you want and need more directly and giving feedback were two verbal communication skills associated with more positive relationships.

In addition to these suggestions, you will learn two important guidelines for effective verbal communication in the section that follows. These include being willing to share and using specific language.

Guidelines for Effective Verbal Communication

BE WILLING TO SHARE

In order for communication to be successful, both a sender and a receiver are required. When it is your turn to be the sender, you can encourage open lines of communication by adopting a willing attitude to let others know what you think, feel, want, and need.

Opening yourself to others can be risky, simply because you do not always know what kind of response you will receive. That is why sharing usually occurs in stages. Individuals generally begin their relationships by sharing information that focuses on mutual interests, like sports or hobbies, and then gradually develop greater confidence in expressing opinions and feelings.

Some of the advantages that result from a willingness to share include establishing trust, minimizing misunderstandings, and encouraging openness from the person with whom you are communicating.

USE SPECIFIC LANGUAGE

One very essential way to ensure understanding when you communicate with others is to use specific language. Before sending a message, most of the time you have an idea in your head that you want to communicate. However, just because the idea is clear to you does not mean that the idea will be clear to the receiver as well. For example, when the boss says to a worker, "You are not being careful enough when you fill out the shipping order," what does the statement imply? Does the boss mean information on the order is missing, incorrect, or incomplete? The worker can only guess at the intended meaning unless the worker questions the boss further. The potential for misunderstanding increases when communicators use language that is general rather than specific.

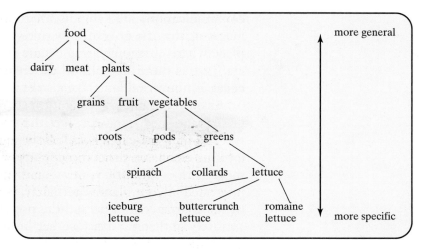

FIGURE 4.2 ■ Abstraction Ladder

Imagine a customer bringing a car into an automotive repair shop, complaining that there is a "strange noise" coming from the front end of the car. Before completing the job order, the service writer will more than likely question the customer further to determine how the noise sounds, how frequently it occurs, under what conditions it becomes noticeable, and so on. Getting the customer to be more specific is the first step in identifying the cause of the problem and finding a way to fix the automobile.

When you interact with others, you must choose from a wide range of language options. Those options include words that are very broad or general as well as those words that are very precise or specific. In some instances, being general may be perfectly suitable. For example, if a classmate tells you, "I am headed to work after class," you generally do not question the classmate further to find out where the classmate works, how long it takes to get there, and so on. However, if the classmate asks you to pick him or her up after work for a bite to eat, you obviously will need to get the name of the company, the exact address, and an approximate time it takes to get there. Although general language saves time, specific language promotes understanding.

Take a look at figure 4.2 to get a better idea of the relationship between general and specific language.

Nonverbal Communication Defined

Nonverbal communication can be defined as "all types of communication that don't involve the exchange of words" (Rogers & Steinfatt, 1999, p. 67). In many ways, it is like verbal communication in that your nonverbal communications are symbols for thoughts and feelings, they communicate meaning, they are governed by rules, and they are influenced by context—the place where communication occurs and the relationship between the speakers. Just as there are cultural differences in verbal language, cultural differences in nonverbal language also exist (Martin & Nakayama, 2000).

Like words, nonverbal communication can also influence the believability of your messages. Consider the statement, "Of course, I'm interested in the plan you are proposing." If the person who says this to you is busy answering emails on the computer, never looks up at you, and makes the statement with a sarcastic tone, would you really believe that the person was interested in your plan? Alternately, Professor Karen Bradley argues that one of the characteristics behind the popularity of Oprah Winfrey is that she is "entirely authentic" because her body movement and voice reinforce each other (Argetsinger & Roberts, 2007, p. D03).

Principles of Nonverbal Communication

Nonverbal communication is present everywhere and makes up the bulk of the messages you send. In fact, how would you try not communicating to someone nonverbally: Turn your back, hide your face in your hands, and stand at the far end of the room? These behaviors would, indeed, communicate your desire to not communicate! Albert Mehrabian (Mehrabian & Weiner, 1967) found that 55 percent of the meaning people send is contained in facial expressions, 38 percent of the meaning is contained in the voice, and only 7 percent of the meaning is contained in the actual words. More current estimates put the nonverbal messages at about 2/3 and verbal messages at about 1/3 (Burgoon, 1994). Sometimes the nonverbal message is all you need. For example, peering into the locker rooms of two teams who have just finished playing in a championship game would probably be sufficient for you to know which team won. The idea that your nonverbal communication is ever present and substantial cannot be denied.

A second principle is that people often do very little to learn and understand about nonverbal communication. As a part of your education, you were provided lessons in speech and grammar but may not have had occasion to learn about the nonverbal dimensions of your communication, unless you took a course in interpersonal skills. Consequently,

Facial Expressions and Body Language Convey Meaning

Edward Hall, who did extensive research in the areas of nonverbal behaviors, described elements of nonverbal communication as the "hidden dimension" (1990) and the "silent language" (1973). Because these nonverbal messages are unspoken, their hidden meaning often goes by unnoticed. However, greater awareness of how to interpret nonverbal messages can help you understand the silent language that is a major part of human interaction.

A third principle is that nonverbal messages are sent in advance of verbal messages. Before you even open your mouth, your facial expressions, your clothes, your walk, your body posture, your skin color, your hairstyle, etc. are communicating much about you. This is true even if the message sent is not what you intend to communicate. Consistent with this principle are estimates that job interviewers have a strong sense about whether to hire you or not within the first 45 seconds of an interview. Jack Griffin (1998) offers the following suggestions for communicating in powerful ways, including nonverbally, in advance of your first verbal message in U.S. business settings. These suggestions follow.

- Make an effective entrance into a room.
- Walk tall.
- Enter the room with a purposeful stride.
- Give a firm (but not too strong) handshake.
- Smile.

A fourth principle is that most nonverbal messages are about people's identities, their emotions, and their relationships. Trust is also tied to a person's nonverbal communication. Your style of dress, hairstyle, and body ornaments such as rings, tattoos, piercings, and so on, are reflections of a certain identity you want to portray: aspiring sales professional or heavy metal rocker. Your nonverbal messages also primarily communicate your emotions. How would you nonverbally communicate your thoughts about the new customer relations guidelines? It would be difficult. However, you could express your excitement, your dismay, your fear, or your anger at that plan with different facial expressions.

In addition, your nonverbal messages communicate much about your relationships. The distance you stand from a group of co-workers, your body posture when you are with them, and your eye contact all send messages about how you feel when interacting with them.

Finally, trust is increased when your verbal and nonverbal messages complement one another. For example, sharing your feelings openly with

Business Greeting in the United States

others while maintaining a relaxed posture, frequent eye contact, and a comfortable distance increases your believability. In contrast, nonverbal behaviors that contradict your spoken messages may create suspicion and distrust.

The last principle is that nonverbal communication, like verbal communication, is culture-bound. Cultural differences exist in how people greet each other, what gestures mean, how far or close people stand to each other when interacting, and so forth. Many people often assume, however, that nonverbal communication is universal, an assumption you would be wise to avoid. Because this is such an important principle, the next section of this chapter will include cross-cultural examples of the various types of nonverbal communication.

Types of Nonverbal Communication

Although language differences are more obvious, effective communicators must also recognize the great variability that exists in the "hidden dimension" of their communications: their nonverbal messages (Hall, 1990). This section will briefly describe seven types of nonverbal variations: chronemics (use of time), proxemics (use of space), oculesics (eye contact), kinesics (gestures and facial expression), haptics (touch), vocalics (vocal variations), and personal style.

To begin, variations exist in how people regard time—referred to as chronemics. Time is a valuable commodity to most Americans as evidenced in all the ways they talk about time. You are probably very familiar with phrases like losing time, killing time, and saving time. Time is so important that you may stop a really valued activity, such as having a good conversation with a friend, because "time is up." Time can also be a part of the total message. When a message is shared, how urgently it is shared, and how much time it takes to communicate the message all affect the total meaning. Although cultural differences influence your interpretation of time, you also need to understand that individuals have a personal sense of timing. Some people seem to be constantly rushed, whereas others exhibit a more laid-back attitude toward time. Some people focus on one thing at a time, whereas others pride themselves on doing multiple tasks at the same time.

Proxemics is a second nonverbal element. This nonverbal variation refers to the distance you stand when talking with others as well as how you regard territory. Edward Hall (1969) and others have noted different uses of space for North Americans. Intimate messages are shared from physical contact to about 18 inches; personal messages are shared from 18 inches to four feet; social messages are communicated at a distance of 4 to 12 feet; and public messages are shared beyond 12 feet. Also, messages match the distances. For instance, you are more likely to share confidential information in the intimate zone than in the public zone.

Compared to people in the United States, people from other cultural groups maintain a shorter distance when communicating with others. For example, Eastern Europeans generally stand closer to one another when speaking than do Americans. When someone is standing too close for comfort, you may react defensively. You probably have noted how people interact when forced into a small space such as an elevator. Verbal communication comes to a halt, and individuals fidget, looking down or at the numbers indicating the floor location of the elevator—but almost certainly avoiding eye contact.

Territoriality refers to your relationship to fixed space. Your seat in a classroom, your work area, or your favorite chair at home are all examples of fixed spaces that you regard as your own for specific periods of time. You mark your territories in a number of ways, often with personal belongings such as a coat, purse, or backpack. Interestingly, you may be surprised if not disturbed, when you see someone has taken over your space. In summary, you need to be aware of personal space and territory when interacting with others.

Related to territoriality are variations in eye contact—termed **oculesics**. Most Americans generally like a "soft" eye contact where people make eye contact with each other but look away from time to time. In other cultures, such as in China or Japan, there is very little eye contact made, especially with people considered superiors. Alternately, in some cultures gaze is more intense. Combining a short interpersonal distance and intense stare makes most Americans feel very nervous. However, for Middle Easterners, generally, the "eyes are the windows to the soul," and a short personal space combined with a "looking through" the eyes helps them to read another person's true messages.

Kinesics refers to the many behaviors of the body: postures, gestures, body orientation, and facial expressions. Hand gestures are by no means universal. Consider, for example, the gesture for hitchhiking—thumb up, all other fingers curled into the palm. This gesture can also signal approval such as "thumbs up" but also is an equivalent to the social "middle finger" in South Africa. As one other example, although people all smile in the same language, the meaning of that smile changes. Unless you know the person, you would only smile at someone in the Middle East if the person were engaging in some embarrassing behavior.

Touch, also referred to as **haptics,** is another powerful form of communication that can share a range of feelings. A hug or pat on the back, for example, evokes different emotions than would a slap in the face. Although touching behaviors take many forms, you must also interpret them in light of culture, status, gender, and personality traits. The boss's hand on an employee's forearm may signal,

Our Body Language
Speaks Volumes

Unfortunately, Some Stereotypes Stem from Personal Style Choices

"Pay attention." A supportive hand to the shoulder may signal, "I'm here," whereas similar signals may communicate, "Move over."

Accidental touching is usually accompanied with an apologetic "Excuse me." Likewise, you probably know a few people who are "touchers," even when their behavior may make others feel uncomfortable. Guidelines for appropriate touching vary from one culture to another. However, in the workplace, when touch is a part of communication, it should be purposeful and clear to both the sender and receiver. It might be wise, then, to avoid any kind of touching behavior until you understand more fully the culture of the organization.

Although most people regard touch as appropriate among close friends and family, it was, until recently, reason for being arrested in China. Conversely, in Argentina, as well as in much of Latin America, a hug—called an "abrazo"—and a kiss is a typical greeting even among strangers.

Vocalics is the study of vocal messages with regard to rate, pitch, quality, and volume. Consider all the ways you could say something while varying these vocal elements to influence the overall meaning of the message. How would the sentence "I'm on fire" change if said quickly, with a high pitch, and in a loud voice versus if said in a slow, soft, low, and sexy voice? It is also interesting to note that Americans are often regarded as way too loud in comparison to the vocal volume deemed appropriate in other cultures.

Personal style refers to your appearance and includes body hair, body odor, body decorations such as tattoos, and body shape, as well as clothing and personal artifacts. People assign meanings to your body type, skin color, manner of dress, hairstyle, and accessories. Think about the initial stereotypes you may have when you see someone with a nose ring, a Mohawk haircut, or hundreds of tattoos. Unfortunately, some people do not see past these obvious aspects of an individual's personal style to see the traits, character, and skills of the person.

Guidelines for Effective Nonverbal Communication

Now that you are more familiar with the principles and variations of nonverbal behavior, you may want to examine some guidelines for effective nonverbal communication. Perhaps the most important guideline is to realize that you cannot read people "like a book" given their nonverbal messages alone. All nonverbal messages must be verified. Sometimes you simply do not know what a particular nonverbal behavior means.

A helpful verbal strategy for checking understanding is to describe the nonverbal behaviors you observe. For example, you might say, "I noticed that all of a sudden you've grown quiet and are looking away." Your observation can be coupled with an interpretation of what you think the behavior means. Together, your remarks might sound something like this: "When

I asked you about the closing of the Lee account, you became quiet and looked away as if you didn't want to comment." Recognize that your statement does not mean that the person will respond truthfully, but your remarks give the person a chance to explain the nonverbal messages.

A second guideline is to consider the messages you are communicating nonverbally. Obviously, it is best to assure a match between your verbal and nonverbal messages. It is also essential to recognize how your emotional state can be revealed in your nonverbal messages. Sometimes your feelings about a person or an idea will override any spoken words that you convey. For instance, if you tell a colleague you have time to talk and are simultaneously glancing at your watch, you will be sending mixed messages. Such conflicting messages can easily create confusion.

A third guideline is to recognize the impact that status and power have on your nonverbal communication. People who have greater status, and usually greater power, often communicate their status in subtle but effective ways. Generally, this status might be evident in the clothes they wear, the posture they assume, and the office space they occupy. On the other hand, you might also think about how a person of lower status or power might communicate nonverbally in the presence of such a person. The person with lower status might engage in the following behaviors: open the door for the other, allow the higher status person to lead the conversation, sit in silence for a longer period of time, dress up a bit more when meeting with the person, and so on.

A fourth guideline is to observe nonverbal communication in clusters. That is, people rarely send one nonverbal message. People generally send several messages at the same time. To accurately understand what is being shared nonverbally, you need to read as many of these nonverbal messages as possible. For example, when trying to understand a colleague's reaction to suggestions you offered in a meeting, pay attention to the colleague's tone of voice, eye contact, and facial expression in addition to what he or she says.

A final guideline is to be cautious when making generalizations about the meaning of nonverbal cues. Allen and Barbara Pease's (2006) book, *The Definitive Book on Body Language,* offers practical suggestions for interpreting nonverbal behavior. The body speaks in many ways, and each message must be interpreted by considering the uniqueness of the individual, the physical and social setting, and the cultural context in which the communication occurs.

Language and Technology

As you might imagine, it is important to understand how language is influenced by technology. On one level, you have to be especially precise and complete when sending electronic messages. The receiver of electronic communications is not able to observe other important elements of the message that often come with face-to-face interactions: tone of voice, facial expression, and body posture, for example.

On another level, consider how email, but especially telephone text messaging, has spawned a whole new language. It uses acronyms as substitutes for whole phrases and passages—which is efficient but possibly confusing until someone understands these acronyms fully.

Imagine for a moment, that you have just purchased a new cell phone with text messaging. You call a friend, mention your new phone, and soon afterward hang up. You get your first text message. It reads:

Hey bff. How r u? I got a bf! Lol jk G2g ttyl.

Cell Phone Text Messaging Has Its Own Language Usage Conventions

What would you make of that message? Would you know that your friend thinks of you as a "best friend forever"? Would you know that your friend wonders, "how are you" and is telling you about her "boyfriend"? Hopefully you also had to "laugh out loud" since your friend was "just kidding," and now has "got to go," and will "talk to you later."

Using these acronyms with those who have little access to or familiarity with them or texting in a formal work or school situation would not be appropriate. However, using such language among close friends with whom you "txt message" all the time would no doubt be appropriate and even fun.

In conclusion, the chapter has ended: Got 2 go. Ttyl. Lol.

Review Questions

1. Describe a time when you experienced a breakdown in communication due to lack of clarity or purposefulness of your, or someone else's, verbal or nonverbal symbols. What did you learn from this experience?

2. Provide a list of three to five of your favorite statements that use figurative language. How might you restate those in a way that they could not be misunderstood?

3. Give an example of one personal characteristic (conservative or liberal, for example) that could be described using several different words depending upon the impact you wish to have on the listener.

4. Explain how place or context affects your communication.

5. List three strategies for sharing verbal messages to help you to achieve shared understanding. Explain why those strategies would be effective.

6. Explain three principles of nonverbal communication that you believe are most important. Tell why these are the most important for you to keep in mind when communicating.

7. Share an example of a difference in verbal or nonverbal communication across cultures.

8. Given the list of guidelines for effective nonverbal communication, what steps will you take in the future to assure that nonverbal messages are clear and purposeful?

9. Discuss how you feel about your ability to send messages, both verbally and nonverbally. What are your strengths? What areas need improvement?

Key Terms and Concepts

Chronemics   90
Connotation   83
Contextual Meaning   83
Denotation   83
Dialects   84
Figurative Language   83
Haptics   91

Jargon   85
Kinesics   91
Language   79
Nonverbal Communication   87
Oculesics   91
Personal Style   92
Phonemes   82

Pragmatics   83
Proxemics   90
Semantics   83
Syntax   82
Territoriality   91
Vocalics   92

Web Activities

Visit the following interesting sites to find out more about nonverbal communications and their related meanings.

- http://members.aol.com/nonverbal2/diction1.htm
- http://nonverbal.ucsc.edu/

To help you understand the meanings of words, check out this webpage:

- http://www.prefixsuffix.com/

For fun, search for word games such as the following and test your skills:

- http://www.theproblemsite.com/default.asp

Assignments

ASSIGNMENT 4.1: FIGURATIVE LANGUAGE

Directions: Figurative language adds a certain flavor to any communication. However, such language can be a problem for those who do not understand its meaning. For each of the following statements, draw a picture of what the statement means if taken literally. Then try to explain what the figurative language means so that it could be more clearly understood by a wide range of communicators. Space is provided for you to add one example of figurative language of your own.

Figurative Language	Literal Drawing	Alternative Statement
I've hit a brick wall.		
She has feet as big as boats.		
My boss really blew his top.		
My supervisor has a heart of gold.		
Be careful when playing cards with him. He's a shark.		
Try to avoid splitting hairs.		
(Add your example here.)		

ASSIGNMENT 4.2: CONNOTATION IN LANGUAGE

As described in this chapter, connotation refers to the wider, usually emotional, responses people have to the words being used. You can choose different words to describe the same thing, but the words chosen can have a different impact. In the 1980s, for example, the United States supported a group of people who attempted to overthrow the democratically elected government in Nicaragua. Then President Ronald Reagan, who at the same time had called a ballistic missile a "peacekeeper," called these people "freedom fighters." To the government in Nicaragua, they were "terrorists" or "rebels." The choice of words invokes a particular positive or negative response.

Directions: For this activity, take the words that are in italics and replace them with more favorable words to invoke a positive, or at least less negative, response. For example:

Statement: Our sales have *hit bottom*.
Restatement: Our sales have slowed.

Statement: That new worker is *opinionated*.
Restatement:

Statement: The union is *stubborn* in negotiations.
Restatement:

Statement: When it comes to bonuses, our company is *miserly*.
Restatement:

Statement: Two words describe my neighbor: *ancient* and *nosy*!
Restatement:

Statement: My significant other is *pushy* when talking about marriage.
Restatement:

What is the most important lesson(s) you have learned from this activity?

ASSIGNMENT 4.3: SPECIFIC VERSUS GENERAL LANGUAGE

Directions: In addition to developing accuracy in your communication, you must also strive for clarity in your messages. Following is a series of words that will enable you to distinguish between general and specific language. For each pair of words, place an "X" next to the word that is more specific.

1	Equipment	Computer
2	Refrigerator	Appliance
3	Apartment	Residence
4	Organize	File
5	Exercise	Walk
6	Pulley	Mechanism
7	Letter	Correspondence
8	Vehicle	Automobile
9	Fuel	Diesel
10	Union	Organization
11	Add	Compute
12	Legal document	Contract
13	Solar power	Energy
14	Luggage	Suitcase
15	Business	Store
16	Bank transaction	Deposit
17	Phone book	Directory
18	Window covering	Blinds

ASSIGNMENT 4.4: ABSTRACTION LADDERS

Directions: Another way to sharpen your awareness of the distinction between general and specific language is to rank the following groups of items from the most general (#1) to the most specific (#5). Notice how the meaning changes with the item you rank #5, as it presents the clearest picture.

Ranking	Group 1
	Human biology
	Knowledge
	Biology
	Science
	Reproductive system

Ranking	Group 2
	Transportation
	Land vehicle
	Jeep
	Vehicle
	Four-wheel drive

Ranking	Group 3
	Aerobic exercise
	Swimming
	Physical activity
	Exercise
	Backstroke

Ranking	Group 4
	Work
	Employment
	Computer worker
	Programmer
	Occupation

Ranking	Group 5
	Central Campus
	School
	Education
	Business Building
	Postsecondary

Ranking	Group 6
	Equipment
	Machine
	Brake lathe
	Metal cutter
	Industrial machine

Ranking	Group 7
	Business
	Organization
	Store
	J.F.Ward's
	Department store

Ranking	Group 8
	Carbohydrates
	Nourishment
	French fries
	Potatoes
	Food

Ranking	Group 9
	Cola
	Refreshment
	Nonalcoholic beverage
	Beverage
	Soft drink

Ranking	Group 10
	1/2" Hammer drill
	Power drill
	Mechanism
	Tool
	Power tool

ASSIGNMENT 4.5: NONVERBAL CHARADES

Directions: In a small group of two to four persons, each member will take turns expressing the list of emotions that follows using just facial expressions. It is best if your group is mixed in terms of gender, ethnicity, race, languages spoken, etc. List the order in which you will attempt to share these emotions with the others in your group. Then express these emotions in the order you numbered them. See if the others in your group can detect the order in which you shared them. Take turns doing this activity.

Emotions—List the order in which you will share them, with 1 = first, etc.

_____ Anger   _____ Fear

_____ Disgust   _____ Surprise

_____ Sadness   _____ Happiness

Peer Responses—When finished expressing these emotions, ask your peers what emotions you shared. Write down their guesses here; then reveal the order in which you expressed the emotions.

Peer #1	Peer #2	Peer #3
_____	_____	_____
_____	_____	_____
_____	_____	_____
_____	_____	_____
_____	_____	_____
_____	_____	_____

Discussion:

After all in the group have completed this activity, answer the following: Who was better at communicating emotions? Why? Who was better at detecting emotions? Why? What affect did the gender of the participants or culture of the participants have on these results? What did you learn about communicating nonverbally from this exercise?

ASSIGNMENT 4.6: NONVERBAL INTERCULTURAL DIFFERENCES

In this interaction, you will discover differences in nonverbal communication, specifically related to cross-cultural gestures. In a study by Morris and his colleagues (1980), pictures of gestures were shown to

more than 1,200 people in forty different locales, mostly in Europe. Respondents were asked to describe what each gesture meant.

Directions: In figure 4.3, place a check mark by what you think each of the three gestures communicates. Compare their responses (in figure 4.4) with your own.

FIGURE 4.3 ■ Three Gestures from Morris Study
Source: Morris, 1980.

The Nose Thumb

_____ Mockery   _____ Buzz off

_____ Idiot   _____ You're crazy

_____ Get lost   _____ Up yours

The Ring

_____ O.K. — Good   _____ Orifice

_____ Zero   _____ Threat

_____ Insult   _____ Thursday

The Thumbs Up

_____ Directional   _____ Hitch-Hike

_____ O.K.   _____ One

_____ Sexual insult _____ Obscenity

ASSIGNMENT 4.7: NONVERBAL COMMUNICATION ARTICLES REVIEW

Directions: Read three articles about nonverbal communication. Choose three articles with a similar theme such as gender, gestures and their meaning, the uses of time, touch, deception, or any aspect of nonverbal communication. Then use the following review forms to help you identify key information from the articles. Finally, be prepared to share a short three- to five-minute talk with your class about the topic you chose and what you learned. Use the following outline.

Article Review #1

Title of article:

Author:

Author's credentials:

Source (name of journal, newspaper, or book—include dates, page numbers, volume and issue numbers, publisher, etc.):

3 to 5 Main Ideas:

    A.

    B.

    C.

    D.

Most important thing you learned and want to share with your peers:

Article Review #2

Title of article:

Author:

Author's credentials:

Source (name of journal, newspaper, or book—include dates, page numbers, volume and issue numbers, publisher, etc.):

3 to 5 Main Ideas:

    A.

    B.

    C.

    D.

Most important thing you learned and want to share with your peers:

Article Review #3

Title of article:

Author:

Author's credentials:

Source (name of journal, newspaper, or book—include dates, page numbers, volume and issue numbers, publisher, etc.):

3 to 5 Main Ideas:

    A.

    B.

    C.

    D.

Most important thing you learned and want to share with your peers:

ASSIGNMENT 4.8: CASE STUDY: STANTON'S REPORT

Directions: Imagine you work for a company, Stanton Corporation, that has been struggling financially the last couple of years. The company's profits had been strong, but in the last two years, the profits dropped, employees were laid off, and morale decreased. This year, business has stabilized, but the company is still losing its share of the market, and the company would consider breaking even a good year.

Al-Kor, a business from another country, is considering a major purchase from Stanton, which would provide a substantial boost as well as help increase your company's share of the market. In requesting a meeting with your company, Al-Kor has stated its concern with the financial health of Stanton, having noted the past two-year's downturn.

You have been assigned to be part of a team to discuss the upcoming meeting with representatives from Al-Kor. In addition, you have been asked to write an explanation of Stanton's recent financial status. You want to use language that is honest yet puts your company in the best financial light. Write your explanation, and answer the questions that follow.

QUESTIONS

1. How did you feel about writing the explanation?
2. What was difficult about your task? What was easy?
3. If this were part of your everyday work—generating press releases, making public relations statements, and negotiating on behalf of your company—what would be your strengths? What skills would you need to develop?

FIGURE 4.4 ■ Results from Morris Study
Source: Morris, 1980.

The Nose Thumb Meanings:

1 Mockery   1,058
2 others   14
3 not used   128
(Based on 1,200 informants
at 40 locations)

The Ring Meanings:

1 O.K.—Good   700
2 Orifice   128
3 Zero   115
4 Threat   16
5 others   27
6 not used   214
(Based on 1,200 informants
at 40 locations)

The Thumbs Up Meanings:

1 O.K.   738
2 One   40
3 Sexual insult   36
4 Hitch-hike   30
5 Directional   14
6 others   24
7 not used   318
(Based on 1,200 informants
at 40 locations)

References

Anzaldúa, G. (1987). *Borderlands*. San Francisco: Spinsters/Aunt Lute.

Argetsinger, A., & Roberts, R. (2007). The reliable source. *Washington Post*, May 13, 2007, p. D03.

Burgoon, J. K. (1994). Nonverbal signals. In M. L. Knapp and G. R. Miller (Eds.), *Handbook of interpersonal communication* (pp. 229–285). Newbury Park, CA: Sage.

Chatterjee, C. (1999). Stopping spats. *Psychology Today, 32*(2), 12.

Griffin, J. (1998). *How to say it at work: Putting yourself across with power words, phrases, body language and communication secrets*. Paramus, NJ: Prentice Hall Press.

Hall, E. T. (1990). *The hidden dimension*. New York: Anchor Books.

Hall, E. T. (1973). *The silent language*. New York: Anchor Books.

Hall, E. T. (1969). Listening behaviors: Some cultural differences. *Phi Delta Kappa, 50*, 379–380.

Hayasaki, E. (2007). "Now the giant awakes"; An LA Gang member and a boy drawn to the streets find refuge in writing. Their words enthrall—and unsettle—the teacher-novelist. *Los Angeles Times*, October 20, 2007, p. 1.

Heath, S. B. (1983). *Ways with words*. Cambridge, England: Cambridge University Press.

Lublin, J. S. (2004). To win advancement, you need to clean up bad speech habits. *Wall Street Journal*, October 5, 2004, p. 1 (Section B).

Martin, J. N., & Nakayama, T. K. (2000). *Intercultural communication in contexts*. Mountain View, CA: Martin.

Mehrabian, A., & Weiner, M. (1967). Decoding inconsistent communications. *Journal of Personality and Social Psychology, 6*, 109–114.

Morris, D., Collett, P., Marsh, P., & O'Shaugnessy, M. (1980). *Gestures, their origins and distributions*. New York: Stein and Day.

Pease, B., & Pease, A. (2006). *The definitive book of body language*. New York: Bantam/Random House.

Rogers, E. M., & Steinfatt, T. M. (1999). *Intercultural communication*. Prospect Heights, IL: Waveland Press.

Shute, N. (2007). Chatty Cathy, Chatty Charlie. *U.S. News & World Report*, July 16, 2007, 143(2), p. 30.

Tong, R. (1975). Language of the Buddha. *English Language Teaching, 30*(1), p. 3.

Chapter 5

Listening and Responding

"The most basic of all human needs is the need to understand and be understood. The best way to understand people is to listen to them."

Ralph Nichols

Listening Is Important

University of Wisconsin Police Officer Heidi Golbach knows about the importance of listening (figure 5.1). If you spend five minutes with her, "she'll point out a half dozen of the characters she knows from her daily patrols of [the] lower campus. Spend an hour with Golbach as she makes her rounds, and it soon becomes clear that she knows the names and life stories of almost everyone who spends time near Library Mall, from homeless men to building managers" (Beyler, 2006, p. 1).

FIGURE 5.1 ■ Officer Heidi Golbach, University of Wisconsin *Source:* Used with permission from the University of Wisconsin-Madison.

One Friday, "Golbach started her afternoon confiscating beer from two drunken men, simultaneously making sure they had a place to spend the night. She moved on to Mosse Humanities and the Elvehjem, where she teased a long-time custodian about making a mess, and congratulated a homeless man who had just gotten a grant to return to school. A few minutes and two hugs later, Goldbach was on the Union Terrace, supervising as a tow truck pulled a Hoofers boat trailer that was in danger of falling off the pier" (Beyler, 2006, p. 1).

The article goes on to say about Golbach, who is also pursuing a degree in criminal justice, that "the other officers call her maternal, but she comments, 'sometimes all a person needs is someone to listen to them for five minutes, rather than the long arm of the law reaching out to snag them'" (Beyler, 2006, p. 1).

Heidi Golbach is not alone in recognizing the need for effective listening on the job; Julie, a nurse, also recognizes this need. Julie was one of the nurses that Consultant Terry Taylor worked with and writes about. Taylor collected inspirational stories from nurses like Julie for a book entitled *Nurse Power: Find It, Keep It, Grow It, Share It.* Julie comments, "Nurses need to know how to listen well to their patients, to hear their stories, to be compassionate but also to detect evidence of discomfort, symptoms and other clues to the whole patient" (Taylor, 2006, p. 1).

Julie talks about a patient in her clinical practice who had experienced multiple back surgeries and even with the aid of narcotics was still in excruciating pain. Julie "took time to sit with him while he cried." Afterwards, the patient told Julie "it was more important for him to have someone just listen than to have any other procedure done to him. It was clear he hadn't felt heard by anyone up to that point; most likely the caregivers felt they had nothing more to offer him" (Taylor, 2006, p. 2).

Although the stories of Heidi and Julie represent just two individuals for whom listening is vital to their jobs, you can probably think of examples from other occupations where effective listening is equally important. Consider service personnel who routinely listen to customer complaints, the child care attendant who needs to listen to and comfort an upset

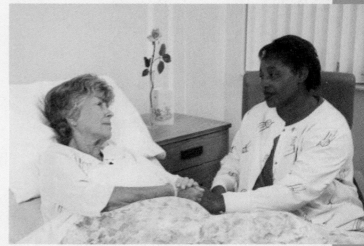

Compassionate Listening Is a Skill That Pays Rich Dividends

toddler, or the sales rep who must identify client needs in order to provide appropriate goods and services.

Apart from the workplace, some research indicates that even within family life, listening may not be given the attention it deserves. The dinner table, a setting for family sharing and listening, appears to represent a bygone era. In an article by Cameron Stracher (2005) titled "Much Depends on Dinner," the author states that "fewer than one-third of all children sit down to eat dinner with both parents on any given night. The statistics are worse if both parents are working and the family is Caucasian (Latino families have the highest rate of sharing a meal). The decline in the family dinner has been blamed for the rise in obesity, drug abuse, behavioral problems, promiscuity, poor school performance, illegal file sharing and a host of other ills" (p. 1).

Stracher (2005) also refers to the National Center on Addiction and Substance Abuse at Columbia University, which found "teens from families that almost never eat dinner together are 72 percent more likely to use illegal drugs, cigarettes and alcohol than the average teen and that those who eat dinner with their parents less than three times a week are four times more likely to smoke cigarettes, three times more likely to smoke marijuana and twice as likely to drink as those who eat dinner with their parents at least six times a week" (p. 1).

From this data, it might be safe to assume that when families don't make time to share a meal, they lose a precious opportunity to connect with one another, missing the chance to share events of the day and affirm the worth of the people with whom they live through attentive listening.

Studies Have Shown a Correlation Between the Decline in Family Dinners and the Rise in Societal Problems

Near the end of the article, Stracher (2005) points out that the family dinner "can't be hastened by new technology or emailed as an attachment to our kitchens. Instead, it's one of the few opportunities for conversation in a noisy world, a place to take a slower measure of our frenzied days. By missing mealtime, we are missing a substantial part of our children's lives. Sooner than we realize, they will not be at our table. Sooner than that, they will not want to have anything to do with us" (p. 2).

You might also be interested to know that about 95 percent of what people learn during their lifetime is learned through their eyes and their ears. In fact, research confirms that 70 percent of your waking day is spent communicating interpersonally, with 45 percent of that 70 percent devoted to listening (*International Journal of Listening,* 2006, p. 5).

Unfortunately, even though you are likely to spend close to half of your communication time listening, your level of listening efficiency may be less than ideal. It is estimated that immediately after listening to a ten-minute message, most listeners have comprehended only about 50 percent of the information. Forty-eight hours later, comprehension dips to approximately 25 percent. These statistics may not be particularly surprising when you acknowledge that not many individuals have received any formal training in listening, maybe as few as 2–5 percent according to some researchers.

No doubt employers and employees alike are recognizing the benefits of listening training in the workplace. Online searches reveal numerous training resources are being marketed from books and CDs to online courses and workshops in an effort to meet consumer demands for listening improvement.

Management-trainer Madelyn Burley-Allen, author of *Listening, the Forgotten Skill: A Self-Teaching Guide,* identifies several tangible benefits for effective listening in the workplace. Take a look at the ones she cites in an online article entitled "Practical Benefits of Better Listening for Leaders and Teams:"

- **A Bond of Respect:** Sincere listening promotes respect, builds rapport, and creates trust between the sender and the receiver.
- **Productivity:** Productivity is increased, and problems are addressed sooner when people engage in sharing and listening before offering advice.
- **Cooler Heads:** Attentive listening helps both the sender and the receiver to maintain composure when handling a crisis or discussing emotionally charged topics.
- **Confidence:** Employees who listen experience increased self-esteem that results from getting along better with others in the workplace.
- **Accuracy:** Listening efficiency promotes retention of important information, resulting in fewer misunderstandings and on-the-job errors (Wilson, n.d., p. 1).

Now that you are more aware of the importance of listening in both your personal and professional life, you are ready to examine the process of listening.

Listening Is a Process

The International Listening Association defines listening as follows:

> Listening is "the process of receiving, constructing meaning from, and responding to spoken and/or nonverbal messages" (ILA, 1996, p. 1).

In order for listening to occur, the outer ear must first catch the sound; this sound then travels through the ear canal into the middle ear, where the eardrum is located. The eardrum creates vibrations that become nerve impulses. These nerve impulses are then sent to the inner ear and converted from acoustical energy into electrochemical energy that the brain recognizes.

The diagram in figure 5.2 illustrates the external, middle, and inner portions of the ear that allow these processes to occur.

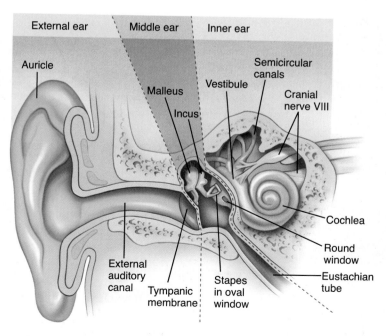

FIGURE 5.2 ■ The Ear

Physical and Mental
Presence?
Source: www.CartoonStock
.com.

You can see that for listening to take place, hearing has to occur first. However, listening differs from hearing in several respects.

First, hearing is involuntary; it happens automatically. Listening, in contrast, involves making a choice. You must decide that you want to listen to a message.

Second, you must prepare yourself to understand the message. This preparation requires you to focus on the message both physically and mentally. Physically, you must position yourself in a way that encourages alertness and that convinces the speaker that you really are paying attention.

Maintaining an alert, upright posture; facing the speaker directly; establishing eye contact; and assuming a comfortable distance all communicate active participation in the listening process. Mental preparation requires blocking out internal distractions, keeping an open mind, discovering interest in the speaker and message, and withholding premature judgments. This combination of physical and mental presence is frequently referred to as **attending**.

Third, listening happens when you decode the message in an attempt to understand what the speaker intended. This decoding process includes understanding the content and the feelings contained within both the verbal and nonverbal parts of the message. Achieving accurate understanding is often difficult because of the numerous factors that influence your thinking. These factors include your expectations, past experiences, personal beliefs, and values, to mention just a few.

Finally, to assure that accurate listening has occurred, you need to respond or provide feedback. Your feedback might take the form of evaluating, interpreting, supporting, questioning, or paraphrasing. You will read more about these responses later in this chapter.

Listening Principles

Once you have a basic understanding of the difference between hearing and listening, along with an awareness of how listening happens, you are ready to review a few basic principles that govern listening.

LISTENING IS LEARNED

When you hear, you are making an automatic response. However, when you listen, you engage skills that must be developed through observation, instruction, and practice. You can learn to be a better listener, and you can help others learn good listening skills by following a few basic guidelines.

You may be interested in the following article by Joshua Uebergang, "You Can Teach (Listening) through Modeling":

You can teach your child to listen by having good listening skills yourself. Monkey see, monkey do. Here are some ideas to help you:

- **Do Not Interrupt**—When someone says something that we disagree with, we love to interrupt and even go the extra step further by proving [him or her] wrong. Hearing what your children say improves their listening skills by encouraging them to not interrupt.

- **Be Together**—Just by interacting with your [children] and building a relationship, they are spending more time with you. The more time you have in their lives, the more influential you become, and the more you interact and talk to them, the more your effective listening skills run over onto your [children].
- **Honesty**—Just like adults, children can see when you are not listening. You need to be attentive and honest in your listening by not tricking them into thinking that you are listening.
- **Have Patience**—You cannot expect your [children] to be patient and attentively listen to you when you cannot be patient yourself. Understand that children take longer than adults to say what they want" 2006, pp. 3–4).

LISTENING IS ACTIVE

The first step to being an active listener involves cultivating an interest in both the speaker and the message. In part, self-centeredness can be a source of disinterest. Particularly in our society, talking is frequently given a greater priority than listening. An article from the *Christian Science Monitor* (2002) raises the question if everybody's talking, who is going to do the listening? Article author Marilyn Gardner states, "When social historians of the future look back on the early 21st Century, they could easily label this the Age of Talk. From round-the-clock TV and radio call-in shows to ubiquitous [ever-present] cell phones, never have so many people made such an effort to banish silence. As cell phone users cup their hands around small black rectangles, press them to their ears, and chat away—on sidewalks and beaches, in restaurants, malls, theaters, and even churches—their new credo has become: I talk; therefore, I am" (p. 14).

I Talk; Therefore, I Am

Yet to be a good listener, you need to place self-interest aside, at least temporarily, and cultivate interest in both the speaker and his or her message. Although not always easy to do, a willingness to listen with interest is certainly an attitude that can be developed with practice.

The second step to becoming an active listener is to focus your attention on the speaker and the message. At one time or another, you may have given others the impression you were listening while your attention was miles away. Maybe you found the speaker boring; perhaps you were worrying about a recent disagreement with a close friend; possibly a favorable weekend weather report had you daydreaming about a day at the beach. Regardless of the reason, faking attention can become a habit where you are present physically but not mentally. This lack of attention can occur when listeners assume that listening is passive rather than active.

The International Listening Leadership Institute (ILLI) cites the problem of faking attention with an excerpt from the best seller, *Tuesdays With Morrie* by Mitch Albom:

When Morrie was with you, he was really with you. He looked you straight in the eye, and he listened as if you were the only person in the world. How much better would people get along if their first encounter each day were like this—instead of a grumble from a waitress or a bus driver or a boss.

"I believe in being fully present," Morrie said. That means you should be with the person you're with. When I'm talking to you now, Mitch, I try to keep focused on what is going on between us. I am not thinking of what's coming up this Friday.

"So many people are so self-absorbed their eyes glaze over if you speak for more than thirty seconds. They already have something else in mind—a friend to call, a fax to send, a lover they're dreaming about. They only snap back to attention when you finish talking, at which point they say 'Uh-huh' or 'yeah, really' and fake their way back to the moment.

"Part of the problem, Mitch, is that everyone is in such a hurry," Morrie said. "People haven't found meaning in their lives, so they're running all the time looking for it" (Steil & Bommelje, 2004, p. 1).

As you can see, Morrie didn't fake attention, and he made the sender feel valued. Although the ability to be present, physically and mentally, may not come naturally or easily, it is certainly a skill you can cultivate with awareness and practice.

LISTENING OCCURS FASTER THAN SPEECH

When you speak, your average rate of speech is around 125 to 150 words per minute. In contrast, when you listen, the average rate of your thoughts can be well over 500 words per minute. You may wonder what the variation between speech-speed and thought-speed has to do with your listening. Given this variation, as a listener, you can comprehend information at a much more rapid rate than you can present information as a speaker. As a result, you have "time left over" to let your mind wander. You can start daydreaming so spontaneously that when you finally return to a speaker's message, you may have missed some important information.

LISTENING REQUIRES EMOTIONAL CONTROL

Your goal in effective listening is to understand the message the way the sender intended. This goal cannot be achieved if you let your emotions get in the way. A variety of triggers can produce strong emotions that interfere with your listening. You may find the subject being discussed is highly controversial; maybe you find the speaker's choice of words to be personally offensive; possibly the topic of discussion arouses defensiveness in you. In all of these instances, listeners may tune out the speaker altogether or be planning a response long before the speaker has concluded. Although "keeping your cool" might be a challenge under such circumstances, failure to do so is likely to result in an inaccurate interpretation of the message.

In addition, loss of emotional control can occur when you make snap judgments about the speaker or the message. Ineffective listeners make evaluations or judgments prematurely, before they have all of the necessary facts. This tendency is sometimes referred to as jumping to conclusions.

Stop and think for a moment about the times you may have jumped to conclusions. Maybe your boss ignored a suggestion you made in a meeting. Did you conclude that he or she was upset with you for some reason? Perhaps a friend was in a hurry to end a phone conversation with you. Might you have assumed this friend didn't want to talk to you? Possibly your spouse has been unusually quiet at the dinner table. Could it be your spouse has something on his or her mind? Although any of these conclusions is reasonable, they all may be incorrect as well.

Your boss might be feeling stressed by added work responsibilities; your friend may have been running late for an important appointment; your spouse could be tired after a demanding day at work. However, if you fail to recognize these incorrect assumptions, you may feel worried about your relationship with the boss, resentful toward your friend, and annoyed with your spouse.

The syndicated newspaper column *Dear Abby* often includes letters that illustrate jumping to conclusions. Here is one you might find interesting, written by a sixteen-year-old teen.

DEAR ABBY:

I am a 16-year-old girl with wonderful parents and a great little sister who is 13. My mom just had a third child. My brother's name is "Nathan." He is 6 months old now, and I don't think any baby could be more loved. Because my mother works part-time, I take care of my brother for a few hours each day. The problem is that when I take him for a walk or to the mall, I am faced with disapproving looks and rude comments from adults who obviously think he is my baby. I see people shake their heads when I walk by, and I hear them mutter about irresponsible teenagers. I don't know how to respond to people like that, but I do know that adults should stop seeing something wrong with every situation they encounter. They seem to think my entire generation is hopeless. This is far from the truth. Abby, how should I deal with this situation when I next encounter it?

SWEET 16, SEATTLE

DEAR SWEET 16:

I know it's far from the truth, and you shouldn't be put in the position where you feel you "must respond" to disapproving looks and rude remarks from strangers. Have a T-shirt made for your little brother bearing the message: "She's My Sister!" (Dear Abby, 1999, p. 2)

Listening Skills: At School, at Work, at Home

LISTENING AT SCHOOL

You may be one among many listeners who need to improve listening skills at school. Amanda is one such listener. Each afternoon when Amanda attends her three-hour psychology lecture, she chooses a seat near the back of the room and gets as comfortable as possible. She takes out her laptop to type in notes from her instructor, making sure to record all of the information on the instructor's PowerPoint slides word for word. When another student asks a question of the instructor, Amanda uses a break in the lecture to check her email. As the instructor resumes her lecture, Amanda hears a concept she doesn't quite understand. Rather than asking for clarification, she figures she can find an answer to her question later in the textbook. After about half an hour, Amanda is feeling some boredom set in and begins wondering how the lecture material is going to help her in her career as a dental hygienist. Before she is aware, Amanda discovers that her distractions have caused her to fall behind in the PowerPoint slides. Feeling confused and frustrated, she decides to surf the net for ideas on a paper she is writing in her ethics class.

Jordan is a fellow classmate in Amanda's psychology class. Aware that his listening skills are not always the best, Jordan sits in the first row or two to avoid unnecessary distractions. Jordan has already printed out the instructor's PowerPoint lecture slides so he can concentrate on what the instructor is saying and not have to worry about taking lots of notes. When another student in the class asks a question, Jordan pays close attention, hoping the instructor's response might help him better understand the lecture content as well. A bit later in the class, Jordan feels some confusion about the exact meaning of a key term the instructor has defined. He raises his hand to seek clarification and jots down the instructor's reply. As an accounting major, Jordan is alert for ideas in the lecture that will help him better understand the personalities of clients and co-workers he will face in the workplace.

You can see from these two examples, Jordan's listening skills are more effective than Amanda's. Like Jordan, if you desire to improve your listening abilities, you must first be aware of the habits that get in the way of good listening. In the case of Amanda, her bad habits include getting too comfortable in the back of the room, trying to take notes word for word, failing to ask for clarification, and yielding to distractions.

However, regardless of what your own bad listening habits may be, you can become a better listener at school by practicing the suggestions that follow (figure 5.3).

FIGURE 5.3 ■ Central Idea and Main Points

Some Listening Techniques Are More Effective Than Others

1. **Come prepared to listen.** This guideline encourages you to familiarize yourself with course content before coming to class. For example, make sure you have completed the assigned reading material so you will have a basic understanding of the information to be discussed. Also, take advantage of any online supplements your instructor may make available to you. Printing out PowerPoint slides the way Jordan did can free you from excessive note taking. In addition, make sure you have the necessary supplies for recording key information, upcoming assignments, and so on. You can use either a spiral notebook or a laptop. Finally, position yourself in the classroom where you can easily see and hear what is going on, along with minimizing distractions. The goal is to remain comfortably alert.

2. **Listen for central ideas and main points.** The central idea presents the **subject** (who or what the speech is about) and a **focus** (the key point the sender intends to make about the subject). Central idea statements usually come near the beginning of a presentation and may be restated near the end of a message. The central idea will present the core of the speaker's message in one sentence. This general statement helps you as a listener identify the speaker's purpose. Here are a few central ideas you may hear instructors deliver in a classroom presentation:

   "Today we are going to discuss Maslow's Hierarchy of Needs."

   "A certifiable weld must meet three specific tests."

   "EMTs use the following guidelines to identify cardiac arrest."

   Detecting the sender's central idea is one of your first tasks as a listener. Once you have discovered the central idea, you will want to find main points.

Main points are components of the central idea that are explained in terms of kinds, steps, or reasons. Often the sender will preview his or her main points after stating a central idea. For example, a nursing instructor may state, "Today we will examine three major curves of the spine: the cervical, thoracic, and lumbar regions." This preview helps prepare you for the information that will follow. Your criminal justice instructor may begin a discussion of major types of felonies by listing violent offenses, property offenses, drug offenses, and white-collar offenses. Other main points may come in the form of steps in a process or reasons for an occurrence. These forms can be illustrated when your culinary instructor previews the steps of a recipe or identifies several possibilities for a soufflé failing to rise.

3. **Use an effective note-taking system.** Although you want to avoid taking notes the way Amanda did, word-for-word, you can take notes effectively to reinforce key concepts. You also need to develop a note-taking system that works for you and is flexible to adapt to the speaker's organization. Outlining is one such strategy. Nursing students learning about congenital birth defects, for example, may hear a presentation explaining the effects of Goldenhar Syndrome. The outlined notes may look like this:

Goldenhar Syndrome affects everyone surrounding the defect.
　Goldenhar Syndrome affects the patient.
　Goldenhar Syndrome affects the family.
　Goldenhar Syndrome affects the friends.

More specific details could be added to each main point with memorable introductory and concluding statements.

You may want to try mapping the information the way you would draw the solar system with the sun in the center and the planets orbiting the sun. These visual maps are good for establishing relationships between central ideas and main points. A firefighter/EMT heard a lecture on the types of wounds and created the map shown in figure 5.4.

Information about the characteristics of each type of wound could be added to lines extending out from the "planets."

As another alternative, you may choose to list main points to the left of the page and supporting details to the right to create a "logic tree" or "fish diagram." A culinary arts student made such a diagram when noting information about preventing food-borne illness (figure 5.5).

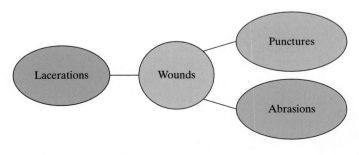

FIGURE 5.4 ■ Wound Map

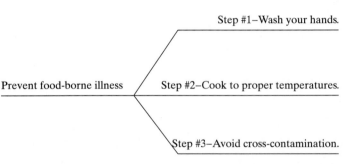

FIGURE 5.5 ■ Fish Diagram

You can also create your own memory devices to help you remember. Auto body students were told how to use A, B, and C type fire extinguishers safely with the acronym PASS.

Pull, Aim, Squeeze, Sweep = PASS

Regardless of the system you use, try to capture the central idea and the main points in a way that helps you recall that information. Most important, you must be flexible in your note taking and adjust to the topic and organizational style of the sender.

LISTENING AT WORK

Jessie had just started a new job at a local hardware store. He was really excited about the job because his supervisor said she would assign him hours that fit his school schedule. Also, the store was located close to home, so Jessie had only about ten minutes of travel time from home to work.

His first day on the job, Jessie's supervisor told him to unpack a recent shipment of exterior paints and to stock them on the appropriate shelves in the front half of the store. The supervisor gave him specific instructions about stacking the paint cans so they would be clearly visible to customers and easy to reach. Unfortunately, Jessie wasn't paying as much attention to the directions as he should have and ended up stacking the cans with only three of the colors clearly visible from the customer aisle. A few hours later, the supervisor spotted the paint cans and reprimanded Jessie for not following directions.

Not Listening in the Workplace
Source: www.CartoonStock .com.

Although Jessie's error was easy to fix, he certainly didn't make a positive impression with his supervisor. However, sometimes the result of ineffective listening in the workplace can have catastrophic results. In their book, *Listen Up,* authors Barker and Watson (2000) describe the story of a power plant worker who was told not to use an elevator because a fire had broken out five stories above. Unfortunately the worker hadn't listened. He entered the elevator, only to lose his life when the elevator shaft exploded (p. 56).

Although most poor listening at work does not have such dire consequences, think for a moment about the lost productivity, strained relationships, and lowered morale that occur when workers fail to listen to one another.

Fortunately, however, many employees in the workplace are highly effective listeners. Chris Stebnitz is one of them (figure 5.6). A 1995 graduate of the University of Wisconsin-Whitewater, Stebnitz received the International Listening Association's "Listening in the Business Sector Award" (Schmidt, 2007).

Stebnitz took over his grandfather's building business as owner and was responsible for developing a "procedural listening process for his company,

FIGURE 5.6 ■ Chris Stebnitz, Recipient of Award from International Listening Association

which he trained his associates and employees to use in their day-to-day work" (Schmidt, 2007, p. 1).

"The focus of procedural listening is to facilitate improvement of listening skills within the company through a unique and tailored discipline of listening and documentation. The goal of the technique is to ensure that all of the client's needs and wants are heard and understood, as well as documented and distributed throughout the organization" (Schmidt, 2007, p. 8).

"The process came about in response to customer surveys received by the company a few years ago, which found clients desired a builder who was willing and able to communicate effectively even more than one who offered a competitive cost" (Schmidt, 2007, p. 8).

Although you may not be an award-winning listener like Chris Stebnitz, you can certainly become an outstanding listener in your place of employment. Consider the following suggestions, which offer you ways to improve listening at work:

1. **Be attentive.** This first suggestion might seem fairly obvious. However, given all of the distractions that can occur at work, paying attention to others is not as easy as you think. Consider Les, a supervisor in a small company that produces Simply Natural, a line of organic snack foods. Les prides himself on his ability to multitask and maintain a high level of efficiency on the job. He also established an open-door policy so workers could freely approach him whenever they had a problem to discuss. However, Kate and Perry, two marketing reps for the company, recently confronted Les with some concerns they had about Les's communication style. They commented that although they feel free to stop by Les's office, he is generally on the computer while they are talking to him. Consequently, they don't feel as if they have his full attention. After some honest sharing, Les agreed to put his computer work aside when Kate and Perry come in to discuss company matters.

   Les learned from this experience that he had to stop what he was doing in order to give co-workers his undivided attention. Next, he made sure to move out from behind his desk to a chair alongside the co-workers. He also tried to establish frequent eye contact, in addition to head nods, as a way of showing that he was physically and mentally present. As a result of these changes, Les found that his listening skills improved, and his co-workers felt that what they had to say mattered.

2. **Be opportunistic.** Listeners who are opportunistic view listening at work as a chance to solve problems, strengthen interpersonal ties, encourage creativity, and facilitate networking. Kelly is a good example of an opportunistic listener. Working the front desk of a large hotel gives her plenty of time to communicate with guests when they are checking in and out. A few weeks ago, Kelly encountered a disgruntled customer who was exhausted after a long flight and eager to check into his room. Unfortunately, Kelly could find no record of his reservation in the computer system, and the hotel was fully booked due to an out-of-town convention.

Upon hearing that the hotel had no room available for him, the customer became hostile with Kelly, insisting that the hotel was to blame for not booking the reservation he made online.

At first, Kelly found herself becoming defensive, yet she knew that arguing back with the customer would serve no practical purpose. In addition, she realized that this difficult encounter could give her an opportunity to solve a problem and possibly ensure future business from this customer. She reminded herself to take a few deep breaths and patiently listen to the customer with an open mind while he vented his frustration. She also tried to put herself in the customer's place, and found herself gradually feeling more empathy for his situation.

After the customer had calmed down, Kelly checked the hotel computer again, only to discover that the reservation had been booked for the following day instead of the day the man arrived. Although she couldn't tell for sure who was responsible for the booking error—the hotel or the customer—Kelly got on the phone to other nearby hotels and found a vacancy just a short distance away. Kelly booked the room, sincerely apologized to the customer, and offered him a meal voucher so he could enjoy a complimentary dinner before departing for the other hotel. She also arranged to have the courtesy van pick up the customer's luggage and drive him to the other hotel after he had finished dinner.

Hotel Check-In Sometimes Offers Communications Challenges That Require Skill and Finesse

3. **Give and receive feedback.** As you may recall from Chapter 1, feedback is essential to promote understanding between a sender and a receiver and can occur in a variety of forms. For example, you may seek feedback from a supervisor on ways to improve your job performance and ensure advancement opportunities. If you work in a supervisory capacity, you are likely to provide feedback to your subordinates in an effort to keep them updated on company policies and procedures. In today's competitive job market, companies also encourage feedback from clients and customers in order to remain on the cutting edge as providers of goods and services.

According to Gregory Smith, author of *Employee Involvement Campaigns* (2008), "Getting employees' ideas is no longer an option. If your organization is going to be competitive, it is mandatory you involve the minds, hands, and ideas of everyone in your organization. Getting employees involved not only yields valuable ideas and suggestions, but also the increased morale of workers who feel like they are being listened to results in a more productive and satisfying work environment" (p. 1).

Further in the article, Smith describes an employee suggestion program called an Idea Campaign. He tells of several organizations who tried this campaign in an effort to obtain employee feedback on "how to improve productivity, cut costs, and improve worker motivation" (p. 1).

"At Eglin Air Force Base, the campaign ran for two weeks where both civilian and military personnel were asked to submit ideas that could reduce waste and inefficiency or increase productivity. Eglin received a tremendous surprise when workers generated $400,000 worth of cost savings ideas and new ways to generate revenue. Harley-Davidson ran a similar program, saving $3,000,000 in one 30-day program. The U.S. Park Service made over 12,000 suggestions with an approval rate of 75 percent" (Smith, 2008, pp. 1–2).

LISTENING AT HOME

In some ways, listening at home is more difficult than listening either at school or at work. At both school and work, the price for failing to listen appears to have more negative consequences. Ineffective listening at school could cost you a high GPA, whereas ineffective listening at work could cost you your job.

Like many others, you may take those with whom you live for granted. You may count on the fact that if you don't listen to your parents, your spouse, your siblings, or your children, somehow they will overlook your inattention.

Keep in mind, however, that although failing to listen at home may not result in material losses, the quality of your relationships can certainly suffer.

David and Claudia Arp in their article, *You're Not Listening* (2008), state, "Not listening plays a big part in problem marriages. Counselors hear over and over again statements like: 'He never listens to me,' or 'She doesn't understand how I feel'" (p. 1).

They continue, "If poor listening is a sign of a troubled marriage, then good listening is a characteristic of a healthy marriage. When others say, 'Hey, tell me more' and really listen to us, we feel important, understood, and accepted" (Arp & Arp, 2008, p. 1).

You will find the following tips helpful when you work to improve your listening skills at home.

1. **Take time to listen.** Today's families are often so busy juggling work, school, and social obligations that they have little time just to sit and talk to one another. Rosa and Derek are a couple who found themselves in this situation.

Rosa works part-time as an instructional assistant, and Derek works full-time as a landscape supervisor while pursuing an associate degree at a local community college. The couple also has a six-year-old son and an eight-year-old daughter. Lately Rosa has been feeling frustrated about the lack of quality family time. Between her job, driving the children to soccer practice and music lessons, and trying to keep up with day-to-day household chores, she seems to have little time for anything else.

In addition, she and Derek have begun to argue more over minor irritations, and the children are more preoccupied with TV watching and video games when they come home from school.

Finally, Rosa decided to sit down and talk to Derek and the children about her feelings. Together they decided to make some changes. Thursday night became "family night." Derek picked up pizza on his way home from work,

Family Night Promotes Harmony and Fun among Family Members

and the four of them had dinner and sat and talked about their day at work or school. After dinner, the four of them enjoyed a different group activity each week. One week the activity involved a nature walk at a local park; another week the family went to a recreation league baseball game.

Rosa admits that although their lives can still be hectic, each of them has come to look forward to Thursday nights and the opportunity these evenings provide for quality sharing and productive listening.

2. **Practice effective attending behavior.** Although many suggestions are offered to help you become a better listener, real improvement requires a caring attitude, an attentive physical presence, and a responsive mental presence (figure 5.7). These suggestions can be used when you are communicating with family.

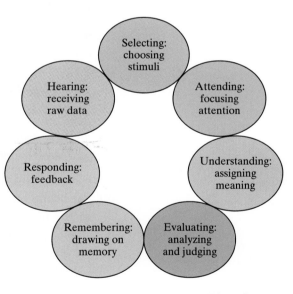

FIGURE 5.7 ■ Listening Process

The central attitude important to listening effectively is, "I *want* to understand you." Until you make this decision as a conscious choice, you will be easily distracted from the important listening task at hand. This attitude is rooted in concern for the well-being of those with whom you live. Until you go beyond your own personal preoccupations and focus your concentration on the family member who has something to say, effective listening will be haphazard at best. This attitude is fostered by the ability to empathize with the sender. Empathy requires you to put yourself in the sender's place, to view the world from his or her perspective, to ask yourself, "If I were you, how would I feel?" Although some individuals seem to be more empathic by nature, empathy is something anyone can develop with practice.

After you've made the decision to really listen, proper attending behavior will signal your physical and mental presence. Attending behaviors are a combination of the attitude already mentioned and actions that communicate your involvement with the sender, demonstrating your interest and concern. Your eye contact, posture, and interpersonal distance will be signs of your physical attention. Your eye contact must be for a sufficient length of time, of an appropriate intensity, and frequent enough to suggest genuine involvement with the sender. In addition, your body orientation and posture must reveal alertness and a willingness to participate fully in the communication process. Finally, the distance you maintain with the sender must create a comfortable rapport so the sender feels at ease and willing to share.

Your caring attitude and physical presence will help you establish a mental presence that focuses your attention on the sender and reduces both external and internal distractions. A mental presence that fosters good listening requires you to put aside your own preoccupations and concentrate fully on what the sender is saying. Such concentration increases your ability to understand the sender and to empathize with his or her feelings.

3. **Respond appropriately.** In your relationships with family members, appropriate responding completes the listening process. This step involves your ability to sense what kind of feedback will ensure understanding of the message and communicate your genuine interest in the sender. In some instances, you may find that providing comfort and reassurance are just what the sender needs. In other instances, you might decide to question the sender further in order to seek additional information. If the sender has requested your opinion or advice, you can offer either one in the context of your feedback. Perhaps you feel the need to restate what the sender has said as a way of encouraging further sharing.

Keep in mind, however, that responding appropriately is important not only at home but at school and at work as well.

In the next section, you will read more about the most commonly used responses. This information will enable you to provide the kind of feedback that promotes understanding, strengthens relationships, and communicates your sincere interest in the sender.

Responding Skills

Whether you are listening at school, work, or home, your choice of response becomes especially important when someone shares a personal or professional problem. In such situations, you have an opportunity to respond in several ways. Your response reflects your reaction to the situation as well as your intentions and may encourage open communication and problem solving or

Evaluating—Judging	Evaluating—Solving, Advising
• Values as good or bad, right or wrong	• Shares solution
• Passes judgment	• Offers advice
— That was stupid!	— Why don't you . . . ?
— Only a fool would. . . .	— You really should . . .
	— If I were you, . . .

inhibit further sharing and understanding. Take a closer look at the choices that are available to you as you react. Does your response help you to listen? Does your response help the person with the problem?

Suppose Pat, your classmate and friend, comes to you and relates the following: "I don't know about this program. I thought I made a wise choice going into dental hygiene, and now I find out how many science courses are required. I've never been much good in science, and I'm concerned about not making it through the program." As you respond to Pat's problem, you may feel evaluative or judgmental, curious, concerned, analytical, supportive, or empathic. The feelings and reactions that you have can be shared clearly with Pat if you are aware of the different responses that are available to you.

Research has identified several types of responses. The following is a partial list of common responses that you can choose from as you provide feedback to the concerns of others.

When you choose an evaluating response, you will be either judging and evaluating, or advising and solving the sender's concerns. These two types of evaluating responses, those that judge and those that advise, are the most common choices for many listeners. When your response judges, it says what is right or wrong, good or bad. Examples might be: "That was stupid!" "That's right!" "You're great!" "That's important!" Your response that advises will offer a solution to the person's problem by telling him or her what to do. Examples might include these: "If I were you I would . . ." "You really should . . ." "You ought to . . ." "Why don't you . . ." Your evaluating response to Pat might be, "You're in over your head. I'd bail out as fast as I could if I were you and go into another program."

Your interpreting response will analyze, explain, or teach the sender about the cause of his or her concern. Your interpreting response explains why something happens, or states a cause(s) for actions and feelings by adding information not stated in the original problem. Examples might include these: "You may feel that way because . . ." "She probably did that because . . ." "Maybe the reason this problem came about is due to. . . ." Your interpreting response to Pat might be, "It could be that you're jumping to conclusions about your ability before you've given those science courses a chance."

Interpreting

- Explains reason for feelings or behaviors
- Finds causes not in the problem
- Explores the motives
  - She said that because. . . .
  - You're doing that to. . . .

Supporting

- Reassures, pacifies
- Reduces intensity of feelings
- Can be "false" or "genuine"
  — Everybody has bad days.
  — I'm sure you will . . . .

Questioning

- Gains more information
- Clarifies meaning
- Selects open or closed
  — When did that happen?
  — What did you do then?

Paraphrasing

- Summarizes content and/or feeling
- Uses the listener's words
  —You feel . . . because . . . .
  —So you're saying . . . .

Your supporting response is designed to reassure, pacify, or comfort. When you choose a supporting response, you attempt to make people feel better; cheer them up; or offer help, encouragement, or comfort. Probably one of the most effective, supportive responses you can make is one that states how you are able to help in terms of being available and offering your services, time, or possessions. Examples that you may use include: "I'm sure things will be better . . ." "Look at the progress you have made since . . ." "We all feel that way once in a while . . ." "If there is any way I can help . . ." "I'd be willing to come over and help you with . . ." Your supporting response to Pat might be, "I feel that way about some of my math courses. I've taken advantage of tutoring in our Learning Center."

Your questioning response probes, clarifies, inquires, or seeks more information. You may choose from two types of questions, open or closed. Open questions require more than a yes or no answer and encourage greater freedom of response, whereas closed questions can be answered with a yes or no. Examples of open questions that you might use include: "What makes you think that?" "How long have you felt that way?" "Where were you?" "What do you mean by that?" Your questioning response to Pat might be, "Exactly what kind of science courses does the program require?"

Your paraphrasing response summarizes, restates, or reflects. When you use a paraphrasing response, you show what you've understood by restating in your own words what you think the speaker meant or by summarizing the content and/or feelings in the message.

Examples of paraphrasing responses might be these: "You mean you're feeling . . ." "So what you are saying is . . ." "In other words . . ." "If I understand, you've . . ." Your paraphrasing response to Pat might be, "You're unsure of your own ability in some of the courses and are wondering whether you made the right choice about dental hygiene?"

An important point for you to remember is that these responses are not right or wrong. You can use each response in effective interaction with those who have problems. With practice, you will develop the skillful and appropriate use of these responses.

Using Response Styles

Approximately 80 percent of all the feedback you give to senders can be categorized as evaluating, interpreting, supporting, questioning, or paraphrasing responses.

You will find the evaluating response appears to be the one used most frequently when senders share problems with listeners. The high frequency of the evaluating response may be the result of your feeling responsible to solve senders' problems by offering advice or believing that you know what is in the senders' best interests. In contrast, paraphrasing tends to be used least often, and this response may be one that you have to learn to use.

Your feedback will be more effective when you develop the ability to use all of the responses, rather than over-using, or inappropriately using only one of the responses. According to psychologist Carl Rogers, if you use any response 40 percent of the time or more, people tend to see you as always responding that way. Consequently, if you use a large number of evaluating responses in communication, others may perceive you as being judgmental and close-minded, which can lessen your effectiveness as a listener.

Certain guidelines can enable you to use the response styles more effectively. In addition, senders give you some cues to let you know when a particular response is helping the sender to deal with a problem. When senders come to you with problems, try to keep in mind the following suggestions (figure 5.8):

Response	Intent	Example
Evaluating, judging	Values as good/bad or right/wrong.	That's stupid. You're right! What a jerk!
Evaluating, advising	Shares solution or offers advice.	If I were you . . . You really should . . .
Interpreting	Explains why something happens, gives reasons not stated in problem for feelings or behaviors.	You may feel that way because . . . S/he probably did that because . . .
Supporting	Reassures, pacifies, reduces intensity of feeling.	I'm sure things will be better . . . Look at the progress you've made since . . .
Questioning	Gains more information, clarifies meaning, expands details.	What makes you think that? How long have you felt . . . ?
Paraphrasing	Shows what you understand, restates in your own words what you heard. Summarizes content and/or feelings with reflecting skills.	You mean you're feeling . . . So what you are saying is . . . If I understand you . . . You feel . . . because . . .

FIGURE 5.8 ■ Response Style Summary

Evaluating: Your evaluating response normally does not help a sender in coping with a problem unless the sender specifically asks for your advice. If advice is requested by a sender, you can feel more confident that the sender is ready to accept your advice and is less likely to blame you if your advice does not work out. An indication that your advice is working occurs when the sender willingly accepts the advice, almost as if it represents a solution the sender hadn't previously thought of. If the sender openly disagrees with your advice or responds with "Yes, but . . ." and proceeds to explain why your advice won't work, chances are your evaluating response is not being effective.

Interpreting: This response works best when your intention is to offer insight into the problem's causes. Your interpreting response also tends to work more effectively when stated non-absolutely, such as "Maybe you feel this way because . . ." or "Perhaps you're feeling undecided as a result of . . ." This tentative language acknowledges that you may not be completely accurate in your analysis, and therefore, potential defensive or argumentative reactions in the sender are less likely to occur. If the sender agrees with your interpretation, this response is working. If the sender disagrees and proceeds to tell you why you're wrong, your interpreting response is unsuccessful.

Supporting: Support and reassurance work best when the sender has already determined how to solve the problem and simply needs the strength and encouragement that your support can provide. If this response is working, the sender will accept your words of comfort and assume a more relaxed nonverbal posture; if not, the sender may say something like, "But you don't really understand."

Questioning: When your need for additional information is genuine, questioning works best. If you ask questions, ask them one at a time; ask them only as often as necessary; keep them open-ended. You may also want to ask questions that make the sender think more deeply about the problem such as, "What might be some underlying causes of this problem?" "How do you feel about this?" "What do you think you can do about that?" If questioning is having the desired effect, the sender will gladly provide the information requested; if not, the sender may begin sharing less by offering one-word responses or answering a question with a question.

Paraphrasing: When a sender communicates a problem to you, your paraphrasing response reveals a sincere desire to understand the sender's thoughts and feelings. When you paraphrase, the sender then can talk through the problem and arrive at a solution in an atmosphere of acceptance. If your paraphrasing is effective, the sender will continue to share thoughts and feelings in greater depth or correct you if your understanding is inaccurate. If the sender retreats and begins to share less, paraphrasing is probably not being successful.

As a final reminder, effective listening is invaluable at school, work, and home. Like any skill, your listening can improve with practice and patience. As you take advantage of the suggestions discussed in this chapter, you will be on your way to enhancing your interpersonal relationships both personally and professionally.

Review Questions

1. Briefly explain any three specific situations where listening will be an important part of your life.
2. Describe the steps in the listening process.
3. How is listening defined in your text?
4. Explain four listening principles that are discussed in your text.
5. List three tangible benefits of effective listening in the workplace.
6. Discuss several ways listening differs from hearing.
7. Identify the note-taking style described in the text that you find most effective to increase your understanding. Explain why this style works for you.
8. Describe when you would use each of the response styles and how you would know whether or not each was effective.

Key Terms and Concepts

Central Idea   111

Main Points   112

Attending Behavior   118

Evaluating   122

Interpreting   122

Supporting   122

Questioning   122

Paraphrasing   122

Web Activities

Visit the following interesting sites to find out more about listening in action.

- The International Listening Association offers several interesting resources at http://www.listen.org/Templates/facts.htm.
- See listening skills in action; read the stories about two rabbis who have mastered the art of listening at http://www.hasidicstories.com/Stories/Pesach_

Mendel/advice.html or http://www.hasidicstories.com/Stories/Later_Rebbes/shortest.html.

- Test yourself and enjoy an interactive review of listening barriers at http://www.wisc-online.com/objects/index_tj.asp?objID=CCS2506.

Assignments

ASSIGNMENT 5.1: LISTENING SELF-ASSESSMENT

1. On a scale from 0 to 100, how would you rate yourself as a listener?

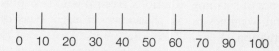

| 0 | 10 | 20 | 30 | 40 | 50 | 60 | 70 | 90 | 100 |

Place "X" to indicate rating.

2. How do you think others would rate you as a listener? Use the following letters and scale to indicate where you think the following people would rate you as a listener:
   A. Your best friend
   B. Your boss
   C. Co-workers
   D. Subordinates
   E. Significant other

```
|  |  |  |  |  |  |  |  |  |  |
0  10  20  30  40  50  60  70  90  100
```

Place letters to indicate ratings.

3. What kind of bad listening habits do you have? Indicate how frequently you do the following:

Listening Habits	Frequency
	A lot..........Very little
Call the subject uninteresting	5....4....3....2....1....0
Criticize the speaker's delivery	5....4....3....2....1....0
Disagree with the speaker's message	5....4....3....2....1....0
Listen only for facts	5....4....3....2....1....0
Try to outline everything	5....4....3....2....1....0
Fake attention to the speaker	5....4....3....2....1....0
Tolerate distraction	5....4....3....2....1....0
Avoid difficult material	5....4....3....2....1....0
Overreact to emotional words	5....4....3....2....1....0
Waste the thought/speed advantage	5....4....3....2....1....0

4. What two terms best describe you as a listener?
   A.

   B.

5. Describe your listening behavior in four different types of listening situations. Record your strengths and weaknesses as a listener in each type of situation.
   A. Listening to directions or work assignments

B. Listening for factual information (lecture material)

C. Listening for opinions

D. Listening for feelings

6. List three changes that would improve your listening skills.
   A.
   B.
   C.

ASSIGNMENT 5.2: LISTENING SKILLS TEST

Directions: Follow the instructions below to complete the Listening Skills Test at this website: http://www.psychtests.com/tests/alltests.html.

1. Boot up a computer at home or in any of the labs on campus.
2. Open Internet Explorer or Netscape.
3. Type URL in the address box and press Enter.
4. Scroll down the complete list of tests to the My Profile Premium Tests.
5. Double-click on the Listening Skills Test.
6. Scroll down to "Non-members take the test" and click on "Go."
7. Respond to each of the 57 items on the test.
8. Click on "Score" when completed.
9. Review your test results.
10. Print out a copy of your results to submit to your instructor.

And/Or

Obtain a six-factor profile of your listening by clicking on this link: http://www.highgain.com. Choose the "Free Self-Test." Answer the questions and submit your results to your instructor.

ASSIGNMENT 5.3: LISTENING REPORTS

Complete one of the following two assignments:

Listening Article Report

Find a magazine or Internet article about some aspect of listening. Write a summary of the main points and key supports of the article, and present your summary to the class in a two- to three-minute presentation.

or

Listening Habit Report

Relate a two- to three-minute story describing how you used good listening habits to accomplish a task at work or at school. Describe who was involved, what the project was, and the good listening habits that you used to complete the job.

ASSIGNMENT 5.4: RESPONSE STYLES QUESTIONNAIRE

Directions: Read each of the following ten situations, and write a response that is typical of what you normally say as a listener. Then go back and read the sample responses for each situation. Circle the letter of the sample that most closely resembles the intention of the response you've written, even though the wording may be different. If there are no matches, circle the one that sounds like something you might say in response to the problem.

After you complete the Response Styles Questionnaire, answer the questions posed in the Response Styles Analysis Worksheet. Finally, practice making each type of response by completing the Response Styles Practice Worksheet.

1. *The union just told us we have to take another 10 percent cut in pay because the company is in bad economic straits. I don't know what I'm going to do. With a family of three kids to support, it will be hard making ends meet.*

Your Response:

_____

_____

A. You have no right to complain. Just be thankful you've got a job.
B. I know what you mean. My company cut back on our vacation time because of financial problems.
C. It sounds like you're feeling depressed about that salary loss.
D. You may be concerned because you've never been forced to budget your money before, and you're not sure how to go about it.
E. How much was the other cut you had to take?

2. *I'm seriously thinking about the boss's offer to have the company send me to school part-time to upgrade my skills. But I don't know—I was never much of a student in high school, and I don't know if I've got what it takes to go on to a community college.*

Your Response:

_____

_____

A. What do you mean when you say you weren't much of a student in high school?
B. You're having doubts about your ability to succeed in school?
C. You'll be sorry if you don't take the boss up on this offer, especially since the company agreed to pay for it.
D. Most people have apprehensions about returning to school. But you can make it!
E. Perhaps you're worried about being embarrassed in front of the boss if you don't get all A's and B's.

3. *I'm really having a hard time getting along with the new supervisor. He's the company owner's son, and he seems to feel he can push everybody around because his mom owns the business.*

Your Response:

_____

_____

A. How has he been pushing you around?

B. If I were you, I'd go and complain to the owner about it.

C. I get the idea you're unhappy with the way this supervisor is handling the people in your department.

D. It could be that he feels the need to prove his supervisory ability to his mother.

E. If you can just hang in there a little longer, the situation is bound to improve.

4. *I just can't talk to my parents anymore since I told them Terry and I are getting married. They are always asking questions about where I go and what I do. They keep track of me like I am a two-year-old. I don't know what's happened to them.*

Your Response:

_____

_____

A. Why don't you tell them to butt out? They shouldn't be hassling you.

B. What do they want to know?

C. You sound really upset about this.

D. They're probably just finding it hard to let go of you now that you're getting married.

E. Lots of parents are like that all the time. I'm sure it will pass.

5. *Lupe, I hate it when those customers call and say their appliances aren't working after we just fixed them. Half of the people barely know how to plug them in, much less run them. Then I get stuck listening to all their problems on the phone.*

Your Response:

_____

_____

A. They really do get you upset; don't they?

B. What was wrong with that last caller?

C. Just tell them to read their owner's manual.

D. Sometimes they worry more about something when it's new or fixed. That's why they call so much.

E. I got the same grief when I had your job; you'll get used to it.

6. *The crew on the line keep inviting me to join them at a bar after work. I feel obligated to go, being the new employee and all. Sometimes I can't afford to buy a round, but everybody usually buys one. I hate to be rude, so what do I do?*

Your Response:

_____

_____

A. Don't go just because you feel obligated. That's dumb.

B. Perhaps you think you need to do this to feel accepted by them.

C. So you're worried about fitting in with the crew on the assembly line, but you're not sure you can afford being one of the group?

D. Where do you usually go anyway?

E. I was in the same situation at the last place I worked. I guess it's the normal thing to do when you're new on your first job.

7. *I really like working here. The opportunities are great; the conditions are excellent; the pay is good. I've learned a lot. But Kerry, that perfectionist boss we have . . . I just can't seem to do enough right. There's always something wrong with the work I've done.*

Your Response:

_____

_____

A. Hey, you'll get through okay. I'm sure Kerry will see that you're working up to your potential.

B. You think the boss demands too much from you?

C. Kerry's boss used to treat him the same way. Kerry probably thinks that's what a good boss does.

D. What did Kerry say to you last night?

E. If I were you, I'd find something else to do or somebody else to work for.

8. *My boss is really rude. Three months ago I asked if I could have a vacation in early July and was told yes. I've made all kinds of plans to go out west, and now the boss said that if I go, I'll be fired.*

Your Response:

_____

_____

A. After promising you vacation, your boss has threatened action if you take it?

B. Why do think the boss changed so suddenly?

C. I'd go to a union officer and file a grievance.

D. A lot of the workers around here feel the same about their boss.

E. The company must have just gotten a new order in, and now they need your help.

9. *It's really hard being the only female in an all-male shop. All the employees who don't think I'm serious about diesel mechanics tease me to death.*

Your Response:

_____

_____

A. You're being too sensitive about the issue. Just ignore their remarks.
B. That must really be a hassle. If there's anything I can say or do to help change things, just let me know.
C. What do they say that is most irritating when they tease you?
D. You seem fed up with the other employees' comments.
E. Maybe they're intimidated by a woman in this occupation.

10. *It's totally useless! Everywhere I go for jobs, I'm told that nothing is available or that I don't have enough experience. How can I get any experience unless somebody is willing to give me a chance?*

Your Response:

_____

_____

A. What kind of jobs are you applying for? What are your qualifications?
B. You want to work, but you lack the needed experience?
C. You're going about it all wrong. You should go to school and get an advanced education in that area.
D. The economy is in such a mess that employers have a greater pool of potential workers. They can now afford to be really choosy.
E. You're only one of many people in the same boat.

Response Styles Analysis

Answer the following questions about your response styles.

1. What was your dominant style of your written responses?
2. Did the dominant written style match with the selected style? If not, explain the differences.

3. Describe the dominant response style used by each of the following:
   a. Your significant other
   b. Your boss
   c. Your major instructor
   d. A family member
4. How will your knowledge of response styles affect the messages you send?
5. How will your knowledge of response styles affect the feedback you give to messages you receive?

ASSIGNMENT 5.5: RESPONSE STYLES PRACTICE

Directions: For each of the following three situations, write an example of all five responses.

1. "This co-worker in my car pool is constantly criticizing and complaining about the other people at work. I'm getting sick and tired of these comments. I never hear anything positive about anybody."
   Evaluating:
   Interpreting:
   Supporting:
   Questioning:
   Paraphrasing:

2. "Wow, I just got fired. My boss walked up to me, gave me my last paycheck, and told me that they didn't need me any longer. I didn't even get an explanation why."
   Evaluating:
   Interpreting:
   Supporting:
   Questioning:
   Paraphrasing:

3. "What do you do when somebody wants to borrow your tools or test equipment? This new assembler doesn't have everything that's needed for the job. I don't mind lending some of my stuff, but I can't keep up with my own work without the tools I need. I hate to be selfish, but I don't know what to do."
   Evaluating:
   Interpreting:
   Supporting:
   Questioning:
   Paraphrasing:

ASSIGNMENT 5.6: CASE STUDY: LISTENING TIPS

Case 1

You tell your supervisor that you are taking a communications class. The supervisor begins to rant and rave that people always say she is a poor listener. She asks you for your opinion and then goes to her computer and begins to answer emails. Using information from this chapter, describe the listening barriers evident in this example. Additionally, give your supervisor three specific suggestions for improving her listening style.

Case 2

A friend, who is also a classmate, is talking with you about some challenge he is having on the job. His grades have been affected by the situation at work. He goes on to suggest that the stress is taking a toll on his personal life, too. Based on what you have learned from this chapter, list five behaviors that would show that you are an empathic listener.

References

Arneson, K. W. (2002, January 13). The fine art of listening. *New York Times*, p. 4A.34. Retrieved March 1, 2007, from http://proquest.umi.com/pqdweb?index=7&did=99347887&SrchMode=1&sid=2&Fmt=3&VInst=

Arp, D. & Arp C. (2008). *You're not listening.* Retrieved February 8, 2008, from http://womentodaymagazine.com/ relationships/listen.html, p. 1.

Barker, L. & Watson, K. (2000). *Listen up: How to improve relationships, reduce stress, and be more productive by using the power of listening.* New York: St. Martin's Press.

Beal, M. L. (2006). Contributions of a listening legend. *International Journal of Listening*, p. 27.

Beyler, L. (2006, November 2). Police officer stresses listening skill. Retrieved January 9, 2008, from http://www.news.wisc.edu/10361

Dear Abby. (1999, September 8). Adults jumping to conclusions trip on misconception of teen. *Dear Abby on uExpress.* Retrieved March 14, 2007, from www.uexpress.com/dearabby/?uc_full_date=19990908

Dietsche, V. K. (2000, December 13). Effective note taking improves your GPA. Retrieved February 16, 2007, from http://jerz.setonhill.edu/Writing/academic/notes2.htm

Gardner, M. (2002, February 6). Everybody's talking—who's left to listen? *Christian Science Monitor,* p. 14. Retrieved March 1, 2007, from http://www.highbeam.com/doc/1G1-82527373.html

High Gain. (n.d.). Listening at work. Retrieved February 9, 2007, from www.highgain.com/html/listening_at_work.html

Listening Facts. (1996). International Listening Association. Retrieved March 9, 2007, from www.listen.org/Templates/facts.htm

Nichols, R. G. (2006). The struggle to be human. *International Journal of Listening*, pp. 4–12.

Schmidt, M. (2007, October 7). UW-W grad Stebnitz earns listening award. *Daily Jefferson County Union*, pp. 1, 8.

Science Instructional Graphics. (n.d.) The ear. Submitted by Nicky Chen. Retrieved February 23, 2007, from www.coe.uh.edu/archive/Science/science_graphics/sciencegr18.html

Smith, G. P. (2008). *Employee involvement campaigns: Capturing employee ideas and suggestions.* Retrieved February 6, 2008, from http://www.chartcourse.com/articleidea.htm, pp 1–2.

Steil, L. & Bommelje, R. (2004). *Learn how to be present.* International Listening Leadership Institute. Retrieved March 30, 2007, from http://casts.webvalence.com/sites/ListeningLeader/Broadcast.D20000103.html

Stracher, C. (2005, July 29). Much depends on dinner. www.dinnerwithdad.com. Retrieved February 9, 2007, from http://ad.doubleclick.net/adi/opinionjournal.wsj.com/taste_general;;pTile=2;;u=SatJan06120. . .

Taylor, T. (2006, December 01). Nurse's story: Julie—listen. *The Nurses' Journal.* Retrieved January 9, 2008, from http://2theheartofthematter.blogspot.com/2006/12/nurses-story-julie-listen.html

Uebergang, J. (2006, December 20). Teaching your child listening skills. *Improving our "signals" and "beings."* Retrieved January 9, 2008, from http://www.earthlingcommunication.com/blog/teaching-your-child-listening-skills.php

Wilson, B. (n.d.). *Practical benefits of better listening for leaders and teams.* Retrieved April 6, 2007, from www.businesslistening.com/leadership_listening-skills.php

Chapter 6

Interpersonal Relationship Skills

Learning **Objectives**

At the end of this chapter, you should be able to meet the following objectives:

1. Identify the importance of interpersonal relationships.
2. Recognize elements of supportive and defensive communication climates.
3. Describe the differences among assertive, aggressive, and nonassertive communication.
4. Describe the characteristics of each element in assertion messages.
5. Provide examples of the four parts of an assertion message.

"The greatest good you can do for another is not just to share your riches but to reveal to him his own."

Benjamin Disraeli

Interpersonal Relationships Are Important

An article about relationships that appeared in a local newspaper began with this lead-in:

> You're born. You have parents or guardians. Relationships.
> You get a job. You get co-workers. Relationships.
> You flirt with a cutie at the grocery story. You go on a date. Relationships.
> You enroll in college. You meet a classmate. By now, you see where this is going.
> Relationships are an inevitable part of life. No matter your situation, you will be connected to someone else.
> One or two of your relationships may be estranged, and perhaps, not all of your relationships are as simple and traditional as the above examples. But chances are you have relationships that you value and want to keep healthy (Price, 2007, March 17, p. 1).

You have relationships with family members, friends, and co-workers. Although these relationships may range from intimate to casual, they all enrich your life in a variety of ways.

As a student, Sandy Hefty discovered a relationship that enriched her life when she met Loretta Olson. In the introduction of a speech titled *A Friend in Need*, Sandy describes Loretta: "'[She] sometimes gets confused and does some pretty bizarre things. For instance, sometimes she puts her ice cream in the refrigerator instead of the freezer, and sometimes she feeds her cat chocolate chips instead of cat food. You see, Loretta is an 85-year-old woman who suffers from Alzheimer's disease. She was preceded in death by her husband and only child and now is trying to live on her own the best that she can. You may be wondering how somebody as confused as Loretta could possibly keep living on her own, but she does.

"'During my freshman year, I volunteered six hours a week to help Loretta remain independent in her home. Due to forgetfulness associated with Alzheimer's disease, my main duty as a volunteer was to help Loretta with her cooking and house cleaning, which she often forgot to finish on her own.'"

After she began volunteer work with Loretta, Sandy learned that millions of elderly Americans are in need of help in order to remain independent in their own homes (Hefty, n.d., p. 1).

Sandy concluded her speech by encouraging those in the audience to consider volunteering themselves, commenting on the personal gratification that such efforts provide.

Milwaukee psychologist Kelly Smerz, who specializes in relationships, states, "It's important to maintain a number of relationships in your life. No one person can be everything . . . It's healthy to have friends, have co-workers and be involved with other people and have different needs met in different ways. We have the opportunity to be really and truly known by someone else, and in turn, a relationship provides us with an opportunity to really know ourselves" (Price, 2007, March 17, p. 1).

Robert is another individual who discovered the benefits of interpersonal relationships. Recently displaced from his job as a welder in a large manufacturing plant, Robert began to experience recurrent episodes of depression. A single parent with a teenage son, Robert felt isolated from the companionship he had enjoyed at work for close to twenty years.

Several months after his job loss, Robert took a part-time position as an intern-trainee at a local wildlife rehabilitation center in his community, caring for injured and orphaned animals. Although he found the work enjoyable, he was especially grateful for the chance he had to forge new friendships with the center staff. He noticed too that his episodes of depression began to lessen and eventually disappeared. Commenting to a fellow staff member, Robert shared that the opportunity to interact with supportive co-workers brought renewed meaning to his life.

Regardless of the type of relationship, however, communication is a key element to ensure interpersonal satisfaction.

According to an article titled *Workplace Communication* (2004), "One of the key foundations of any successful workplace is being able to communicate effectively. It can help people receive and share information better, define and understand goals, and even avoid the negative effects of conflict and confusion. Studies also show that good communication can build rapport, enhance relationships, promote self-confidence and have a positive overall effect on the working environment" (Shepell, 2005, p. 1).

These benefits can be experienced not only in the workplace but in families and among friends as well. Research indicates that those relationships that thrive and make life worthwhile are supportive in nature. In the next section, you will read about the difference between supportive and defensive relationships.

Supportive and Defensive Relationships

You may have noticed how some work groups are warm and friendly whereas others are cold and impersonal, how some families interact well together and others experience a lot of stress. You may even have felt the "vibes" that tell you the kind of climate that you are in.

You need a sound basis for deciding what communication will enhance your relationships and what messages will destroy them. Many years ago, Jack Gibb examined the characteristics of communication climates to determine what factors made some situations positive and others negative.

Dr. Gibb was a distinguished psychologist and consultant for five decades, working with "all forms of organizations, from corporations and governments to schools, churches, and hospitals." He is viewed as the "original proponent of the importance of trust in team dynamics and organizational behavior, and the effect of trust on creativity" (Gibb, 1991, p. 1).

His research gave us the following characteristics for supportive and defensive communication climates (figure 6.1).

You will see that all of these elements of supportive and defensive climates are valid factors in determining the effectiveness of your communication. Let's examine what each element says about your communication.

Supportive Climates	Defensive Climates
Description	Evaluation
Problem Orientation	Control
Spontaneity	Strategy
Empathy	Neutrality
Equality	Superiority
Provisionalism	Certainty

FIGURE 6.1 ■ Gibb's Characteristics of Communication Climates

Description refers to messages that explain your feelings, your reactions, and your needs to others. Statements like, "I am confused by your comments," "I was surprised when you interrupted me," and "I need to take a break" are all examples of descriptive remarks. On the other hand, **evaluation** judges, blames, or criticizes another person. Notice that evaluative comments often begin with the pronoun "you." "You gave me unclear directions," "You were rude to that customer," and "You never listen when I talk to you" are all evaluative messages.

Problem orientation is a point of view you share with another that says "we" have a problem, and we can find a solution. We can work together to meet both parties' needs. Mike, who works in architectural drafting, used the problem orientation approach when he confronted his co-worker, Sam. While the personnel in Mike's department routinely listen to music as they work, Sam has been bringing in CDs of music Mike finds distracting. Mike approached Sam to see if they could work out a compromise about music selection. They agreed to play several CDs all of the workers enjoy, and Sam brought in his mp3 player with ear buds to listen to other music he enjoyed. In contrast, those who attempt to exert **control** in a conflict situation expect the other person to change their behavior. You probably see that controlling does not result in a win-win outcome and is likely to trigger resentment for the person on the losing end of the solution.

Spontaneity refers to a genuine, natural way of communicating with honesty and openness. Anne works as a cashier at a local food cooperative, and co-workers and customers alike are drawn to her spontaneous communication style. Anne routinely inquires about the well-being of those with whom she interacts and looks for opportunities to share mutual interests and concerns. Given Anne's sincerity, it is no wonder that fellow employees welcome the chance to work with her, and customers will often choose her checkout lane over those of other cashiers. **Strategy,** on the other hand, involves manipulation, tricks, or a planned script rather than free-flowing, open communication. Individuals whose communication is strategic rather than spontaneous may feel uncomfortable showing others who they truly are.

Empathy communicates respect, understanding, and acceptance to another; it involves your ability to put yourself in another's place. Empathic people consider, "If I were you, how would I feel?" Rudy is a disabled veteran with a great deal of empathy for others. Because of his own experiences, Rudy spends time with other vets who are recuperating from injuries at a local military base hospital. Rudy comments that although these veterans receive outstanding medical care, what they also need is someone to talk to about their feelings. He believes that the empathic listening he provides is critical to the healing process both physically and emotionally. Unlike empathy, **neutrality** expresses a lack of concern with a detached, impersonal tone. Neutrality can result from lack of first-hand experience, making it difficult for you to understand someone else's feelings. However, neutrality can also occur from self-centeredness and an unwillingness to be fully attentive to the sharing of others.

Equality shares a sense of value and mutual respect regardless of power, status, or position. If you approach others with a sense of equality, you perceive their inherent worth, regardless of differences that may exist between you and them. Elizabeth is a supervisor in a company that designs natural fiber children's clothing. Although she is responsible for managing a team of twenty-five diverse employees in her department, she treats all of them with the same consideration she would exhibit to her peers. Elizabeth takes her employees' suggestions seriously and solves problems collaboratively with them in an effort to sustain a supportive climate. In contrast to equality, **superiority** involves looking down on others, creating feelings of inadequacy, fault, or failure. Elizabeth has discovered that other managers in the plant who approach their subordinates with a sense of superiority also experience more disgruntled employees, lower morale, and reduced rates in productivity.

Provisionalism refers to an open-minded view of new ideas, trying new behaviors, and seeking new solutions. Creative solutions to problems that occur in your workplace, at school, or at home are made possible in an atmosphere of provisionalism. Interestingly, the open-mindedness represented by this attitude has actually led to some unexpected scientific discoveries. For example, "in 1938, 27-year-old Roy Plunkett set out to invent a new refrigerant. Instead, he created a glob of white waxy material that conducted heat and did not stick to surfaces. Fascinated by this 'unexpected' material, he abandoned his original line of research and experimented with this interesting material, which eventually became known by its household name, 'Teflon.'

"In principle, the unexpected event that gives rise to a creative invention is not all that different from the unexpected automobile breakdown that forces us to spend a night in a new and interesting town, the book sent to us in error that excites our imagination, or the closed restaurant that forces us to explore a different cuisine. But when looking for ideas or creative solutions, many of us ignore the unexpected and, consequently, lose the opportunity to turn chance into a creative opportunity" (Michalko, 2008, pp. 2–3).

Unlike provisionalism, **certainty** is characterized by a closed-minded, know-it-all view of the world with no need for changes. People who adopt this attitude limit themselves from experiencing the satisfaction that creativity brings to life and interpersonal relationships.

This list of qualities for supportive climates becomes the foundation for the four-part assertion messages that you will be reading about later in this chapter. By learning to express yourself in a supportive rather than a defensive way, you open the door to improving the communication climate in all of your relationships.

Developing an Assertive Style

BE ASSERTIVE

Your ability to be assertive is a key element in developing a supportive style. Assertive communication is best understood when compared with aggressive and nonassertive communication. Consider the following definitions:

- **Assertiveness:** Stating what you think, feel, want, or need in a way that is direct, honest, and respectful of others.
- **Aggressiveness:** Stating thoughts, feelings, wants, or needs directly and honestly but in a way that is disrespectful of others.
- **Nonassertiveness:** Respecting others while stating your thoughts, feelings, wants, or needs indirectly or not at all.

Keep in mind, too, that each of these approaches to interpersonal communication brings with it advantages and disadvantages. Let's take a brief look at the pros and cons.

Assertive communication allows you to share information openly, honestly, and respectfully while allowing others to do the same. This interpersonal approach builds trust, helps prevent conflicts, and enables you and the persons with whom you communicate to get important needs met. However, becoming more assertive requires an awareness of the skills involved and then consistent practice of those skills. As you probably already know, change of any kind can bring with it a period of discomfort. The same is true when you seek to change some of the ways in which you communicate. Consequently, as you practice new assertive behaviors, be prepared to feel uncomfortable for a time. In addition, co-workers, friends, and family have become accustomed to your present communication style. When you make changes, these individuals may feel uncertain about how to respond to you. They will need time to adjust to the changes as well.

Aggressive communication can certainly be a way of getting your needs met. It can also be somewhat effective in preventing conflict; most people would prefer to avoid confrontations with individuals who are highly aggressive. On the other hand, those who are aggressive frequently pay a

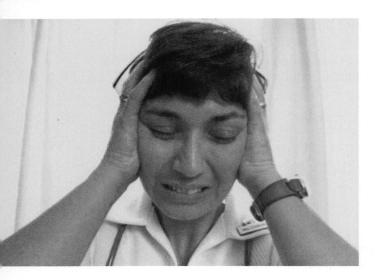

Would You Say This Person Is Probably a Type A or a Type B?

Are You Nonassertive?

price for this interpersonal approach. Often aggressiveness is associated with what is called type A behavior patterns. Some psychologists suggest that those prone to type A behavior suffer from insecurity and low self-esteem. As a result, they exhibit characteristics such as impatience, irritability, anger, and aggressiveness.

Several decades ago, two cardiologists, Dr. Ray Rosenman and Dr. Meyer Friedman, established a connection between personality and coronary heart disease. The people they used in their studies were classified as either **type A** or **type B**. In contrast to type A, type B individuals tend to be easygoing, relaxed, patient, and affectionate. What Rosenman and Friedman discovered was that type A individuals were "70% more likely to suffer from coronary heart disease, even if they had no prior history of the disease" (American Institute for Preventive Medicine, 2001, p. 1). You may want to take a few minutes to determine whether you are a type A by going to Systematic Stress Management's website and Choosing are you a type a at http//aipm.wellnesscheckpoint.com/library/banner_main/asp? P=29892EASME2.

Nonassertive communication has advantages and disadvantages as well. Individuals who are nonassertive avoid conflict are perceived as easy to please, and may be cooperative team players. On the other hand, nonassertive individuals frequently fail to get their needs met, feel resentful about always giving in to others, and suffer low self-esteem from refusing to stand up for themselves. In addition, communicating with people who are nonassertive can be frustrating because they rarely share their true thoughts and feelings. Another fact to consider is that habitual nonassertive communication can lead to stress. Think about a time, for example, when you experienced a disruption of communication. Maybe you had an argument with a significant other and ended up not speaking for several days. Interestingly, prolonged absence of communication can have a direct relationship to stress-related health problems.

According to preliminary results of a University of Michigan study, Dr. E. Harburg and associates report that, "Couples in which both the husband and wife suppress their anger when one attacks the other die earlier than members of couples where one or both partners express their anger and resolve the conflict" (Harburg, 2008, p. 1).

By now, you probably have concluded that the assertive approach is the most conducive to a supportive style of communication. In order to assess your level of assertiveness, you might want to complete the inventory shown in figure 6.2.

Finally, you may find the chart in figure 6.3 to provide some helpful distinctions among the nonassertive, assertive, and aggressive approaches to communication.

How Assertive Are You?

Do you find it easy to be assertive, or does speaking up for yourself make you feel uncomfortable? The following assessment will give you an opportunity to identify how assertive you are.

Assign a score from 1 to 5 for the following statements. Choose 5 for those statements that are **always** true for you, 4 for those that are **usually** true for you, 3 for those that are **sometimes** true for you, 2 for those that are **rarely** true for you, and 1 for those that are **never** true for you.

Score   **Statement**

1. I look forward to meeting new people in social situations.

2. I say "no" to others without feeling guilty.

3. I express strong feelings such as hurt, frustration, or irritation.

4. I ask for help and information from others when I need it.

5. I welcome the opportunity to learn new things and try new activities.

6. I admit to my own mistakes without feeling guilty.

7. I share my beliefs without judging those who disagree with me.

8. I listen to the honest opinions of others without feeling threatened.

9. I tell others when their behavior is unacceptable to me.

10. I speak up confidently in group settings.

11. I express anger or disappointment without blaming others.

12. I think my needs are as important as those of others.

13. I state my beliefs even when the majority disagrees with me.

14. I am able to delegate tasks to others.

15. I value my own experience and wisdom.

Total Score

Scoring Key

(75 to 65) If you scored in this range, you are consistently assertive. You are able to voice your own opinions, thoughts, and feelings to others while respecting the right of others to do the same.

(64 to 54) If you scored in this range, you generally are assertive but would do well to identify those areas in which you are less confident or direct in telling others what you think, feel, want, or need.

(53–43) If you scored in this range, you are reasonably assertive in some areas but considerably less so in other areas. For example, although you might feel fairly comfortable expressing your honest opinions to a close friend or family member, you refrain from voicing your views in a group setting, particularly if you know others disagree with you. You could improve your score by learning and practicing assertive communication skills.

(42–32) If you scored in this range or lower, you may be more inclined to avoid situations that offer you opportunities to be assertive. However, do not feel discouraged. Remember that becoming assertive is a skill that can be developed with practice and patience. You will discover that making such an effort will not only increase your self-confidence but will enhance your interpersonal relationships as well.

FIGURE 6.2 ■ How Assertive Are You?

Source: Adapted from Am I Assertive? http://www.cmcsb.com/Am%20I%20Assertive.html.

	Nonassertive	Assertive	Aggressive
Voice	Sometimes "wobbly" Tone may be "singsong" or whining Over-soft or over-warm Often dull and in monotone Quiet, often drops away at end	Steady and firm Tone is middle range, rich, and warm Sincere and clear Not over-loud or over-quiet	Very firm Tone is sarcastic and sometimes "cold" Hard and sharp Strident, maybe shouting, rises at end
Speech Pattern	Hesitant and filled with pauses Sometimes jerks from fast to slow Frequent throat clearing	Fluent, few awkward hesitancies Emphasizes key words Steady, even pace	Fluent, few awkward hesitancies Often abrupt, "clipped" Emphasizes blaming words Often fast
Facial Expression	"Ghost" smiles when expressing anger, or being criticized Eyebrows raised in anticipation (for example, of rebuke) Quick-changing features	Smiles when pleased Frowns when angry, otherwise "open" Features steady, not "wobbling" Jaw relaxed	Smile may become "wry" Scowls when angry Eyebrows raised in amazement/disbelief Jaw set firm Chin thrust forward
Eye Contact	Evasive Looking down	Firm, but not a "stare-down"	Tries to "stare-down" and dominate
Body Movements	Hand-wringing Hunching shoulders Stepping back Covering mouth with hand Nervous movements that detract (for example, shrugs and shuffles) Arms crossed low for protection	Open hand movements (inviting to speak) "Measured pace" hand movements Sits upright or relaxed (not slouching or cowering) Stands with head held up	Finger pointing Fist thumping Sits upright or leans forward Stands upright, head in the air Strides around (impatiently) Arms crossed high (unapproachable)

FIGURE 6.3 ■ NonAssertive, Assertive, Aggressive
Source: http://tutorials.beginners.co.uk/images/articles/429/image3.gif.

Four-Part Assertion Messages

One of the most useful skills that can enhance your interpersonal communication is the four-part assertion message. This skill can be used when you need to confront others with behavior that is interfering with your work, consuming your time, harming your possessions, costing you money, or causing you extra work.

Rather than approaching a co-worker angrily, for example, you can use this skill to present the facts of a problem situation in a clear, objective way that minimizes defensiveness and encourages a positive resolution. Your assertive skills are based on the assumption that conflict is best managed through a problem-sharing approach that makes use of your direct, honest, and appropriate messages. The qualities for building your workplace relations, which include clarity, respect, assertion, and flexibility, will be valuable in your personal and professional lives. Your skills can be developed through the acquisition of specific tools and the cultivation of positive, supportive attitudes. The challenge to you, the communicator, is to incorporate these tools and attitudes into your natural communication system so that you are honest, open, and genuine in your communication.

Four-part assertion messages include the following parts:

Behavior Description	■ A factual description of the behavior causing the problem.
Feeling Message	■ A statement of your feelings in response to the behavior.
Consequence Statement	■ An identification of the tangible consequences you are experiencing as a result of the behavior.
Request Statement	■ A statement of request as a possible solution to the problem.

Imagine for a moment that you have been giving a co-worker with transportation problems a ride to work for the last two weeks. On at least three occasions, this co-worker has been late getting out to your car, resulting in you being five to ten minutes late punching in. You're concerned about how this lateness will impact your job. You decide to approach this co-worker with the following four-part assertion message:

"Chris, you've been late three times in the last two weeks when I've come to pick you up (**Behavior Description**). I'm feeling anxious about this situation (**Feeling Message**) because your lateness has caused me to punch in five to ten minutes late (**Consequence Statement**). I need to have you be on time, or you will have to make other transportation arrangements to get to work (**Request Statement**)."

Notice that your message does not accuse, judge, or threaten the co-worker. Your message simply describes the problem, identifies the problem's effect on you personally, and states what you need to have happen if you are to continue picking the co-worker up. Now the decision of how to respond is up to the co-worker.

Although these four-part assertion messages can be highly effective in problem situations, they can also be used when you want to acknowledge positive behavior. Consider, for instance, a turn of the tables—Chris wants to state appreciation for the rides you have been providing. Chris's message might sound something like this:

> "Since you've been giving me a lift to work for the last two weeks (**Behavior Description**), I have felt really grateful (**Feeling Message**) because I didn't have to spend an extra hour a day bussing it (**Consequence Statement**). I hope I can count on you for one more week until I get a car of my own (**Request Statement**)."

In the sections that follow, you will find more detailed explanations of these four-part elements, along with opportunities to develop experience in using this skill.

BEHAVIOR DESCRIPTIONS

Many four-part assertion messages begin with behavior descriptions, statements designed to share your observations of another's action in specific and observable terms. How you interpret other people's behavior influences your thoughts and feelings. If someone's behavior violates your personal rights, prevents you from meeting your needs, or causes you unnecessary inconvenience, you may think you are being treated unfairly and respond with feelings of frustration, irritation, or annoyance.

Expressing your feelings is certainly healthy, both physically and psychologically, but such expressions can be even more useful if you let a receiver know what behavior you are reacting to. You cannot force a person to change behavior that is having a negative impact on you, but you can increase the chances of a person changing the behavior voluntarily when you describe that behavior in specific, factual, nonjudgmental terms.

Notice the difference between saying to someone, "You've really been inconsiderate lately," as compared to, "You've borrowed my reference manuals twice this week without asking me if I needed to use them."

In the first instance, your receiver may not only become defensive at being called inconsiderate but also may have no idea what behavior led you to make that judgment. In the second instance, the receiver now knows precisely what behavior you are reacting to, minus the personal judgment you made about the behavior.

The receiver is more likely to ask permission to borrow your manuals next time (which is really what you wanted all along) because you've clearly identified the behavior, and you've avoided any evaluation of character, motives, or intentions, thereby reducing defensiveness. You can never know for certain what motivates people to behave as they do, so it's wise to simply describe the behavior you observe with your senses and then identify how you are feeling in response to that behavior.

Behavior descriptions should meet the following criteria:

- Behavior descriptions should report only behaviors you can observe with your senses.
- Behavior descriptions should exclude any evaluation of the behavior or statement of what you believe may be the feelings, motives, or intentions that prompted the behavior.
- Behavior descriptions should be specific and tentative rather than general and absolute (avoid words like "always" and "never").

As a final note, you may find it helpful to describe others' behaviors that affect you positively and not just negatively. For example, let's say your friend makes the following statement to you: "When you canceled your plans to go up north last weekend so you could help me move, I was really grateful because I couldn't have done it alone." This comment shares a very specific behavior, along with personal feelings and results of the behavior. You would probably feel more appreciated for your actions if your friend makes this kind of statement rather than simply saying, "Thanks for helping me move."

Describing others' behaviors that affect you positively not only reinforces such behaviors but also promotes relationships in which feelings of warmth, caring, and appreciation are fostered.

Problems with Behavior Descriptions In *People Skills*, Robert Bolton explains the following most common problems that individuals encounter when sending behavior description messages to others:

- Using general, "fuzzy-termed" statements.
- Presenting inferences about the other's motives, feelings, or attitudes, etc.
- Including character assassination, profanity, or other loaded words that introduce judgments into the description.
- Using absolute terms, such as *never, always, or constantly*.
- Extending the description to include more than one specific act, thus making it too lengthy or "windy" (pp. 145–147).

FEELING MESSAGES

In your life, you have experienced a wide range of emotions. Psychologists theorize that those individuals who skillfully express emotions to others tend to experience a higher degree of physical and psychological health, which is often the result of more satisfying interpersonal relationships, than those individuals who do not. You could lessen misunderstandings, reduce stress, and avoid unnecessary conflict if you learned to voice your feelings constructively at home and in the workplace. The skill of expressing feelings doesn't imply sharing your deepest inner emotions with everyone and anyone. The inappropriate expression of your feelings can be just as destructive as the failure to express any feelings at all. However, more people seem to fall into the category of under-expressing rather than over-expressing their feelings; therefore, your goal is to achieve a balance between these two extremes.

Four general guidelines can help you to determine when expressing your feelings is appropriate. Your feelings should be expressed:

- In ongoing relationships such as parent–child, husband–wife, friend–friend, etc.;
- When there is a greater likelihood of helping the relationship rather than harming it;
- In the face of conflict that threatens the relationship;
- When the expression of those feelings moves gradually to a deeper level of sharing.

Knowing when to express your feelings is not enough. Equally important is knowing how to express them. Your constructive feeling messages will contain these elements:

- An "I" message that makes it clear to a receiver that you are claiming ownership of and accepting responsibility for the feelings you are expressing;
- Identification of the precise feeling you are experiencing such as hurt, annoyance, happiness, uncertainty, confidence, etc.

The following examples in boldface lettering show how these elements can be combined into effective expressions of feelings:

- "When you use my car and then don't refill the gas tank, **I feel irritated.**"
- "**I'm so pleased** with the seven extra hours you've put in on the reports."
- "When you tried to talk to me during the meeting, **I got really upset** because I missed the change in work hours the supervisor was explaining."

In the beginning, you may feel awkward and mechanical using this skill, but with practice, feeling messages will become a part of your overall style of communication and become a natural way of responding to the people with whom you interact.

Problems with Feeling Messages   Several problems can occur with feeling messages. The following list describes some of the problems you may encounter with expressing your feelings.

- Misplaced ownership occurs when you substitute "that," "it," "you," or "they" for "I." You assign the responsibility for the feeling to some external event or person. Consider these examples: "You upset me when you say things like that"; "It makes me unhappy when you ignore me." Without the personal "I" message, your unskillful attempts can sound like accusations or blaming statements.

- "Feel" is often used when you mean "think." When "think" can replace "feel" with no change in meaning, then you are sharing ideas rather than feelings, as in, "I feel the Packers will win on Sunday." You would not likely say, "I think depressed about the test results."

- Rather than share how you do feel, sometimes you may tell how you don't feel. For instance, you may say, "I don't feel confident about that new procedure." This problem can be eliminated with statements that share how you do feel: "I feel confused about that new procedure."

- Future feeling statements forecast feelings you will have in a few minutes or when some condition is met. Saying how you would or will feel after something happens doesn't share how you are feeling right now. Contrast these two statements: "I would be happy if you could finish that report by the beginning of the week," versus "I am worried about making the deadline for that report."

- When you say "I feel like" or "I feel that," chances are you will not name a feeling. Most likely you will report an action you feel urged to take, present some figure of speech, or offer some advice. Consider the way these statements fail to express an emotion: "I feel like giving up" or "I feel that you should change the set-up on that project."

- Trite expressions, such as, "I'm sorry" or "I'm afraid," lose their meanings as feeling messages when you overuse them.

- When you combine skillful feeling messages with unskillful messages, the resulting mixed message will be confusing at best. Rather than challenge the listener to sort out these conflicting messages, you should strive for clear, skillful feeling messages. Consider the unclear result of a message like this: "I am worried about your attendance. Why don't you think about how your missing work affects others?" The first part of the message expresses concern while the last part presents an attacking question.

As you begin to write and share your feeling messages, try to become comfortable saying, "I feel . . .", "I get . . .", or "I am . . ." Then try to zero in on the single word that names the feeling you are experiencing. Try to avoid the problems mentioned earlier with skillful feeling messages.

CONSEQUENCE STATEMENTS

All of your actions have consequences; these consequences affect your life in many ways, both positively and negatively. This simple fact comes home to you in countless ways. Your job performance, when reviewed, can be the source of reward or punishment. Your conduct on the job can either favorably impress or turn off co-workers. Your behavior in public places can win the respect of family and friends, or it can get you arrested. What you do can have a very definite impact on others and your relationship with them.

The consequences of your actions can be tangible and concrete, or they may be intangible. Thomas Gordon, Robert Bolton, and other communication experts have written about the importance of tangible and concrete effect statements when sharing concerns with others. They note the strengths of telling others how their behavior has real, lasting effects on your **time, money, work, possessions,** and **effectiveness on the job.** To this list you can add **health** and **safety** because people do act in ways that endanger or enhance your health and safety. You need to comment about the times when others act in these manners. Tangible, concrete effects can be measured in terms of gains, savings, or losses. As such, tangible consequences represent the most convincing form of persuasion by showing how someone's behavior affects you directly.

Consequences describe specific, tangible effects on your:

- Time
- Money
- Work
- Possessions
- Effectiveness
- Health and safety

Different from the tangible, but in many ways no less important, are the intangible effects that occur when others take action that has a definite effect on your life as well. The feelings you enjoy or suffer through, the sense of accomplishment or being cared for, and the notion of power or belonging can directly or indirectly spring from your reaction to the behavior of others. Hearing that someone loves you, that your teenager is getting body piercing, or that a good friend is moving away may produce effects that cannot be measured by a clock, in your pocketbook, or in

All Behavior Has
Consequences

your productivity, yet the intangible consequences affect you in very significant ways.

Tangible and intangible effects may be positive or negative. They can save, enhance, add to, or enrich; on the other hand, they similarly can cost, diminish, waste, or destroy. Effective communication requires the sharing of consequences, both positive and negative, tangible and intangible. Consequence statements provide information that clarifies your feelings and makes your messages more appropriate to the receiver.

Your tangible consequence statements will answer the question "why?" They provide a "because" for observations and feelings. Here are some examples of your statements:

- "... because I have to pay money that I don't have."
- "... because I have to spend extra time repairing the equipment."
- "... because I couldn't hear the customer."

These, of course, are your tangible, negative effects; they could also be positive:

- "... because I saved money and time when you repaired my computer."
- "... because I saved extra work and trips when you helped me move across town last week."

In short, consequence statements inform others of the effects their behavior is having on you. These statements need to be direct, honest, nonthreatening expressions of your reactions to their behaviors.

REQUEST STATEMENTS

Being able to communicate through the use of behavior descriptions, feeling messages, and consequence statements is necessary if others are to understand you better and react to you more positively. By combining behavior descriptions, feeling messages, and consequence statements, you will often get people to modify their actions in a way that reduces the concern at hand. For example, you tell your roommate, "I feel irritated when you leave your clothes lying around the living room in our apartment because I have to spend my time and energy to put your clothes where they belong." This may be the first time that your roommate has come to know that such behavior is affecting you negatively. Your roommate may respond with, "Oh, I'm sorry; I didn't know that bothered you. You never said anything before, so I thought it was okay. Now that I know it irritates you, I'll make sure I put my clothes in my own room."

Getting people to modify their behavior is your goal, and if others change without having to be directly asked, great, fantastic! However, sometimes people don't realize that their behavior is having a negative effect on you, even when you tell them, or they do not know how to relieve the irritation that you're experiencing. In such situations, request statements are the next logical messages you will want to send. Requests are polite statements that directly and specifically ask someone to modify his or her behavior in a way that gets your needs met and that maintains the quality of the relationship. Your requests may seek the permission of others for your actions, "I would like to have off on Saturday the 18th." Requests may ask for help from others, "Can you help me understand this diagram in the service manual?" Some requests may ask for cooperation from others, "Let's work toward a solution of the work schedule, one that meets all of our needs."

The essential parts of a request statement are as follows:

- Requests should be direct. You must state directly what you need, want, or would like to see happen.
- Requests must be specific. You need to tell others exactly what you are asking them to do.
- Requests must allow for a freedom of response. You need to be open-minded enough to realize that people may say "no" to your request because they are unable or unwilling to do what you ask.

You also need to listen to alternative suggestions from others that may meet both your needs as effectively as your original request.

With these three qualities, your requests will be courteous and polite rather than sounding like demands. Remembering to include a **please** can make your request more welcomed. Your request statements are most helpful for interpersonal relationships when they directly ask the other, specifically express your needs, openly accept alternative suggestions, and actively encourage a freedom of response.

Sending Four-Part Assertion Messages

Now that you are familiar with the four parts of assertion messages, let's examine how you can combine them to present your concerns to others in a conflict situation. Four-part assertion messages will help you share valuable information about what happened, how you feel about the situation, how you are affected by the other person's behavior, and what changes you would like to have happen. By sharing this information and listening to the other person's responses to these combined assertion messages, you can discuss the conflict in a productive way. Preparing these messages takes practice. Following is an example of a four-part assertion message.

Four-Part Assertion Message Sample   The person who relieves you at work has demanding family responsibilities and is constantly coming in late. This person is your friend, so you don't want to tell the boss. Three times, however, you've missed some important engagements because you left work too late. You've mentioned something before in passing, but this person keeps showing up late, including right now.

Your four-part assertive message will include the following:

Behavior Description	You came to work 25 minutes late today, and this is the third time in the past two weeks.
Feeling Message	I feel perturbed that I have to stay late but also trapped because I think I can't do anything about it.
Consequence Statement	I have to miss some important engagements and spend my free time at work when I'd rather be somewhere else.
Request Statement	I would like to know how much longer this is going to continue and if there is some way I can be notified earlier when you can't be to work on time.

Combined into one statement, your four-part assertion message would sound like this:

"When you came to work 25 minutes late today, and this is the third time in the past two weeks, I felt perturbed and also trapped because I have had to miss some important engagements. I would like to know if there is some way I can be notified earlier when you can't be to work on time."

Keep in mind that your interpersonal relationships play a vital role in all of your interactions at work, home, and school. Although the sharing you do with others can range from small talk to personal feelings, all forms of sharing are most effective when they occur in a supportive environment. This environment is created when you communicate directly, honestly, and assertively. Although the development of these skills may take time and practice, the results will yield healthier, more satisfying relationships with others.

"We're agreed then - no more purring or tail wagging until our demands are met."

Review Questions

1. Give three of the reasons presented in your text for why relationships are important.

2. List six elements of the supportive climate. Give a workplace example for a time when you have witnessed each.

3. Describe the differences among assertive, aggressive, and nonassertive communication.

4. Identify the characteristics of each element of the four-part assertion message.

Key Terms and Concepts

Aggressiveness 135

Assertiveness 135

Behavior Description 140

Certainty 134

Consequence Statement 144

Control 133

Defensive 132

Description 133

Empathy 133

Equality 134

Evaluation 133

Feeling Message 141

Neutrality 134

Nonassertiveness 135

Problem Orientation 133

Provisionalism 134

Request Statement 145

Spontaneity 133

Strategy 133

Superiority 134

Supportive 133

Type A Behavior 136

Type B Behavior 136

Web Activities

- Consider taking any of the following self-assessments of your relationships at http://www.psychtests.com/tests/relationships/index.html.

- For a complete list of tests from Psychtests, visit http://www.psychtests.com/tests/alltests.html.

- Examine the many aspects of your relationships by consulting the Relationship Institute at http://www.relationship-institute.com/.

Assignments

ASSIGNMENT 6.1: BEHAVIOR DESCRIPTIONS

Behavior Description Recognition Practice

Behavior descriptions should meet the following criteria:

- Behavior descriptions should report only behaviors you can observe with your senses.

- Behavior descriptions should exclude any evaluation of the behavior or statement of what you believe may be the feelings, motives, or intentions that prompted the behavior.

- Behavior descriptions should be specific and tentative rather than general and absolute. Avoid words like "always" and "never."

Directions: Some of the following statements describe only observable behavior whereas others go beyond and deal with motives, feelings, attitudes, etc. Put an "X" next to those statements that describe specific behaviors only.

_____ 1. You never pay your fair share.

_____ 2. You waste my time with stupid questions.

_____ 3. You gave me a dirty look for telling an ethnic joke at the party.

_____ 4. You asked for directions to the customer service center.

_____ 5. You told me that you got a new job offer and may leave here.

_____ 6. I just saw you punch in on Stewart's time card.

_____ 7. You were really annoyed when I wouldn't change vacations with you.

_____ 8. You called the service department and said Job #2217 was ready.

_____ 9. This morning you interrupted me while I was on the phone with a customer.

_____ 10. You look at the newspaper when I am talking to you.

_____ 11. You were rude to that customer.

_____ 12. You took the parts from your machine and put them in the boxes without checking them for the correct size.

_____ 13. You twisted the way the accident occurred to fit your version.

_____ 14. You changed my work schedule on Friday for next week's work.

_____ 15. You ignore safety policy so you can get the job done faster.

Writing Behavior Descriptions Practice

Use specific, clear language to write six behavior descriptions of your own. These should present behaviors that please you in three situations and behaviors that upset you in the other three situations.

Behaviors that please you:

1.

2.

3.

Behaviors that upset you:

1.

2.

3.

ASSIGNMENT 6.2: FEELING MESSAGES

Feeling Messages Recognition Practice

Feeling messages contain these elements:

- Feeling messages include an "I" message, that makes it clear to a receiver that you are claiming ownership of and accepting responsibility for the feelings you are expressing.

- Feeling messages identify the precise feeling you are experiencing (hurt, annoyance, happiness, uncertainty, confidence).

Directions: Following are 15 statements, some of which describe feelings directly and specifically. Put an "X" next to those statements that clearly describe what the speaker is feeling.

_____ 1. I feel it's time for us to take a break.

_____ 2. I'm really grateful you loaned me your car while mine was being repaired.

_____ 3. I get annoyed when you turn up the television while I'm studying.

_____ 4. My feelings are hurt when you tell me I'm inconsiderate of others.

_____ 5. You are such an easygoing person.

_____ 6. This darn fighting all the time is a pain.

_____ 7. Apart from all the work I have to do, I feel a sense of accomplishment with this job.

_____ 8. I'm surprised that you asked for a raise.

_____ 9. I don't feel good about being here; Sam's always complaining about something.

_____ 10. I feel that going on second shift if you don't have to is really stupid.

_____ 11. I feel you could practice more.

_____ 12. When you're late from work, I feel concerned.

_____ 13. I am clumsy—always have been, always will be.

_____ 14. I feel like I'm on top of the world.

Writing Feeling Messages Practice

Directions: Refer to the worksheet titled "Writing Behavior Descriptions Practice" you completed in Assignment 6.1. For each of the behavior description statements you wrote, add an appropriate feeling message. Use the form, "When you _____, I feel _____."

1. When you _____
   _____, I feel _____.

2. When you _____
   _____, I feel _____.

3. When you _____
   _____, I feel _____.

4. When you _____
   _____, I feel _____.

5. When you _____
   _____, I feel _____.

6. When you _____
   _____, I feel _____.

ASSIGNMENT 6.3: CONSEQUENCE STATEMENTS

Consequence Statement Recognition Practice

Consequence statements report the effects of others' actions on you in tangible, concrete terms.

- Telling others how their behavior has had real, lasting effects on your *time, money, work, possessions, and effectiveness or health and safety* shares your consequences with them.

- These tangible, concrete effects can be measured in terms of gains, savings, or losses. As such, they represent the most potent form of consequence by showing how someone's behavior affects you directly.

Directions: Label the following statements "T" for tangible or "I" for intangible.

_____ 1. . . . because I have to spend money on repairs.

_____ 2. . . . because my feelings are hurt.

_____ 3. . . . because my calculator doesn't work anymore, and I need it.

_____ 4. . . . because I was unable to complete the work on time.

_____ 5. . . . because I could be injured if we have an accident.

_____ 6. . . . because I have to spend three hours redoing the work.

_____ 7. . . . because I can't go as fast as you do.

_____ 8. . . . because I'm late for work and get docked for pay.

_____ 9. . . . because I'm embarrassed to say I don't know.

_____ 10. . . . because I get annoyed and aggravated.

_____ 11. . . . because that makes me look bad.

_____ 12. . . . because then people won't believe me.

_____ 13. . . . because I think you don't like me.

_____ 14. . . . because my standing in the community is lessened.

_____ 15. . . . because I lose my place and have to start over.

Writing Consequence Statements Practice

Directions: Provide tangible consequence statements for the following messages:

1. When you don't lock out the power on the machine, I feel concerned because I _____
_____.

2. When you said that you would be moving on to a new job at the end of the week, I was worried because I _____
_____.

3. When you start talking to me as you are walking into another room, I get upset because I _____
_____.

4. When you talk to me when I'm on the phone with a customer, I feel frustrated because I _____
_____
_____.

5. When you cleaned the apartment, I was elated because I _____
_____.

6. When you borrow my car and return it empty of gas, I'm aggravated because I _____
_____.

7. When you offered to change work assignments with me, I was grateful because I _____
_____.

8. When you poured the antifreeze in the oil fill spout, I was annoyed because I _____
_____.

9. When you smoke cigarettes in our enclosed work area, I feel uncomfortable because I _____
_____.

10. When you said I didn't need a new computer, I was relieved because I _____
_____.

ASSIGNMENT 6.4: REQUEST STATEMENTS

Request Statement Recognition Practice

Request statements require the following three essential parts:

- Request statements should be direct. You must state directly what you need, want or would like to see happen.

- Request statements must be specific. You need to tell others exactly what you are asking them to do.

- Request statements must allow for a freedom of response. You need to be open-minded enough to realize that people may say "no" to your request because they are unable or unwilling to do what you ask. You also need to listen to alternative suggestions from others that may meet both your needs as effectively as your original request.

Directions: Place an "R" next to those following statements that make direct and specific requests. Those statements that are not specific and direct requests should be left blank.

_____ 1. Please hand me that file folder on the desk.

_____ 2. Thanks to your late arrival, we couldn't start the safety training on time.

_____ 3. Would you kindly return the insurance enrollment forms by Friday this week?

_____ 4. The outgoing message on the answering machine needs to be updated.

_____ 5. Would you go to Quality Plating to pick up the reconditioned parts that I have on order?

_____ 6. Since I've been putting in overtime at work, could you please help getting supper on the table?

_____ 7. Employee to boss: "You know, it's been almost a year and a half since I had my last raise."

_____ 8. If you could, I'd like you to pick me up for work tomorrow because my car won't be repaired until Wednesday.

_____ 9. I want to talk to you about the low rating you gave me on my work evaluation last month.

_____ 10. Wouldn't it be a good idea to move on to the next item on the agenda? This meeting is running too long already.

_____ 11. I'd like you to let me know before you use that new numerical control machine so that I can see how it works.

_____ 12. What do you know about the settings on this new copier?

_____ 13. Can you help me file this batch of office equipment requests that came in this morning?

_____ 14. Would it be possible for you to change vacation days with me next week?

_____ 15. Why can't I have the same assignments as everybody else? I can do everything they can.

Writing Request Statements Practice

Directions: Provide a behavior description and an appropriate request statement for the stem sentences that follow:

1. When you _____, I ask that _____.

2. When you _____, would you?

3. When you _____, I want you to_____.

4. When you _____, could you please_____?

5. When you _____, I would like for you to _____.

6. When you _____, please_____.

ASSIGNMENT 6.5: FOUR-PART ASSERTION MESSAGE SELF-ASSESSMENT

Directions: Mark the correct letter to identify each of the statements 1–16 below.

Mark "A" for behavior descriptions; or

Mark "B" for skillful feeling messages; or

Mark "C" for tangible consequence statements; or

Mark "D" for request statements.

_____ 1. "Because now I have to replace three panels."

_____ 2. "I want you to help position this piece and then tack it in place."

_____ 3. "When you said there would be time to finish this, . . ."

_____ 4. "Could you please change machines with me?"

_____ 5. "I am so relieved about that."

_____ 6. "Please decide whether you will accept the job or not."

_____ 7. "I'm surprised about the idea you presented."

_____ 8. "I will have to hire someone to fix my car."

_____ 9. "When you leave my test equipment out in the snow, . . ."

_____ 10. "I am going to have to spend over three hours analyzing the problem."

_____ 11. "I have to recalculate the charges."

_____ 12. "When you leave scratches and pit marks in the new lens, . . ."

_____ 13. "Please help me align the new part before break."

_____ 14. "When you said, 'No!' you would not switch vacations with me, . . ."

_____ 15. "I get so fearful with this equipment."

_____ 16. "I feel angry when that happens."

_____ 17.–20. Write a four-part assertive statement that includes the assertive statements you have studied. Label each of the components of your response.

ASSIGNMENT 6.6: FOUR-PART ASSERTION MESSAGES PRACTICE

Directions: Following are three practice situations for sending four-part assertion messages. For each situation, you are asked to be open-minded and think of both sides of the conflict. Then you are asked to write the elements needed to make four-part assertive messages in these situations.

Situation #1

Ardon Caterers tells you that they will cater your graduation party for $1,500, including set-up and clean-up. After the party, you receive a $100 clean-up charge from the hall that you rented, claiming Ardon did not adequately clean the facility. You contact Ardon to resolve this issue.

FIGURE 6.4 ■ Ardon's Bill

Write your four-part assertion message below.

Behavior Description:

Feeling Message:

Consequence Statement:

Request Statement:

Situation #2

You're concerned about a co-worker at the company where you're both employed. You've become very good friends, but you notice that your friend has come to work seemingly depressed several times in the last few weeks since being denied a recent promotion. When you asked about this behavior, your friend yelled at you and told you to mind your own business. You believe this person needs your friendship more than ever.

FIGURE 6.5 ■ Co-worker Concern

Write your four-part assertion message below.

Behavior Description:

Feeling Message:

Consequence Statement:

Request Statement:

Situation #3

Your employer had told you that your vacation request was approved. Two days before the vacation is to begin, you have heard through the grapevine that your vacation request is to be denied. You've already made extensive plans to travel and will lose money if you have to cancel. Your supervisor is now telling you about the denial of your time off.

FIGURE 6.6 ■ No Vacation

Write your four-part assertion message below.

Behavior Description:

Feeling Message:

Consequence Statement:

Request Statement:

ASSIGNMENT 6.7: WHEN TO USE FOUR-PART ASSERTION MESSAGES

Directions: Brainstorm answers for the following questions for each assertive option.

	When Should I Use . . .?	What Is the Unspoken Message When I Use . . .?	What Reactions Would Signal That This Is Effective?	What Reactions Would Signal That This Is Ineffective?
Behavior Description				
Feeling Message				
Consequence Statement				
Request Statement				

FIGURE 6.7 ■ Brainstorm Answers

ASSIGNMENT 6.8: CASE STUDY: PERSONAL APPLICATION

Directions: Describe a conflict that you have experienced at home, work, or school.

Your Conflict:

_____

_____

_____

_____

_____

_____

Write your four-part assertion message below.

Behavior Description:

Feeling Message:

Consequence Statement:

Request Statement:

References

American Institute for Preventive Medicine. (2001). Introduction to type A & B behavior patterns. Systematic stress management. Retrieved May 17, 2007, from http://aipm.wellnesscheckpoint.com/library/banner_main.asp?P=29892EASME2, p. 1.

Am I assertive? (n.d.). Retrieved May 17, 2007, from http://www.cmcsb.com/Am%20I%20Assertive.html

Bolton, R. (1979). *People skills: How to assert yourself, listen to others and resolve conflicts.* Englewood Cliffs, NJ: Prentice Hall.

Frohlich, D., Whittaker, S., & Daly-Jones, O. (1994). *Informal workplace communication: What is it like and how might we support it?* Retrieved November 8, 2005, from http://www.hpl.hp.com/techreports/94/HPL-94-23.pdf

Gibb, J. (1991). Taken from the jacket material of *Trust*, 1991 edition. Retrieved February 15, 2008, from http://www.geocities.com/toritrust/jack_r_gibb.htm

Harburg, E. (2008). *A good fight may keep you and your marriage healthy.* Retrieved March 14, 2008, from http://www.ns.umich.edu/htdocs/releases/story.php?id=6286

Hefty, S. (n. d.). *A friend in need.* Retrieved February 15, 2008, from http://www.myrafritzius.com/per-fin.htm

Michalko, M. (2008, January 14). *Finding the unexpected.* Retrieved February 22, 2008, from http://www.amazon.com/gp/blog/post/PLNKBGYJ84KGJFKA

Nonassertive, Assertive, Aggressive. (n.d.). Retrieved May 17, 2007, from http://tutorials.beginners.co.uk/images/articles/429/images3.gif

Price, L. (2007, March 17). Relationships: Reach out to know others, yourself. *Milwaukee Journal Sentinel.* Section E, p. 1.

Shepell, W. (2005). Workplace communication: *HealthQuest.* Retrieved November 8, 2005, from http://www.warrenshepell.com/articles/hq_04spring.asp

Chapter **7**

Conflict Resolution

Learning **Objectives**

At the end of this chapter, you should be able to meet the following objectives:

1. Identify the importance of conflict in interpersonal relationships.
2. Define the five types of interpersonal conflicts.
3. Recognize the five styles of conflict management.
4. Identify conflict strategy guidelines.
5. Respond appropriately to criticism.

"In the middle of difficulty lies opportunity."

Albert Einstein

Conflict Is Important

"Brigit M. just graduated from a public college in southern New Jersey with a 4.0 GPA. Putting herself through college with a full course load, she worked 25 to 30 hours a week off campus as a waitress plus 8 to 12 hours a week on campus as a writing and economics tutor. She had a scholarship, but, as she says, 'You think a full scholarship is great, but it doesn't cover books, transportation, and health care costs.' She was lucky to have a flexible employer who was willing to accommodate her course schedule. But the time juggle was still difficult: 'It was hard to come home from work at 11:00 P.M. and still have to write a paper that was due for an 8:30 A.M. class.'

"Brigit is one of almost six million working students in the United States. Many of these students do much more than put in a few hours in the school cafeteria or library. They cannot afford a college education without working long hours at one or more off-campus jobs, taking on heavy students loans, and using credit cards to fill in the gaps" (Mutari & Lakew, 2003, p. 1).

You may be able to relate to the challenges that Brigit faced. Working to support yourself and perhaps a family, carrying a demanding class load, and trying to find time for a personal life can provide fertile ground for both internal and external conflict.

Although the term *conflict* can be defined in a variety of ways, you may find the following definition helpful before you read further in this chapter:

> Conflict is the internal or external tension that occurs when you experience difficulty in meeting important needs.

Let's take a closer look at what this definition is saying by examining another situation you may find familiar.

Aaron was a student enrolled in an associate degree nursing program at a local community college. He found himself struggling in his anatomy and physiology class to the point that by midsemester, he was risking failing the course. As a result, he made the decision to withdraw from the course and take it again the following semester. However, Aaron faced a conflict. His parents had been helping to finance his education, and he assumed they would be furious to find out he dropped the course and lost out on the tuition money that was not refundable. Consequently, he held off telling his parents the news. This situation weighed heavily on his

mind, creating **internal tension,** or stress. He suspected too that once he did inform his parents about the class, **external tension** would occur in the form of a family argument. In addition, he feared that his parents might be reluctant to help him out financially with future schooling, an **important need** that he had.

Situations like Aaron's and Brigit's are not at all unusual. They are, in fact, representative of challenges that many of you face. Although both of these instances involve school and financial issues, you are likely to confront other sources of conflict as well. Working with a difficult boss, experiencing relationship problems with a spouse, or dealing with a problematic child are just a few other examples of conflicts you may encounter.

However, in the middle of difficulties, opportunities exist as well. You may be surprised to discover that difficulties, like conflict, actually provide opportunities to experience a variety of benefits too. "Without conflict, attitudes, behavior, and relationships stay the same, regardless of whether they are fair. Conflict reveals problems and encourages those problems to be dealt with. Whether they are dealt with constructively or destructively depends on how the conflict is handled" (Brahm, 2004, p. 1). In other words, when you manage conflict effectively, you increase the likelihood of positive change in all areas of your life.

An article titled "Conflict Resolution" by Frances Picherack (2003) provided the following comparison of managed conflict versus out-of-control conflict.

MANAGED CONFLICT	OUT-OF-CONTROL CONFLICT
Strengthens relationships and facilitates team building.	Damages relationships and discourages cooperation.
Encourages open communication and cooperative problem solving.	Results in defensiveness and hidden agendas.
Increases productivity.	Wastes time, money, and resources.
Deals with real issues and concentrates on win-win resolutions.	Focuses on fault-finding and blaming.
Calms and focuses toward results.	Is often loud, hostile, and chaotic.
Supports respectful workplace and client relationships and a client satisfaction/service orientation.	Results in considerable workplace/client dissatisfaction and missed opportunities for service recovery.
Facilitates an environment of openness and permission for service recovery and improvement.	Creates/sustains an environment of denial and missed opportunities for continuous improvement.

Source: Picherack, 2003, p. 8.

The benefits of conflict that is managed effectively can also be seen on an international scale. Some time ago, National Public Radio aired a report by Anne Garrels titled *U.S. Soldiers Try to Bridge a Sectarian Gap in Iraq*. The report told about U.S. Army Captain Eric Peterson, stationed in the district of north Gazalia, a fault line between Shiite and Sunni extremists. Garrels commented that, "Sunnis and Shiites once lived together in Gazalia. It was a pleasant, leafy area populated by professionals. In the past couple of years, Sunni extremists have terrorized Shiites. Shiite militias, in turn, have threatened and killed Sunnis.

"As a result, this once peaceful neighborhood became a slum, with blocks and even streets defined by sect. Some families moved only a few yards to be with their own. Many houses were abandoned as residents fled the area altogether" (Garrels, 2007, p. 1).

In view of this situation, 29-year-old Captain Peterson decided to try an experiment that involved calling a meeting between local Sunni and Shiite leaders. At the start of the talks, each side described the abuse inflicted by the other side. Peterson interrupted, and through an interpreter stated that the point of the talks was to move forward in an effort to restore peace to the area. Garrels stated, "Despite the inauspicious beginning and a certain amount of posturing, these men got down to business quickly, surprisingly quickly. They agreed they should choose one small area—maybe just a couple of streets—to show that with Peterson's protection, people can return to their homes and that Shiites and Sunnis can live together again." Mr. Abu Assama, a Sunni resident of Gazalia, stated, "Let us start with a square block and make it a model for the rest of the blocks. We, the three to four good men, cannot clean up a neighborhood. It is impossible. But we can start with a square block." (Garrels, 2007, pp. 1–2).

Garrels concluded her report by stating that "even though these men know the risks, the local leaders keep on with their talks. They agree to weekly meetings. It's a first step" (Garrels, 2007, p. 2).

Now imagine for a moment if all government leaders and military personnel approached sectarian conflicts in the manner of Captain Peterson—with optimism, determination, and one small step at a time. The dream of a peaceful global community might not be as seemingly impossible as most think.

Conflict Types

By now, you are probably more aware that conflict is both important and inevitable in your relationships. Joel Edelman and Mary Beth Crain in *The Tao of Negotiation* (1994) have identified the most common causes of conflicts at work. They found that poor performance of an employee is seldom the cause of conflict, but rather, the five leading causes of conflict are as follows:

1. Misunderstanding–miscommunication
2. Disrespect or disregard for other people

3. Conflicting egos

4. Impatience

5. Fear and insecurity over loss of control (p. 238).

Any of these factors can cause conflict in the workplace. Regardless of the cause, experts tell us that many types of conflicts challenge us every day. Verderber and Verderber in *Inter-Act* (1998) describe several different types of conflicts that we typically encounter: pseudo conflicts, fact conflicts, ego conflicts, and value conflicts (pp. 337–340). In addition to these types, conflicts can also be centered on needs.

Some conflicts are called **pseudo conflicts.** As their name suggests, they are not real conflicts, but are only perceived as conflicts. Pseudo conflicts can result from two causes: faulty assumptions and false dilemmas. Take the situation that occurs when you and your partner agree to clean the office on Friday afternoon. At noon on Friday, you see your partner leave the building. Your first reaction may be that your partner is ducking out on the cleaning job. When you assume that your partner left you to clean by yourself, you may be setting yourself up for a pseudo conflict. Although you may be right in your assumption, your partner may have gone shopping for cleaning supplies. Mistaking assumptions for facts may explain many pseudo conflicts.

Pseudo conflicts that result from false dilemmas occur when the parties involved see only two choices as solutions to a problem. For example, assume your boss has invited you to attend a twenty-hour violence prevention workshop, and you have a full schedule of inventory duties to complete. You may see only two choices: either attend the workshop and fall behind on the inventory or complete the inventory and disappoint the boss. In reality, other choices may be available: attend the workshop and ask for help with the inventory or explore the possibility of rescheduling the workshop until the inventory is complete.

Fact conflicts are at hand when individuals disagree about information that could easily be verified. What the tolerances are for machining a particular part, who has the best ERA record in the national league, and how many miles per gallon hybrid cars get are all questions that can be answered by consulting some reference. Rob and Sara recently experienced a fact conflict when they were assigned a collaborative project in their sociology class. Their instructor required the class members to choose a partner and seek to prove or disprove the following statement: "Individuals who live together before marriage have a higher divorce rate than those who do not live together before marriage." Rob felt that the statement was true because he knew of several couples who had cohabitated before marriage and divorced shortly thereafter. Sara, on the other hand, believed that couples would be more compatible in a long-term relationship if they lived together first. Rob and Sara had several heated discussions about their assigned topic until they realized that they would have to put their personal biases aside and do some objective research to uncover statistical data that either supported or disproved the position. Unfortunately, some people choose not to seek answers; rather, they turn fact conflicts into ego conflicts.

Ego conflicts occur when a dispute centers on status or power. The initial arguments may be over some factual question that could be answered easily. However, the ego conflict results when you argue over who has the "right" facts. The question of who hit the most home runs in the major leagues last year becomes who knows more about baseball, you or me? Rather than solving problems or answering questions, those engaged in ego conflicts spend their energy proving their self-worth, their power, or their status to others. Don and Jared were co-workers involved in an ego conflict. Don had been employed by a small graphic design company for several years and was hoping for a promotion. Jared was a recent graduate from the local community college with a graphic arts degree. Although Jared had far less on-the-job experience, he had lots of creative ideas and enthusiasm. Don felt threatened by Jared's talents and was often critical of Jared's contributions when the two of them worked together. Fortunately, unlike many ego conflicts, this one was managed effectively. After several weeks, Don took the courageous step and shared his feelings of inadequacy with Jared. To Don's surprise, Jared disclosed that he valued the years of knowledge and skills Don brought to the job. As a result of Don's honesty, the two workers were able to capitalize on one another's strengths.

Ask, Don't Tell by Gary Cohen & Corey Sauer

Value conflicts focus on personal beliefs that you hold near and dear. You may value the right to organize workers and engage in collective bargaining. You may believe that employees should have the right to choose their own health care providers. Perhaps you have difficulty with the way your co-worker treats customers. These issues are in the realm of value conflicts. Value conflicts frequently surface in personal relationships. For example, Debbie and Ammar have been dating for several months and really enjoy one another's company. They have discussed the possibility of a long-term commitment, but both are concerned about their different religious faiths. Debbie was raised in a traditional Christian family and is very devoted to her church. Ammar, on the other hand, comes from a Hindu background and is equally devoted to his faith. Both are concerned about the religious differences they bring to their relationship, particularly if they decide to have children. Although neither Debbie nor Ammar can concede to the other's religious values at the present time, they have agreed to honor one another's differences. They also have decided that if their relationship becomes more serious, they will need to resolve their value differences in a way that allows both to maintain personal integrity.

Need conflicts usually occur when the needs of one individual are at odds with the needs of another. When you need a tool to finish a job and so does your co-worker, when you need time to complete a project for work and your spouse needs your help right now, or when you need to schedule a meeting at two o'clock and your team member can't be there until three, you have a conflict of needs.

Sometimes need conflicts are easily resolved by redefining or restating the needs in a way that allows a mutually satisfying solution. For example, although you may need to start the meeting at two o'clock, you could schedule your team member's presentation later on the agenda. You can give your spouse the help he or she wants right now, if your spouse helps you with your project afterwards. Finally, if you can't share a tool in order to finish your job, maybe one of you could borrow someone else's. Often the needs of each person can be met if those needs are specifically stated and clearly understood by both.

These conflict types can overlap and complicate situations by masking the real issues and make status, values, or assumptions more important than problem solving. You may have personally witnessed the mixture of need conflicts, value conflicts, and ego conflicts. You may have felt uncomfortable as you watched others argue and attack one another. You have perhaps questioned the benefit of conflict or wondered what good could come from such behavior. Unfortunately, many conflicts are poorly managed, and people often let conflicts bring out the worst in them and their relationship. Therefore, you will find it helpful to review the various styles of conflict management that are discussed in the next section.

Conflict Management Styles

You will also discover that in addition to different types of conflict, people exhibit various styles when attempting to manage conflict. These styles include avoiders, accommodators, forcers, compromisers, and collaborators (figure 7.1).

Avoiders steer clear of conflict for a variety of reasons. If you are an avoider, you may lack the time, energy, confidence, or skills to engage in conflict. In addition, you may be fearful that the conflict will escalate, or you may be doubtful that the parties involved can get their needs met. Avoiders try to stay away from conflict by leaving the situation, changing the subject, or simply agreeing to disagree without discussing the issues that precipitated the conflict.

Although constant use of avoidance is not recommended, you may choose this style as a means of buying time in order to think through the problem, as a way of temporarily defusing strong emotions, or as a means of limiting your involvement in a conflict that does not seem worth the time or effort required to resolve it. On the other hand, avoidance may keep you from seeking a long-term solution to a conflict.

Accommodators allow others to determine the outcome of the conflict. As an accommodator, you might prefer to maintain relationships by meeting the needs of others. You will "give in" to keep the peace. Accommodators value smooth relationships and don't want to make waves or cause trouble for anyone. Accommodation may be most appropriate when the issue in conflict is not that important to you or when it is easy to make concessions to others. Repeated attempts to accommodate others, however, may result in resentment and failure to get your own needs met.

How do people behave in conflicts?

- Avoiders
- Accommodators
- Forcers
- Compromisers
- Collaborators

FIGURE 7.1 ■ Conflict Styles

Avoiders

- See conflict as hopeless and useless.
- Are impersonal or distant.
- Remove self mentally or physically.
- Lack commitment to finding solutions.

Accommodators

- Believe conflict is destructive.
- Overvalue maintaining relationships.
- Undervalue own needs.
- Don't make waves.
- Want peace at any price.

Forcers expect to get their needs met regardless of the costs. For the forcer, winning may provide a sense of accomplishment. In conflicts, you may put your needs first and sometimes with little or no regard for the needs of others. You might see conflict as a win-or-lose situation in which you must be the winner. Forcers typically employ persuasion with emotional appeals, strong deliveries, and persistence to get their needs met. They frequently are more interested in implementing their solution to a problem rather than listening to the opinions, needs, and feelings of others. Forcers are often impatient with others who do not see things their way. Although forcing can lower morale, jeopardize relationships, and stifle creativity, in some situations, you might find this approach to be appropriate. For example, when decisions have to be made quickly or when a crisis must be addressed, forcing may be your most reasonable option.

Forcers
• Believe winning is the only thing.
• Love challenge and achievement.
• Express anger when others don't agree.
• Are willing to sacrifice others who don't agree.

Compromisers think that those involved in the conflict must each be prepared to give up something in order to reach a solution. Choosing the role of compromiser, you expect to settle for less than what would meet your needs. Compromisers subscribe to the principle, "We must both give a little." Compromisers usually employ maneuvering, negotiating, and trading in an attempt to find a solution. Finding some middle ground may provide a partial solution to a conflict. However, unmet needs may still remain, and for those involved, the commitment to the solution will be only lukewarm at best. Sometimes, however, you may choose to compromise because the compromise represents a solution both you and the other party can "live with." This latter result is particularly acceptable when the nature of the disagreement isn't of vital importance to you or the other party.

Compromisers
• Believe half a loaf is better than none.
• Want each side to gain something.
• Use voting or bargaining to decide.
• Avoid the real issues.

Different from compromisers, **collaborators** believe that both parties can and will get their needs met. The underlying belief of collaborators is that if you understand one another's needs, you will be able to find a way to meet both parties' needs. The question is not whose needs will be met, but rather how you will meet the needs of both parties. Collaborators share specific information about what they need and listen to understand what the other party needs. Trust and openness make searching for possible solutions a creative experience. Both parties feel committed to the process and the solution because both sets of needs are met. This style has the advantages of promoting collaboration, creativity, and commitment. However, collaborating can seem unattainable to you when the needs of those involved are not clearly stated or understood. In addition, you will discover that collaboration takes time, a willingness of both parties to work together, and the belief that there is a mutually satisfying solution.

Collaborators
• Believe both parties can meet their needs.
• See conflict as a natural way to meet needs.
• Want to hear the needs of the other.
• View the other as equal in a conflict.

Keep in mind that each conflict style may be appropriate in different circumstances and that you must learn to assess how well each style is meeting

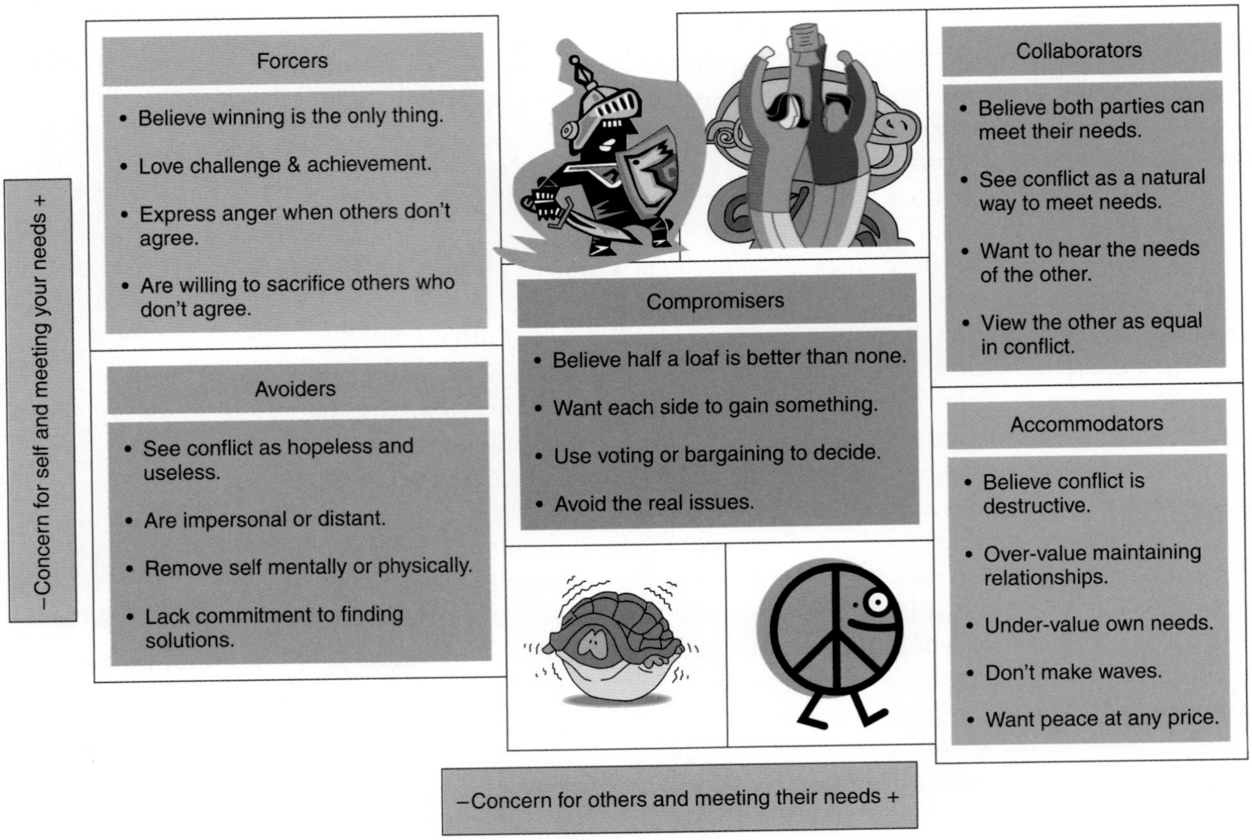

Concern for self and meeting your needs +/−

Forcers

- Believe winning is the only thing.
- Love challenge & achievement.
- Express anger when others don't agree.
- Are willing to sacrifice others who don't agree.

Avoiders

- See conflict as hopeless and useless.
- Are impersonal or distant.
- Remove self mentally or physically.
- Lack commitment to finding solutions.

Compromisers

- Believe half a loaf is better than none.
- Want each side to gain something.
- Use voting or bargaining to decide.
- Avoid the real issues.

Collaborators

- Believe both parties can meet their needs.
- See conflict as a natural way to meet needs.
- Want to hear the needs of the other.
- View the other as equal in conflict.

Accommodators

- Believe conflict is destructive.
- Over-value maintaining relationships.
- Under-value own needs.
- Don't make waves.
- Want peace at any price.

−Concern for others and meeting their needs +

FIGURE 7.2 ■ Managing Conflict Model

your needs and those of the other person. In addition, if a particular style is not working, you need to be flexible and try another style. You probably have seen people switch from being forcers to being avoiders, compromisers, or accommodators depending on how they read the situations. In addition, conflict styles may be used habitually, or they may be a conscious choice. Examine the styles shown in Figure 7.2 to determine which you use most frequently in your attempts to manage conflict.

Conflict Strategy Guidelines

In addition to recognizing the different styles of conflict management, you may find the following guidelines to be particularly helpful in dealing with conflicts.

1. **Recognize the "enemies" that can limit your ability to manage conflict effectively.**

   ■ Your first enemy is your desire to explain your side of the conflict first.

   ■ Your second enemy is failure to listen attentively to the other person's perspective.

- Your third enemy is fear of losing control, losing what you value, looking foolish, or turning out to be wrong.

- Your fourth enemy is the misconception that someone must win and someone must lose. In other words, you fail to recognize the possibility of a win-win solution (Billikopf, 2001, p. 4).

2. **Identify your needs and those of the other person.** This step keeps you focused on the issue that is causing the conflict. In addition, identification of needs is necessary before you can start brainstorming for possible solutions. Finally, this step encourages you to be empathic about the needs of the person with whom you are experiencing conflict, making the possibility of a win/win solution more likely.

3. **Plan what you want to say.** It's a good idea to give consideration to the way you want to word your confrontation with the other person. Thinking back to Chapter 6, you will find the four-part assertion message format to provide you with a template for phrasing your remarks. Remember to describe the behavior you find troublesome, identify your feelings, state the tangible consequences of the behavior, and make a request. Your comments might sound something like this:

   When you take personal calls on your cell phone while there are customers waiting in line (**Behavior**), I feel stressed (**Feeling**) because I have to cover the service desk by myself (**Tangible Consequence**). Would you please wait until your break to use your cell phone? (**Request**).

4. **Choose the right time.** Make sure you confront the other person at an opportune time. This step means both you and the other person should be relaxed, free from distractions, and prepared to spend the time needed to address the conflict.

5. **Take turns speaking and listening.** It is very important that both you and the other person feel free to share your concerns and feelings with one another. In addition, it is equally critical that you both listen open-mindedly rather than defensively to each other. Taking time to paraphrase one another is an excellent way to encourage the active listening required for collaborative problem solving.

6. **Set the stage for finding a solution.** This guideline encourages you and the other person to work collaboratively to find a solution. Brainstorming is a good way to begin this process. Focus on generating creative solutions that can meet your needs and those of the other person. Remember too that effective brainstorming emphasizes quantity rather than quality of ideas, at least initially. Then after you have a list generated, you and your partner can evaluate the list in order to determine which solutions seem most workable.

7. **Express appreciation.** Once a solution has been reached, thank the other person for his or her participation in resolving the conflict. This final step is a form of celebration that says, "We did it!" Ending your discussion

on a positive note also strengthens the relationship and increases the likelihood of effective collaboration for future conflicts, should they arise.

Ogden Nash, born in Rye, New York (1902), wrote:

To keep your marriage brimming,
With love in the loving cup,
Whenever you're wrong, admit it;
Whenever you're right, shut up.

Responding to Criticism

You probably have been criticized at one time or another. Maybe you made a mistake or forgot to do what you were directed to do. Perhaps you have experienced being criticized by someone who just wanted to have control over you, maybe an older brother or sister. Sometimes your co-worker may act like he or she is your boss and use criticism to control your behavior. At other times, when you hear criticism, it is vague, and you may not know if the criticism is for a valid reason or if it is purely manipulative. How you respond to criticism depends on the kind of criticism you hear.

Dealing with criticism and responding nondefensively may be one of the most difficult challenges you face as an effective communicator. The natural tendency to become defensive when you are criticized may result in a negative, upward spiral of defensiveness, which may provoke insults, put-downs, and hurt feelings.

Manuel Smith, in his book, *When I Say No, I Feel Guilty* (1975), described three types of criticism you may encounter: manipulative, valid, and vague criticism (figure 7.3). Smith then recommended three specific communication techniques you can use to cope effectively with these criticisms. These three skills are fogging, negative assertion, and negative inquiry.

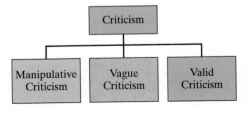

FIGURE 7.3 ■ Criticisms

FOGGING

Fogging is a technique of calmly acknowledging unfair criticism without agreeing or disagreeing with it (figure 7.4). You are then allowed to make a judgment of what to do with the criticism: believe it, challenge it, or discard it. Fogging is based on the assumption that you, not your critic, are the ultimate judge of criticized behavior.

For example, to the co-worker who says, "Your uniform is a mess," you might respond by saying, "Perhaps my uniform could look more professional." This fogging response shows that you are listening and acknowledged the criticism without being defensive or without agreeing. Your indifferent, matter-of-fact tone of voice communicates the unspoken part of fogging: "I'll decide."

Acknowledges Manipulative Criticism

Fogging:

- Fogging presents a nondefensive, indifferent response to manipulative criticism.

- Fogging seeks to acknowledge the criticism.

- Fogging does not agree or disagree.

FIGURE 7.4 ■ Fogging

Fogging, then, is a way of acknowledging the criticism without "buying into" it.

NEGATIVE ASSERTION

Negative assertion is a technique where you strongly agree with valid criticism without having to apologize or give excuses (figure 7.5). This technique has the dual effect of allowing you to acknowledge your shortcomings and to reduce your critic's negative feelings. Negative assertion is based on the assumption that "to err is human," and the best way to deal with your mistakes is to strongly agree with the criticism.

For example, after you offered to pick Jan up from work, you completely forgot until an hour later. When you finally arrived, Jan said, "You forgot to pick me up. I nearly froze my toes off waiting for you." Rather than giving excuses, it might be best to say, "I did forget to pick you up. That's the dumbest thing I've done all week." This response strongly agrees with the criticism without offering excuses, placing blame, or becoming defensive. Negative assertion helps you accept your mistakes and learn from them.

Strongly Agrees with Valid Criticism
Negative Assertion:
• Strongly agrees with valid criticism.
• Admits mistakes.
• Announces the critic right.
• Adds what you have learned from the mistake.
• Expresses a sad, regretful tone.

FIGURE 7.5 ■ Negative Assertion

NEGATIVE INQUIRY

Negative inquiry is a technique of actively questioning your critic for specific information about vague criticism (figure 7.6). Your goal is to clarify the criticism. If you find that the criticism is valid, you may discover it helps you to improve, and if you believe that it is manipulative and unfair, you will exhaust your critic's concerns and thereby reduce defensiveness. The assumption behind negative inquiry is that through active questioning, you can determine if the criticism is valid or unfair. Your concerned, curious tone of voice should say, "I'm confused; I need more information." Your question might sound like these: "What is it about my performance that is a problem?" "How do you think I should have handled that customer?" or "What specifically did I do wrong?" These questions help the critics explain in greater detail the nature of the criticism and disclose their needs to you.

As this chapter concludes, keep in mind that although conflict can be a source of stress in relationships, it also provides opportunities for a variety of benefits as well. You are more likely to experience these benefits when you are aware of the types of conflicts you may encounter, along with the various styles of conflict management. Adhering to the conflict strategy guidelines and coping with criticism effectively provide other valuable techniques to make conflict work for you.

Clarifies Vague Criticism
Negative Inquiry:
• Clarifies the intent of vague criticism.
• Shares a puzzled, confused tone.
• Seeks further information.
• Uses questions.

FIGURE 7.6 ■ Negative Inquiry

Review Questions

1. This chapter discusses several benefits that can result when you are faced with an interpersonal conflict. Describe an interpersonal conflict you have experienced and explain which of these benefits occurred as you attempted to resolve the conflict.

2. Explain the difference among the five types of interpersonal conflicts.

3. Match the letter of each conflict management style in Column A with the appropriate characteristic in Column B. (Refer to the "Managing Conflict Model.")

Column A
a. Forcers
b. Collaborators
c. Compromisers
d. Avoiders
e. Accommodators

Column B
___ 1. Want peace at any price.
___ 2. See conflict as a natural way to meet needs.
___ 3. Want each side to gain something.
___ 4. Lack commitment to finding solutions.
___ 5. Believe winning is the only thing.
___ 6. View the other as equal in a conflict.
___ 7. Believe conflict is destructive.
___ 8. Use voting or bargaining to decide.
___ 9. Love challenge and achievement.
___ 10. Are impersonal or distant.

4. Discuss the values that each of the following conflict strategy guidelines offers you when faced with a conflict:
a. Recognize the "enemies" that can limit your ability to manage conflict effectively.
b. Identify your needs and those of the other person.
c. Plan what you want to say.
d. Choose the right time.
e. Take turns speaking and listening.
f. Set the stage for finding a solution.
g. Express appreciation.

5. Define three different types of criticism and the three different ways of responding to criticism.

Key Words and Concepts

Accommodator   162
Avoider   162
Collaborator   163
Compromiser   163
Ego Conflicts   161
Fact Conflicts   160
Fogging   166
Forcer   163
Need Conflicts   161
Negative Assertion   167
Negative Inquiry   167
Pseudo conflicts   160
Value Conflicts   161

Web Activities

Visit the following interesting sites to find out more about conflict, conflict styles, and coping with criticism.

- For an hour-long audio seminar on Empathic Listening from the University of California's Conflict Management Skills webpage click http://www.cnr.berkeley.edu/ucce50/ag-labor/7labor/13.htm.

- For a free survey that will calculate your preferred method of dealing with conflict, check out the Adult Personal Conflict Style Inventory at http://peace.mennolink.org/cgi-bin/conflictstyle/inventory.cgi.

- To increase your understanding of giving and receiving criticism, take a look at website http://www.uwsp.edu/education/wkirby/ntrprsnl/critic.htm.

- Shauna Shipley of Human Resources Inc. presents an hour-long training program on Conflict Management at http://scythe.uits.indiana.edu/~r547dex4/shipley/index.html.

Assignments

ASSIGNMENT 7.1: DETERMINE CONFLICT STYLES

CONFLICT QUESTIONNAIRE

Directions: Proverbs state traditional wisdom. The following proverbs and statements reflect traditional wisdom for resolving conflicts. Read each carefully. Using the scale given below, indicate how typical each proverb or statement is of your actions in a conflict.

5–Very typical of the way I act in a conflict.

4–Frequently typical of the way I act in a conflict.

3–Sometimes typical of the way I act in a conflict.

2–Seldom typical of the way I act in a conflict.

1–Never typical of the way I act in a conflict.

____ 1. Soft words win hard hearts.

____ 2. Come now and let us reason together.

____ 3. The arguments of the strongest always have the most weight.

____ 4. You scratch my back, I'll scratch yours.

____ 5. The best way of handling conflicts is to avoid them.

____ 6. When one hits you with a stone, hit him with a piece of cotton.

____ 7. A question must be decided by knowledge and not by numbers if it is to have a right decision.

____ 8. If you cannot make a person think as you do, make him do as you think.

____ 9. Better half a loaf than no bread at all.

____ 10. If someone is ready to quarrel with you, he isn't worth knowing.

____ 11. Smooth words make smooth ways.

____ 12. By digging and digging, the truth is discovered.

____ 13. He who fights and runs away lives to run another day.

____ 14. A fair exchange brings no quarrel.

____ 15. There is nothing so important that you have to fight for it.

____ 16. Kill your enemies with kindness.

____ 17. Seek till you find, and you'll not lose your labor.

____ 18. Might overcomes right.

____ 19. Tit for tat is fair play.

____ 20. Avoid quarrelsome people—they will only make your life miserable.

Adapted from Lawrence and Lorsch (1967).

ASSIGNMENT 7.1 (CONTINUED) CONFLICT QUESTIONNAIRE SCORE SHEET

Directions: Record your scores for selected items in the table below:

Forcer		Accommodator		Avoider		Compromiser		Collaborator	
Items	**Scores**	**Items**	**Scores**	**Items**	**Scores**	**Items**	**Scores**	**Items**	**Scores**
Item 3		Item 1		Item 5		Item 4		Item 2	
Item 8		Item 6		Item 10		Item 9		Item 7	
Item 13		Item 11		Item 15		Item 14		Item 12	
Item 18		Item 16		Item 20		Item 19		Item 17	
Total		Total		Total		Total		Total	

Which conflict style has the highest score?

In what situations do you use this style?

Which style has the lowest score?

In what situations do you use this style?

How satisfied are you with your choices of conflict styles?

What changes would you like to make in your selection of conflict styles?

ASSIGNMENT 7.2: MANAGING CONFLICT SELF-ASSESSMENT

Directions: Circle T (true) or F (false) to indicate which of the following statements best describes how you would respond in each of these situations. Although you may not agree with either choice, you must select either true (T) or false (F). Your first response will be your best.

Statements	1	2	3	4	5
1. When our opinions, wants, or needs are different, I would rather discuss the differences than try to persuade the other person that I am right and he or she is wrong.	F				T
2. When our opinions, wants, or needs are different, I would rather disagree openly and discuss our differences than agree with the other's point of view.				F	T
3. When asked to complete a difficult job, I would rather postpone the work indefinitely than follow orders without discussion.		F	T		
4. When our opinions, wants, or needs are different, I would rather try to persuade the other person to my thinking than withdraw from the discussion.	T		F		
5. Sometimes it's better to agree and seem to go along with something without discussion than to avoid saying anything about a controversial subject.		T	F		
6. When we disagree, I would rather say that I may be half wrong than try to persuade the other person that I am totally right.	F			T	

Statements	1	2	3	4	5
7. When our opinions, wants, or needs are different, I would rather give in completely than try to change the other person's thinking.	F		T		
8. I would rather put off an apparent disagreement than discuss our different points of view.			T		F
9. When we disagree, I like to meet the person halfway rather than give in completely.		F		T	
10. Sometimes it's better to agree without discussion than to try to persuade the other person I'm right.	F	T			
11. When we disagree, I prefer to admit that I am half wrong than not say anything and end the discussion.			F	T	
12. When asked to perform a job that I do not like to do, I would rather postpone the work indefinitely than make someone else do the task.	F		T		
13. When we disagree, I like to persuade the other person to my thinking rather than to split our differences.	T			F	
14. When our opinions, wants, or needs are different, I would rather discuss our differences to seek a mutually acceptable solution than leave the discussion without a resolution.	T	F			
15. When asked to do a job that I don't like to do, I would rather postpone the work indefinitely than discuss my feelings and attempt to find a solution we can both agree on.			T		F

Statements	1	2	3	4	5
16. When our opinions, wants, or needs are different, I would rather try to persuade the other person that I am right than discuss our differences.	T				F
17. When we disagree, I would rather admit that I am half wrong than discuss our differences.				T	F
18. Sometimes it's better to agree without discussion than to give up half of what I believe to reach an agreement.		T		F	
19. When our opinions, wants, or needs are different, I would rather discuss our differences than give in without a conversation.			F		T
20. When our opinions, wants, or needs are different, I would rather try to persuade the other to my thinking than give up my point of view by not discussing it.	T	F			
21. When we disagree, I would rather try to find a solution that satisfies both of us than to let the other person find a solution without my input.			F		T
22. When we disagree, I would rather try to persuade the other person than give in completely.	T	F			
23. When asked to do a job that I don't want to do, I would rather agree to do just half the work than to find a solution that is satisfactory.				T	F

Adapted from Salinger Films (1983) Managing Conflict.

Scoring Instructions

1. Count the number of items circled in each of the five columns. Record your totals in the boxes that follow item 23. Multiply each score by 10.

1	2	3	4	5

x-10

2. Chart your score on the graph below. Place an "X" next to your score for each of the five strategies. Draw a straight line connecting the "X's" from one column to the next. This will give you your conflict management strategy pattern.

	1 Force	2 Accommodation	3 Avoidance	4 Compromise	5 Collaboration
120					
110					
100					
90					
80					
70					
60					
50					
40					
30					
20					
10					
0					

ASSIGNMENT 7.3: MAKE A PREDICTION

Directions: Join together with three or four other classmates in a group and make a prediction as to what the outcome would be when the style across the top meets the style along the side of the table below. (Note the shaded areas do not need to be filled in as they are duplicates of predictions that you will make in the neutral or unshaded areas.)

Predict the Outcome	Forcer	Accommodator	Compromiser	Collaborator	Avoider
Forcer					
Accommodator					
Compromiser					
Collaborator					
Avoider					

Once your group has made its predictions, answer the questions that follow:

1. What did you learn about conflict management as a result of making these predictions?

2. What steps could you take to manage conflict effectively with someone who has a different style than your own?

ASSIGNMENT 7.4: CONFLICT RESOLUTION ROLE-PLAYING

Directions: You will gain an understanding of the advantages and disadvantages of various conflict styles by role-playing the styles and dealing with others who are also role-playing the various styles. The class will be divided into groups of three. Each group will meet in a different room or area to discuss a conflict that appears in the instructor's manual.

Round #1

This assignment involves two rounds of role-playing in which two students will discuss the problem, and an observer will note their progress. In the first round, two students will be assigned parts for the discussion and a conflict style to role-play. The students engaged in the discussion will try to come to some resolution for the conflict using the roles that they are assigned. During this round, the observer will note the conflict styles exhibited by both of the students, note the attitudes expressed by them, and identify what behaviors resulted in cooperation or competition throughout the discussion.

Round #2

After about fifteen minutes of role-playing, the instructor will start each pair of students in the second round. In this round, both students will be collaborators and seek to find a mutually satisfying solution to the problem playing their respective roles. Students will alternate between sharing their needs and listening to the needs of the other. During this round, the observer will note who stated his or her needs clearly, who paraphrased the other's needs, who asked clarifying questions, and whose behaviors resulted in cooperation or competition throughout the discussion.

After both rounds are completed, the groups will return to the classroom, and the observers will share their notes with the class.

Finally, all participants should individually jot down an answer to the following questions:

1. What did you learn about conflict resolution from your involvement in this activity?
2. What did you learn about the conflict styles you either role-played or observed during this activity?

Your instructor will have everyone in the class report his or her responses to the questions.

ASSIGNMENT 7.5: RESPONDING TO CRITICISM

Directions: Use the assignment that follows to practice fogging, negative assertion, and negative inquiry, the three techniques for dealing with criticism (figure 7.7). For each situation below, determine if the criticism is manipulative, valid, or vague, and then write your response according to the type of criticism that you have identified.

1. Our report is due on Thursday, and I have all of the sections but yours. We agreed to exchange copies so we could rehearse today. I'm worried our grades will be lowered if we don't have the entire report done.

   Type of Criticism: _____. *Your response:* _____.

   _____

   _____

   _____

2. You've been taking breaks that are too long this past week. We give each employee ten minutes for break, and you were gone at least fifteen minutes yesterday, Tuesday, and today. What's the story here anyway?

   Type of Criticism: _____. *Your response:* _____.

   _____

   _____

   _____

3. This is the fourth time this week that I have had to work a double shift because you called in sick. I can't keep up with my school assignments when I'm working these extra hours.

   Type of Criticism: _____. *Your response:* _____.

   _____

   _____

   _____

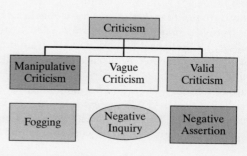

FIGURE 7.7 ■ Respond to Criticism

4. Your multitasking is really getting to me. Whenever I'm talking to you, you have that blasted headset on. You say, "I hear you! I hear you!" I don't think you are paying any attention at all.

Type of Criticism: _____. *Your response:* _____.

_____

_____

_____.

5. I asked you to start dinner because I would be working late, and when I get home, nothing has been done. I'm getting tired of your lack of cooperation.

Type of Criticism: _____. *Your response:* _____.

_____

_____

_____

ASSIGNMENT 7.6: CASE STUDY: TALK IT OUT

Manchester College in North Manchester, Indiana, developed a program titled, "Let's Talk it Out." The aim of the program is to help "elementary students learn to talk through their problems, demonstrating respect for other opinions and conflict resolution" (Kornegay, n.d., p. 1).

As a part of this program, "23 Manchester College students trained 121 first-graders and 96 second-graders in conflict resolution skills. The project is part of a Manchester College course, Intercultural Communication, taught by Associate Professor Mary P. Lahman" (Kornegay, n.d., p. 1).

One Manchester College student involved in the program commented, "I am proud of the fact that I am giving these kids an opportunity to think before they act, and hopefully keeping them from getting into trouble. If the kids can retain the information, it will really help them in life" (Kornegay, n.d., p. 2).

QUESTIONS

1. Do you think programs like "Let's Talk It Out" could help curb school violence? Why or why not?

2. If you were a college student involved in a training program like this one, what content would you like to see included in the curriculum?

3. Based on your own experience in learning to deal with conflict, what personal advice would you offer these elementary students?

References

Billikopf, G. (2001). *Conflict management skills.* Retrieved January 4, 2008, from http://www.cnr.berkeley.edu/ucce50/ag-labor/7labor/13.htm

Brahm, E. (2004, September). *Benefits of intractable conflict.* Retrieved January 9, 2008, from http://www.beyondintractability.org/essay/benefits/

Edelman, J. & Crain, M. B. (1994). *The Tao of negotiation: How you can prevent, resolve, and transcend conflict in work and everyday life.* New York: HarperBusiness.

Garrels, A. (2007, May 17). *U.S. soldiers try to bridge a sectarian gap in Iraq.* NPR. Retrieved May 23, 2007, from file://E:\New Book\NPR.htm

Kornegay, J. (n.d.). *Manchester kids learn how to talk it out from MC students with a mission.* Manchester College, IN. Retrieved January 9, 2008, from http://www.manchester.edu/oca/PR/Files/News/LetsTalkItOut0605.htm

Lawrence & Lorsch. (1967). *Conflict questionnaire.*

McDowell, R. (2003). *AFSC's current Iraq projects.* Wage Peace Campaign. Retrieved January 9, 2008, from http://www.afsc.org/iraq/guide/work-in-iraq.htm

Mutari, E. & Lakew, M. (2003, January 1). *Class conflict: Tuition hikes leave college students in debt and torn between paid work and coursework.* Retrieved January 9, 2008, from http://goliath.ecnext.com/coms2/gi_0199-973060/Class-conflict-tuition-hikes-leave.html

Picherack, F. (2003, May 29). *Conflict resolution.* Retrieved January 4, 2008, from http://www.grad.ubc.ca/gradpd/guides/conflict.html

Salenger Films, Inc. (1983). *Managing conflict: How to make conflict work for you.* Santa Monica, CA.

Smith, M. (1975). *When I say no, I feel guilty: How to cope—Using the skills of systematic assertive therapy.* New York: Dial Press.

Verderber R. F. & Verderber K. S. (1998). *Inter-Act: Using interpersonal communication skills.* (8th ed.) Belmont, CA: Wadsworth.

Chapter **8**

Teamwork

"Teamwork divides the task and multiplies the success."

Unknown

Teamwork Is Important

"Frankly, the prognosis didn't look good for 21-year-old Nissa Stenz the day her motorcycle crashed into the side of a dump truck south of Fond du Lac.

"The accident happened at about 11 A.M. on June 12, with Stenz's cycle slamming into the side of the dump truck, which was headed east on County Trunk F, according to a Fond du Lac County Sheriff's Department report. A helmet that Stenz had been wearing flew off upon impact. Within minutes, area First Responders, paramedics, Sheriff's Department authorities and the Flight for Life helicopter out of Milwaukee were rushing toward the scene"(Schaenzer, 2007, p. 1).

Seriously injured, Stenz miraculously survived and recovered from the accident. "From the dispatchers who received the 911 call regarding the crash to the First Responders and paramedics who arrived on the crash scene to the medical personnel with Flight for Life to the surgeons at Froedtert and the therapists at St. Agnes Hospital—multiple people played a part . . ." (Schaenzer, 2007, p. 2).

The story of Nissa Stenz (figure 8.1) evokes gratitude for the dedicated teams that consider saving lives just a part of their daily jobs. Without the commitment of individuals who work collaboratively in various contexts, companies wouldn't prosper, schools wouldn't succeed, and families wouldn't thrive. If you take a few moments for thoughtful reflection, you are likely to agree that teamwork exists all around you.

According to an Internet article titled *New Teams in the Workplace,* "Teamwork . . . an idea as American as the hot dog or baseball . . . will be the compelling theme of the 21st century. The people who succeed will be those who get high marks in 'works and plays well with others.' And the successful organizations of the future will be customer-focused, team-based organizations" (Parker, 2000, p. 1).

The movement toward self-directed work teams in American business and industry first gained increasing popularity in the early 1980s with the philosophy of W. Edwards Deming and the emergence of TQM (total quality management). TQM was an effort on the part of management to involve teams of workers in the process of continuous improvement. In other words, workplace teams played a critical role in seeking new and better ways to produce a product or provide a service for the benefit of the company and the customer alike.

More recent than TQM, Six Sigma has provided a methodology for ensuring quality (figure 8.2). In particular, this method "strives for near perfection" by "eliminating defects in any process—from manufacturing to transactional and from product to service" (Six Sigma 2000–2003, p. 1).

"General Electric, one of the most successful companies implementing Six Sigma, has estimated benefits on the order of $10 billion during the first five years of implementation" (Six Sigma 2000–2003, p. 1).

FIGURE 8.1 ■ Nissa Stenz, Motorcycle Accident Victim whose Life Was Saved by Good Communication and Teamwork
Source: Republished courtesy of The Reporter (Fon du Lac, Wis.)

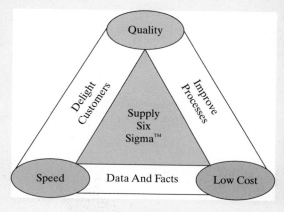

FIGURE 8.2 ■ Six Sigma
Source: http://www.strategicvalueanalysis.com/

Consider the following illustration about another organization that has succeeded as a result of teamwork.

"The cavernous room resembles a secret underground command center. Rows of video monitors line the edge of a giant screen with cylindrical images of the earth highlighted in bright flashing colors. A raised platform in the center of the room houses two technicians behind endless columns of keyboards and telephones. On the outer edge of the room is a glass wall sealing off a large conference room that looks out into the buzz of activity. A national defense center? A clandestine intelligence gathering operation? No. This is just part of a corporate information systems operation for a company passionate about taking care of customers, exceeding quality standards, and staying on the leading edge of its business.

"Hewitt Associates, headquartered outside Chicago, is one of the largest benefit administration firms in the world. In the last five years they have more than doubled in size to 10,000 associates (they don't call them employees) in 34 countries with over 2,400 clients. How did they achieve such success? One of the key elements in their growth has been their attention to providing high quality service to customers. The formula is simple. Growth and profit are directly linked to effective leadership and empowered employees" (Molloy, 2000, p. 1).

The success story of Hewitt Associates is just one of many where organizations combine leaders and employees to collaborate as teams and energize not only company profits but the workplace climate as well.

In addition, although most teams in today's workplace interact face-to-face, computer technology has provided a medium for team members to interact in ways that transcend both time and space. These work groups are often referred to as virtual teams. Computerized discussion groups provide an opportunity for virtual teams to collaborate across the globe. Although this technology is unlikely to replace the personal contact that face-to-face teams represent, it does offer a new dimension for working collaboratively, a dimension that requires not only team-building skills but technical skills as well.

The strength of workplace teams should not really come as a surprise to you. After all, human beings are "social animals" who tend, in general, to gravitate toward groups. You play sports in groups, worship in groups, and seek social interaction in groups.

Given the likelihood that work teams are here to stay and that they possess the resourcefulness to exert a powerful influence in the workplace, you would do well to examine your abilities to function as an effective team player.

Virtual Teams in the Workplace

Benefits of Teams

Tendra was assigned to a team for a persuasive presentation in her oral communications class. Each team in the class consisted of five to six members. The teams were instructed to select a topic of interest to them and subdivide the topic among the members. Each member was then expected to research and prepare an eight-minute speech on his or her topic. They chose the subject of global warming.

During the next few weeks, Tendra and her classmates spent time in the library gathering materials and then meeting with one another to share the information they had collected.

Once they all had developed preliminary outlines of their speeches, they met at Tendra's house to design a series of PowerPoint slides to accompany their presentation.

After the team did a successful presentation for the class, Tendra commented that working together produced a host of benefits. Tendra discovered that she learned more about global warming from the input of her team members than if she had researched the topic alone. In addition, she commented that the willingness of her team to help one another throughout the preparation process bolstered confidence and enthusiasm for the assignment. She also stated that she was grateful for the friendships that developed among her team members.

The benefits Tendra experienced from team participation are quite common. In fact, in companies that use self-directed work teams, there seems to be a consensus about the benefits that result. For one, as a team member,

Student Work Teams
Offer Many Advantages

your morale is likely to be higher and absenteeism less of a problem. These benefits are generally the result of a greater sense of empowerment that you enjoy as a team member. Second, your customers' satisfaction increases since your team focuses on ways to improve the quality of the goods and services it provides. Third, you will discover that decisions can be made quicker and problems addressed at the source, in part because teams often have the luxury of giving their attention to a single issue. However, these benefits are largely realized when a team is functioning effectively. In the next section, you will examine the characteristics of effective workplace teams.

Analysis of Effective Teams

Before you identify the factors that contribute to an effective team, whether that team is one in which members function face-to-face or one that interacts virtually by way of computer networks, let us first define the word *team*.

A team is a collection of interdependent individuals who work together, generally over a period of time, in order to achieve a common goal. Teams are sometimes referred to as committees or task forces in certain organizations. But regardless of how these groups are labeled, their function remains essentially the same.

In some instances, you may be part of a team organized to address a specific concern in the workplace, and when that concern has been satisfactorily addressed, your team is disbanded. One company, for example, was planning on switching insurance carriers. A team was formed to explore other potential carriers and to weigh the pros and cons of these alternative carriers in terms of premiums, types of coverage, choice of providers, and so on. After these comparisons were made, the team members presented their findings to management, along with their recommendations. Once management had reached a decision, the team was no longer necessary.

In other cases, however, you could be part of a team with an ongoing objective. Consider a company team whose function is to plan semi-annual in-service training for employees. This team is likely to operate on a permanent basis.

Regardless of whether your team functions for a short period of time or for an extended period of time, the factors that enhance its performance remain the same. Following are some of these factors:

1. **Clear goals.** In order for your team to function optimally, the members have to operate on the basis of clearly defined goals. In certain instances, your team may be given a specific goal or series of goals before even beginning to work. The team mentioned earlier that was assigned to assess alternative insurance carriers on the basis of set criteria (e.g., premiums, types of coverage, etc.) represented a team with goals already defined for them.

   On the other hand, your team might have less tangible goals presented to it and have greater responsibility for establishing its priorities. If your team is directed to examine ways of increasing company sales as its primary goal, the members may have to identify a series of preliminary goals first. Your team members may decide that their first objective is to design a market survey to assess the current needs of their customers. After the survey has been designed, they may need to determine how the survey will be administered and the results tabulated, and so on. In this latter instance, you and your other team members will need to be very clear on the preliminary goals required before an overall objective can be reached.

2. **Capable team members.** In addition to having clearly defined goals, you and your team members must be capable. Generally, team members should possess sufficient technical expertise in their respective fields so that they can make meaningful contributions to the group. Many companies see to it that teams are comprised of members from various departments in order to broaden the base of technical knowledge. Also, you and your team members should be good problem solvers and critical thinkers. Much that goes on within a workplace team involves careful analysis of data and decision making, so your ability to think critically and solve problems logically are indispensable team skills. In addition, you must have good communication skills. The success of any team endeavor is largely dependent upon the members' abilities to voice their ideas clearly and concisely and to listen objectively to opposing points of view. Finally, in order to be truly capable participants, you and the other members need to receive training in the teamwork process.

   Sometimes overly zealous companies who are eager to implement strategies like Six Sigma assign their employees to teams and expect them to perform without sufficient instruction. It should not be surprising when, under such circumstances, teams experience less than satisfactory results.

3. **Commitment to excellence.** For your team to be truly successful, members must be committed to achieving excellence. In large part, this commitment stems from the belief that the goals you are working to achieve are worthwhile and will in some measure contribute to overall company, employee, and customer satisfaction. As a result of this commitment, you will be more willing to put the team's interests above your own personal interests and to engage in the process of continually evaluating your own effectiveness and that of the team.

4. **Outside recognition.** If your team is operating effectively, all the members can derive great personal satisfaction from the work they are accomplishing. However, such personal satisfaction is often not sufficient to keep the team highly motivated and productive. What members also need is some form of outside recognition, usually from the company management. Consider, for example, a worker who is doing his or her job superbly but gets little or no recognition from the boss. Contrast this situation with one where another worker is doing an equally outstanding job but receives acknowledgement and appreciation from the boss. Which of the two workers is most likely to sustain his or her quality of work? Most would probably say the latter. The same principle holds true in a team setting. If your team receives management's recognition, all participants will tend

to feel that the work they are doing is of greater value than teams that receive no recognition at all. In addition, this recognition can occur when management actually implements the ideas your team has generated or acts upon a decision your team has made.

5. **Collaborative climate.** A climate or atmosphere most conducive to productive teamwork is one in which you and the other members have established rapport with one another. This type of climate results when trust has been built among the members, and they feel free to share information openly and honestly. Another factor that enhances the climate occurs when you and your team members feel valued. Feelings of value result when individual members are listened to, respected, and acknowledged for their contributions by other members on the team. Finally, a collaborative climate develops when you experience interdependence with one another. Members need to know, for example, that they can count on one another to get the job done. They also need to have worked out a system of conflict resolution strategies so that problems can be managed while relationships remain intact. Keep in mind too that a collaborative climate is not only fostered within the team but must be supported by the culture of the organization itself. In other words, management from the top down must be committed to promoting an environment that makes teamwork possible.

Effective Teams Have

1. Clear goals
2. Capable team members
3. Commitment to excellence
4. Outside recognition
5. Collaborative climate

Stages of Team Development

Like most interpersonal relationships that develop over time, so too do team members develop a working relationship among themselves over time. Beth Camp, in her book *Effective Workplace Writing* (1997), discusses five stages of what she calls the "life cycle" of any work group or team (figure 8.3). The first is the **form stage.** In this stage, your team's members become organized, identify the strengths and weaknesses of the group, define their task, establish meeting times, and so on. The second is the **norm stage.** This stage requires you and your team members to clarify goals, determine norms for the meetings, fine-tune team tasks, assign who will do what by when, and set standards for the work that will be produced. Stage three is the **work stage.** The primary purpose of this stage is for your team to begin substantive work on its goals. This stage involves gathering information to complete the task and beginning to evaluate team performance as the work proceeds. Stage four is called the **storm stage.** Since conflict is an inevitable part of team interaction, you and fellow members now begin to resolve any disagreements that may occur over performance, the quality of work produced, or the deadlines that have been established. The final stage is the **perform stage.** At this point, your team has completed its assigned task and is ready to present the work to the intended audience (p. 14).

During this entire developmental process, you can observe two distinct phenomena occurring. First, you can see the actual work that is being accomplished by your team members. This work follows a pattern of identifying tasks, assigning work to individual members, gathering the necessary information, evaluating and refining the work, and then producing the final product. But in addition to the work that is being accomplished, you can observe a second phenomenon occurring—the development of relationships among your team members. As your team begins working together, the members develop a rapport among themselves. This rapport is critical to the success of your team since it provides a climate in which your team members can work harmoniously and productively. In the next section, you will examine some of the specific skills that enhance this type of climate.

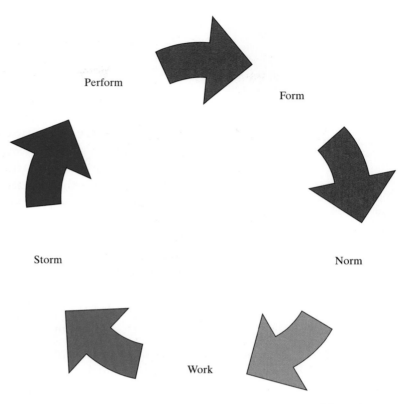

FIGURE 8.3 ■ Team Stages

Positive Participation Skills

You have probably experienced the satisfaction that comes from working with others whose company you enjoy. Working relationships that are supportive and nurturing make your job easier, increase your level of creativity, and energize your performance. This same principle holds true in a team setting. Teams where members feel a genuine sense of belonging are much more likely to be productive than teams where members feel a lack of connection to one another. In order for a team to maximize its productivity, members must possess attitudes and exhibit behavior that fosters the kind of climate described earlier. The following is a list of the factors that enable you to be a positive participant. See figure 8.4 for a summary.

Accountability: One of the most important qualities team members can possess is a sense of accountability. Being accountable means you are

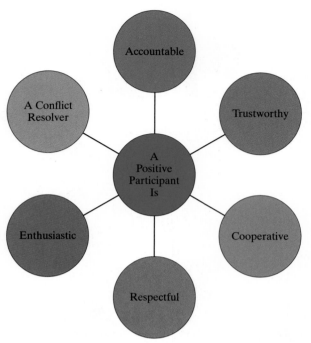

FIGURE 8.4 ■ Positive Participant

Cooperation Leads to a Mutually Satisfying Outcome

responsible. You and your team members need to be clear on their responsibilities to the group and to assure one another that each member can be counted on to fulfill those responsibilities.

Trustworthiness: Members must also exhibit that they are worthy of trust. In part, trustworthiness results when you and the members of your team are accountable. However, in addition, trust is built when you and fellow participants are open and honest with each other, honor confidences, and refuse to participate in gossip about other members of the team.

Spirit of Cooperation: For any team or group to be successful, the members must be cooperative. You will discover that teams are often comprised of diverse individuals, with conflicting points of view, and cooperation is generated when you and the other members are willing to be flexible, open-minded, and able to compromise when necessary.

Respectfulness: Along with cooperation, you and your team members must have respect for each other. Although members may be very different from one another, each member deserves to be treated with respect. Respect is evidenced when participants are given the opportunity to voice their views and are listened to fairly, when differences among members are celebrated for the richness they bring to the group, and when all members demonstrate courtesy in their interactions with fellow team members.

Enthusiasm: When you and your team members approach collaborative work with interest and enthusiasm, an energy is unleashed that keeps the team focused and on track. Enthusiasm also stimulates creativity and makes whatever work the team must address more enjoyable.

Willingness to Resolve Conflicts: Even among the most amiable teams, conflict is likely to occur from time to time. You will find that these conflicts can range from disagreements about the work being done to differences of opinion that seem irreconcilable. Regardless of the source of the conflict, however, effective teams have a variety of strategies for working through conflicts while keeping relationships intact. With practice, you and your team can even come to view conflicts as opportunities for growth.

Up to this point, you have explored fundamental principles and ideas that underlie teamwork. Now you are ready to identify some specific techniques for implementing workplace teams. The following section will focus on four primary techniques. First, you will examine the process of organizing a work team; second, you will determine member and leader responsibilities; third, you will identify a problem-solving strategy for resolving team conflicts; and finally, you will review a strategy for recording the team's progress in the form of meeting minutes so the information can be shared with others.

Organize the Team

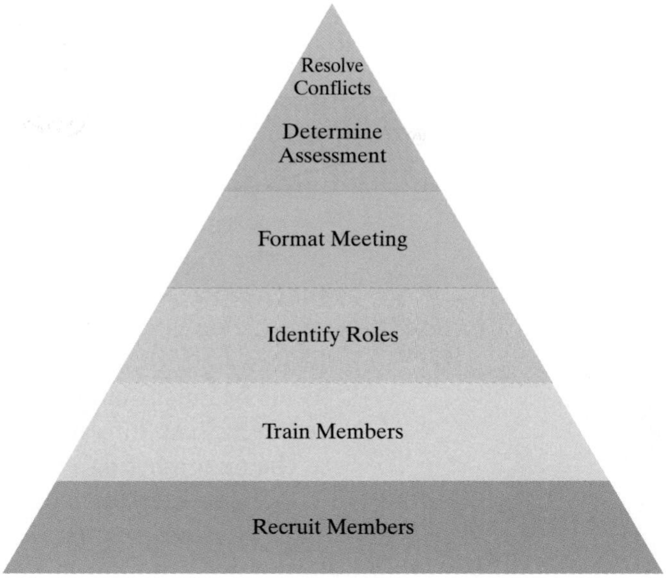

Let's begin by identifying how a work team might be organized (figure 8.5). Prior to such organization, a company must have determined the need for the existence of a team approach. This need is frequently the result of a shift in management philosophy that seeks to involve all employees in the process of continuous improvement so that customers may be served well, workers may experience greater satisfaction, and management may realize higher levels of productivity. In addition, a company must ensure that adequate time, resources, and support will be provided so that teams can function as optimally as possible. Once these preliminary considerations have been addressed, the team organizational process can begin.

FIGURE 8.5 ■ Team Organization Steps

The first step in the team organization process involves **recruiting members.** Ideally, recruitment should be voluntary, if at all possible, to ensure interest among the members. A second approach is to allow you and other workers to choose from a variety of teams being organized so individuals do not feel compelled to participate without any available options. Next, an ideal number of participants on a team is either five or seven. This odd number eliminates the possibility of tie votes. Also, this number reasonably assures a fair representation of varied points of view and reduces the manageability problems that are more likely to occur with larger groups of participants. Finally, recruitment efforts should encourage diversity among members, both personally and professionally. For example, members representing several departments would be more desirable than all members from the same department. Likewise, a mix of men and women, along with participants from different racial, ethnic, and cultural backgrounds would enhance your team as well.

The second step in team organization is **training the members.** As was mentioned earlier, if you have never been a team participant before, you cannot be expected to perform ideally without some prior instruction. To begin, you need to understand the company's philosophy and goals and to be shown how the various teams' efforts will support that philosophy and those goals. Second, you should be provided suggestions for maximizing your productivity within the team. These suggestions might involve discussion of member responsibilities, available styles of leadership, strategies for managing conflict, and so on. Next, your team needs to be given clear direction as to its purpose. Those purposes reveal the work the team needs to accomplish such as developing an ad campaign for a new product, designing a customer feedback form, or evaluating several lines of computer software the company is considering purchasing. Finally, some companies provide "ongoing" training for team members to continually fine-tune their participation skills.

Other companies will assign a mentor to each team so that if problems and concerns arise during the team's work, a mentor can step in and provide whatever assistance might be necessary for you and others.

The third step in team organization is **identifying roles.** Once a team has been assembled and the members trained, it is now time for the team to determine the roles that each member will play. You will notice as you participate on a team that some teams prefer to assign roles to members. For example, one member might be assigned to record meeting minutes; another may serve as timekeeper; a third member may be responsible for reserving meeting rooms and facilities. Sometimes these roles are maintained for the duration of the team. Other times the roles may rotate among members. In addition to these kinds of functional roles, you, along with others, may be expected to conduct research, seek information, meet with other company teams, and report back at the next meeting in order to facilitate decision making.

The fourth step in team organization is **selecting a meeting format.** At this step, your team must decide how often it will meet, when it will meet, and how long it will meet in order to accomplish its assigned task. In addition, you and other members need to determine whether or not it will be necessary for you to follow a strict agenda, to be governed by *Robert's Rules of Order,* and so on.

The fifth step in team organization is determining a **team assessment method.** For your team to be successful, the members *periodically* need to take stock of how they are doing. Some teams may choose to develop a simple assessment form that members can complete anonymously. This form can include criteria to assess the quality of the work, the effectiveness of the meetings, and the nature of the personal interactions. Some teams do a quick check of their performance by having members write on a 3×5 note card one example of something the team is doing well (such as staying on schedule with their work) and one example of something that could be improved (such as being more careful not to interrupt other members when they are making a contribution to the discussion). Other teams whose members value their openness with each other may simply take time to voice their personal assessment of team performance. Regardless of which method your team selects, members should also determine the frequency of these assessments. For a team that will be functioning for only a short period of time, these assessments might be conducted every meeting or two in some brief form. For teams that are ongoing, every few weeks may be sufficient.

The sixth step in team organization is identifying **methods of conflict resolution.** It is very important for your team to acknowledge in the early stages of its work that conflict is an inevitable part of group interaction. You and your members also need to recognize that these conflicts can be substantive (i.e., dealing with the nature of the team's work) or personal (i.e., dealing with how the members interact with each other). In addition, you should appreciate the variety of conflict resolution strategies that can be chosen, depending upon the circumstances. For example, if your members are finding it difficult to reach a decision on a matter they are discussing, they may choose an approach which involves defining the problem, analyzing the problem, brainstorming for a list of solutions, evaluating the solutions, etc. (Note: This reflective approach will be explained more fully later in the chapter.) If the conflict involves personalities, your team may decide to have the member or members concerned schedule a private meeting with a team mentor.

Member and Leader Responsibilities

Once your team has been organized, you and the other members need to be aware of individual responsibilities. We've already discussed, in general, some of the positive participation skills that all members must exhibit. In this section, however, you will explore the tasks faced by members and leaders in more specific detail. Let's look at the responsibilities of members first.

Members: To begin, as a member, you need to attend meetings regularly and be on time. When a member is absent, extra time may be required by other members and/or the leader to inform the absent member about what took place during his/her absence. In addition, when members are late for meetings, they may delay available work time while others wait for them to arrive or cause disruption of a meeting that may have already begun.

Next, you should come to meetings prepared. Preparation requires you to review the agenda prior to the meeting so you are familiar with the topics to be addressed. Also, you should come to the meeting with any previously assigned work completed so you are ready to make productive contributions to the discussion.

In addition, you need to stay involved during the course of the meeting. Involvement means that you must remain alert, interested, and eager to contribute your ideas to the discussion. You should also seek clarification by raising questions when necessary and encourage more reticent members of the team to make contributions of their own.

Finally, you need to adhere to the meeting protocol established by the team. For example, if a policy has been established that each member can speak *only* once until each other member of the team has had the chance to speak one time as well, you need to honor this limitation. Perhaps the team has opted to follow *Robert's Rules of Order*. In such a case, you need to be familiar with these rules so the meeting can run more smoothly.

Leaders: When you think of leaders, you may think of corporate executives, government officials, or union organizers. However, leaders come from all walks of life, as the following example illustrates.

Ginger Dosedel is a self-described military brat and the wife of an Air Force officer. But she never thought she'd turn her living room into a makeshift military depot, that is, until her 12-year-old son Mike spoke up.

"He saw the soldiers on television in a hospital gown, and he told me, 'Mom, you should sew for them—they need someone to sew for them,'" recalls Dosedel.

Mike knew firsthand his mom would be up to the job. He's a survivor of a rare bone cancer, and periodically needs surgery to help his right leg grow to the proper length. Over the course of many surgeries, Ginger has altered his pants and shorts to accommodate the special brace he occasionally must wear.

"People don't look at you as much when you have something that covers it," says Mike.

Mike got to know some injured troops during his last hospital stay at Walter Reed Army Medical Center in Washington. He figured they would appreciate the tailored clothes, too. And that's how Sew Much Comfort was born.

Sew Much Comfort now has over 1,000 volunteers working together to advance Ginger's effort. (Jordan, 2006, pp. 1–2)

This story of Ginger Dosedel and her volunteer organization is an amazing example of teamwork (figure 8.6). The enthusiasm of one individual inspired hundreds to commit their time and resources to a worthy cause that continues to enrich the lives of others.

You may not find yourself in a leadership role with effects as far reaching as those of Ginger Dosedel, but you certainly can find plenty of opportunities to cultivate your leadership skills.

If you ever participated in a team project at school, served on a problem-solving committee at work, or volunteered with a local community group, you were on fertile ground for experiencing the responsibilities of leadership.

Some leaders are designated. These individuals are assigned their role, frequently because of their status, experience, or expertise. Other leaders emerge

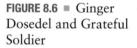

FIGURE 8.6 ■ Ginger Dosedel and Grateful Soldier

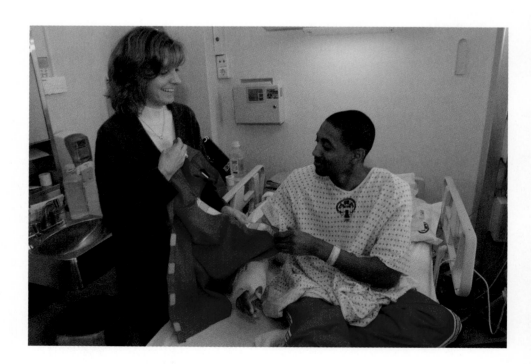

from within the group or team. These leaders who surface naturally may have a particularly strong commitment to the team's goal; they might display effective communication skills; they possibly reveal special talents that solicit confidence from the other team members. Finally, certain teams find their members sharing leadership tasks where all participants accept responsibility for the efficient functioning of the group.

In addition, you will find that regardless of the kind of leadership that operates within a group, the tasks expected of a leader are fairly consistent.

First, as a leader, you will set meeting agendas and see to it that these agendas are distributed to the other members in advance of the meeting. These meeting agendas typically include when and where the meeting will take place, what topics will be discussed and the order in which they will be discussed, how much time will be allotted for each topic, and who will be attending the meeting.

Second, you need to encourage participation. To do so, you must often raise questions to initiate discussion, call on specific members to make contributions, and draw out members who tend to be more hesitant to speak in the group. In addition, make sure that all members are given equal opportunity to voice their ideas and opinions freely and without censure.

Third, keep the discussion on track. In order to accomplish this responsibility, you want to make sure that members stick to the agenda and may appoint a timekeeper to assure that all agenda items are covered during the meeting. If the discussion strays from the topic at hand, you need to adeptly steer the discussion back in the right direction to avoid wasting valuable time.

Fourth, clarify and summarize frequently. During the course of discussion, many different ideas and viewpoints may be voiced. A skillful leader is

Encourage Participation

able to paraphrase this information to verify understanding for the group and to provide a smooth transition to the next topic of discussion.

Fifth, facilitate problem solving. Much of the work that takes place within a workplace team involves problem solving. Successful leaders are able to lead the team through a logical, systematic sequence of steps that ensure satisfactory resolution of the problems the team is facing.

Sixth, bring closure to the meeting. A skillful leader is able to wrap up the meeting with a quick summary of the team's accomplishments, to identify what issues still need to be addressed, and to set the next meeting time so members can plan their schedules accordingly.

Problem-Solving Skills

How a team decides to solve problems is largely dependent upon the nature of the problem as well as the type of relationships the members have with each other. Although several strategies are available for problem solving, take a look at one of the most versatile methods of problem solving called the reflective approach (figure 8.7). This approach requires the full participation of all members and involves an attempt to reach a consensus. The seven steps of this process are not new. In fact, they have been in use for more than half a century and were originally developed by John Dewey.

The first step is to **define the problem.** Before you and your team can even think about resolutions, all members need to have a clear understanding of the problem they are facing. For example, if your team has been asked to develop an employee training program for new computer software to streamline the monthly inventory, the members clearly have a two-part problem: What is the best instructional method to provide this training? And what specific information needs to be included in the training?

The second step is to **analyze the problem.** This step demands that you and the other participants explore the problem in greater depth to determine its scope. Oftentimes, this step requires some outside research or investigation before the problem can be explored from all angles. In the case of the software-training program discussed earlier, team members may discover that this new software is somewhat challenging to use for some of the employees. They might also determine that a significant number of senior employees are resistant to the new program when they have been using a simpler program for so many years. Both of these issues need to be considered when the team moves on to a discussion of possible solutions to the problem.

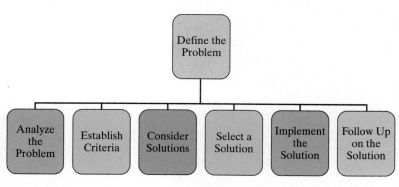

FIGURE 8.7 ■ Problem Solving

The third step is to **establish criteria for a solution.** Here your team needs to prepare a list of requirements a solution must meet. For instance, the software training must be done outside normal working hours; certain cost restraints of

Consider Possible
Solutions

the training must be kept in view; follow-up support must be made available after the training for employees who need it; the approach selected must be persuasive enough to "win over" those employees resistant to change, etc.

The fourth step is to **consider possible solutions.** This step is where brainstorming takes place, and you and your team members are able to exercise some creativity. The goal of brainstorming is to generate as many solutions as possible, keeping in mind the criteria that were established in step three. As members suggest solutions, these solutions can be jotted down or typed into a laptop. It is important that all solutions volunteered by members be acknowledged without any criticism or evaluation at this point. Members will have time to reflect on the viability of proposed solutions in the next step. You will note that the software-training program involves a two-part problem (i.e., what instructional method to use and what information to include in the training). Consequently, when considering possible solutions, members would do well to create two separate brainstormed lists, one for each part of the problem. Alternatively, you and the team may even want to cycle through this seven-step process entirely with one part of the problem only and then return to the start of the cycle for the second part of the problem.

The fifth step is to **select a solution.** Now your team is ready to examine the solutions that were generated in step four. To begin, you and your members need to weigh each suggestion on the basis of the criteria cited in step three. For example, if one suggestion proposes that the company use DVDs to train the employees, the team might collectively decide that a hands-on approach would be better for all trainees. In addition, the team might decide that two or more of the proposed solutions be combined. Consequently, the team may opt to combine the suggestion for a hands-on approach (suggestion one) along with the use of a "buddy system" (suggestion two) so that employees with less computer experience are paired up with a more experienced employee for hands-on training.

The sixth step is to **implement the solution.** This step occurs only after your team has a detailed plan for putting its proposed solution or combination of solutions into effect. In some cases, the team itself will actually implement the plan, assigning specific tasks to individual team members, establishing time lines for implementation, and so on. However, with the computer software training, your team will more likely be expected to submit a detailed plan to management for implementation.

The seventh and final step is **follow up on the solution.** This step requires either your team or management to evaluate the success of the solution after it has been implemented. Employee feedback forms would be an excellent way to assess employee satisfaction in response to the software training. Based on these responses, the team or management could make adjustments in the training, if necessary, to ensure even greater success in the future.

Share Team Results

One final tool that your team needs is a way of keeping records of its work as the work progresses. Since most teams will meet routinely until they have reached their goals, they will want to document what takes place at each meeting for the benefit of themselves and perhaps those outside the group, such as management or even other teams.

The primary vehicle for this kind of communication is meeting minutes. This form of communication typically keeps record of the following information: the date, place, and time of the meeting; a list of members present and sometimes those absent; a list of topics that were discussed; a brief description of decisions made and/or follow-up actions required; the date of the next meeting; the time the meeting adjourned; and a signature of the member who prepared the minutes.

Your team might appoint an official recorder to take meeting minutes. In other instances, this duty will be rotated among the members. After the meeting, the recorder will usually type the minutes on the computer, print copies for all who need them, and then distribute them for review. Some teams will have a laptop computer available during the meeting so that minutes can be entered into the computer by the recorder.

Whoever prepares the minutes for your team should keep them clear, concise, accurate, and easy to read. Typically, boldface headings are used to separate key issues the team discussed. The information is single-spaced within paragraphs and double-spaced between them.

The best way to understand a typical format for meeting minutes is to examine the sample in figure 8.8.

As you can see from the chapter you have just read, teams play a vital role in today's workplace, along with providing many benefits. However, in order

Wellness Team Meeting
April 14, 2009
Conference Center Room B

Members Present:

Sara Alby	Jeff Bogart
Randy Carter	Sue Frazier
Karen Olson	Martin Peterson
Robert Wilson	

The meeting of the Wellness Team began at 9:45 A.M. and was chaired by Karen Olson. The agenda was reviewed, and members agreed to the time allotments for each topic of discussion.

Company Health Fair: Robert Wilson reported that the company health fair would take place on May 18 in the Conference Center Auditorium. He stated that employees, their families, and the community would have access to a variety of free screenings including blood pressure, cholesterol, vision, and hearing, etc. Local area health care providers are also being scheduled to do thirty-minute presentations at various intervals during the course of the fair. To date, Dr. Richard Weber, a local chiropractor, has volunteered to discuss proper lifting techniques to reduce back injuries. Nurse practitioner Sandy Christel has agreed to speak on ways to relieve workplace stress. Tom Kendall, a fitness trainer, will talk about getting in shape for the summer. Robert informed the team that he would let them know more about community organizations that would have booths at the fair by the next meeting.

Stress Management Speaker: Sue Frazier reported that the stress management speaker who spoke to employees last month was well-received. One hundred ten employees attended the lunch-hour presentation. Feedback forms indicated that employees would welcome more special programs like this in the future. Sue asked the team to think about other topics of interest for such programs and to bring back ideas for the next meeting.

Hazardous Waste Disposal: Randy Carter reported that the State has issued new guidelines for disposal of hazardous industrial waste. He said that those guidelines are available in the Health and Safety Office for employees who need copies for their departments.

Smoking Cessation Classes: Sara Alby reported that June 12 is the company "Smoke Out" Day. All smokers are encouraged to quit for a day. Those who are interested in remaining smoke-free can sign up for a series of three smoking cessation classes offered by the public health department. These classes are free to all employees, and the first one will take place in Conference Center Room C from 4:00–5:00 P.M. beginning June 12. The participants will decide on subsequent class meetings.

Next Meeting:
The next meeting is scheduled for 9:45 A.M. in Conference Center Room A on July 16.

Meeting Adjourned at 11:00 A.M.

Respectfully Submitted,

Jeff Bogart

FIGURE 8.8 ■ Meeting Minutes

to function effectively, team organization requires careful thought and planning. Both members and leaders must be aware of the skills and responsibilities required to ensure a collaborative environment and a successful outcome to the team effort. Although problems are an unavoidable part of group participation, using the reflective approach can resolve issues before they become unmanageable. Finally, sharing the results of a team's efforts through meeting minutes offers a permanent log of the hard work and personal satisfaction that is the outcome of committed members.

Review Questions

1. Give an example of each of the five factors that can enhance team performance.
2. Describe the seven-step problem-solving strategy based on the ideas of John Dewey.
3. List the information required for accurate meeting minutes.
4. Name four of the positive participation skills required of team members.
5. List four responsibilities of team leaders.
6. Give an example of three of the responsibilities that team members have.
7. Name the steps in the team organization process.
8. After a team is organized, it will go through several stages. List the five stages.

Key Terms and Concepts

Accountability   183
Analyze the Problem   190
Capable Team Members   181
Clear Goals   180
Collaborative Climate   182
Commitment to Excellence   181
Consider Possible Solutions   191
Define the Problem   190
Determining a Team Assessment Method   186
Enthusiasm   184
Establish Criteria for a Solution   190

Follow Up on the Solution   192
Form Stage   182
Identifying Roles   186
Implement the Solution   192
Meeting Minutes   193
Methods of Conflict Resolution   186
Norm Stage   182
Outside Recognition   181
Perform Stage   183
Recruiting Members   185
Reflective Approach   190
Respectfulness   184

Select a Solution   191
Selecting a Meeting Format   186
Six Sigma   177
Spirit of Cooperation   184
Storm Stage   183
TQM   177
Training the Members   185
Trustworthiness   184
Willingness to Resolve Conflicts   184
Work Stage   182

Web Activities

- NASCAR fans and/or firefighters in training may enjoy the article Chief Mike Chiaramonte, a thirty-five-year member of the Lynbrook (N.Y.) Fire Department, has posted at http://firechief.com/volunteers/firefighting_nascar_teach_us/.
- PsychTest.com offers several self-assessments to gauge your Team vs. Individual Orientation and your ability to contribute in a team setting with its Team Roles Test at http://www.psychtests.com/tests/alltests.html.
- The jackpot for team resources may be found at "Teamwork Links: selected reviews of teamwork websites" at http://reviewing.co.uk/toolkit/teams-and-teamwork.htm.

Assignments

ASSIGNMENT 8.1: PARTICIPATION STYLE SELF-ANALYSIS

As you might imagine, workplace teams can be comprised of many diverse individuals. This diversity can be related to one's position within the company, educational background, gender, race, ethnicity, and so on. In addition, team members can also represent different styles of participation. Those among you who have participated in any kind of group or team setting know that some members like to "take charge." Others prefer to sit back and watch things happen. Some are outstanding critical thinkers who carefully scrutinize all the ideas that are generated in the group. Others are socially outgoing and good at maintaining group harmony. The list of these participation styles is probably endless, and all of these styles can offer valuable contributions to the effectiveness of the group or team.

This self-analysis exercise is designed to have you, as well as your team members, determine your predominant participation style. Knowing your own style and those of your teammates can enable the entire team to capitalize on one another's strengths and compensate for one another's weaknesses.

Directions: To complete this self-analysis, read the groups of statements that follow. For each group, select the characteristic that most applies to you by checking the H, A, O, or M. Although more than one characteristic may apply, choose the one that comes closest to describing your behavior in a group.

When you are finished with the self-analysis, tally your score and read the explanation of what your score says about your participation style. Finally, take some time for all of your team members to share their results with one another.

When getting started with a team:

It's most important to get to know my teammates. ____H

It's most important to have a clear vision of the team's purpose. ____A

It's most important to have the team set up a work schedule. ____O

It's most important to get down to business as quickly as possible. ____M

When working together with a team:

It's most important that we all get along with each other. ____H

It's most important that we think logically before making decisions. ____A

It's most important that we use our time wisely. ____O

It's most important that we remain enthusiastic about our work. ____M

When considering ideas with a team:

It's most important that all members have a chance to share ideas. ____H

It's most important that all ideas are subject to critical thinking. ____A

It's most important that we use a systematic order of discussion. ____O

It's most important that we foster creative ideas. ____M

When handling conflicts with a team:

It's most important that we resolve those conflicts harmoniously. ____H

It's most important that we consider all the facts first. ____A

It's most important that we follow a problem-solving strategy. ____O

It's most important that we resolve conflicts quickly. ____M

When attempting to feel personal satisfaction with a team:

It's important to have established positive relationships with members. ____H

It's important to have done our work with careful attention to detail. ____A

It's important to have done our work in an orderly, time-efficient way. ____O

It's important to feel energized by our accomplishments. ____M

Now that you have completed the self-analysis, tally the number of times you chose each of the various answers:

H ____   A ____   O ____   M ____

Most of you should have a predominant score in one of these four categories. Read on for a description of these participation styles.

H = Harmonizers: This group of participants tends to be outgoing and to thrive on developing satisfying interpersonal relationships. Consequently, harmonizers are eager to establish rapport with their teammates, maintain harmony within the group, encourage all members to share their ideas, and resolve conflicts amicably. However, the harmonizers' tendency to be very sociable can sidetrack them from the work that needs to be accomplished. In addition, their gregarious nature may put some members off, especially those who are more reserved by nature.

A = Analyzers: This group of participants is represented by those who are logical, critical thinkers. Analyzers want to know what the team is expected to do and pride themselves on their ability to think clearly and logically. They also tend to be attentive to detail and prefer to solve problems by carefully considering all of the facts. Due to their analytical nature, these individuals may appear to be cold and distant, especially to harmonizers. Also, their linear way of thinking may be frustrating to those team members who are more creative thinkers.

O = Organizers: This group of participants is characterized by those who are highly efficient. They prefer to operate on a set schedule, using time wisely. Therefore, they feel most productive when meetings are conducted in an orderly, predictable fashion. They also like to solve problems systematically. Organizers are also good at keeping the team "on track" by sticking to the set agenda. Because of their highly efficient nature, organizers may become impatient with those who take a more relaxed approach to their work. In addition, they may lack needed flexibility when it comes to adjusting meeting schedules or agendas.

M = Motivators: This group of participants is highly enthusiastic, energetic, and eager to work! Motivators are also creative thinkers and innovators. They are always on the lookout for doing things in new and better ways. When it comes to conflicts, motivators want to resolve them quickly in order to return to the task at hand. However, due to their somewhat overly zealous nature, motivators may be impulsive in their decision making. Also, their high energy might be agitating to others on the team who are more low-key.

ASSIGNMENT 8.2: SELF-ANALYSIS OF TEAMWORK

Directions: After you have worked for a period of time with an actual workplace team or in a team with your classmates, take a few moments to reflect on your experience by completing the following evaluation form. Rank the statements as follows: **1 = Yes; 2 = Partially; 3 = No.** When you have completed the form, tabulate your score and determine your score's value.

1	2	3	1. The team was clear about its intended purpose (i.e., what members were expected to accomplish).
1	2	3	2. The team encouraged open discussion about how the work should be divided so that all members were satisfied.
1	2	3	3. The team established a work schedule so all members knew what they were expected to do and by when.
1	2	3	4. All of the members came prepared for the work that needed to be done each time they met so the time was used productively.
1	2	3	5. The team found a style of leadership that all members were comfortable with, whether that leadership was provided by one member or shared among the members.
1	2	3	6. The team was able to work out any conflicts that may have occurred among members so that the team never lost sight of its goal.
1	2	3	7. All members were respectful of others on the team.

1	2	3	8. All members were willing to help one another out whenever necessary.
1	2	3	9. Team members felt confident about all of the work they had accomplished at the completion of their task.
1	2	3	10. The members seemed personally satisfied with their team experience.
			Total points

Scoring Key:

10–12 Excellent
13–15 Good
16–21 Average
22+ Needs Improvement

ASSIGNMENT 8.3: INTERVIEW A WORK TEAM

Directions: This activity is designed to help you gather information from an existing workplace team and to identify some of the ways in which members work together to achieve their goals. Interview someone who currently participates in a workplace team, maybe a co-worker, family member, or close friend. Use the following questions to structure your interview. Based on your interview prepare a two- to 3-minute oral report of your findings to the class. Turn in a typed copy of the interview to your instructor.

Name of Company _____
Team Name _____
Interviewee _____ Date _____

1. What is the purpose of the team?
2. How was the team formed (e.g., Were members assigned, or did they volunteer to participate)?
3. What kind of diversity is represented among the team members (e.g., different positions within the company, different racial and/or ethnic groups, etc.)?
4. What kind of training in team building did the members receive?
5. Does the team have a designated leader, or is leadership shared among the members?

6. Aside from the role of leader, do members hold any other roles (e.g., recorder of minutes, timekeeper, etc.)?
7. How frequently does the team meet?
8. How are meetings conducted (e.g., by following an agenda, using *Robert's Rules of Order*, etc.)?
9. How are team conflicts resolved?
10. What is the overall level of satisfaction with the team experience?

ASSIGNMENT 8.4: TEAM ARTICLE REVIEW

Directions: Find a two- to three-page magazine or Internet article on teamwork. Make a copy of the article of your choice. Read the article carefully; note the central idea (thesis), main points, and supporting facts. Prepare a typed summary of the article's content and a personal reaction to it. Prepare a two- to three-minute oral report of your summary and reaction for your class. Submit a copy of the article and summary to your instructor.

Article Title _____
Publication Title _____
Date of Publication _____
Author _____

Summary:

Reaction:

ASSIGNMENT 8.5: CASE STUDY: A PROBLEM-SOLVING EXERCISE

Directions: The following exercise is designed to give you practice solving problems using the seven-step reflective approach explained in this chapter. Your instructor will divide the class into three teams. Each team will be assigned one of the following problems. The teams will be responsible for completing the following steps:

Define the problem.

Analyze the problem.

Establish criteria for a solution.

Consider possible solutions.

Select a solution.

Implement the solution (i.e., explain how the solution could be implemented).

Follow up on the solution.

Record the information your team generates as you complete these steps. Review the sample presented on pp. 190–192 to determine what data is required for each step.

You will be given twenty minutes to complete this process. Then each team will present its findings to the rest of the class.

Problem #1

Your company has been concerned about the increasing rise in insurance premiums. Under the present health care plan, employees currently pay 10 percent of the insurance premiums, and the company covers the rest. Employees are free to seek care from the doctors of their choice and pay a $250 deductible, after which the insurance company pays the remainder of any medical charges for the rest of the calendar year. Your company has informed employees that continued rises in premiums will result in employees having to pay a greater percentage of those premiums, along with a higher deductible. Your team has been assigned to investigate possible solutions to this health care cost problem.

Problem #2

A new hire in your department is a female working in a traditionally male-dominated career field. This new employee has recently been complaining about some of the calendars and "artwork" other male employees have hanging in their work cubicles. She has commented that these materials are sexist and a form of harassment. The male employees feel they have every right to display materials of their choice in their own work areas. The department supervisor has expressed concern that this new female may file sexual harassment charges unless this issue is addressed. Your team has been assigned to come up with possible solutions that will satisfy all of the parties concerned.

Problem #3

Due to hard economic times, your company has recently lost a contract from one of its major clients. The loss of this contract is likely to result in less work for your company. Consequently, your company's management has been hinting at the possibility of layoffs. Management has asked your team to determine if there are any other solutions to this work shortage aside from layoffs. Management has said that they will be open to any reasonable alternatives your team may identify.

References

Camp, B. (1997). *Effective workplace writing*. Chicago: Irwin Mirror Press.

Jordan, R. (2006, April 14). Tailoring clothes for the troops. *NBC News*. Retrieved March 20, 2008, from http://www.msnbc.msn.com/id/12303651/

Molloy, W. F. (2000). A simple formula for success. *Team Building News*. Retrieved March 20, 2008, from http://www.teambuildingnews.com/ideas/ideas.html

Parker, G. (2000, January 5). *New teams in the workplace*, reprinted from U.S.1. Retrieved June 14, 2001, from http://www.glennparker.com/Freebees/new-teams.html

Schaenzer, A. (2007, October 26). Local woman is Flight for Life's 25,000th airlift. *The Reporter*. Retrieved March 20, 2008, from http://www.fdlreporter.com/apps/pbcs.dll/article?AID=/20071026/FON0101/710260440/1985

Six Sigma. (2000–2003). *Six Sigma – What Is Six Sigma?* Retrieved November 24, 2003, from http://www.isixsigma.com/sixsigma/six_sigma.asp

Chapter **9**

Preparing the Informative Presentation

"The best way to sound like you know what you're talking about is to know what you're talking about."

Unknown

Informative Presentations Are Important

Step Right Up
Your Room Is Waiting For You

One of People's Greatest Fears Is of Public Speaking.
Source: The Eggleston Group.

Stephen Eggleston, author of an article titled "Fear of Public Speaking" (2005), described his earliest experience facing an audience: "My first public humiliation came when, as a top-heavy mushroom in the second grade play, I fell off the stage. I hid for weeks. Kids are more cruel than any other species of animal, since they tell the truth. Surely I would never be a whole human being again. I might as well have died. Two days later, all of the other kids had forgotten the whole thing" (p. 1).

Eggleston's performance as a mushroom was just the first of many public presentations he was destined to give. Further in the article, he commented, "The real great awakening came quite a few years later when I realized that umpteen million years from now, when the sun grows to burn the Earth to a cinder, that stupid mushroom is not very important in the cosmic sense" (Eggleston, 2005, p. 1).

"I stopped worrying about what people would think about me when I realized how seldom people think about anyone but themselves. There is no real trick to public speaking; there is only confidence. If you cannot begin by having confidence in yourself, you must begin by having confidence in your message" (Eggleston, 2005, p. 1).

Eggleston went on to become a highly successful public speaker. "His seminars, keynotes and training programs on presentations, speaking, management, quality, technology, and the Internet are popular among small business and Fortune 100 companies alike" (Eggleston, 2005, p. 3).

Although you may not have the opportunity to speak publicly on a regular basis, you will discover that in today's workplace, the ability to communicate effectively is one of the most important skills employees can possess.

Joe Grenier, representing Toastmasters International—a worldwide organization that teaches effective public speaking and leadership skills—commented that the work Toastmasters does "has never been more important."

"A lot of young people have spent a lot of time in front of the computer, and they don't have the social skills to make a presentation to a lot of people," said Grenier, a product support manager for Caterpillar, Inc., in Peoria, Illinois. "But as they go into the working world, many are being thrown into those roles. They need the skills, and they find themselves lacking" (Hogan, 2005, p. 1).

Not surprisingly, the kind of presentations Grenier is speaking about are more likely to intimidate you than other forms of communication,

"I'm a little nervous ... you see,
I didn't expect to be thrown to the wolves."

especially if you find your public speaking skills lacking. "According to *The Book of Lists,* the fear of speaking in public is the #1 fear of all fears. The fear of dying is #7! Over 41% of people have some fear or anxiety dealing with speaking in front of groups" (Laskowski, 1996, p. 1).

It is because of this prevalent fear of public speaking that an organization like Toastmasters International has become so popular (figure 9.1). Toastmasters clubs meet in most major cities of the United States at different times and locations during the week and offer a supportive and affordable way for those interested to practice their public speaking skills. "There are currently over 230,000 members of 11,500 clubs located in 92 different countries throughout the world, and the organization is still growing." In *The Toastmasters International Guide to Successful Speaking,* authors Slutsky and Aun state that, "Over 3 million people have gone through the Toastmasters program. Clubs generally meet weekly." They also point out, "Some clubs meet inside an organization and are distinguished as corporate clubs, including IBM, Apple Computers, AT&T, Bank of America, Coca-Cola Co., Disneyland, Eastman Kodak, Hewlett Packard Co., Kraft, Inc., Rockwell International, Levi Strauss & Co., the United States Armed Forces, and hundreds of others" (Slutsky & Aun, 1997, pp. x–xi).

Slutsky and Aun go on to point out, "There is perhaps no greater skill that can help you build your career or business better than effective public speaking. Whether you're speaking to a small committee of ten decision makers or an arena filled with 10,000 future leaders, knowing how to present your point of view persuasively can make the difference between merely surviving or thriving in a vastly competitive environment" (Slutsky & Aun, 1997, p. 1).

Once you have been hired, the forms that your workplace communication can take are many and varied. These forms may include resolving a customer complaint, working collaboratively within a team, or asking for a raise. However, workplace communication is not limited to interpersonal or group settings alone. As Grenier pointed out, you may be expected to speak more formally by delivering presentations.

FIGURE 9.1 ■ Toastmasters
International Emblem

Informative speeches are one of the most common presentations you are likely to encounter in the workplace. Introducing a new product to potential customers, providing on-the-job training to a group of new employees, presenting a progress report for your team to several managers, or building company/community relations by addressing a local Rotary Club are all examples of informative presentations you might be called upon to make.

However, you might find yourself in a position to deliver an informative presentation outside of the workplace as well. Think for a moment about the classes you are currently taking that require informative presentations. Perhaps as a student in law enforcement, you must deliver an informative speech to your classmates on Homeland Security or crisis intervention; if you are enrolled in culinary management, you may deliver an informative speech on choosing fresh herbs to enhance meal preparation; as an interior design student, you may explain a room makeover that you created, complete with floor-cover samples and swatches of window treatment fabrics.

In addition, as a participant in community or church organizations, you might be called upon to speak informatively. For example, if you are a volunteer firefighter in your town, you may be asked to deliver fire prevention tips to local schoolchildren. Possibly you belong to a garden club where you present information on growing daylilies to other club members. You may be asked to teach a Sunday school class or offer a treasurer's report for the annual church picnic. You can see that informative speaking opportunities can come in many different forms, depending on your involvement in outside activities.

So that you can count yourself among those who are confident about speaking informatively in public, whether at work, at school, or in your community, the remainder of the chapter is designed to get you started. In the sections that follow, you will learn more about identifying types of informative presentations, selecting appropriate topics, analyzing your audience, determining your specific purpose, and formulating your central idea.

Types of Informative Presentations

As mentioned earlier, informative speeches are one of the most common types of presentations you are likely to deliver. Whenever you explain, instruct, or report, you are speaking informatively. Although informative speeches can be classified in a variety of ways, consider the following four categories: tools/mechanisms, processes or procedures, incidents, and ideas. Let's take a closer look at each of them.

TOOLS/MECHANISMS

This type of informative presentation focuses primarily on inanimate objects that serve a particular function. Although the distinction between tools and mechanisms can be somewhat confusing, you might find it helpful to think of tools as handheld devices that you use to accomplish some kind of work.

FIGURE 9.2 ■ Adjustable Wrench and Blackberry

Hammers, wrenches, trowels, stethoscopes, handcuffs, and cleavers are all examples of tools used in various occupational settings. In contrast to tools, mechanisms can be more complex, with multiple parts. Examples of mechanisms include food processors, heart monitors, computers, brake lathes, and so on (figures 9.2 and 9.3).

Regardless of whether you are speaking about tools or mechanisms, you will probably include the following information in your presentation:

1. A physical description (including size, shape, dimensions, parts)
2. A functional description (explaining what the tool/mechanism is used to accomplish)
3. An operational description (describing how the tool/mechanism works)

Informative speeches about tools or mechanisms help users better understand the composition and purpose of these devices. You could deliver this type of informative presentation to employees or customers who might be using the device you are explaining.

PROCESSES OR PROCEDURES

This type of informative speech explains how something works (processes) or how something is done (procedures). Let's take a brief look at the distinction between the two.

Process speeches aim to help the audience understand how something works or happens, particularly complex processes. Nurses frequently have to explain to patients and their families how a specific diagnostic test will be performed. Both patients and their relatives will feel more at ease, for instance, when they understand how magnetic resonance imaging (MRI) works prior to a scan being done. Chefs may need to explain to their kitchen staff how foodborne illnesses occur in order to ensure safety of the patrons they serve (figure 9.4).

In contrast to process speeches, procedure presentations instruct the audience step by step so the audience members can perform the procedure themselves. This approach is the typical "how to do it" speech.

FIGURE 9.3 ■ Food Processor
Source: Used with permission from www.FixItClub.com

You will deliver a procedure speech whenever you provide on-the-job training to co-workers on a new piece of equipment or machinery. Physical therapy assistants may instruct a patient and his or her family on specific exercises to do following a workplace injury. Instructors may clarify a procedure for handling plagiarism (figure 9.6).

INCIDENTS

Incident speeches provide the audience with information about a particular event or occurrence. The incidents you speak about could be relatively recent, or they may represent a historical event. The intent of this type of informative speech is to re-create the incident for the audience to experience. Following is a list of details that incident speeches often contain.

1. A timeline of the incident (what happened first, next, then)
2. A description of the physical setting in which the incident occurred
3. A description of the people who were involved
4. An explanation of the results following the incident

Police officers are required to provide courtroom testimony of incidents in which arrests occurred. Such testimony can offer considerable challenges to officers since the court appearance may not take place until months or even years after the arrest. Even so, the officer must give a factual account of the incident under oath.

In one of our classrooms, a panel of students did an informative presentation of the 9-11 incident (figure 9.5) in which the panelists recounted who were the terrorists, who were the victims, and what happened from start to finish. Cleverly, at the end of the presentation, panel members had classmates in the audience report one by one where they had been and what they had been doing when they heard the news about the Twin Towers. All of the audience members were able to recall exactly. This presentation underscored that such a tragic incident would not likely be forgotten for a long time.

IDEAS

The final type of informative speech centers on ideas. Here you have the opportunity to share concepts, beliefs, attitudes, and opinions with your audience. Now remember that when sharing ideas, you are not attempting to persuade your audience to think the way you do. Rather, you are sharing a more personal side of yourself with your listeners.

For example, maybe you have chosen to snack on more healthful food. As a result, you decide to share with your classmates different snacks you've been eating instead of the more common candy bars, chips, and soft drinks. You could also tell them how these new choices have made you feel.

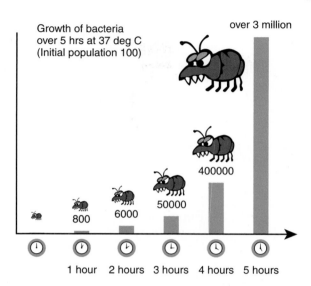

Growth of bacteria over 5 hrs at 37 deg C (Initial population 100)

over 3 million

400000

50000

6000

800

1 hour 2 hours 3 hours 4 hours 5 hours

FIGURE 9.4 ■ Food Bacteria *Source:* Based on Hanna Instruments Catalogue, volume 27, p. 13.3.

FIGURE 9.5 ■ Aftermath of 9-11

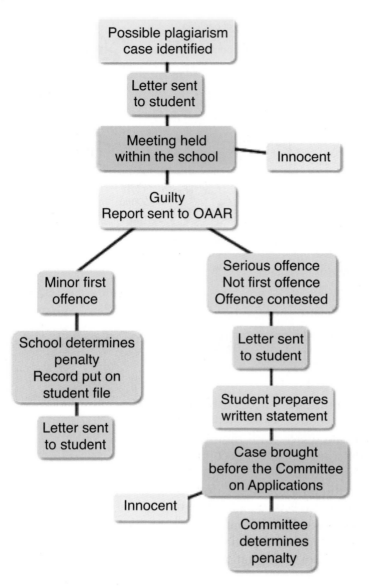

FIGURE 9.6 ■ Procedures for Handling Plagiarism *Source:* The University of Leeds.

Maybe you deliver an informative speech about some volunteering you did at a homeless shelter and how the experience impacted your life. Possibly you inform your audience of the ways a "can-do" attitude helped you overcome some challenges in your personal life.

Of all four types of informative speeches, the ideas speech comes closest to persuasion. However, if you maintain your primary focus on delivering information, you will resist the temptation to convince the audience about your ideas.

Analyzing the Audience

No matter what type of informative speech you have the opportunity to present, a key step in your preparation process is analyzing your audience. Experts in the field of public speaking tend to agree that the single most-frequent question listeners have when they come to a presentation is, "How will this information be of value to us?" In other words, your audience wants to know why they should take the time to listen to you. It is your responsibility, therefore, to make the speech relevant to the audience's needs, concerns, and interests. Consequently, you will need to spend some time finding out about your audience.

To begin this process, you will want to determine the demographic composition of your listeners. **Demographic** characteristics are observable or measurable. They include factors such as age, race, ethnicity, gender, socio-economic status, and so on. Market researchers rely on demographic data to identify target audiences; census data is assessed on the basis of demographic considerations; pollsters make projections from the demographic information they solicit.

However, there is more to your audience members than their vital statistics. Characteristics such as attitudes, interests, values, likes, and dislikes can be equally important considerations. These factors are sometimes referred to as **psychographics** and may be less obvious than demographic traits.

Although personal observation can be a helpful starting point for audience analysis, many speakers administer surveys to their audience members ahead of time to determine both demographic and psychographic dimensions of their listeners. The following sample audience analysis form is what our students use as they begin their speech preparation process.

AUDIENCE ANALYSIS FORM

Discuss the following questions with several members of your classroom audience:

- What do you already know about my topic?
- What is your attitude toward my topic?
- What would you expect to hear in a speech about my topic?
- What would you most like to learn about my topic?
- How could you use information about my topic?
- Are there any terms or concepts that you might find confusing about my topic?
- What would make my topic interesting to you?
- Are there any issues related to my topic that you find offensive or that would make you uncomfortable?

Once you have collected some data on your audience, keep in mind that all of the remaining choices you make about your speech should be based upon the composition of your listeners. In other words, your goal is to create what is called an "audience-centered" speech. This term means that all of your decisions—from the way you approach your topic, to the method of organization you use, to the types of visuals you design—should be based upon your audience. For if you were speaking about on-the-job safety to a group of employees, you might want to include information about how to avoid injury, what to do if an injury occurs, and how to qualify for compensation during recuperation from the injury. In contrast, if you were speaking about this same subject to managers, you would want to discuss how to spot and correct dangerous working conditions, how to provide safety training for employees, and how to avoid liability for employee injuries.

Once you have an understanding of your audience, you are ready to identify what is commonly called your specific purpose.

Determining the Specific Purpose

Specific purposes identify the desired audience response at the conclusion of your speech. In other words, what do you want your listeners to know, think, or do after they have heard your presentation?

Although you do not actually state the specific purpose in the context of your speech, you use this statement to give direction to the development and organization of your information.

To be effective, a specific purpose statement should meet the following guidelines:

1. It should be a complete sentence.
2. It should contain only one key idea.
3. It should be stated in measurable terms.

Let's take a brief look at each of these guidelines.

Complete Sentence: Typically, specific purpose statements begin like this: "At the end of my speech, my audience will. . . ." Then you supply the desired audience response. For example, "At the end of my speech, my audience will be able to list the four steps for safe lifting (figure 9.7)." This statement is a complete sentence, unlike the following, "The four steps for safe lifting."

One Key Idea: You'll notice that the specific purpose stated previously has only one key idea that includes the steps required for safe lifting. If the speaker had stated, "At the end of my speech, my audience will be able to list the four steps for safe lifting and also identify several exercises for strengthening the back," he or she would have more than one key idea.

Measurable Terms: When you state your specific purpose in measurable terms, you ensure the likelihood of reaching your speaking goal. Notice how the next example fails to express the speaker's goal in measurable terms:

"At the end of my speech, my audience will have a better understanding of safe lifting practices."

This example lacks measurable terms because the speaker would find it difficult to actually measure whether or not the audience understood safe lifting practices as a result of the speech. On the other hand, when the speaker states that the audience will "list" the four steps, now he or she has a strategy for assuring the audience's comprehension.

FIGURE 9.7 ■ Safe Lifting
Source:
www.natasafety1st.org

After you have phrased your specific purpose statement, you are ready to construct one of the most important elements of an effective presentation, your central idea, sometimes called the thesis.

Formulating the Central Idea

Think of the central idea as the core or foundation of your presentation. A central idea states, in a single sentence, the essence of the speech. It needs to be clear, concise, and focused for the audience. So important is this central idea that the effectiveness of the entire presentation is largely dependent upon it. It tells the audience what the speech is all about and prepares your listeners for the information that is to come. Here is an example: "You can take steps to protect yourself against identity theft" (figure 9.8). Notice that this central idea begins with the word "you." Phrasing a central idea in this way lets your audience know that the information is focused on them.

The central idea appears in the introduction of the speech, setting the stage for the audience and helping you to develop and organize the body of the presentation. In order to create a clear, concise central idea, you need to keep in mind the following criteria:

1. **A central idea must be expressed as a sentence.** In other words, central ideas cannot be stated as phrases or titles of a speech. Consider the following example: "How to Handle Customer Complaints." This is a phrase that could also serve as the title of a speech. However, it does not represent a sentence and is, therefore, not a central idea. Revised to form a central idea, it might sound something like this: "Handling customer complaints requires strong communication skills." As you can see in the latter example, the focus of the speech is much clearer. The audience now knows that the presentation will address the communication skills needed to handle customer complaints skillfully.

2. **A central idea should not be expressed as a question.** Questions such as "Do you know how to handle customer complaints?" might be used to arouse audience interest in the introduction of the speech, but like phrases or titles, questions do not set the stage for the specific information that is to follow.

3. **A central idea should contain only one key idea.** "Laptop computers are a convenience for business travelers, and they are also quite affordable." This example contains two key ideas. It attempts to address not only the

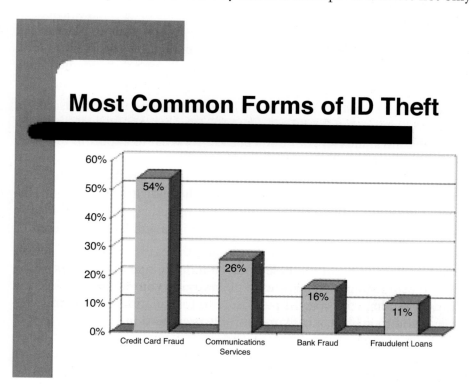

FIGURE 9.8 ■ Identity Theft
Source: http://www.ftc .gov/os/2000/07/images/ idtheft6.gif.

convenience but also the affordability of laptops. You will do better to confine your presentation to a **single key idea.** In this case, you could eliminate the part about laptops' cost and deal solely with their convenience. If, however, you really wanted to cover both issues, you could rephrase the central idea to read: "Laptop computers offer several advantages for business travelers." With this revision, the central idea still has only one key idea, the advantages. Then in the body of the speech, you might include among those advantages convenience and affordability.

4. **A central idea consists of a subject and a focus.** The **subject** of a central idea represents who or what the speech is about. "Handling customer complaints requires strong communication skills" is a speech whose subject is handling customer complaints. The **focus**, on the other hand, represents the key idea of the speech. In other words, what do you wish to emphasize about the subject? With this example, the focus is on strong communication skills. The focus allows both you and your audience to predict the main points in the body of the speech.

   Given this particular focus, you could safely assume that the rest of the speech will discuss the communication skills that employees need to handle customer complaints. It is also important that subjects and focuses be neither too general nor too specific. Consider this example: "Technological advances in the workplace have changed the way workers work." This central idea has a subject (technological advances) and a focus (changed the way workers work) that are both too general and, therefore, lack direction for both you and the audience. Consider this improved version: "Email systems have revolutionized the way workers communicate with each other."

   Notice that both the subject and the focus have been sharpened. In contrast, a central idea that is too specific leaves you with no place to go. Take this example: "The view function on email allows workers to look at a document without actually opening it." Although this statement may be true, there is little more that you could say about this function.

5. **A central idea should be stated in the introduction and the conclusion.** In the introduction, you first attempt to capture listener interest and then state the central idea so your audience knows what to expect in the body of the presentation. The central idea is stated once again in the conclusion for two reasons. First, such restatement reinforces the importance of the information you have just shared with the audience. In addition, listeners remember most what they hear last. Including the central idea in the closing remarks helps to ensure that this idea will be remembered.

In summary, keep in mind that developing the skills required to deliver effective presentations can increase your confidence and success both personally and professionally. The process of analyzing your audience, selecting a topic, determining your specific purpose, and formulating your central idea will enable you to achieve a truly memorable presentation.

Review Questions

1. List three reasons why informative presentations are important.
2. Describe four types of informative presentations you may have to give.
3. Explain why analyzing your audience is essential for your informative presentation.
4. List two types of information to be included in your audience analysis.
5. Describe three guidelines for writing an effective specific-purpose statement for your informative presentation.
6. List five guidelines for formulating the central idea of your informative presentation.

Key Terms and Concepts

Audience Analysis 207
Central Idea 208
Demographics 206

Focus 210
Psychographics 206

Specific Purpose 207
Subject 210

Web Activities

Visit the following interesting sites to find out more about informative presentations:

- http://www.genesismission.org/educate/kitchen/foodthought/Informative.pdf
- http://homepage.powerup.com.au/~mamalade/TMspeeches.htm#toinform

Find out more about Toastmasters International at their homepage:

- http://www.toastmasters.org/

See what Rick Clements has developed to promote Toastmasters International at:

- http://www.geocities.com/athens/acropolis/3558/Achiever.htm#speaking

Check out the following sites for possible informative presentation topics:

- http://www.informativespeechtopics.info/
- http://www.speech-topics-help.com/informative-speech-topics.html
- http://www.presentationhelper.co.uk/informative_speech_topic.htm

Assignments

ASSIGNMENT 9.1: BRAINSTORMING TOPICS

You've probably done brainstorming before in other classes. Brainstorming can be done alone or in small groups. The goal is to generate a pool of ideas, and in this assignment, the ideas will provide you with possible topics for an informative presentation. It can help

if you begin the brainstorming process with a framework. Try the following approach.

Directions:

1. Take a blank sheet of paper, preferably 8½ × 11, and divide it into four columns.
2. Create headings for each of the four columns. Label Column I Tools/Mechanisms, Column II Processes/

Procedures, Column III Incidents, and Column IV Ideas. Review the section in this chapter that discusses these four types of informative presentations.

Spend fifteen or twenty minutes listing possible topics under each of these headings. Try if you can to list at least ten topics under each heading. Put your list away; come back to it a day or two later, and continue adding some more topics.

Think about jobs you hold or have held, hobbies or interests you pursue, and life skills for which you have an aptitude. These can form the basis for generating a topic list. Be sure to save your list because you will be using the ideas you generated in some of the assignments that follow.

ASSIGNMENT 9.2: MAP YOUR TOPIC

Directions: For two of the topics that you listed in your Assignment 9.1, Brainstorming Topics, prepare a Mind Map (figure 9.9) to develop more connections to additional subjects. Mind maps are visual representations

of the ideas you generate. You start your map with a general topic area in the center of your paper and then branch off from there with related information. When you finish your map, you'll view at a glance a variety of topics and subtopics that can be developed into speech outlines. If you feel particularly creative, you can design your map with colored markers and pictures as you see in the following illustration. Check out the following website for more specific directions on mind-mapping: http://www.mind-mapping.co.uk/make-mind-map.htm.

ASSIGNMENT 9.3: AUDIENCE ANALYSIS

Directions: For two of the topics that you listed in your Assignment 9.1, Brainstorming Topics, prepare an Audience Analysis Survey to gather information about your audience. Include questions that will help you collect both demographic and psychographic data. Then distribute the survey to your audience as you begin the speech preparation process. After you collect

FIGURE 9.9 ■ Mind-Mapping
Source: http://www.buzan.com.au/images/ExercisesforDestressing_big.jpg.

the completed surveys, tabulate the results and use the information to help you in planning your presentation. You may want to refer back to the sample audience analysis form illustrated in this chapter to get you started.

ASSIGNMENT 9.4: SPECIFIC PURPOSE STATEMENTS

Directions: For five of the topics that you listed in your Assignment 9.1, Brainstorming Topics, write specific purpose statements that identify what you want your audience to do when you have finished your speech.

Remember, a specific purpose statement represents what you want your audience to have accomplished after they have listened to your presentation. In other words, what do you want your audience to know, think, or do by the end of your speech? Given the topic of behavior-based job interviewing, your specific purpose statement might sound something like this: *At the end of my speech, I want my audience to be able to prepare for behavior-based interview questions.*

You do not actually share your specific purpose with the audience. The specific purpose simply acts as a guide for you in determining the desired outcome of your speech.

1. _____

_____

2. _____

_____

3. _____

_____

4. _____

_____

5. _____

_____

ASSIGNMENT 9.5: WRITING CENTRAL IDEAS

The central idea or thesis is the controlling idea that identifies the essence of your speech. It contains a **subject** and a **focus**. The subject states who or what the speech is about, and the focus identifies the key information you intend to discuss about your subject. Consider this central idea: "Behavior-based job interviews require careful preparation." The subject is **behavior-based job interviews,** and the focus is the **careful preparation** required. You may find it helpful to remember that the focus predicts the main points that will be developed in the body of the speech. Note too that central ideas are always expressed as complete sentences rather than as questions or phrases.

Part A

Directions: Underline the subject once and the focus twice for each of the following central ideas.

1. New cars can be purchased with a number of expensive options.
2. Keeping physically fit takes continuous effort.
3. Many healthful benefits are provided by organic fruits and vegetables.
4. Whoever smokes cigarettes is asking for trouble.
5. The variety of disposable products available to consumers is mind boggling.

Part B

Directions: Rewrite the following phrases or questions so they become central ideas.

1. How can you become a better student?
2. The high cost of building your own home.
3. Are you aware of the benefits of regular aerobic exercise?
4. How television violence affects young children.
5. Buying a used car wisely.

Part C

Directions: Choose three central ideas from **Part A** or **Part B**, and do the following:

1. Write a specific purpose statement.
2. Write the central idea.

Specific Purpose _____

Central Idea #1 _____

Specific Purpose _____

Central Idea #2 _____

Specific Purpose _____

Central Idea #3 _____

ASSIGNMENT 9.6: THE INFORMATIVE SPEECH

In Chapters 10, 11, 12, and 13, you will be learning about additional steps in the speech preparation process. Your instructor may have you read those chapters before you begin working on a presentation of your own. However, the following informative speech assignment is presented so that you can lay the groundwork for your presentation. As you complete the upcoming chapters, you will continue your preparation until you have completed the assignment and are ready to deliver the presentation in class.

The goal of this assignment is to deliver a five- to seven-minute informative speech on a topic of your choice. You should have a number of possible topics to consider from the brainstorming list you completed earlier. You can also check out the websites listed at the end of this chapter for additional topic ideas.

Next is a list of steps for you to follow:

1. Analyze your audience.
2. Select an appropriate topic.
3. Determine your specific purpose.
4. Formulate your central idea.
5. Develop your main points.
6. Gather information to support your main points.
7. Choose effective verbal and visual supports.
8. Organize your information into an outline.
9. Create a reference page of your sources.
10. Practice your delivery.

ASSIGNMENT 9.7: CASE STUDY: TOASTMASTERS

You have read that Toastmasters International is an organization where individuals can develop and improve their public speaking skills. As a marketing student at a local community college, you realize that you will be assigned a number of presentations in your classes this semester, and you think Toastmasters might be a valuable resource for you.

Find out what Toastmasters is all about by going to the organization's website at www.toastmasters.org and then answer the following questions:

1. What is Toastmasters?
2. Why should you consider joining Toastmasters?
3. What resources are available through Toastmasters?
4. Where is the nearest Toastmasters group in your community?

References

Eggleston, S. (2005). *Fear of public speaking: Stories, myths and magic*. Retrieved March 7, 2008, from http://www.the-eggman.com/writings/fearspk1.html

Hogan, D. (2005, August 8). *Not born with a gift of gab? There's help available: Tips for public speaking*. Retrieved July 19, 2007, from http://jobs.aol.com/article/?id=20050808184609990032

Laskowski, L. (1996). *Overcoming speaking anxiety in meetings & presentations*. Retrieved June 11, 2001, from http://www.ljlseminars.com/anxiety.htm

Slutsky, J. & Aun, M. (1997). *The Toastmasters International guide to successful speaking*. Chicago: Deaborn Financial.

Chapter **10**

Organizing Informative Outlines

Learning **Objectives**

At the end of this chapter, you should be able to meet the following objectives:

1. Develop main points for your informative presentation.
2. Select a pattern of organization for your main points.
3. Create an outline for your informative presentation.
4. Identify the role of transitions in an informative presentation.

"Good order is the foundation of all good things."

Edmund Burke

Developing Main Points

Kim began her semester as a new student at a local community college. After the first week or two, she found herself struggling to keep her life organized. Between a demanding class schedule with several hours of homework each night and her part-time waitress job at Pizza Heaven, she was having a hard time keeping track of all her responsibilities. Terry, a fellow classmate and friend, suggested that Kim invest in a personal electronic organizer. He told her that he had been using one for several months and was able to stay on top of his demands at school and work. Kim decided to follow Terry's advice and found that in a few weeks, she was feeling more in control of her life too.

Interestingly, if you are having trouble getting your life organized, you can actually hire someone to help you. The National Association of Professional Organizers provides this service. If you go to their website at www.napo.net/, you can access a list of select specialty services. The organization can help you organize your home, your time, your garage sale, or your public speaking.

Although you may not seriously consider hiring a professional to help you get organized, you will likely agree that being organized makes you more efficient, eliminates unnecessary stress, and enables you to enjoy what you do.

Just as in all areas of your life, organization can increase your effectiveness as a public speaker as well. Think for a moment about a few of the best speakers you have ever heard. These individuals might have been classroom teachers, motivational presenters, or experienced politicians. One skill they all probably had in common was the ability to organize their ideas clearly.

Your task as a speaker is the same—to take the information you have gathered for your speech and structure it in a way that will enable your listeners to follow along. The best place to begin is by identifying your main points.

IDENTIFY THE MAIN POINTS

Once the central idea has been written, you can determine the main points for the body of the presentation. You will remember from Chapter 9 that a central idea contains a subject and a focus. The subject identifies your topic, and the focus states a key idea about your topic. Just as central ideas must meet these two criteria, main points have a set of criteria they must meet as well.

DEVELOPING MAIN POINTS

State main points in sentence form.

Choose between three and five main points.

Include only one idea for each main point.

Establish a direct connection with the central idea.

Make the main points parallel.

Include balanced information in all main points.

1. **State main points in sentence form.** This means that main points cannot be questions or phrases. When you express your main points as sentences, you take steps to ensure that you will be communicating a complete thought instead of a fragmented one. Let's say, for example, that your central idea states, "You can help save the life of a possible stroke victim by following three major steps."

   Main Point A: *Have the victim repeat a simple sentence.* Notice that you are informing the audience what to do, as opposed to phrasing the main point as a question or fragment: Can the victim speak? (question) or Getting the victim to speak (phrase). These latter two examples are less clear than the first one.

2. **Choose between three and five main points.** Somehow three seems to be a magic number when it comes to main points in a speech. Audiences tend to remember multiples of three most easily. Of course for topics that are quite complex, you may need to incorporate additional main points. However, try not to use more than five. If you exceed five main points, your audience is likely to have more difficulty retaining the information you present.

3. **Include only one idea for each main point.** This third guideline is especially important to guarantee clarity in your speech. For instance, you wouldn't want to have Main Point A of your speech read like this: *Have the victim read a simple sentence, and see if the victim can stick out his or her tongue.* By combining two ideas, you are likely to create some confusion for your listeners. You would be better off dividing the two into separate main points.

4. **Establish a direct connection with the central idea.** The central idea of your speech serves as a predictor of your main points. When audience members hear that they can help a possible stroke victim by following three major steps, they will be primed for an explanation of those steps in the body of your speech. Consequently, you will want to make sure that all of your main points do, in fact, develop that central idea. Including a main point such as "Strokes occur for a variety of reasons" doesn't relate to the central idea and shouldn't be included in the speech.

5. **Make the main points parallel.** When main points are parallel, they are worded similarly. Take a look at the following example of parallel structure.

(Central Idea): **Quality customer service is easy to provide.**

Main Point 1: Quality customer service includes treating the customer with respect.

Main Point 2: Quality customer service includes listening to customer needs.

Main Point 3: Quality customer service includes providing customer satisfaction.

Notice how each of these three main points begins with the words "Quality customer service includes." This setup for your main points adds style to your speech, makes the information easier to remember, and creates coherence in your outline.

6. **Include relatively balanced information in all main points.** This final guideline suggests that all of your main points be developed with the same amount of information. For example, if you spend three minutes on your first main point and less than a minute on your last two, your main points probably lack balance. If one or two of your main points are quite short, perhaps you could find a way to combine them, or maybe you have to reconsider alternative main points. Just keep in mind that when you select main points for an audience, you are basically telling your listeners that all of the main points are equally important. You communicate that importance by keeping your points balanced.

Selecting a Pattern of Organization

As an informative speaker, you must make sure that the main points in the body of your presentation are logically organized. Numerous patterns of organization can be used to give presentations a coherent structure. Some of the most common patterns of organization for informative presentations are chronological, topical, or spatial. Let's examine each.

CHRONOLOGICAL

Chronological patterns organize information in a time sequence. This pattern is typically used when the speaker is delivering a set of instructions, describing steps in a process, explaining a series of events that happened over time, or retracing history. You could use a chronological pattern to explain the steps for inserting a Foley catheter; you could use a time sequence to explain how a TASER X26 stops a suspect, or you could trace the decline of the labor movement in this country using a chronological pattern.

TOPICAL

Topical patterns divide information into logical categories or groupings. This pattern classifies your main point by types or kinds. You may describe the options for office furniture as being traditional, contemporary, or eclectic, or you could report to company employees the various choices of health care coverage: traditional major medical, PPO, HMO, or self-insured. The order of your topical listing may be from the most common to the least common (as with household fires) or the most important to the least important (as with the responsibilities of an emergency room nurse).

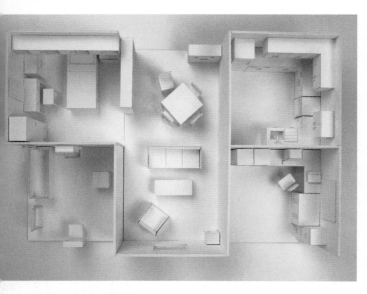

FIGURE 10.1 ■ Spatial Patterns

A topical pattern may also work for your presentation on the three key elements of design, as you could discuss line, color, and texture in each of your main points. Another application for the topical pattern occurs when you discuss the types of job placements available to human services graduates by devoting a main point to social work, placement counseling, and community outreach careers.

SPATIAL

Spatial patterns organize ideas on the basis of physical location or how something is put together (figure 10.1). You may report the incidents of aggravated assaults by discussing crimes from the East Coast, the Midwest, and the West Coast. When you are asked to conduct a tour of your business, you will likely discuss the layout of the various departments within the company. When you introduce a new piece of machinery to a group of workers you will likely describe the machinery in terms of its component parts and their relationship to each other.

Creating the Outline

Once you have developed your main points and determined the most appropriate pattern of organization, you are ready to create your outline. An outline provides the framework for putting all of your information together in a logical sequence. Although outlines can take a variety of forms, depending upon the nature of your subject and purpose, generally outlines consist of three primary parts: the introduction, the body, and the conclusion. The introduction captures your audience's attention and identifies the nature and purpose of your presentation. The body provides main points with the verbal and visual supporting information and evidence to make your presentation clear and convincing. The conclusion brings closure to the presentation by summarizing and providing appropriate closing comments. Let's look more closely at each part.

THE INTRODUCTION

The introduction acts as a preview for the remainder of the speech. You'll want to begin your presentation by capturing the audience's attention. Creating interest can be accomplished in several different ways. You may cite some startling facts, tell a brief story, ask a rhetorical question, use a quotation, refer to the audience and/or the occasion, or include appropriate humor. Whatever device you choose, the goal is the same—to motivate the audience to listen.

Here are some examples of attention-getting strategies you could use for a presentation on credit card debt among college students.

Startling Facts: A survey done by Nellie Mae, a lender of educational loans, found that "78% of undergraduates (aged 18–25) have at least one credit card. Ninety-five percent of the graduate students surveyed had at least one card. Undergraduates carried an average balance of $2,748 while graduate students carried an average balance of $4,776." In addition, "of the 78% of undergraduates with a card, 32% have four or more cards; 13% have credit card debt between $3,000–$7,000; and 9% have credit card debt greater than $7,000" (Holub, 2003–2004, p. 1).

Story: "WASHINGTON (CNN)—Before his recent graduation from college, Jason Britton confronted his mounting credit card bills, worked to pay off thousands of dollars in debt and got on with his life. Sean Moyer and Mitzi Pool took another path.

Your Speech Introduction Should Capture Audience Attention

Moyer, a University of Oklahoma junior, had earned the minimum wage as a part-time salesman and gift wrapper in a department store. Yet, by the time he hanged himself in his bedroom closet, he had 12 credit cards and had amassed $10,000 in debt on them. Moyer, who died in February 1998, still gets credit card offers in the mail, his mother told CNN.

"Pre-selected credit line of up to $100,000 from Chase (Manhattan Bank)," Jane O'Donnell said, reading off the envelope of a letter that arrived for her son last week. "He owed Chase when he died. And we get these at least once a month, so it never stops."

Pool had only three cards, but they were maxed out, and $2,500 is a heavy debt load for an 18-year-old. The University of Central Oklahoma freshman also hanged herself, her checkbook and credit card bills spread out on her dorm bed" (CNN.com, 2001 p. 1).

Rhetorical Question: How would you react if you received statements from several credit card companies stating that you had maxed your line of credit and owed $10,000?

Quote: "Georgetown University sociologist Robert Manning, who studied credit card debt among college students, maintains that marketing of the cards on campuses 'now poses a greater threat than alcohol or sexually transmitted diseases'" (CNN.com, 2001 p. 1).

Refer to Audience/Occasion: It's the start of another semester and a time of expenses for us

Greater Threat

as students. We have tuition to pay and textbooks to buy—in addition to covering other necessities like rent, food, and car insurance. No problem! We just take that little plastic card out of our wallets and charge our bills. Such an easy way out—that is, until the credit card statement arrives at the end of the month.

Humor:

Kids do the darnedest things.

For example, six-year-old Bennett Christiansen of Aurora, Illinois, managed to get his own credit card from Bank of America.

Amy Christiansen, the child's mother, said that all of her family members had been receiving offers of credit in the mail—including Bennett. For a bit of fun, she allowed Bennett to fill out and send in one of the applications addressed to him.

In a totally unexpected development, Bennett soon received a credit card with his name on it, even though he'd listed his birth date as 2002 and his income as $0. The child's card carried a $600 credit limit.

Bank of America insists that they do not target or give credit to minors, but Mrs. Christiansen was understandably concerned about the ease with which her child obtained his first credit card. She'd better stay on her toes; Bennett's 3-year-old sibling has also received offers of credit. (Creditor Web, 2008, p. 1).

After you have captured the interest of your audience, you will want to show them that the information that follows in the body of your speech will be of value to them. In other words, let them know that what you have to say is worth their time and attention. You should try to show some tangible gain that will result for them such as saving time or money, enhancing health or safety, or increasing personal or career effectiveness. For the topic of credit card debt, you might tell your audience, "This presentation can help you avoid the devastating consequences of credit card debt that many college students experience." With a statement like this, it is a good bet that most of your listeners will want to hear more about your topic.

Third, you must state the central idea or thesis. A well-written central idea communicates the gist of the speech in a single sentence and lets the audience know what you hope to accomplish. A central idea for the subject of credit card debt could sound something like this: "Avoiding credit card debt is easier than you think." Now your audience is aware that they will learn about some simple ways to keep themselves out of debt.

Finally, you need to preview the main points that will be developed in the body of your speech. As stated earlier in this chapter, you should limit your main points to about three, and generally not more than five. Here is what you might say to preview your main points: "To avoid credit card debt, you need to limit your use to one card, cut back on your spending, and pay your account on time." Once these four steps have been accomplished, you are ready to move on to the body of the outline.

THE BODY

The body of the outline contains your choice of main points, along with supporting material. Supporting material consists of information that makes your main points interesting, understandable, and believable. You could use explanations, examples, statistics, stories, testimonies, and comparisons. All of these verbal supports will be discussed in Chapter 11. For now, keep in mind that it is a good idea to use several supports for each main point and to use a variety of different supports throughout your speech. For example, using only statistics in your speech is likely to bore your audience. However, if you also incorporate some inspiring stories, a few memorable quotes or testimonies from experts, and several imaginative comparisons, you will have a more balanced speech that keeps your audience involved.

It is also important for you to make a smooth connection between one main point and the next. This connection is made largely by the use of **transitions**—words or phrases that create a bridge between ideas. You've undoubtedly heard speakers say "first, next, then" to signal movement from one thought to another. Other examples of transitions include "in addition," "consequently," "therefore," "however," "finally," and so on. Besides the use of these common transitions, speakers may comment on how one main point relates to the next one.

For instance, a speaker might say, "Now that you understand the importance of proper lifting techniques, we will examine those techniques one step at a time." You should also know that transitions are used not only in the body but throughout the entire speech as well. In fact, they exist in all of the necessary parts of the outline. See figure 10.2 for examples of transition words.

Transition words are like road signs. They help the listeners understand the direction of your thought. Here is a chart of example transition words you can use to guide your listeners through your presentations.		
Above all	Finally	Meanwhile
Accordingly	First, Second, Third	Moreover
Actually	First and foremost	Next
Afterward	For instance, For example	No doubt
All things considered	For this reason	Of course
Another	From here on	On the other hand
Arguably	Furthermore	Otherwise
As a consequence	However	Paradoxically
As a matter of fact	In addition	Presently
As a result	In any case	Presumably
At any rate	In conclusion	Regrettably
At the same time	In fact	Similarly
At this point	In my opinion	Still
Be that as it may	In other words, as it were	Strangely enough
By, and, or	In the first place	Then
By and large	In the meantime	Therefore
By the same token	In the same way	Too, also
Consequently	Incidentally	Ultimately
Even so	Ironically	

FIGURE 10.2 ■ Transition Table
Source: Wichita State University, College of Education.

I. **Introduction**
   A. Gain attention
   B. State need for information
   C. State central idea
   D. Preview of main points

II. **Body**
   A. First main point
      1. Verbal support
      2. Verbal support
      3. Verbal support
      Transition
   B. Second main point
      1. Verbal support
      2. Verbal support
      3. Verbal support
      Transition
   C. Third main point
      1. Verbal support
      2. Verbal support
      3. Verbal support

III. **Conclusion**
   A. Review main points
   B. Restate central idea
   C. Close memorably

FIGURE 10.3 ■ Skeletal Outline

THE CONCLUSION

The final part of the outline is the conclusion. This section contains three major parts: a summary of the main points, a restatement of the central idea, and memorable closing remarks. Although the conclusion represents the final portion of a presentation, do not underestimate its importance. The conclusion gives you a chance to review your key information one final time, as well as an opportunity to close the presentation memorably. Interestingly, some of the most noteworthy lines in famous speeches have occurred in the conclusion. In addition, research indicates that what audiences hear last, they remember most. Unforgettable conclusions are what bring audiences to their feet, motivate them to take action, and stir powerful emotions within their hearts.

After you have reviewed the main points and central idea, you can then end with a quotation, a brief illustration, a provocative question, a humorous anecdote, or a reference to an attention-getter that was used in the introduction. Most importantly, you should be brief and to the point, not allowing the conclusion to drag on. In addition, no new information should be introduced in this final portion of the speech. Figure 10.3 shows a skeletal outline form.

In several of the upcoming chapters, you will learn more about putting together a successful presentation. Now that you have a better understanding of what it takes to organize an informative outline, you will be ready to select verbal and visual supports, gather information to develop your outline, and prepare for delivering your speech to a live audience.

Review Questions

1. List six criteria for effective main points in your informative presentation.
2. Explain the differences among the three patterns of organization for your main points.
3. Identify three main elements of your informative presentation outline.
4. Explain what transitions are and why they are important for a successful informative presentation.

Key Terms and Concepts

Body 223
Chronological 219
Conclusion 224
Introduction 220
Parallel Form 218
Spatial 220
Topical 219
Transitions 223
Verbal Supports 223

Web Activities

Check out this helpful website on public speaking from the Standard Deviants:

- http://www.pbs.org/standarddeviantstv/episode_res_public.html

This website will give you a helpful checklist for informative speech preparation:

- http://homepage.smc.edu/martin_ben/Checklist.htm

Review guidelines for effective introductions and conclusions on the PowerPoint slides at this website:

- http://www.hawaii.edu/gened/oc/intro_concl.ppt

Assignments

ASSIGNMENT 10.1: DEVELOP MAIN POINTS

You will need to determine the main points that will develop your central idea and help you accomplish your specific purpose. Try to limit your speech to three main points. These main points should meet the following criteria:

1. Be expressed as complete sentences.
2. Contain only one key idea per point.
3. Develop the central idea.
4. Be stated in parallel form.

For example, the central idea on behavior-based job interviewing might include these three main points:

A. Behavior-based interview responses include a challenge from your past experience.
B. Behavior-based interview responses include an action that met the challenge.
C. Behavior-based interview responses include the results that occurred from the action.

Directions: Choose three central ideas from **Part C of Assignment 9.5—Writing Central Ideas** and write three main points for each central idea.

Central Idea

#1 _____

Main Point

A _____

Main Point

B _____

Main Point

C _____

Central Idea

#2 _____

Main Point

A _____

Main Point

B _____

Main Point

C _____

Central Idea

#3 _____

Main Point

A _____

Main Point

B _____

Main Point

C _____

ASSIGNMENT 10.2: SCRAMBLED OUTLINES

Outline #1 Golfing

Match the sentence number to the informative talk outline form in the following table.

1. Now that everyone in your group has hit off the tee, we can focus on the fairway.

2. The essence of golf etiquette is respect for your fellow golfers.

3. The key to golf etiquette is respect for your fellow golfers.

4. I will describe how you can show respect for your fellow golfers 1) on the tee, 2) through the fairway, and 3) on the greens.

5. Respect your fellow golfer through the fairway.

6. Story of 6½-hour round of golf at Brown Deer Park.

7. By following these guidelines you can avoid 6½-hour-nightmares of frustration and ensure that everyone can play a fast, enjoyable round of golf.

8. Respect your fellow golfer on the greens.

9. Statistics from National Golf Foundation (visual): As a result of this situation, there is an increasing need for improvements in player relations.

10. Respect your fellow golfers on the tees.

11. As I have shown here, by respecting your fellow golfers in all three areas of the course–the tees, the fairways, and the greens–you improve the quality of your game.

12. Now that your group is approaching the green, let's examine how you can show respect there.

Introduction	Second Main Point #
Attention-Gaining Device #	Transition #
Need for Information #	Third Main Point #
Central Idea #	
Preview of Main Points #	**Conclusion**
Body	Review of Main Points #
First Main Point #	Restate Central Idea #
Transition #	Closing Statement #

What pattern of organization was used in this presentation? _____

Outline #2 Certifiable Weld

Match the sentence number to the informative talk outline form in the following table.

1. The testing procedure is the final requirement in producing a certifiable weld.

2. Metal preparation is useless if the wrong welding technique is used.

3. A certifiable weld must meet three requirements.
4. Metal preparation is of prime importance in producing a certifiable weld.
5. Rhetorical questions about weldments in buildings, aviation, industry.
6. The welding technique is also a prime requirement in producing a certifiable weld.
7. So the next time you walk into a building, fly in an airplane, or take a job in a factory, rest assured that certifiable welds are all around you.
8. After the metal has been prepared and welded, it must be tested.
9. These three requirements (metal preparation, welding, and testing) must work together to produce certifiable, safe welds.
10. I will be explaining the importance of each one of these requirements (metal preparation, welding, and testing).
11. A certifiable weld must meet three requirements.
12. Peace of mind comes from understanding the requirements of a certifiable weld.

Introduction	Second Main Point #
Attention Gaining Device #	Transition #
Need for Information #	Third Main Point #
Central Idea #	
Preview of Main Points #	**Conclusion**
Body	Review of Main Points #
First Main Point #	Restate Central Idea #
Transition #	Closing Statement #

What pattern of organization was used in this presentation? _____

ASSIGNMENT 10.3: GROUP PRACTICE OUTLINES

Your instructor will divide the class into several small groups and assign a pattern of organization to each group (chronological, spatial, or topical).

Work with your group to create an outline for an informative presentation using the assigned pattern of organization with one of the following four topics:

Tools/Mechanisms

Processes or Procedures

Incidents

Ideas

Follow these steps to prepare your outlines:

1. Select a topic appropriate for your group's pattern of organization.
2. Construct an outline for your presentation.
3. Copy your outline onto poster paper.
4. Present your outline to the class.
5. Observe how others used different patterns to develop their informative presentations.

ASSIGNMENT 10.4: INFORMATIVE OUTLINE DRAFT

Start your informative presentation outline by completing the following template:

INFORMATIVE PRESENTATION OUTLINE

I. **Introduction**

Attention Device

Need for Information

Central Idea:

_____

Initial Summary of Main Points

II. **Body**

Main Point #1: _____

Support:

Support:

Support:

Transition

Main Point #2: _____

    Support:

    Support:

    Support:

  Transition

Main Point #3: _____

    Support:

    Support:

    Support:

III. Conclusion

    Final Summary of Main Points

    Restate Central Idea

    Closing Statements

ASSIGNMENT 10.5: CASE STUDY: VITAL SPEECHES

Directions: Go to your library and find a speech that interests you in *Vital Speeches of the Day,* or you can also access the following website to obtain a speech from this publication: http://www.accessmylibrary.com/coms2/browse_JJ_V024.

After reading the speech, identify the central idea, main points, and pattern of organization.

References

CNN.com. (2001). Credit cards on campus get bad marks by some. Retrieved August 9, 2007, from http://www.cnn.com/US/9906/09/college.kids.debt/

Creditor Web. (2008, June 20). Bank of America issues credit card to boy, age 6. Retrieved October 31, 2008, from http://blog.creditorweb.com/index.php/2008/06/20/bank-of-america-issues-credit-card-to-boy-age-6/

Holub, T. (2003–2004). Credit card usage and debt among college and university students. *ERIC Digest*.
Retrieved August 9, 2007, from http://www.ericdigests.org/2003-2/credit.html

Chapter 11

Verbal and Visual Supports

"The deepest sin against the human mind is to believe things without evidence."

Thomas H. Huxley

Types of Verbal Supports

You just finished your first semester at the local community college, maintaining a stellar GPA and making the dean's list. Although excited about your accomplishments, you are apprehensive about the economics class you have to register for in the fall. You've heard it is a difficult course. Lonnie, a friend and classmate, has already taken economics, so you figure Lonnie can tell you which of the two instructors teaching this course would be most suited to your learning style.

Lonnie tells you that Mr. Johnson, the instructor he had, is well organized, puts all assignments on the Internet, and uses PowerPoint in his lectures. Lonnie says that this instructor also has a great sense of humor and is willing to provide extra help for students outside of class. Mr. Johnson's exams are difficult though, primarily consisting of essay questions. He informs you that only about 15 percent of his class got A's on the exams. In addition, Lonnie explains that he spent two to three hours each night on homework assigned by Mr. Johnson.

Lonnie has also gotten feedback from some of his friends who had Ms. Rawson, the other economics instructor. These friends liked Ms. Rawson's interactive teaching style. She has students participate in lots of small group activities, including role-playing experiences. In addition, her class is required to do two oral reports during the semester, along with take-home exams. Although Ms. Rawson assigns less homework, Lonnie says that his friends spent fifteen to twenty hours preparing each of the two oral reports.

Now that you have a bit more information, you may find it easier to decide on an economics instructor. Notice that Lonnie provided you with a comparison between the two instructors, described a bit about their teaching styles, and offered some numerical data on grading and homework hours. Without such details, making a decision would be more difficult.

As you begin preparation for an effective oral presentation, just like Lonnie you have to offer your listeners plenty of details to ensure their understanding of your message. These details are generally referred to as supporting material and can be both verbal and visual (figure 11.1).

In both cases, the function of verbal and visual support is to make the information more interesting, more understandable, and more believable. When searching for appropriate supports, speakers should begin by inventorying their own level of knowledge. In other words, ask yourself, "How much do I already know about my topic based upon personal experience?" In most instances, you will discover that you have a variety of facts, examples, stories, and so on that you can incorporate into a presentation. In addition, you may also need to seek outside resources in the form of company files, annual reports, product information, and so on. Regardless of their source, however, supporting materials fall into several general categories.

Verbal Support	Visual Support
Explanations	Objects or Models
Examples	Charts or Graphs
Statistics	List s
Stories	Tables
Testimonies	Photographs
Comparisons	Diagrams

FIGURE 11.1 ■ Verbal and Visual Supports

EXPLANATIONS

This form of verbal support defines, analyzes, or describes. Definitions involve clarifying technical or complex terms that may not be familiar to the audience. If you have occasion, for instance, to provide on-the-job training for a group of new employees, you will probably have to familiarize them with the jargon that is used among more experienced workers. Analyses break down complex processes or concepts into their component parts to ensure understanding. If an experienced nurse were instructing a group of nursing assistants about how to take a blood pressure, the nurse would have to explain that process step by step. Descriptions provide detailed pictures for an audience by explaining how something looks, sounds, feels, smells, or tastes. A company sales representative would likely use descriptions when introducing a new line of orthopedic mattresses to potential retailers, explaining the construction, appearance, and feel of the mattresses. Likewise, an accounting student may find mutual funds easier to understand with the following explanation that includes a definition and analysis.

A mutual fund is defined as follows:

> An open-ended fund operated by an investment company which raises money from shareholders and invests in a group of assets, in accordance with a stated set of objectives. Mutual funds raise money by selling shares of the fund to the public, much like any other type of company can sell stock in itself to the public. Mutual funds then take the money they receive from the sale of their shares (along with any money made from previous investments) and use it to purchase various investment vehicles, such as stocks, bonds and money market instruments. (InvestorWord, 2008, par. 1)

EXAMPLES

Examples are typical instances used to clarify a point. They work particularly well when used in groups of two or more. A health care professional speaking to a community group about the value of regular aerobic exercise might suggest walking, biking, or dancing as suitable choices. An interior designer speaking to several customers about window treatments may mention mini blinds, pleated shades, or sheers as possibilities. A culinary student doing a presentation on balanced nutrition might use examples from the food pyramid illustrated in figure 11.2.

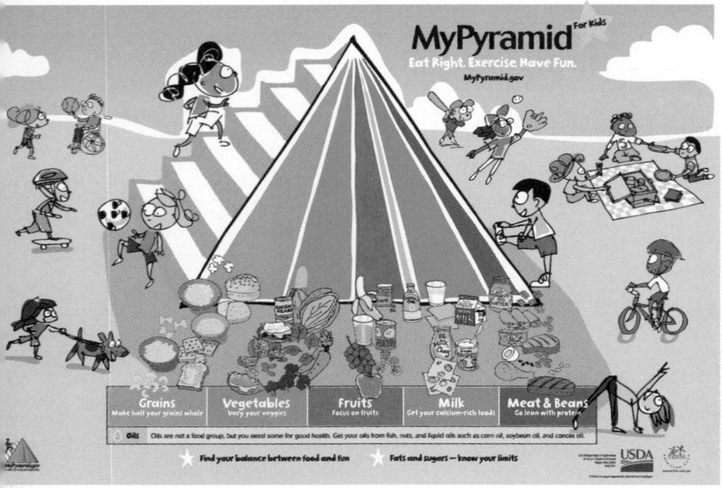

FIGURE 11.2 ■ Food Pyramid

STATISTICS

Statistics are numerical facts that show relationships. For instance, if you were attempting to convince a group of managers that sales had been steadily increasing over the last quarter, you would probably use statistics to prove the point. Statistics can be highly convincing forms of evidence, but to use them effectively, you need to follow certain guidelines. To begin, always cite the source of your statistics, including the date. They have much more credibility when the audience knows how they were obtained. Next, display them visually if you can. Reading off a list of statistics is less effective than presenting them on a graph or chart where your listeners can actually see the information. Also, it is better to round your statistics off if possible. Instead of saying, "We had 2,962 in attendance at the annual convention," consider saying, "We had close to 3,000 attending the annual convention." Figures that are rounded off are more memorable to an audience.

Chip and Dan Heath in their best seller, *Made to Stick: Why Some Ideas Survive and Others Die* (2007), note that "Statistics are rarely meaningful in themselves. Statistics will, and should, almost always be used to illustrate a relationship. It's more important for people to remember the relationship than the number" (p. 143). The Heath brothers go on to tell how you are far more likely to be killed by a deer than a shark, despite the reports of shark attacks in the press around the world. Statistics from the Florida Museum of Natural History, for example, state that you are 300 times more likely to be killed in a deer-related car accident than by a shark attack (Heath & Heath, 2007).

Finally, even though statistics can be persuasive forms of support, don't overdo them. Overwhelming your listeners with statistics decreases the effect of the information.

STORIES

These verbal supports take the form of short narratives or anecdotes. They can be factual, or they can be hypothetical. Factual stories report incidents that have actually occurred. If you relay an experience that involved satisfying a difficult customer, the experience would obviously be factual. On the other hand, hypothetical stories are imaginary but believable. If you wanted the audience to think about how they would respond to a difficult customer, you might first create an imaginary scenario for the audience to reflect upon. Stories can be highly effective forms of captivating audience interest for the beginning of your presentation.

Dale Carnegie, a famous developer of self-improvement and corporate training materials, advised his students to start every speech with a story. The engaging quality of sharing a common experience sets the tone and establishes rapport for the information that follows. Stories can be extended to run through an entire presentation. Information can be shared in an interesting manner with flows and pauses to keep the audience completely focused on your presentation. In addition, the sensory details of a story provide connections to the memories of audience members, making the point of your story unforgettable. Moreover, most listeners enjoy a well-timed story in the context of a speech.

Two examples from *Vital Speeches of the Day* show how effective stories can be when used to begin speeches. Stephen Bertman, professor of Classics at the University of Windsor, Ontario, used a story to begin his keynote address to a Canadian symposium. Notice the interest generated in the first paragraph of the story.

> Over fifty years ago on the evening of July 4, 1947, an incident occurred in the desert near Roswell, New Mexico. According to those who claimed to have seen the wreckage, an aircraft crashed that was not of this world. Fragments were found of an extraordinarily lightweight metal that, after being crushed by the hand, could spring back to its original shape. On one metal fragment an inscription was found written in a strange script unlike any other writing system on earth. Near the wreckage, survivors were found, but they were not human in form—survivors who would die soon after without telling their tale. What had crashed at Roswell was a spacecraft from another galaxy, or even from another dimension, an extraterrestrial vehicle that had taken an incredibly long voyage across both space and time. Of course, all of this is denied by official government sources. But what if it all did happen? What if it was all true? (Bertman, 2000, p. 1).

Stories also help you picture situations you have not experienced. Chip and Dan Heath suggest that stories can be your simulators for problem solving, learning new skills, and applying new concepts (Heath & Heath, 2007). A law enforcement student included the following slow-motion story in her persuasive speech titled, "Slow Down":

> **How fast can you die?** Here is a slow-motion, split-second story of what happens when a car going 55 mph hits a solid, immovable tree.
>
> **1/10th second**—The front bumper and chrome grillwork collapse. Slivers of steel penetrate the tree to a depth of 1½ inches or more.
>
> **2/10th second**—The hood crumples as it rises, smashing into the windshield. The spinning rear wheels leave the ground. Fenders come into contact with the tree, forcing the rear parts out over the front doors. BUT the driver's body continues to move forward at the vehicle's original speed. At this point, the driver, 160 lbs., now weighs about 3,200 lbs.
>
> **3/10th second**—The driver's body is now off the seat, torso upright, broken knees pressing against the dashboard. The plastic and steel frame of the steering wheel begins to bend under his terrible death grip. His head is now near the sun visor, his chest above the steering column.
>
> **4/10th second**—The car's front 24 inches have been demolished, but the rear end is still traveling at an estimated 35 mph. The driver's body is still traveling at 55 mph. The heavy engine block crunches into the tree. The rear of the car, like a bucking horse, rises high enough to scrape bark off low branches.
>
> **5/10th second**—The driver's fear-frozen hands bend the steering column into an almost vertical position. The force of gravity, now increased to 20 times normal, impales him on the steering post. Jagged steel punctures lungs and intercostal arteries. Blood pours into his lungs.
>
> **6/10th second**—The driver's feet are ripped from his tightly laced shoes. The chassis bends in the middle, shearing body bolts. The driver's head smashes into the windshield. The rear of the car begins its downward fall, its spinning rear wheels digging into the ground, adding another forward force.
>
> **7/10th second**—The entire writhing body of the car is forced out of shape. Hinges shear; doors spring open. In one last convulsion, the seat rams forward,

pinning the driver against the cruel steel of the steering column. Blood leaps from his mouth; shock has frozen his heart. He is now dead.
Total elapsed time: **7/10ths of one second.**

(James Madison University, Ratio of Fatalities to Speed)

TESTIMONIES

Quotes from experts in a given field constitute testimonials. Experts are those who have extensive experience and knowledge in a specific area. The observations of lay people, who may have casual exposure with limited knowledge in a field, are better suited to anecdotes or stories than to testimony. A company's nurse practitioner might promote a seminar on worker safety by using a quote from the National Institute for Occupational Safety and Health on work-related injuries.

> Acute trauma at work remains a leading cause of death and disability among U.S. workers. Trauma is defined as "an injury or wound to a living body caused by the application of external force or violence." Acute trauma can occur with the sudden, one-time application of force or violence that causes immediate damage to a living body. (NIOSH)

If you decide to use testimonials, be sure your choice meets the following criteria. First, the person you are quoting should, in fact, be a legitimate expert. Second, it is helpful if the audience is familiar with the expert. If not, you should share the speaker's credentials. The audience doesn't need to know the expert personally but should be aware of his/her expertise. Finally, make certain you quote or paraphrase the expert accurately.

You may cite a food and nutrition specialist for testimony about causes of food poisoning in catered foods. Her opinions, coupled with her credentials, make her a convincing source for your presentation. If you were attempting to persuade your audience about the need to have safer standards for fruits and vegetables, you might quote Sally Greenberg, senior counsel at Consumers Union. She offered the following testimony to the Food and Drug Administration:

> In the last five months more than 200 consumers in 26 states ate spinach contaminated by E. coli. Five incidents were fatal, and over 100 required hospitalization. Another E. coli outbreak came from shredded lettuce, with at least 150 people falling ill.
>
> The safety of the food we buy is a fundamental expectation of consumers, and government must use its standard-setting, investigative and enforcement powers to see that this expectation is fulfilled. (ConsumersUnion.org, 2007, April 13, p. 1)

COMPARISONS

Comparisons attempt to show similarities between objects, ideas, and concepts. Typically, if you were introducing the audience to new or unfamiliar information, you would use comparisons by linking the new to something with which the audience is already familiar. For example, if you were training co-workers to use new computer software, you might compare it to software they are currently using. As a sales rep, you could show potential customers how a new piece of machinery compared to an older model. Both of these are examples of literal comparisons. They show how items of the same class are alike. Publications like *Consumer Reports* compare products in order to help readers make purchasing decisions.

You can also use a figurative comparison to explain an unknown concept in terms of a more familiar one. The human heart is like a fuel pump in a car, or the hard drive of a computer is like a phone directory. These figurative comparisons help the listeners understand new concepts. Consider the comparison made last winter by a student who was also a luge athlete in the Winter Olympics (figure 11.3). The student explained the event, the equipment, and the ride using an interesting figurative comparison.

> Riding the luge sled is like leaning back on your chair to the point where you are about to tip over backwards, yet you balance on the back two legs of the chair. Do you know the feeling? On the luge, you have that feeling at 80 miles per hour! Wow!

Consider another memorable comparison made by one scientist who stated how difficult it would be to land a spacecraft on Mars. This scientist compared the feat to hitting a specific window in the Empire State Building with a projectile launched from Los Angeles.

FIGURE 11.3 ■ Luge Racer

Types of Visual Supports

Supporting materials that develop your presentation are not only verbal but may be visual as well. The inclusion of visual aids enables the audience to "see" what you are talking about. By coupling verbal and visual support, you can powerfully reinforce the information you are presenting (figure 11.4). For example, if you were trying to persuade co-workers to contribute to the United Way Campaign, you might use statistics to illustrate how the funds are allocated among various social agencies. However, if you incorporate a pie chart to visually divide the funds, the listeners would have a more memorable picture of the figures.

FIGURE 11.4 ■ Visual Aids

Visuals can be used in a variety of forms. Those forms include some of the following: objects or models, charts or graphs, lists or tables, photographs or diagrams.

OBJECTS OR MODELS

As visual support, objects include real-life examples of your subject. For instance, musical instruments, mechanisms, tools, and even living creatures add realism and authenticity to your presentation. Objects can be an effective form of visual support when they are easily transported, skillfully manipulated, and clearly seen by your entire audience. In some situations, you may need to enhance the view of your object by projecting its image so others can see it more clearly.

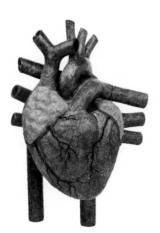

When objects are not available or are too awkward for comfortable use, models of your subject can be effective visual supports. Scaled replicas, life-like reproductions, and miniature mock-ups are common types of models you could use. The 3D model shown in figure 11.5, for example, is helpful for nursing students to understand the structure of the human heart. One website that offers life-like replicas for your presentation is 3-D-Models.com.

FIGURE 11.5 ■ Heart Model

CHARTS OR GRAPHS

If you have numerical or statistical data to share with your audience, you can create charts or graphs. These visual supports summarize numerical data, show relationships, and describe trends. You can choose from several types of charts or graphs, such as bar, pie, line, column, etc. The statistics on drunk drivers (see figure 11.6) become clearer when presented with visual support in the form of a bar graph.

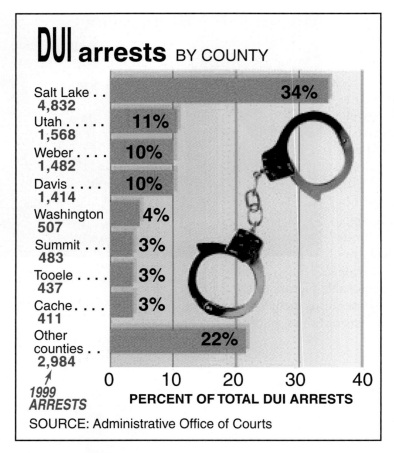

FIGURE 11.6 ■ DUI Bar Graph
Source: Deseret News.

LISTS OR TABLES

Information presented in lists can include a series of examples in a bulleted list, steps of a process in a numbered sequence, or a list of reasons why you should vote for a referendum as found in a persuasive brochure. Lists help to simplify the information, reducing it to the kernels that are easy to remember.

Tables provide a summary of information that would take pages of text to explain. Data is presented in rows and columns in a clear, direct manner so that relationships, values, and categories are easily identified for your audience. Consider how clearly information is presented in the Periodic Table of Elements (see figure 11.7).

PHOTOGRAPHS OR DIAGRAMS

Pictures put a face on your subject. They can provide vivid, colorful, emotional dimensions to your visual support. In addition, they are easy to prepare and edit with programs like Photoshop, convenient to transport, and can be projected for all to see. Diagrams allow you to simplify complex information by showing relationships visually. An electrical schematic, an exploded view of a firearm, or installation instructions for

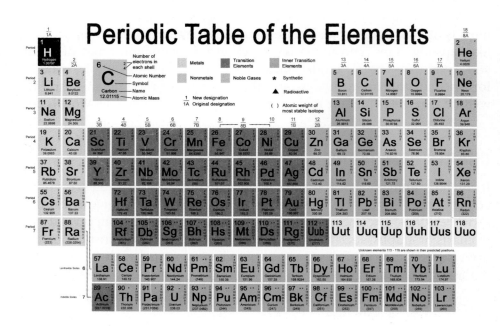

FIGURE 11.7 ■ Periodic Table of the Elements

your on-demand hot water system all make use of diagrams. Notice too how photos and diagrams work together to emphasize a major difference between two hybrid automobiles when carlist.com presented the new Toyota (see figure 11.8).

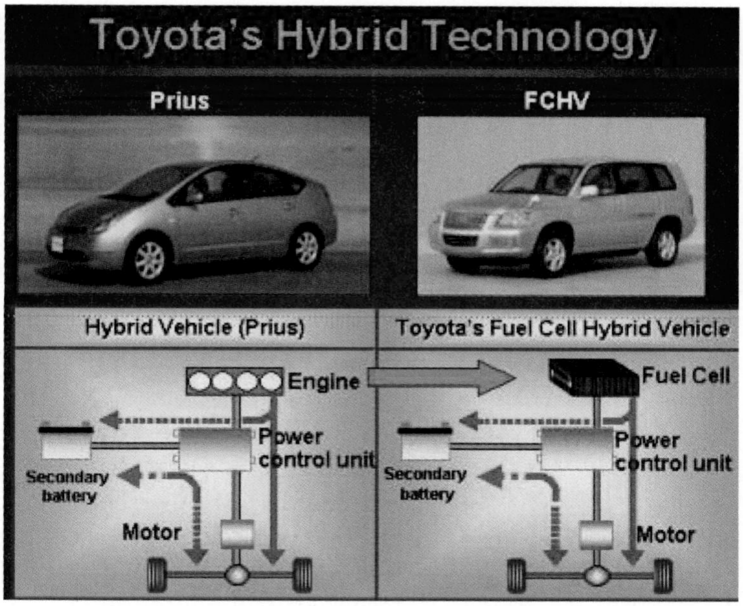

The media for presenting these visuals can be equally diverse. They include flip charts and poster boards, slides, DVD's, computer-generated graphics, and handout materials.

Deciding on the type of visual and the choice of media for presentation is dependent upon several factors. First, what is the nature of your subject? Highly complex information, for example, might demand the use of slides coupled with handout materials the audience can take with them at the conclusion of the presen-

FIGURE 11.8 ■ Toyota Hybrid Diagram

tation. Simpler, more straightforward information might be easily presented on a flip chart.

Second, what is the audience's level of sophistication? Audiences that are accustomed to hearing professional speakers may come to expect a PowerPoint presentation. Other audiences may be easily accommodated with the use of poster boards.

Third, where will the presentation take place? A large lecture hall might necessitate the use of computerized displays. A small meeting room might be suitable for objects and models that the audience can examine up close.

Finally, what purpose is the visual intended to serve? If the visual is intended to provide step-by-step instructions of some process workers need to follow, a DVD that can be viewed again at a later date might work well. If, on the other hand, the visual is intended to record information from an audience brainstorming session, a flip chart or white board may suffice.

Regardless of a speaker's choice of visual, however, certain guidelines must be followed in order to maximize the visual's effectiveness.

Four Factors Influence Your Selection of Visual Support

1. The nature of your subject
2. The audience's level of sophistication
3. The place your presentation will occur
4. The purpose the visual will serve

Guidelines for Effective Visual Supports

1. Make sure the visual is large enough for the entire audience to see.
2. Keep the visual simple by resisting the temptation to cram too much information onto a single visual.

3. Create "eye appeal" by using colors, fonts, and graphics in imaginative ways.

4. Have a definite purpose in mind for using the visual.

5. Introduce the visual, explain it, and then put it away.

6. Be certain you have the necessary equipment available and in working order before the presentation.

7. Practice the speech using the visuals.

Visual Supports and Technology

With software like PowerPoint, designing sophisticated visuals has never been faster or easier. No wonder students and working professionals make frequent use of this medium in their presentations.

In addition, modern college classrooms and workplace facilities often provide media carts that allow speakers to project images from DVDs, the Internet, or still photographs.

Although the use of technology to create and project visuals seems like the ideal combination, you might want to consider the suggestions that follow.

1. Avoid the use of visual technology as a substitute for meaningful content in your presentations. It can be tempting to take shortcuts in your outline while expecting the visuals to make up for missing information.

2. Use visual technology to provide additional clarity and interest to your presentation. Some beginning speakers attempt to put their entire speech onto PowerPoint slides and then simply read the text projected on the screen. A better approach involves using visual images that complement rather than repeat what you are saying.

3. More is not necessarily better. Resist the tendency to fill your presentation with one visual after another. Too many visuals can distract your audience from what you are saying and lessen the effectiveness of those visuals as well.

4. Make sure the equipment you are using is working. Nothing can ruin a good presentation more quickly than technical problems that do not allow you to project your visuals.

5. Always have a back-up plan. Be certain you have alternative visuals in case you encounter technical problems. These alternatives might include printouts of your visuals that you can display on a flip chart or files saved in more than one location.

As you begin preparation for a presentation, whether in the classroom, at work, or in your community, keep in mind the suggestions for including well-developed verbal and visual supports. Along with providing interest, understanding, and credibility, you will discover that well-chosen supports increase your confidence as a speaker and make your information memorable for your audience.

Review Questions

1. List three reasons why verbal and visual supports are important.

2. Find an example of each of the six types of verbal supports.

3. Obtain an example of each of the six types of visual supports.

4. Describe the four factors that influence your choice of visual supports.

5. Summarize the seven guidelines for effective visual supports.

Key Terms and Concepts

Charts   237

Comparisons   235

Diagrams   238

Examples   232

Explanations   232

Graphs   237

Objects or Models   237

Photographs   238

Statistics   232

Stories   233

Tables   238

Testimonies   235

Verbal Support   231

Visual Support   237

Web Activities

Find a quotation appropriate for your informative presentation from a webpage with a collection of quotations such as:

- http://www.quotationspage.com/search.php3
- http://www.bartleby.com/quotations/
- http://www.quoteland.com/

- Use Opposing Viewpoints Resource Center or one of the Internet search engines to find statistics for your informative presentation.

- Find visual images for your informative presentation by searching through the possibilities on Google, Ask.com, Excite, AltaVista, AlltheWeb, or Yahoo! images.

Assignments

ASSIGNMENT 11.1: RECOGNIZING SUPPORTS

Identify the following supports as stories, comparisons, examples, statistics, testimony, explanation, or a combination of supports. Where you find more than one type of support in a selection, note all of the supports that are combined.

1. "Years ago I planted a rose garden as a birthday gift for my husband. It was a beautiful garden, and I was astonished that it became even more beautiful as the days and weeks went by. And then suddenly, it seemed virtually overnight, the leaves started to yellow and mildew, and my once beautiful garden became scraggly and brittle. Sputtering with indignation, I called Bachman's Nursery and asserted that the rose bushes they had sold me must have been diseased. You can imagine my shock and disbelief when the rosarian asked me what I'd been using to dust the leaves, and what I'd been using to feed the root system" (Keefeler, 1991, p. 92).

2. "If you want to get a job, you have to prepare to win. Arthur Rubenstein, the world's greatest pianist, once said:

   If I miss one day of practice, I notice the difference. If I miss two days of practice, the critics notice the difference. If I miss three days of practice, the audience notices the difference" (Mackay, 1991).

3. "Many electro-technologies are so efficient that using them saves energy <u>even after allowing for conversion losses.</u> Here are some cases:
   - Produce steel with an electric arc instead of a blast furnace. Energy savings: 50 percent.
   - Make glass with an electric melter instead of a flame. Energy savings: 65 percent.
   - Dry paint with infrared electric heat rather than gas ovens. Energy savings: 90 percent.
   - Cook in a microwave oven instead of a gas oven. Energy savings: 90 percent" (Kuhn, 1991).

4. "Professor Hans Selye, the world's foremost authority on human stress, defines stress as 'the body's nonspecific response to any demand placed on it, pleasant or not.' We often recognize these nonspecific responses in a rapid pulse, increased blood pressure, frequent illness, unusual susceptibility to infection. Sometimes it appears as brooding, fuming, shouting or even in increased use of alcohol, tobacco, or drugs. In some it's as severe as ulcers or a heart attack; in others, like one of my daughters (who takes after her dad in this), it's fingernail biting" (Weaver, 1991).

5. "No surgeon would be asked to operate on several bodies at one time; no lawyer would be expected to try a number of cases simultaneously. However, teachers are routinely required to instruct large sections of students with different backgrounds, abilities, motivations and learning styles. The consummate teacher is one who is able to adjust the learning environment in ways that develop the potential of each student. With the multitude of variables in every classroom, it is regrettable, but not surprising, that some students fall through the cracks. But what is amazing is that even the average teacher does so well in instructing individuals under conditions that would be considered intolerable in most other professions" (Estes, 1991).

6. "The *Economist* magazine once calculated that there were about 250 million people on earth at the birth of Christ. They had a per capita annual income roughly equivalent to 460 of today's dollars. That was the standard of living that could be supported by human labor, assisted by animals, wind and fire: just 460 dollars a year. By the late 18th Century, nearly 2,000 years later, world population had increased to about 750 million. Humanity still depended on the same four forms of energy. And per capita income was still just $460. No progress in 2,000 years in energy or in income. . . . In the next 200 years, per capita income would increase eight-fold. World per capita income is $3,750. In the U.S., it's about $18,000" (Kuhn, 1991).

7. "Three weeks ago, I attended a tennis camp in Arizona. I've played tennis most of my life, but I'm still not as good as I want to be. So I go to camps, I read books, I watch videotapes, I take lessons, and I watch great players play. I do everything I can to keep trying to get better. One morning at camp I was assigned to play a doubles match. The way it works is that four people show up, and partners are decided by spinning a racquet. When I got to the court, the others were already there, and one of the fellows was visibly upset. It seems he didn't want to be paired with a certain party who happened to be ninety-two years old! I didn't have any particular preference about partners, and, as luck would have it, I wound up with the ninety-two-year-old. I was wondering how things would work out, but I shouldn't have worried. The first two sets, we hammered our opponents 6-1, 6-1"(Mackay, 1991).

8. "Women account for 47 percent of the labor force and receive more than half of all bachelor's degrees, yet continue to be paid significantly less than their male counterparts. Obtaining a college degree does not protect a woman from pay inequity. Women with college educations are still paid only 72 percent as much as men with the same level of education. Overall, the average woman is shorted approximately $250,000 over the course of her career due to the wage gap. This loss of revenue for women is unacceptable and needs to be addressed."

   "The wage gap greatly decreases women's daily buying power, affects their ability to pay for quality childcare, prevents them from saving for retirement, and hinders them from receiving livable Social Security benefits based on their wages. In addition, the wage gap serves to keep women working minimum or sub-minimum wage jobs and their families in poverty. Pay discrimination not only affects women, but also puts their families, children and dependents at a disadvantage" (NOW, Women in Red, 2007).

ASSIGNMENT 11.2: ONE-POINT SPEECH

Practice selecting and using different forms of verbal and visual supports by developing a one-point speech that has at least three different verbal supports and two different visual supports.

Directions: Using the Internet as a resource, type "informative speech topics" in the Google search box and select a topic from any of the lists you find.

Once you have selected a topic, determine what terms or concepts need explanation, examples, or stories to make them clearer for your audience.

Next, consider how comparisons, testimony, or statistics could help clarify your point.

Finally, decide how you could use visual supports to reinforce two of the three verbal supports you have selected. Search Google Images, AltaVista Images, Yahoo! Images, or your favorite search engine's images for visuals to strengthen your verbal support.

ASSIGNMENT 11.3: CASE STUDY: THE PERSUASIVE AD

Find an effective advertisement either online or from a magazine. Analyze the visual appeal in the ad, and identify the verbal supports that are used. Bring your ad to class, where you will be assigned to a group of three or four other classmates. Each person in the group should share his/her ad with the others. The group will then select the ad they believe is the most effective. All of the groups will display their chosen ad to the class and explain the rationale for their choice.

References

AFL-CIO. (n.d.). Equal pay. Retrieved April 26, 2007, from http://www.aflcio.org/issues/jobeconomy/women/equalpay/EqualPaybyOccupation.cfm

AFL-CIO. (n.d.). Executive paywatch. Retrieved February 1, 2007, from http://www.aflcio.org/corporatewatch/paywatch/

Arnold, C. (2007, April 18). Workplace ethics begin with the boss. NPR. Retrieved April 18, 2007, from http://www.npr.org/templates/story/story.php?storyId=9642184

Bertman, S. (2000, January 15). Greek epic. *Vital speeches of the day*, p. 1.

Davidson, A. (2007, April 18). Bloggers debate code of conduct. NPR. Retrieved April 18, 2007, from http://www.npr.org/templates/story/story.php?storyId=9642178

DUI Multiple Offenders. (n.d.). *Department of Public Safety, Driver License Division*. Retrieved April 13, 2007, from http://deseretnews.com/photos/b0722dui.gif

Estes, D. (1991, August 15). In praise of teaching. *Vital speeches of the day*.

Food Pyramid. (n.d.). Retrieved April 13, 2007, from http://www.pennhealth.com/health_info/nutrition/food_pyramid.gif

Greenberg, S. (2007, April 13). Consumers union calls for mandatory safety measures for fresh produce. Retrieved April 27, 2007, from http://www.consumersunion.org/pub/core_food_safety/004399.html

Heath, C. & Heath, D. (2007) *Made to stick: Why some ideas survive and others die*. New York: Random House.

InvestorWord.com. Retrieved January 19, 2008, from http://www.investorwords.com/3173/mutual_fund.html

James Madison University. (n.d.). *Ratio of fatalities to speed*. Retrieved April 1, 2007, from http://www.jmu.edu/safetyplan/vehicle/generaldriver/speed.shtml

Keefeler, J. B. (1991, November 15). Managing changing organizations: Don't stop communicating. *Vital speeches of the day*, pp. 92–96.

Kuhn, T. R. (1991, August 15). Energy, efficiency, ingenuity. *Vital speeches of the day*.

Luge Photo. (n.d.). Retrieved April 20, 2007, from http://news.bbc.co.uk/olmedia/1795000/images/_1795747_luge_run300.jpg

Luge Sled Diagram. (n.d.). Retrieved April 20, 2007, from http://www.hansensled.com/specs.htm

Mackay, H. B. (1991, August 15). How to get a job. *Vital speeches of the day*.

Model Heart (n.d.) Retrieved April 13, 2007, from http://www.3-dmodels.com/3d-model_files/371m765.htm

National Organization of Women. (2003, April 4). Women in red! Equal pay day is April 15. Retrieved April 26, 2007, from http://www.now.org/issues/economic/alerts/04-04-03.html

NIOSH. (n.d.). Traumatic occupational injuries. National Institute for Occupational Safety and Health. Retrieved April 6, 2007, from http://www.cdc.gov/niosh/injury/

Toyota's Hybrid Technology. (n.d.). Retrieved April 13, 2007, from http://www.carlist.com/autonews/2004/image/toyota_hybrid_diagram.jpg

Weaver, R. L. (1991, August 15). Self-motivation. *Vital speeches of the day*.

Chapter **12**

Gathering Information

Learning **Objectives**

At the end of this chapter, you should be able to meet the following objectives:

1. Recognize the sources of information.
2. Record information.
3. Document sources of information.
4. Avoid plagiarism.

"Research is to see what everybody else has seen, and to think what nobody else has thought."

Albert Szent-Gyorgyi

Sources of Information

Sonia was assigned an informative speech for her communications class. Eager to share some facts about her native India with her classmates, Sonia chose the topic of arranged marriages. Although she was knowledgeable on the subject, the assignment required her to use three outside authoritative sources as well. Sonia began her investigation in the campus library, feeling somewhat overwhelmed by all of the resources available. With help from the reference librarian, Sonia started her search using various electronic databases and then moved to the library's reference section. After several hours of research, Sonia had more than three sources for possible inclusion in her presentation. Feeling confident about her ability to organize an interesting speech, Sonia headed off to begin a review of the materials she had found.

Like Sonia, you too have likely been given speech assignments that demanded research. You probably also know that the process of locating evidence to develop your main points can be a time-consuming process. Jay Budzik, a graduate student at Northwestern University, must have been aware of the effort that research takes when he developed a "personal information management system that can turn your PC into a research librarian by collecting information relevant to your project" (Watson, 1999, p. 1).

The system, referred to as Watson, "actually reads the documents you are working on and uses its understanding of your subject matter to search the Web for pages and sites most relevant to your work. . . . The system then sifts through the pages to remove outdated material and redundancies, thus providing useful information while reducing the volume of results" (Watson, 1999, p. 1).

Although you may not have a system like Watson to help you with researching your own speech, you can simplify your task by becoming more familiar with the major resources contained in your college library.

As you begin the information search for your speech, take some time to determine what you already know about your subject. Personal knowledge of a topic can be a good starting point from which you begin your exploration of other sources. Most of the research you do will include print and electronic media. We'll look at print sources first, including books, reference materials, and periodicals.

PRINT SOURCES

More developed

Books   When seeking information to develop a speech outline, many if not most students turn to the Internet because of the speed and convenience electronic technology provides. However, don't overlook the value of books you can find in your campus or community library.

You may discover that books offer several advantages over electronic sources. First, books develop a topic in greater detail than a Web article, for instance. You will likely find multiple chapters dealing with your topic from which you can pick and choose facts that you need. Second, books you find

Print Sources Offer Several Advantages over Electronic Sources

in the library are more inclined to provide credible evidence, unlike certain Web-based articles; remember, just about anyone can put just about anything on the Web. Third, books are readily accessible, permanent sources of information in hard copy. You simply use your library's online catalog to locate books according to subject, author, or title. Then after finding the call numbers of the books that interest you, go to the appropriate shelves and help yourself. You can also access electronic books via your library's card catalog. These electronic books can be called up on your home computer and read online, a convenience that may save you valuable travel time.

When Sonia was looking for books in the library, she discovered a compelling one entitled *Arranged Marriage: Stories* by Chitra Divakaruni. The book chronicled a collection of stories about Indian-born girls and women who sought to find balance between Indian societal beliefs and desires of their own. Sonia felt that using illustrations from the book would give her speech a poignant and very personal touch to create empathy among her listeners.

Reference Materials   Although a form of print sources, reference materials are somewhat different than books. As you probably know, reference materials cannot be checked out of the library. They remain on the shelves for everyone to use at any time. In addition, these resources contain more limited information, often in condensed form. Dictionaries, encyclopedias, almanacs, directories, government documents, statistical abstracts, and so on are classified as reference materials. If you are looking for some specific information such as definitions of terms, current statistical data, or demographic profiles, reference materials can be very useful. They are generally located in a designated section of the library apart from other shelved books.

In the reference section of her campus library, Sonia found the *Worldmark Encyclopedia of Cultures and Daily Life.* In it she found a comparison of arranged marriages between southern Indians and northern Indians. The encyclopedia stated, "In the north, marriage partners are usually unrelated, and there are specific rules determining how close a blood-relationship is permitted. In southern India, however, cross-cousin marriage is the norm. The preferred match for a man is his maternal cross-cousin—his mother's brother's daughter" (*Lodrick,* 1998, p. 291).

Periodicals   Periodicals include newspapers, magazines, and journals. College libraries generally carry a wide selection of periodicals that can be accessed in hard copy, just like books. One advantage of these sources is they are current. In addition, you can easily determine the credibility of these sources. Publications like the *New York Times, U.S. News & World Report,* and *American Journal of Nursing* are generally respected as reliable sources of information. Although libraries may not permit you to check out the most current periodicals on the shelf, you are able to check out back issues that are also relatively recent.

Moee current

Sonia located an interesting article on her topic from the *Journal of Counseling and Development.* The article was titled "Marriage Satisfaction and Wellness in India and the United States: A Preliminary Comparison of Arranged Marriages and Marriages by Choice." Sonia suspected that many of the non-Indian students in her communications class would assume that an arranged marriage would result in less satisfaction and well-being than a marriage by choice. However, Sonia found a comparative study that showed "no support for differences in marital satisfaction or love aspects of wellness" between arranged marriages in India and marriages by choice in the United States (Myers, Madathil, & Tingle, 2005, p. 189).

ELECTRONIC SOURCES

Electronic sources are commonly used by students preparing for speech presentations. The Internet provides a world of facts at the touch of a finger, all in the comfort of your own home. However, keep in mind that not all electronic sources are created equally. The two most common are library databases and the Web.

Library Databases   Library databases are a collection of indexed information that you can access on your computer, typically in printable form. Libraries subscribe to these databases from reputable sources that include a wide variety of newspapers, magazines, and professional journals. Research databases you are likely to find through your campus library include EBSCOHost, Facts.com, InfoTrac, and ProQuest, to name a few. These databases are user-friendly, and you will be guided step by step through the process of searching for articles related to your topic. The articles you find may be full-texts or just abstracts of the article. Two major benefits of these databases include the ease with which they can be accessed and the credibility of the sources they reference.

The online journal *Women and Language* provided Sonia with a statistic that "an estimated 95% of all Hindu marriages in India are still arranged marriages" (Chawla, 2007, p. 5).

Electronic Sources are Easy to Access.

World Wide Web More frequently referred to as the Web, the World Wide Web is "a part of the Internet accessed through a graphical user interface and containing documents often connected by hyperlinks" (Merriam-Webster Online, 2007–2008, p. 1). You will find literally billions of Web pages on the publicly indexed Web. Given the magnitude of information on the Web, it is no wonder you may use this resource as a quick way to find information for class assignments.

However, because "so much information is available, and because that information can appear to be fairly 'anonymous,' it is necessary to develop skills to evaluate what you find. When you use a research or academic library, the books, journals and other resources have already been evaluated by scholars, publishers and librarians. Every resource you find has been evaluated in one way or another before you ever see it. When you are using the World Wide Web, none of this applies. There are no filters. Because anyone can write a Web page, documents of the widest range of quality, written by authors of the widest range of authority, are available on an even playing field. Excellent resources reside alongside the most dubious" (Kirk, 1996, p. 1).

If you decide to use the Web as a source of information for your speech, make sure you assess any article you find with care. See figure 12.1 for good Web searching tips. Consider the author of the article and what you know about his or her credentials. The same applies if the article is published by a group or organization. Might the author or publisher have any biases that would affect the accuracy of the information? Also identify when the article was last updated so you can determine the currency of the facts presented. In addition, see how the facts you find in the article compare with other facts you may find in reliable sources like books and

FIGURE 12.1 ■ Web Search
Tips

**Waukesha County Technical College's Library offers the following guidelines
for evaluating your online sources:**

Tips for Good Web Searching

Point One: How reliable is the authority of the site?

Who has created this website? Are they clearly identified? Can I contact them? Are
they fully qualified and knowledgeable on the topic? What is their education,
reputation, etc.? An example of a good authority on medical information is: The
National Library of Medicine.

Point Two: What's the purpose & objectivity of the site?

What is the purpose of this site? Is it trying to inform, sell me something, entertain, etc.?
Am I being given all relevant information? Does it seem one-sided or biased in any way?
What opinions are being expressed?

Point Three: How is the content of the site?

Is the information on the site original? Or is it someone else's work? Does the
information appear factual? Is it clear & easy to understand? Is the site properly
noted with footnotes and other references?

Point Four: How current is the website?

Is the information up to date or current? Does it contain the most recent information
available? When was it last updated? Are there inactive links on it?

Point Five: Does the website meet your needs?

Does it contain information that you are truly in need of? Is it meeting your needs?

professional journals. Remember, as a
public speaker, you have an ethical responsibility to report information that
is accurate and free of biases.

Recording Information

Once you have found credible information to support your main points, you will
want to record it for inclusion in your
presentation. Some speakers have found
bibliographic cards (see figures 12.2
and 12.3) and evidence cards helpful for
this task.

Bibliographic cards provide the essential information for creating a bibliography or reference page for your sources.
You record each of your sources on a

Source: www.CartoonStock.com.

Whitcomb, Susan. *Resume Magic: Trade Secrets of a Professional Resume Writer.* St. Paul: JIST Works, 2006.

FIGURE 12.2 ■ Sample MLA Bibliographic Card

Whitcomb, S. (2006). *Resume magic: Trade secrets of a professional resume writer.* St. Paul: JIST Works.

FIGURE 12.3 ■ Sample APA Bibliographic Card

| *Support Type* | Definition of Biometrics |
| *General Subject* | Biometrics |

Evidence

Biometrics is an automated method of recognizing a person based on a physiological or behavioral characteristic. Among the features measured are face, fingerprints, hand geometry, handwriting, iris, retina, vein, and voice. Biometric technologies are becoming the foundation of an extensive array of highly secure identification and personal verification solutions.

Source: An introduction to biometrics

FIGURE 12.4 ■ Sample Evidence Card

separate index card. Then when you have all of your cards prepared, you can alphabetize them according to the authors' last names and type your final bibliography or reference page. Two of the most common formats for bibliographies are the Modern Language Association, or MLA, and the American Psychological Association, or APA. Your instructor should indicate which format he or she prefers.

In contrast to bibliographic cards, evidence cards are used to record specific information you have selected from your authoritative sources (see figure 12.4). You will create these evidence cards as you research your topic. Then when your research is complete and you are ready to construct your outline, you can simply sort through your cards to determine what evidence you want to use and where you want to use it in the speech. The following information is generally found on evidence cards:

- **Support Type**
- **General Subject**
- **Evidence**
- **Abbreviation of Source**

(*Note:* You do not have to provide detailed information of your sources since that information has already been recorded on your bibliographic cards.)

Listing Your Sources

Information that you are using for support needs to be documented in a way that provides the source and publication details, enabling anyone to check the authenticity and accuracy of the information you are presenting. Many styles of documentation are used, and your instructor will specify which you are to use. For most courses, you will be assigned either American Psychological Association (APA) documentation or Modern Language Association (MLA) documentation. Several websites that show examples of citations for your different sources, your reference page, and your in-text citations are included under Web Activities at the end of this chapter.

Figure 12.5 lists some quick-and-easy features to look for when you use APA for your reference page.

Figure 12.6 lists some quick-and-easy features to look for when you use MLA for your list of works cited, and figures 12.7 and 12.8 show examples of reference citations in APA and MLA styles respectively.

You know you're using APA when . . .

- Your reference page has the title References
- Your references are listed in alphabetical order using the author's last name, editor, or title as the alphabetizer
- Your authors do not have a first name, only an initial
  Cheesebro, T., O'Connor, L., Rios, F.
- Your first entry is followed by a date in (parentheses)
  Smith, B. (2008). *Document your life: You can't live without it.* New York: Harpers.
- Your titles are *italicized*
- Your title uses sentence capitalization
  Implementing biometric security, not *Implementing Biometric Security*
- Your second and third lines have a five-space hanging indent and are double-spaced
- Your entries with an author are alphabetized by the author's last name
- Your entries without an author are alphabetized by the first word of the title, excluding a, an, or the
- Website entries have the hyperlink underlining removed and appear in black type

FIGURE 12.5 ■
APA Checklist

You know you're using MLA when . . .

- Your reference page has the title Works Cited
- Your references are listed in alphabetical order using the author's last name, editor, or title as the alphabetizer
- Your authors do have a first name
  Cheesebro, Thomas, O'Connor, Linda, & Rios, Francisco
- Your dates appear at the end of your citations
- Smith, Bryan. *Document Your Life: You Can't Live Without It.* New York: Harpers, 2008.
- Your titles are <u>underlined</u>
- Your underlined titles have capitalized the main words in them
  Implementing Biometric Security, not *Implementing biometric security*
- Your second and third lines have a five-space hanging indent and are double-spaced
- Your entries with an author are alphabetized by the author's last name
- Your entries without an author are alphabetized by the first word of the title, excluding a, an, or the
- Website entries have the hyperlink underlining removed and appear in black type

FIGURE 12.6 ■
MLA Checklist

References

Bolles, R. N. (2007). *What color is your parachute?* Retrieved September 13, 2007, from http://www.jobhunters bible.com/

Martin, C. (2005). *Perfect phrases for the perfect interview: Hundreds of ready-to-use phrases that succinctly demonstrate your skills, your experience and your value in any interview situation.* New York: McGraw-Hill.

Whitcomb, S. (2006). *Resume magic: Trade secrets of a professional resume writer.* St. Paul: JIST Works.

FIGURE 12.7 ■ Sample
APA Reference Page

FIGURE 12.8 ■ Sample
MLA Works Cited Page

Works Cited

Bolles, Richard. *What Color Is Your Parachute?* 2007. 13 Sept. 2007
<http://www.jobhunters bible.com/>.

Martin, Carole. *Perfect Phrases for the Perfect Interview: Hundreds of Ready-to-use
Phrases That Succinctly Demonstrate Your Skills, Your Experience and Your
Value in Any Interview Situation.* New York: McGraw-Hill, 2005.

Whitcomb, Susan. *Resume Magic: Trade Secrets of a Professional Resume Writer.*
St. Paul: JIST Works, 2006.

Avoiding Plagiarism

By carefully documenting your sources, you have taken a major step in avoiding plagiarism in your speech. Plagiarism occurs when you use the works of others in your presentation without crediting the source. Failure to credit your sources when you quote, paraphrase, or borrow ideas from those sources is a serious violation of ethical public speaking.

Plagiarism can actually result in a variety of ways. The most blatant form involves a speaker delivering an entire speech written by someone else. Thankfully, this type of plagiarism is comparatively rare. In contrast, you may find two other forms more common. One includes taking bits and pieces of material from a single source while failing to credit that source. Another form results when a speaker takes information from several different sources and pieces them together without providing proper citation.

In addition to including a Works Cited or References page with your outline, during the delivery of your speech, you need to mention your authoritative sources specifically.

The best way to reference your sources during your delivery is to provide a lead-in phrase before you cite your evidence. Some examples of how to accomplish these citations are as follows:

"According to Richard Bolles in his book *What Color Is Your Parachute.* . . ."

"A research study conducted in 2008 by Northwestern University's Intelligent Information Laboratory concluded. . . ."

"The People for the Ethical Treatment of Animals website stated in December 2008 that. . . ."

The extra attention and care you take to follow these suggestions will ensure that your speeches are free of plagiarism. In addition, you will be perceived by your audience as a credible speaker with the highest of ethical standards.

As you finish this information-gathering chapter, you will likely agree that researching, evaluating, recording, and documenting information for a speech can be a time-consuming process. However, with practice, you will become more confident and efficient in using these steps. In addition, the time and effort you invest in this part of speech preparation will go a long way to ensure a successful presentation.

Review Questions

1. Describe three different types of print sources of information.
2. What is a library database? Name three such databases you might use to research your speech.
3. Identify the five tips for good Web searching.
4. Using the five tips for good Web searching, evaluate three sources of information for your speech assignment.
5. Create a bibliographic citation for your textbook in either the MLA or APA format.
6. Explain the difference between a bibliographic card and an evidence card.
7. Describe three ways that plagiarism can occur in a speech presentation.

Key Terms and Concepts

APA 250

Bibliographic Cards 249

Evidence Cards 250

Library Databases 247

MLA 250

Periodicals 247

Reference Materials 246

References Page 252

Web 248

Works Cited 250

Web Activities

The following links may help you develop skill in recording information and sources accurately.

- Click on the following link to view examples of MLA works cited or APA reference page citations for every imaginable source: https://www.baker.edu/library/handouts/apa.pdf

- Knight Cite provides a very helpful website for making your MLA work cited or APA reference page entries. It can be found at http://www.calvin.edu/library/knightcite/index.php.

- Citation Machine puts your information into MLA or APA notation for you. Be sure to select either MLA or APA as other formats are also presented at http://citationmachine.net/.

- UC Berkeley–Teaching Library Internet Workshops offers a helpful resource for evaluating Web pages, including techniques to apply and questions to ask at http://www.lib.berkeley.edu/TeachingLib/Guides/Internet/Evaluate.html.

- For a wealth of information on a variety of topics, check out How Stuff Works at http://www.howstuffworks.com/.

Assignments

ASSIGNMENT 12.1: FIND YOUR SOURCES

Find at least one printed source and two different electronic sources of information for your informative presentation topic.

ASSIGNMENT 12.2: EVALUATE YOUR INFORMATION

Use the WCTC Library's "Tips for Good Web Searching" in this chapter to evaluate your information from the three sources in Assignment 12.1.

ASSIGNMENT 12.3: LIST YOUR SOURCES

Prepare a list that arranges at least three of your sources in alphabetical order using APA reference page or MLA works cited format.

ASSIGNMENT 12.4: CASE STUDY: TRIVIAL PURSUIT

Directions: To give you more practice in using print and online resources for research, your instructor will divide your class in groups of three or four. Each group will be sent to your college library to find answers to the following trivia questions and to record the sources of your answers in MLA or APA bibliographic format.

1. What does a prestidigitator do?
2. Who did James Buchanan beat in the 1856 presidential election?
3. What city in northeastern France was the place of origin for a famous cheese?
4. What is unique about the menu at San Francisco's Millennium Restaurant?
5. In 1903, what did Dr. George Crile invent, and how is it used today?
6. When the Nobel Prize was established in 1901, there were only five awards. Which award was added in 1968?
7. What is the main ingredient in andouillette?
8. How many quarter horses are owned in the state of Tennessee?
9. Many modern medicines originated from medicinal plants. Which medicine came from the willow bark?
10. When your car has a mass air flow problem, what should you do?

References

Chawla, D. (2007, Spring). I will speak out: Narratives of resistance in contemporary Indian women's discourses in Hindu arranged marriages. *Women and Language, 30*(1), 5–19.

Kirk, E. E. (1996). Evaluating information found on the Internet. Johns Hopkins University. Retrieved October 5, 2007, from http://www.library.jhu.edu/researchhelp/general/evaluating/

Lodrick, D. (1998). *Worldmark encyclopedia of cultures and daily life.* Detroit, Michigan: Gale Research.

Merriam-Webster Online. (2007–2008). Retrieved March 14, 2008, from http://www.merriam-webster.com/dictionary/World%20Wide%20Web

Myers, J. E., Madathil, J. & Tingle, L. R. (2005, Spring). *Journal of Counseling and Development, 83,* 183–190.

Watson solves mystery of searching information on the Web. (1999, October 19). *ScienceDaily.* Retrieved March 14, 2008, from http://www.sciencedaily.com/releases/1999/10/991019074447.htm

Chapter **13**

Delivering Presentations

Learning **Objectives**

At the end of this chapter, you should be able to meet the following objectives:

1. Understand the importance of delivery.
2. Cope with speaker anxiety.
3. Recognize delivery styles.
4. Practice delivery.
5. Identify four vocal elements of delivery.
6. Describe three nonverbal elements of delivery.

"There are always three speeches, for every one you actually gave. The one you practiced, the one you gave, and the one you wish you gave."

Dale Carnegie

Delivery Is Important

Juan was enrolled in a speech course at the local community college. Although outgoing with his friends and family, Juan had never liked speaking in front of groups. However, Speech 101 was required, and Juan had to complete it if he hoped to obtain his associate's degree.

His first assignment was a three-minute personal experience talk. He decided to tell his classmates about the summer he did volunteer work for the Hunger Task Force.

In anticipation of his presentation, Juan spent the next week outlining the information he wanted to share and practicing his delivery. He noticed, however, that every time he worked on his speech, he felt the symptoms of anxiety— the racing heart, faster breathing, discernable perspiration. Juan wondered how he was going to get through his speech when he was already feeling such nervousness.

Finally, the day arrived. Juan was third in his class to speak. As he approached the lectern, he felt the same uncomfortable symptoms he had experienced during his practice and preparation sessions. Afraid of embarrassing himself in front of his audience, Juan raced through his delivery, reading almost entirely from his note cards. When he finally sat down, Juan felt exhausted and discouraged, uncertain how he was going to make it through the rest of the semester and the other speeches that lay ahead.

If you find yourself recalling situations when you felt like Juan, you are not alone. Many celebrities and gifted artists have struggled with performance anxiety. Early in his career, singer Rod Stewart had such a severe case of nervousness that he sang an entire song while hiding behind a stack of speakers. Barbra Streisand forgot the lyrics to a song she was singing in public and stopped doing live performances for almost three decades (Enright, 2007). Recently, actress Catherine Heigl asked the audience at the Academy Awards where she was presenting to forgive her because she was so nervous.

Although fear of speaking or performing in public is often cited as the number one fear among people, you can successfully learn to manage your own apprehensions about addressing an audience. In fact, your ability to speak confidently before groups is certainly a skill well worth developing, especially in today's workplace.

"More than ever, public speaking—from presenting a status report to a small team to making a sales pitch before a packed room of potential investors—is a necessary skill. Across industries and in companies large and small, being able to convey crucial information credibly and convincingly before groups of all sizes has become as fundamental a job requirement as computer literacy. And being truly adept at it can propel you forward because public speaking gives you a visibility seldom achieved by sterling work alone" (Baskerville, 1994, p. 2).

In the upcoming sections of this chapter, you will discover ways to deliver a speech that captures audience interest, communicates self-confidence, and generates sincere applause. However, before you explore the strategies for an

effective delivery, let's take a look at some of the reasons people fear public speaking and the techniques for coping with this fear.

Coping with Speaker Anxiety

As you read in the opening to this chapter, public speaking is a common fear for many. In fact, some will go to great lengths in order to avoid delivering a speech. Rachel was one of those individuals. A recent graduate with an associate's degree in interior design, she took a position with a highly respected firm that specialized in customized home interiors. Rachel loved working with clients one-on-one where she was able to use her artistic flare and imagination to create warm and inviting living spaces.

Impressed by Rachel's talents, the owner of the firm thought Rachel's innate design abilities and pleasant personality would make her a perfect match for representing the firm at a local women's club meeting to speak about home decorating. When the owner approached Rachel about the idea, Rachel felt panic set in. Although she was perfectly at ease dealing with one or two clients at a time, the thought of addressing a group of 125 women was too much for her to consider. She requested more time to think about the opportunity, hoping she would be able to come up with some excuse for declining the owner's request.

The presentation at the women's club would have been a wonderful chance for Rachel to increase business for the design firm and enhance community relations. However, her fear prevented her from venturing out of her communication comfort zone.

For many, the physical sensations associated with speaker anxiety are the most difficult to bear. Actually, these sensations are very much like those you might experience in any stressful situation. Facing an upcoming exam, dealing with a difficult boss, having an argument with a spouse can all trigger a stress response, sometimes referred to as "fight or flight." Consider what happens to your body in such circumstances.

"The human body responds to stressors by activating the nervous system and specific hormones. The hypothalamus signals the adrenal glands to produce more of the hormones adrenaline and cortisol and release them into the bloodstream. These hormones speed up heart rate, breathing rate, blood pressure, and metabolism. Blood vessels open wider to let more blood flow to large muscle groups, putting our muscles on alert. Pupils dilate to improve vision. The liver releases some of its stored glucose to increase the body's energy. And sweat is produced to cool the body. All of these physical changes prepare a person to react quickly and effectively to handle the pressure of the moment" (Stress, 2008, p. 1).

In reality, when you experience sensations like these, your body and brain are responding normally to a perceived danger or challenge. For example, if you narrowly escape a car accident by quickly swerving your vehicle away from an oncoming motorist, you will be thankful for this stress response. It prepared your body to instinctively react in a way that may have saved your life.

However, speaking in public is not life threatening, and the symptoms of stress you experience are not the result of any true danger. The nervousness you feel before delivering a speech has more to do with how you think about the presentation. You will find it helpful to remember that you cannot have a feeling without first having had a thought. Consequently, one of the first ways to reduce speaker anxiety is to examine the unrealistic beliefs you may have about addressing an audience.

One unrealistic belief you may have is that the audience will be able to sense your nervousness and perceive you as incompetent. In truth, however, most audience members are not nearly as aware of your nervousness as you are. It is not uncommon for a speaker to confess feelings of anxiety after a presentation only to hear audience members comment they didn't even notice.

"It was the classic fight or flight response. Next time, try flight."

Source: www.CartoonStock .com.

Another unrealistic fear can stem from the belief that somehow your delivery must be perfect. Be assured that if you have done your best to get ready for your speech, you can relax and just be yourself. You do not have to be perfect. Who you are is plenty good! Audiences respond to speakers who are genuine, as opposed to those who are stiff and artificial—fearful of making a mistake.

A third unrealistic belief is that you cannot deliver an effective speech because you are not a professional speaker. Remember that confidence in public speaking is built by practice. The more you speak before groups, the more comfortable you will become. Even those individuals who are not experienced speakers can deliver a memorable, heartfelt presentation by speaking with sincerity.

Along with confronting any unrealistic thoughts you might have about speaking in public, you will also find the additional guidelines helpful for coping with anxiety.

First, be well prepared. Some experts say that nervousness can be reduced by 75 percent with sufficient preparation and practice. Second, accept that some tension before a presentation is natural. In fact, it represents a heightened sense of awareness that can be used to add life and energy to your speech.

Third, consider doing some slow, deep breathing prior to speaking. Inhale through the nose for a count of two, counting one-one thousand, two-one thousand. Hold the breath for a second or two, and then exhale through the mouth for a count of four, counting one-one thousand, two-one thousand,

Delivery Improves
with Practice

three-one thousand, and so on. Repeat this cycle three to five times. This breathing exercise can slow your heart rate, reduce nervousness, and help you feel more relaxed.

Fourth, practice positive self-talk. What you say to yourself has a profound effect on how you feel. When you catch yourself engaged in negative self-talk such as, "I'm going to forget what I want to say and look like a fool," immediately replace that message with a positive one. "I'm well prepared; I have note cards with me, and if I forget some information, I'll just pause and take a look at my notes."

Fifth, have a strong introduction. Many speakers find that when they get off to a good start, much of their nervousness dissipates within the first few minutes of the presentation. Finally, remember that much, if not all, of your nervousness is not even visible to an audience. They are there to hear what you have to say and are not really interested in how you might feel at the moment.

In her website, *Facing the Fear,* Kathy Brady addresses several aspects of speech anxiety including "Why Speaking Makes You Sick," "Visualization and Desensitization," "Breathing," "Preparation," "Performance," and "Just How Nervous Are You?" You will find her personable, reassuring approach to speech anxiety helpful as you meet the challenges of your speaking assignments. Brady answers your most basic questions, such as, "What exactly does 'practicing' a speech mean? How many times should you practice your speech? What type of delivery method works best for students with speech anxiety?" She also addresses common concerns that involve volume and pacing, eye contact, and use of the body. Brady's comprehensive website should be your next stop for overcoming speech anxiety: http://www.uwm.edu/People/kabrady/visual.html.

Delivery Styles

Before you begin practicing your speech delivery, you will want to be aware of the various types of delivery that exist. These deliveries include manuscript, memorized, extemporaneous, and impromptu.

MANUSCRIPT

As the name implies, manuscript deliveries are read word-for-word off the printed page. To avoid nervousness, some speakers think that if they write out their entire speech and then read it, they will be less likely to make a mistake. Although their perception may be true on the one hand, on the other hand, they run the risk of delivering a dull, lifeless presentation. Audiences easily become bored by speakers reading to them with little or no eye contact and spontaneity.

On occasion, you may need to read a quote or cite some important data exactly as it is written to ensure accuracy, but to read an entire speech should be avoided at all costs. In addition, with today's technology, speakers may become overly reliant on PowerPoint slides. The end result is a delivery that involves reading from the slides and losing a personal connection with the audience. Keep in mind that if you use PowerPoint, the slides should provide brief visuals to complement the spoken message.

MEMORIZED

To reduce the tendency to read the speech, as with manuscript style, you might think it is a good idea to memorize the speech instead and avoid dependence upon notes. However, even without notes, speakers who memorize their speech still tend to sound stilted and artificial. In addition, you may actually increase your anxiety by worrying about the possibility of forgetting the information you memorized. Although you may choose to memorize a short quote or brief fact or two, committing the whole speech to memory is not the best choice of delivery styles.

EXTEMPORANEOUS

This style is the most versatile of all the styles. It requires you to be thoroughly prepared and well rehearsed, but to deliver the speech in a conversational style with little reliance on notes. With this delivery, the audience feels as if you are speaking to them directly and personally. Obviously, to use this style, you must have a sound grasp of your subject matter and have practiced sufficiently so you can speak with ease. By far, extemporaneous speaking is the most effective delivery style.

IMPROMPTU

As you probably already know, impromptu speaking involves speaking unexpectedly or off-the-cuff. Your manager may ask you to voice your opinion at a meeting; you may need to introduce yourself and to share some of your background with a group of new employees; at a company banquet, you may be asked to "say a few words." These are just some of the instances that require an impromptu delivery. Although it is never a good idea to use the impromptu style for a presentation that demands conscientious prior preparation, it can be a versatile style to cultivate in the situations just described. If you find yourself in an impromptu setting, consider doing the following: state your point briefly, offer any necessary information to clarify your point, and create a concise statement to indicate closure.

Practice Delivery

As you read in the preceding section, the most versatile form of delivery is the extemporaneous style. This style of speaking is carefully prepared and well rehearsed but delivered conversationally. In other words, you know your material so well that you can share it without unnecessary reliance on your outline or speaker's notes. To ensure an extemporaneous presentation, you will find the following guidelines helpful.

Develop a speaking outline: Avoid speaking directly from the detailed outline you prepared. This type of outline is an excellent way to solidify your thoughts and to make sure you are expressing your ideas clearly and specifically. However, speaking from this outline can tempt you to read the information with little audience eye contact. Instead, consider constructing a speaker's outline, note cards, or map. A **speaker's outline** is an abbreviated form of the detailed outline you prepared. It may contain your central idea and main points, along with some key words and phrases to remind you of what you want to say. In other words, this outline serves mainly as a memory jogger and not as a complete transcript of your speech. Such an abbreviated outline will discourage you from becoming overly dependent upon your notes and force you to speak more directly to your listeners. Take a look at the sample speaker's outline shown in figure 13.1.

FIGURE 13.1 ■ Sample Speaker's Outline

I. Introduction

  A. Story about Bonnie
  B. Citation from John Marcus
  C. Successful interviewing requires attention to many details.
  D. Dress, behavior, follow-up

II. Body

  A. Before the interview, dress for success.

    1. Explanation of proper dress
    2. Citation from Molloy
    3. Example of selections

  Transition Now that you are dressed, how should you behave?

  B. During the interview, behave confidently.

    1. Explain posture
    2. Citation from P. Eckman on eye contact
    3. Compare confident to less confident

  Transition When the interview ends, more work needs to be done.

  C. After the interview, follow up with additional contacts.

    1. Explain thank-you note
    2. Statistic on those who wrote
    3. Citation from *Excel* video

III. Conclusion

  A. Pay attention to details: dress before, behavior during, and follow-up after the interview.
  B. A successful interview depends on paying close attention to many details.
  C. Citation from *What Color Is Your Parachute?* by R. N. Bolles.

If you choose to prepare **note cards** instead (figure 13.2), remember some of these tips: number them sequentially; keep the information on each card as brief as possible; write legibly or type them; use boldfacing, underlining, or colored highlighting to make key information stand out; practice your delivery with your note cards; use them as inconspicuously as possible.

I. INTRODUCTION   Note card #1

  A. **Story** about Bonnie
  B. In the months ahead, we will be conducting job searches, the most important part of which is the interview. **Citation** J. Marcus, *Complete Job Interview Handbook.*
  C. Successful interviewing requires attention to many details.
  D. I will be discussing the dress, behavior, and follow-up required for success.

II. BODY   Note card #2

  A. Before the interview, dress for success.
    1. **Explain** proper dress for. . . .
    2. **Citation** from Molloy's *Dress For Success*
    3. **Examples** of combinations that work. . . .

Transition: Now that you are ready for the interview, how should you behave during the interview?

BODY   Note card #3

  B. During the interview, behave confidently.
    1. **Explain** appropriate posture
    2. **Cite** P. Eckman on eye contact
    3. **Compare** confident to less confident applicants

Transition: You may think the interview is over when it ends, but there is more work to do.

BODY   Note card #4

  C. After the interview, follow up with additional contacts.
    1. **Explain** what to write in thank-you note
    2. Placement office **statistics** on those who write. . . .
    3. **Citation** on telephone contact from *Excel* video

III. CONCLUSION   Note card #5

  A. So you can see that you must pay close attention to details before, during, and after the interview.
  B. A successful interview depends on paying close attention to many details.
  C. **Citation** from *What Color Is Your Parachute?* by Richard N. Bolles.

FIGURE 13.2 ■ Sample Speaking Note Cards

If you choose to prepare a **map** for your speaking notes, you will be designing a visual representation of your information. Maps can look like a solar system, with main points orbiting around a central idea, or they may resemble an organizational chart with boxed information arranged in a linear pattern. Inspiration Software is a user-friendly computer program for creating speakers' maps. Figure 13.3 shows a speaking map prepared with Inspiration so you can see what one looks like. If you would like more information about this program, you can go to the website at www.inspiration.com/.

Practice out loud: Once you have prepared a speaker's outline, a set of note cards, or a map, you can actually practice delivering your speech. Effective practice involves going over your entire speech several times out loud. Some speakers make the mistake of simply reading their notes silently. Practicing out loud, however, gives you the opportunity to develop

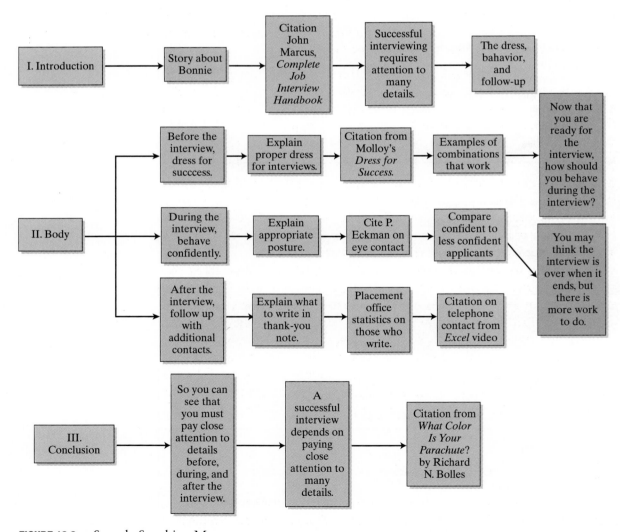

FIGURE 13.3 ■ Sample Speaking Map

a conversational style and to incorporate effective use of eye contact, gestures, posture, and facial expressions.

Practice in front of an audience if you can: Friends, family, and co-workers are often willing to lend an ear and offer constructive feedback as you rehearse. Videotaping can be another excellent tool to help you review strengths and weaknesses in your delivery. In addition, if you are able, try to schedule at least one rehearsal in the room where you will be delivering your presentation.

Practice with your visuals: It is always a good idea to rehearse your speech using your visual aids. Whether you have flip charts, models, or computer-generated graphics, practicing with them will enable you to create a smooth flow as you move from your text to the visuals. Also, as mentioned earlier, if you rehearse in the room you will use for the presentation, make certain any equipment you need is in good working order. Particularly if you are using computer-generated graphics, you will be wise to have a back-up plan in case you encounter computer problems on the day of your delivery. For instance, print out your slides so they can be used on a projection device if the computer fails.

Time your speech: Unless you actually time yourself during rehearsal, you may not know for certain if your speech is too long or too short. For a classroom assignment especially, your instructor might deduct points if the speech doesn't conform to the assignment requirements. By timing yourself during rehearsal, you can determine if you need to add or delete information, as well as slow or pick up your rate of speaking.

Use visualization: Another technique many speakers find helpful as part of their rehearsal involves the use of visualization. Here's how it works. Go to a spot where you won't be interrupted and lie down or sit in a comfortable chair. Close your eyes and take a few slow, deep breaths while releasing any muscle tension you may feel in your body. Then picture yourself delivering your speech in front of your audience. Be very specific and detailed as you visualize this scene in your mind's eye. Imagine what you will be wearing, what the room looks like, who will be present in the audience, and so on. Then see yourself approaching the front of the room, looking out at your listeners and feeling calm and confident. Talk through your entire speech, observing positive feedback from your listeners and experiencing a sense of accomplishment and self-assurance. Try this exercise several times before your actual presentation. The secret of using visualization is to make your mental picture as detailed as possible and to see yourself as being successful.

Vocal Elements of Delivery

Your voice is one of your most unique personal characteristics. Much like a fingerprint, each person's voice contains qualities that set it apart from other voices. In fact, for some time, individual speech patterns have played a part

FIGURE 13.4 ■ Darth Vader, Voice of James Earl Jones

in criminal investigations. Since the tragedy of 9-11, these speech patterns have taken on even greater importance in the field of law enforcement.

"Voice prints are being used to verify the authenticity of terrorists' taped messages, and psychological stress evaluation of their speech provides information about general levels of anxiety and tension of speakers in airports and other ports of entry. Accent and dialect can be used in speaker profiling as one method of determining whether a suspect is traveling from a hostile country. Finally, speech patterns provide important screening information about intoxication, giving law enforcement officers probable cause for detainment and further investigation" (Amazon.com, 2008, p. 1).

In addition to law enforcement agencies using the voice as an indicator of criminal intent, the media also capitalizes on the human voice to sell products, promote causes, and provide entertainment. Think about the distinctive voice of your favorite radio D.J., for example, or the memorable voice of James Earl Jones as Darth Vader in the Star Wars movies (see figure 13.4). Who could forget the voice of Mel Blanc as he portrayed Porky Pig, Bugs Bunny, Barney Rubble, and Daffy Duck? Talented individuals like these were able to make a living as a result of their vocal qualities.

Although you may not be seeking celebrity status using your voice, you can certainly learn to make your voice work for you as an effective public speaker. Remember, 38 percent of the impression you create for an audience comes from your voice. So let's take a closer look at some tips you can follow to create a successful delivery.

Watch your pitch, rate, and volume: Pitch refers to how high or low you speak; rate describes the speed at which you speak; and volume is characterized by loudness or softness of the voice. Ideally, your natural speaking voice is the best voice to use when delivering a presentation. However, you can enhance your voice by varying pitch, rate, and volume. In other words, if your voice is typically low, incorporate a variety of inflections so that you occasionally raise your pitch. The reverse is true if your voice is on the high side; explore opportunities to lower your range from time to time.

Although an abnormally slow rate of speaking can put an audience to sleep, many speakers face the problem of speaking too rapidly, especially if they are a bit nervous. Consequently, it's often helpful to speak somewhat slower than your conversational rate. As for volume, make certain you speak loudly enough to be heard. You can also vary your volume in order to hold audience attention. When making a particularly important point, for example, either raise or lower your normal volume. These kinds of periodic changes keep the audience's attention from drifting off.

Pay attention to articulation and pronunciation: First let's look at the difference between these two. Articulation refers to the clarity with which you speak your words. Failing to speak clearly may result in your audience misunderstanding what you are trying to communicate. Careful articulation becomes more of an issue when you are addressing a large group of people. You want to make sure that those in the back of the room can understand you just as well as those in the front.

Pronunciation, on the other hand, involves placing correct emphasis on the various syllables of a word. If you look in a dictionary, you will discover that some words can be pronounced in more than one way. For example, the word *diverse* can be pronounced with a short "i" or a long "i." Usually the first pronunciation cited is the preferable one. However, most words have a standard pronunciation that you will want to use. In particular, speakers may find difficulty when they are using technical terms. If you need to use technical terms, make certain you are saying them correctly. Consult a good technical dictionary if you are in doubt.

Choose language carefully: Everyday conversation is generally informal. You use informal language when communicating with classmates, co-workers, family, and friends. This type of language also commonly incorporates slang. Here is an example of informal English:

Informal: *Man, I was really bummed by that last psych test. I mean like I didn't even know where the prof got some of those questions from; you know?*

Although informal English is perfectly appropriate in day-to-day interactions, public speaking demands more formal language choices. Take a look at the following same message expressed more formally.

Formal: *I felt discouraged after taking that last test in psychology. In fact, I wasn't certain of the source the professor used to design some of the questions.*

The difference between informal and formal language should be pretty evident from these two examples. It also should go without saying that sexist or racist terms, stereotypes, and profanity have no place in a public presentation.

Avoid nonfluencies: A final consideration to keep in mind is the avoidance of nonfluencies. These are words or vocalizations that serve no purpose. The most common are "you knows" and "ums" and "uhs." Most people use a few of these nonfluencies from time to time in speech, but repeated use of them is distracting and may reveal a lack of confidence. To determine if nonfluencies are a problem for you, tape record or videotape your speech and play it back. You can also have someone listen to your speech rehearsal, paying special attention to the inclusion of "ums," "uhs," and "you knows." If you lose your train of thought during your speech, you will be better off pausing momentarily rather than reverting to nonfluencies.

Nonverbal Elements of Delivery

Finally, your posture, gestures, and facial expressions are major nonverbal elements of your delivery that also require careful consideration.

In reality, your speech delivery begins the moment you leave your seat and approach the lectern. The audience is already paying attention to the way you carry yourself. Communicate assurance by standing tall and walking confidently to the speaker's platform.

Once you have arrived at the lectern, set your speaker's notes down and take a few seconds to establish eye contact with your listeners. You will also feel more comfortable if you balance your weight evenly on both feet rather than crossing one ankle in front of or behind the other or corkscrewing your legs around one another. Notice the posture of the two speakers pictured in figure 13.5. Which speaker looks most ready to deliver an effective presentation?

Your next challenge may involve knowing what to do with your hands and arms. Although you can rest your hands on the lectern, you don't want to lock them in that position for the entire speech. Instead, gesture naturally as you would in more casual conversation. For example, you might raise a hand when you want to emphasize a point. You can use descriptive gestures to illustrate the size or shape of something. Possibly extend your arms with open palms when you want to invite your listeners to consider a particular point of view.

When you practice your speech, make a deliberate attempt to incorporate gestures until you find several that seem comfortable to you. Then insert cues in your speaker's outline, note cards, or map as reminders of where you want to gesture. Although this suggestion might seem somewhat artificial, after several practice sessions, your movements will become more natural.

By all means, avoid any fidgeting, nervous, or distracting gestures that focus your audience's attention away from your message. In addition, keep your hands out of your pockets and free from distracting note cards.

Like posture and gestures, your facial expressions are also important. Perhaps your greatest ally in establishing rapport with an audience is your smile. Use your smile to communicate your friendly desire to share information with your audience.

a)

b)

FIGURE 13.5 ■ Speaker Postures: a) Too Relaxed; b) Ready to Go

Smiles Communicate Beyond Words

Accompany your smile with eye contact that establishes and maintains a visual connection with your audience. The extended eye contact method is a helpful way to make this connection. Look at one or two members of your audience for four to five seconds. Then shift your gaze to another few members of the audience. Continue this rotation until you have created eye contact with your entire audience. In the case of a very large audience, you can use this technique with sections of the audience instead of with specific individuals.

Lastly, let the expressiveness of your face reveal your feelings about the message you are communicating. Think of the way in which your face becomes animated when you run into a good friend, hear a sad story, or receive some surprising news. In these instances, your facial expressions are certainly not static. They change moment by moment with each thought and feeling you experience. In a similar way, let your face tell the audience about your reactions to the information you are sharing. In so doing, you will maintain the interest of your listeners and give them the opportunity to empathize with your own thoughts and feelings.

By following the guidelines offered in this chapter, you will be pleased to experience not only an effective delivery but a feeling of self-confidence that will carry over into all of your interactions with others.

Review Questions

1. Discuss three suggestions for coping with speaker anxiety that you found most helpful in the chapter.
2. List and explain the four different delivery styles.
3. Explain the differences among a speaker's outline, note cards, and a speaker's map.
4. Discuss three suggestions for practicing your delivery.
5. Explain the difference between articulation and pronunciation.
6. What are nonfluencies? Why should they be avoided in your speech delivery?
7. What are the three nonverbal elements of delivery?

Key Terms and Concepts

Articulation   267

Coping with Speaker Anxiety   258

Effective Rehearsal   265

Extemporaneous   261

Formal English   267

Impromptu   261

Informal English   267

Manuscript   260

Memorized   261

Nonfluencies   268

Nonverbal Elements of Delivery   268

Note Cards   263

Pronunciation   267

Speaker's Outline   262

Speaking Map   264

Visualization   265

Vocal Elements of Delivery   265

Web Activities

- Check out the helpful advice for overcoming speaker anxiety at the website http://www.ccri .edu/advising/health_and_wellness/speakers.shtml.
- More help is available for dealing with communication anxiety at *Facing the Fear,* http://www .uwm.edu/People/kabrady/for.html.
- Anxiety Coach offers an interactive exercise to help reduce stage fright at http://www.anxietycoach .com/social2.htm#top.
- This website gives you links to lots of helpful articles on various aspects of public speaking. Check it out! http://www.speaking-tips.com/Delivery/.

- To determine the extent of speaking anxiety that you may be experiencing, visit http://ux.brookdalecc .edu/fac/speech/prpsa.php and complete the Personal Report of Public Speaking Anxiety (PRPSA) Quiz.
- To better understand your reaction to stress, visit the Stress Response website at http://www.wisconline .com/objects/index_tj.asp?objID=AP13804.

Assignments

ASSIGNMENT 13.1: REDUCE SPEAKER ANXIETY

View a DVD about speaker anxiety and note the key suggestions for reducing nervous tension. Bring your summary to the session when your class discusses speaker anxiety.

–OR–

Find an article about speaker anxiety and note the key suggestions for reducing nervous tension. Bring your summary to class for the session when your class discusses speaker anxiety.

In small groups, share your suggestions for overcoming speaker anxiety with other members of your group. Listen to their suggestions. After the discussion, record your group's summary on poster paper provided by your instructor.

Report your group's summary to the entire class. Listen to the suggestions from the other groups.

Finally, prepare a three-step action plan of your own for overcoming your speaker anxiety.

ASSIGNMENT 13.2: FAMOUS SPEECH ANALYSIS

At your school library or speech lab, obtain a DVD recording of a famous speech from the past.

As you listen to and view the speech, note the vocal and nonverbal delivery elements that make the speech effective.

Use the following table to help you focus on these elements:

Criterion	What I liked	What I'd improve
Articulation		
Pronunciation		
Nonfluencies		
Language Suitable to Audience		
Language Formality		
Confident Stance		
Appropriate Gestures		
Visual Rapport (Eye Contact)		
Avoided Distraction		
Overall Delivery		

The part of the speech I liked best was:

The most important thing I learned about speech delivery was:

ASSIGNMENT 13.3: VIDEOTAPE REHEARSAL

Record a rehearsal for a speaking assignment you are preparing for this course or any of your other classes.

Use the following critique table to help you focus on the vocal and nonverbal elements:

Criterion	What I liked	What I'd improve
Articulation		
Pronunciation		
Nonfluencies		
Language Suitable to Audience		
Language Formality		
Confident Stance		
Appropriate Gestures		
Visual Rapport (Eye Contact)		
Avoided Distraction		
Overall Delivery		

The most important thing I learned from the rehearsal was:

The part of the speech delivery I liked best was:

ASSIGNMENT 13.4: CASE STUDY: MANAGING SPEAKER ANXIETY

Your younger brother is scheduled to present an informative speech in class next week, and he has not had much experience giving speeches. He shares with you the great fear and anxiety that he is feeling. Then he says, "You're taking a speech class this semester. What do they tell you about overcoming speech anxiety in your class? How am I ever going to be able to make that speech next week?"

Summarize what you have found in this chapter that would help your brother understand what speech anxiety is, how he might overcome his speech anxiety, and what he needs to do in order to make an effective, informative speech next week.

References

Amazon.com. (2008). *Forensic aspects of speech patterns: Voice prints, speaker profiling, lie and intoxication detection*. Retrieved March 20, 2008, from http://www.amazon.com/Forensic-Aspects-Speech-Patterns-Intoxication/dp/1930056400/ref=tag_tdp_sv_edpp_i

Baskerville, D. M. (1994, May 1). Public speaking rule #1: Have no fear. *Black Enterprise*. Retrieved September 21, 2007, from http://www.encyclopedia.com/doc/1G1-15131799.html

Enright, P. (2007, September 12). Even stars get stage fright. Retrieved March 18, 2008, from http://www.msnbc.msn.com/id/20727420/

Stress. (2008). TeensHealth. Retrieved March 18, 2008, from http://www.kidshealth.org/teen/your_mind/emotions/stress.html

Chapter **14**

Persuasive Speaking

Learning **Objectives**

At the end of this chapter, you should be able to meet the following objectives:

1. Identify the importance of persuasion.
2. Identify the types of persuasive presentations.
3. Describe three elements of persuasion.
4. Explain strategies for persuasive presentations.
5. Recognize patterns of organization for persuasion.

"Persuasion is better than force."

Proverb

Persuasion Is Important

In 1995, Jean-Dominique Bauby, French editor of *Elle* magazine, was forty-three years old when he suffered a massive stroke. Following the stroke, he found himself in a hospital bed completely paralyzed except for his left eye, which became his sole means of communication. "The therapist at his hospital came up with a system. She would read through the letters of the alphabet, and Bauby would blink when she came to the letter he wanted—and thus spell out his message (see figure 14.1). Bit by excruciating bit—by blinking— Bauby dictated a book about his experience, *The Diving Bell and the Butterfly* (NPR, 2007, p. 1). The book later became a film.

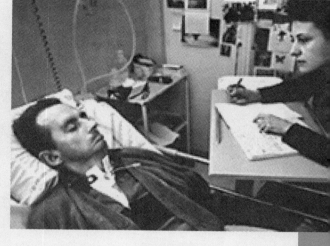

FIGURE 14.1 ■ Jean-Dominique Bauby

The film's director, Julian Schnabel, commented, "I figure if I told this story, I could actually help somebody else, and I could help myself, because I think it's extremely optimistic. I think it's life-affirming. You realize that you can actually do something if you have an interior life . . . that people can have all their faculties, be perfectly healthy and not be alive at all" (NPR, 2007, p. 2).

After reading about the plight of Bauby, you may find it hard to imagine how anyone could face such incredible obstacles and still find it possible to create a meaningful life. Like many films, *The Diving Bell and the Butterfly* carries a strong, persuasive message to the audience. Some viewers might be moved to be extremely grateful for the blessings in their lives; others might find the courage to face their own personal challenges, which seem insignificant in comparison.

In addition to films, you are surrounded by other media designed to be persuasive. Advertisers, for example, count on persuading viewers to buy products, donate to worthwhile causes, or change behavior. Take a look at the ads in figures 14.2 and 14.3. What is your reaction to their persuasive appeal?

Images that appear in ads such as these can be highly effective, but they are not the only media that evoke powerful persuasive appeal. Consider the effect that music, particularly song lyrics, can have on you.

A study of 500 college students published in the *Journal of Personality and Social Psychology* concluded that "Violent song lyrics increase negative emotions and thoughts that can lead to aggression" (Violent Song, 2003, p. 1).

"Researchers from Iowa State University and the Texas Department of Human Services found that aggressive music lyrics increase aggressive thoughts and feelings, which might perpetuate aggressive behavior and have long-term effects, such as influencing listeners' perceptions of society and contributing to the development of aggressive personalities" (Violent Song, 2003, p. 1).

As you can see, understanding persuasion as a communication tool is important because you are influenced by a variety of persuasive messages in the media every day. In addition, employers seek to motivate you to higher levels

FIGURE 14.2 ■ Smoking Is Ugly

FIGURE 14.3 ■ Stop Domestic Violence

"I've hired this musician to play a sad melody while I give you a sob story why I didn't do my homework. It's actually quite effective."

FIGURE 14.4 ■ Sob Story
Source: www.CartoonStock.com.

of performance, friends and family seek to sway your choices, and businesses compete for the dollars you spend. An awareness of this influence can encourage more critical thinking on your part, making you a more discriminating consumer of what you see and hear.

In addition, you often attempt to persuade others when you communicate with them. You may not have gone to the extent that the student in the cartoon in figure 14.4 did to persuade someone to accept your point of view, but chances are you use persuasive communication more frequently than you realize.

Whether you see persuasion as the "art of getting your own way," as the means by which all sales are made, or as the essential force that shapes your government, persuasion is an important component of your day-to-day communication.

You use persuasion to influence a prospective employer that you are the ideal candidate for the job; you use persuasion to convince that "special someone" to have dinner with you; you use persuasion to motivate your children to help out with household chores. These are just a few of the instances when you may find yourself trying to influence the feelings and behaviors of others.

Some communication experts claim that all forms of communication contain an element of persuasion. For example, at a party or social gathering, you may engage in small talk with the other guests. Underlying this small talk is possibly an attempt to be accepted and liked by those with whom you interact. Asking a clarifying question in a classroom is intended to motivate the instructor to provide an answer. Sharing a personal problem with a close friend is often done to prompt encouragement, support, or empathy. What these examples illustrate is that much of your communication with others is prompted by motives that may not be directly expressed or even consciously recognized.

On the other hand, you undoubtedly experience instances when your attempts to be persuasive are much more intentional and direct. For example, during a job interview, you are likely to use skillful responses to an interviewer's questions in order to secure a position you really want. Your desire to get a date with an attractive classmate may motivate you to be particularly attentive and pleasant during conversations with this individual. Your strongest negotiation skills may come to the forefront when you are trying to get the best deal from a car salesperson.

Regardless of whether your communication with others is directly or indirectly persuasive, the ability to use persuasion effectively offers a number of benefits. Take a look at the following benefits:

You become a more skillful communicator: First, you become more adept at establishing your personal credibility. When people perceive you to be trustworthy, dependable, and genuinely concerned about the interests of others, they are more likely to be receptive to your point of view.

Second, you develop greater sensitivity in establishing common ground with your listeners. Those who are the most skillful persuaders are good listeners who make a sincere effort to understand the needs of their audience and then propose shared advantages of a given perspective.

Third, you learn to use vivid language and compelling evidence in supporting your position. Fresh, imaginative word choices coupled with strong, convincing information encourage your listeners to seriously consider what you have to say.

Fourth, you become more proficient in connecting with your listeners emotionally. You make this connection by sharing your emotional commitment to an issue while also sensing your listeners' emotional state and adjusting the tone and intensity or your arguments accordingly (Harrison, 2005–2007, p. 1).

You become a more resourceful researcher: Becoming an effective persuader requires you to support your arguments with credible authoritative resources. Given the availability of electronic media, you may find it easy to turn to the Internet as your primary resource for supporting evidence. But remember that anyone can publish on the Web, so you need to carefully assess the reliability of Web-based information. Some of the questions you will want to ask yourself about Web sources include the following:

ASK YOURSELF ABOUT WEB SOURCES

Who is the author and what kind of credentials does he or she have?

Who published this site? How reliable is the publisher?

How current is the document? When was the site last updated?

How objective is the content? Is the information well documented?

How does the information compare to other sources related to the topic?

In addition, your resourcefulness as a researcher will be enhanced if you examine other sources besides those found on the Internet. Newspapers, periodicals, books, library reference materials, and electronic databases help to round out your selection of resources and provide balance to your research.

You become a more critical thinker: Critical thinking is essential to being an effective persuader. Listeners are more likely to believe your claims if those claims are based upon sound logic. The critical thinker is someone who is able to separate facts from opinions, detect fallacies in reasoning, and determine soundness of emotional appeals. Also, as you improve your critical thinking abilities, you become a better problem solver and a more discriminating decision maker. Critical thinkers are less likely to be misled by propaganda or faulty persuasion.

You become more aware of the importance of ethical communication: To be truly successful in persuasion, you must be highly ethical. Ethical considerations of persuaders include the following:

ETHICAL CONSIDERATIONS

- Having honorable motives
- Being respectful of a listener's point of view
- Evaluating all sides of an issue objectively
- Using information from reliable sources
- Avoiding reasoning fallacies
- Being willing to concede when an opponent has a valid point
- Refusing to manipulate information to advance a personal cause
- Maintaining personal integrity by being honest and trustworthy

You experience increased confidence as a communicator: One of your greatest self-confidence boosters is your ability to stand in front of an audience to express your ideas clearly, calmly, and confidently. Persuasive speaking in particular can bolster self-confidence because of the skills required. You may, for example, find yourself facing an apathetic or hostile audience. Trying to persuade such a group will challenge you to apply all of the persuasive skills you have developed, including those discussed earlier. Projecting credibility as the result of careful research, thoughtful organization, and a courteous delivery can help you win over an audience. And even though not all of your listeners may agree with you at the end of your presentation, they will respect you as a speaker and a person. Such experiences will enable you to confront all forms of communication with greater ease and assurance.

Types of Persuasive Presentations

Throughout your college career and work life, you may be called upon to deliver persuasive presentations in a variety of forms. Sales promotions, motivational talks, proposals, and classroom presentations are just a few that you may encounter. However, regardless of when and where these presentations take place, they can be categorized in three ways: **fact, value**, and **policy**. Let's take a brief look at each of these.

Fact: Topics of fact attempt to establish a relationship or connection between two ideas. For example, you might seek to convince your classmates that smoke detectors save lives, that violent video games influence violent acts, or that regular aerobic exercise results in a longer, healthier life. In the workplace, you might try to convince your supervisor that a new production software package can reduce defects by 37 percent, that medical staff who work more than twelve-hour shifts contribute to a greater incidence of patient errors, or that failure to follow OSHA standards significantly increases workplace accidents.

Value: Topics of value attempt to show an audience that something is good or bad, right or wrong. You may attempt to convince a group of students in a classroom discussion that capital punishment is immoral. As a vegetarian, you might try to persuade your family that a plant-based diet is more humane than a meat-based diet. As a concerned parent, you might attempt to convince the school board that certain reading material being used in classrooms is objectionable.

Policy: Topics of policy call for individuals or groups to take action in response to an existing problem or need. If you try to persuade fellow students to participate in the campus blood drive due to blood bank shortages, you are addressing a topic of policy. Perhaps you will speak before the administration to request an increase in funding for campus computer labs since existing labs cannot accommodate all students. At work, you might propose a change in the employee-evaluation process, request an on-site day care facility, or seek to obtain better health care benefits for retirees—all in response to problems with the status quo.

Being aware of these different approaches to persuasion can give your presentation a sharper focus. In other words, knowing whether your topic is one of fact, value, or policy will assist you in determining the desired outcome of your speech. In addition, when you have a goal clearly in mind, you are better able to select supporting evidence and an organizational format that will increase your chances of achieving that goal.

Although persuasive communication occurs interpersonally, the emphasis of this chapter is on the importance of more formal presentations in a public setting. These presentations might occur in your classroom, in your workplace, or in your community. Whenever you intend to influence your listeners to accept, or at least consider, your point of view, you are speaking persuasively.

FIGURE 14.5 ■ Elements of Persuasion

Elements of Persuasion

Three elements produce potent persuasion: **logos, pathos,** and **ethos** (see figure 14.5). Logos includes the logical appeals found in your persuasive message—the statistics, testimonials, and true stories that give substance to your message. Pathos consists of the emotional appeals used to stir feelings in your audience. Whenever you attempt to evoke emotions like compassion, enthusiasm, concern, and so on, you are using pathos. In addition to logos and pathos, ethos refers to your credibility as a speaker. Ethos is enhanced when you display competence, honesty, and empathy for your audience. These three elements of persuasion team up to make you an effective communicator. Together, logos, pathos, and ethos are like the heat, fuel, and oxygen necessary for fire. Together, the elements of persuasion produce communication that can gain support for your position.

LOGOS

Let's examine logos first. When you try to convince others with logos or logical appeals, be certain to document the source of your information: the author, publication, and dates. If the author is unknown to the audience, share the author's credentials. Select statistics and examples that are current, and choose reputable publications. In addition, try to avoid any logical fallacies.

Logical fallacies are errors in reasoning. As you prepare to present your persuasive message, be careful not to commit any errors of logic that could lead to misunderstandings. Common logical fallacies include: **faulty causation, hasty generalization, either/or thinking, slippery slope,** and **faulty comparison.** Let's take a look at each of these.

Faulty causation occurs when coincidental events are seen as having a cause–effect relationship. Because a machine broke down after the operator completed a specific job does not mean that the job caused the breakdown or that the operator caused the damage. Simplistic cause–effect reasoning has limited application in complicated problem solving.

Hasty generalizations happen when only a few examples are selected to represent the whole of the conclusion. Sampling only a small or unique portion of a universe limits the conclusion that one can derive from the selected sample. To conclude too quickly or without qualifications can result in a hasty generalization. If only two people in this room of twenty-five have part-time jobs, you might conclude incorrectly that few students work while going to school. Or if several of your friends own hybrid cars, you might hastily conclude that hybrid sales are really taking off.

Either/or thinking presents two alternatives when, in fact, many more possibilities exist. Rather than seeing only two choices, the critical listener must look for other possibilities that may not be stated. Whenever an "either/ or" decision is presented, the critical listener must ask what other choices exist.

If a report states, "We must invest in new equipment, or we must subcontract the work to a vendor," careful thought should be given to other alternatives. Perhaps used equipment is available, or a new design could modify our parts' needs.

Slippery slope is a form of if-then reasoning that presents an undesirable "if" coupled with an even more undesirable "then." For example, "If you eat that piece of chocolate cake, then you will totally ruin the diet you're on." "If you don't accept that job offer, you may never work again." In both instances, the consequences of a specific action are exaggerated. Chances are that one piece of cake won't end the diet any more than one unaccepted job offer will end your career.

Faulty comparisons suggest that similarities outweigh differences and unique situations can be treated the same. "Jon and Don are identical twins, so we can treat them the same." Although these brothers may look exactly alike, have the same birthday, and come from the same parents, they have many differences that make each one unique. For instance, Don is outgoing and good in math, whereas Jon is shy and excels in English. Faulty comparisons exist when we focus on similarities and ignore significant differences.

Detecting each of these problems requires careful attention to the details and thoughtful assessment of the message. For a fun exploration of these and more logical fallacies, check out Stephen's Logical Fallacies Index at http://onegoodmove.org/fallacy/toc.htm.

PATHOS

As you attempt to convince others with emotional appeals, you can engage the audience's passion. You can choose from a wide array of feelings such as pride, pity, fear, hatred, hope, responsibility, deference, prejudice, embarrassment, love, admiration, guilt, etc. Your word choice, tone of voice, and selection of material should evoke an emotional reaction in the audience.

Notice how the photo in figure 14.6 from Mothers Against Drunk Driving (MADD) uses motive appeals to influence your beliefs and attitudes.

What is your emotional response when you see this ad? Obviously MADD is making a personal statement about drinking and driving that evokes an emotional response in the audience with very few words.

You may wonder about the source of the emotional appeals used in persuasion. One primary source comes from psychologist Abraham Maslow

FIGURE 14.6 ■ Emotional Appeal

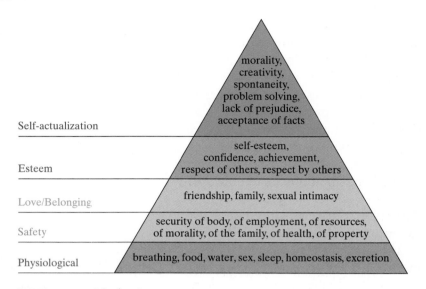

Self-actualization

Esteem

Love/Belonging

Safety

Physiological

morality, creativity, spontaneity, problem solving, lack of prejudice, acceptance of facts

self-esteem, confidence, achievement, respect of others, respect by others

friendship, family, sexual intimacy

security of body, of employment, of resources, of morality, of the family, of health, of property

breathing, food, water, sex, sleep, homeostasis, excretion

FIGURE 14.7 ■ Maslow's Hierarchy of Needs

and his hierarchy of needs. The pyramid in figure 14.7 illustrates human needs from the most primary, which appear at the base, to the more complex, which appear at the tip. Given these needs, persuaders make appeals to their audience in a way that implies if the audience accepts an idea, buys a product, or participates in a cause, these needs will be satisfied.

Let's say, for example, that you are attempting to persuade your audience to volunteer in their community. In your speech, you might focus emotional appeals on the audience's need for love and belonging, illustrating for your listeners how volunteer efforts can forge bonds of friendship with those they serve. Perhaps you want to motivate your audience to buy organic produce. Your appeals in this case would focus on the physiological needs of your listeners, providing factual evidence to support the health benefits of organically grown, pesticide-free fruits and vegetables. Consider your desire to encourage an audience to take a course in public speaking. You might show them how speaking in front of groups enhances self-esteem by building confidence.

ETHOS

Ethos, the third element of persuasion, is created when you show your audience that you possess competence, honesty, and empathy. We'll take a look at each of these.

You can demonstrate your competence in a variety of ways. First, make sure that you are well informed on your subject. Thorough research is necessary to further your cause—your audience is more likely to believe what you are saying if you appear knowledgeable of your topic. Second, be certain that your facts are current and come from reliable sources. Using data from outdated websites or authors who have questionable qualifications and hidden motives are liable to jeopardize your credibility. Finally, you need to present your information clearly and logically. A sound organizational format reveals that you have thought through your arguments and enables your audience to follow the chain of reasoning you have established.

It goes almost without saying that your ethical appeal hinges upon honesty. So how do you convince your audience that you are honest? To begin, never use an argument that you do not believe is true. The goal of persuasion is really about moving closer to the "truth" rather than proving who is "right" or "wrong." Next, choose supporting evidence that is fair and accurate. Some persuasive speakers might be tempted to select only evidence that supports their position, while ignoring facts that weaken their case. Instead, an honest persuader examines all of the facts. Information that weakens your case must be addressed. You will need to respond to conflicting evidence or concede when the opposition has a valid point. Last, keep the tone of your delivery genuine and sincere. When an audience perceives you as straightforward and unpretentious, they are more inclined to see you as trustworthy.

Finally, demonstrate empathy for your audience. If your listeners believe that you care about their interests, needs, and well-being, they will be more open-minded to the information you present. One way to demonstrate empathy is to show that you understand your audience's position. For example, if you are speaking in favor of mandatory drug testing in the workplace, and your audience is opposed, you could let them know that you recognize their concerns about the possibility of violating workers' rights. Another strategy you can use is to show the audience how your ideas will benefit them. Trying to persuade a group of managers, for instance, that they can save time, reduce stress, and increase productivity by using a computerized inventory control system can influence even the most resistant members of the group.

Strategies for Persuasive Presentations

Your persuasive presentations will have a greater impact when you employ some basic strategies that engage your audience and enhance your position. Specifically you will want to establish common ground, delay your thesis, and address your target audience.

First, you must find common ground with your listeners by sharing a common view of the problem, issue, or goal. You may declare that we all want a better quality of life, or better schools, or a healthier environment. An age-old sales technique is to get the customer to agree with the things you say. When your audience's first reaction to what you say is "YES," you have established common ground.

Once you have sincerely established a mutual interest with your audience, don't rush to present your thesis. Build on the common ground that you have established by sharing information about a problem or issue that may have many solutions or causes. Offer detailed examples that "put a face" on the problem. Try to expand the positive response that you received at the start by sharing the extent of the problem. Your thesis or solution will receive a better reception after your audience has seen the development of the issue or problem. By the time you share your solution with the audience, they should be looking for a solution; they should be wondering how you intend to resolve the issues that you have presented.

Your next step is to determine your target audience. Keep in mind that you cannot realistically hope to persuade everyone in your audience. Consequently, you must identify those you are most likely to influence. Some members of the audience will strongly disagree with your position. Others will be neutral or undecided. The remainder of them will agree with your views, and a number of them may fall in between these three categories.

Although your goal as a persuasive speaker might be to get as many in the audience as possible to move to the right on this scale, those who are neutral to moderate in their agreement will become your target audience. This portion represents the listeners you are most likely to persuade.

In addition, sometimes your target audience might be those individuals who have the most power or influence in the group. These audience members are easy to spot by their status, their leadership roles, or their seniority. Other times you may have to research your audience to identify the opinion leaders who are most influential. In addition to identifying the target audience, you also must discover how you can address their preferences, values, and concerns.

In the next section, you will learn about three different patterns of organization that you can use to structure your persuasive presentation. These include Monroe's Motivated Sequence, Advantages–Disadvantages, and Cause–Effect.

Patterns of Organization

MONROE'S MOTIVATED SEQUENCE

You will be pleased to know that your persuasive presentations can be organized to strengthen your effectiveness. One pattern you can use was developed by the late Allen Monroe, former speech professor at Purdue University. By using Monroe's five-step motivated sequence pattern of organization, you will do the following.

MONROE'S MOTIVATED SEQUENCE
I Gain **attention**
II Focus on a **problem**
III Present a **solution**
IV **Visualize** the future
V Gain **action or acceptance**

Each step provides the opportunity for logical appeals, emotional appeals, and ethical appeals. Monroe's original Motivated Sequence has been a successful pattern of organization for over seventy years. We've adapted it slightly as a result of working with students in our classes. Let's examine each step of Monroe's Motivated Sequence.

In the **Attention Step,** you capture your audience's attention by telling a story about the problem, offering a series of examples describing the problem, providing a startling statement to focus on the problem, or asking a rhetorical question about the problem. You try to employ some technique to focus attention on the problem. Be certain to include strong emotional appeals to intensify the importance of the problem.

In the **Problem Step,** you will include four substeps:

A. Stating the problem,

B. Illustrating the problem,

C. Showing the ramifications of the problem, and

D. Pointing out the direct effects of the problem on the audience.

Begin by stating the problem without revealing the solution to the problem. By keeping the audience focused on the problem through its development, you delay giving your solution until the problem is firmly established. After, you have clearly stated the problem, you must explain it and/or illustrate it with documented examples or testimony. If you began the attention step with a story, you may want to add more examples here to illustrate the problem.

After you have stated and illustrated the problem, you will show the ramifications of the problem by telling how serious the concern is, how much it costs nationally each year, or how many will suffer from it worldwide. The ramification of the problem gives the big picture by zooming out to the broadest perspective on the problem.

Capture Attention by Showing Example

Once your audience sees the breadth of the problem, you must point out the direct effects of the problem on the audience. Specifically, you seek to make each member of the audience sense personal ownership of the problem. Also, you may find it helpful to survey your audience as part of your preparation process in order to gain a better understanding of your audience's relationship to the problem.

As you shift from problem to solution, use an effective transition to introduce your central idea. Consider posing possible solutions, or asking what can be done to resolve this issue, or flatly stating that help is available to make the shift from problem to solution.

In the **Solution Step,** you will present five substeps:

Stating the solution (your central idea),

Explaining the solution,

Showing how the solution will solve the problem,

Showing how others have solved problems with this solution, and

Answering the two most likely objections to the solution.

Your audience has been wondering how you will solve the problem that you have established in the first two steps of your presentation. Make certain that you clearly state your solution and emphasize it with pauses, vocal variety, repetition, etc. For example, to address the problem of animal testing to ensure product safety, you may simply state your solution as, "Buy products that are free of animal testing."

Before the audience evaluates your solution, make certain that you explain the solution to clarify who will do what, when, how, and under what conditions. The details that you provide here will answer many questions that listeners may have. If you wanted your audience to boycott products that are developed through animal testing, explain what symbol to look for as they make their purchases.

After you have explained the solution, offer citations, further explanation, or other support that shows how your solution will, in fact, solve the problem. You may find a quote from an expert that attests to the effectiveness of your solution. Testimonials from researchers or activist groups may provide the support you want here.

Present true stories that document the effectiveness of your solution by showing how others have used your solution to solve a problem. Consider providing a list of companies that do not use animal testing.

Anticipate the opposition to your solution by considering the probable resistance. Will the audience see the solution as too expensive, too time consuming, or too difficult? Present your answers to these most likely objections. For the animal testing example, you may need to address these objections: 1) Computer simulation testing is not as accurate as animal testing; 2) man was intended to have dominion over the animals according to the Bible.

Your **Visualization Step** provides the opportunity for you to show what the future will be like through a **hypothetical story.** You may present a positive, negative, or contrasting view of the future. Your positive story describes life five, ten, or fifteen years from now when your solution has been implemented. Your details of this narrative show how the world will be a better place because of the changes adopted today. Or you could choose to present the worst-case scenario and show how terrible the problem will become if your solution is not enacted. Finally, you may elect to tell both stories and emphasize the contrast in how the future may be for your audience. Regardless of which approach you choose, your story offers you a chance to present strong emotional appeals.

In closing your presentation, you will seek **Action or Approval** from your audience by leading, instructing, challenging, or inducing the audience to act on or accept your solution. Present specific directions to be clear about what the audience should do to act on your solution. Make it easy for your audience to commit to your solution. For example, show your audience which labels to look for when purchasing "No Animal Testing" products. Provide a list of companies that do not use animal testing for commonly used products. Hand out bumper stickers encouraging others to join the ban on animal testing of products.

By completing these five steps in Monroe's Motivated Sequence, you will organize a convincing persuasive message. See figure 14.8 as a sample speech prepared by one of our students.

Motivated Sequence	Sample Student Outline
I. Attention Step	What do Waukesha, Paris, London, and Sydney have in common? What costs banks $1 billion a year? An international epidemic of poor network security.
II. Problem Step	A. Insecure networks are an important issue costing millions of dollars. B. Lack of network security leads to identity theft and malicious activities. C. (Statistics) 10 million citizens have fallen prey in the UK; over 10 million in the USA. 41% of Internet users curbed online shopping habits, fearing theft. D. 98% of us use email. Only 1 in 4 change default passwords. 65% have never changed their password.
Transition:	Is there anything you can do? Of the many ways to prevent this, I intend to talk about the most common method.
III. Solution Step	A. Strong passwords make a secure network. B. Strong passwords consist of a minimum of 8 characters, use a combination of alphanumeric (numbers and letters), and are changed at regular intervals. (Testimony) from *Networking—A Beginner's Guide*. C. Beginning of network security breach is the cracking of a user ID and password. Having a strong password definitely makes a network more secure. D. (Comparison) from lastbit.com E. You think this isn't going to happen to you. That's exactly what 10 million other victims thought. You say you don't have time? You'd be spending much more than 30 seconds to get your life back, if you can get it back at all.
IV. Visualization Step	Relaxing one weekend, you get an email saying you are dropped out of course you are getting an A in. You are shocked to find that you can't graduate, because someone logged in as you and dropped you out. Nothing can be done! Don't let it happen to you. Don't wait until it's too late!
V. Action Step	Don't let some stranger dictate your life. Don't fall prey to someone's evil trap. Take control now! Next time you log in make sure you change your password; change it to a strong password and don't disclose it to anyone. The 30 seconds it takes is very little time to ensure peace of mind.

FIGURE 14.8 ■ Motivated Sequence Outline *Source:* Student Speech.

Although we've given considerable attention to the Motivated Sequence, it is not the only pattern of organization that you can use for persuasive speeches.

Two additional patterns you might find useful are Advantages–Disadvantages and Cause–Effect.

ADVANTAGES–DISADVANTAGES

This pattern of organization arranges information based upon pros and cons; it is particularly effective when your audience may not be totally sympathetic to your position. Here's how this approach works.

You begin with the intention to discuss both sides of an issue objectively. This intention means that you do not express your viewpoint in the introduction of your speech. Instead, your central idea or thesis might sound like this:

> Embryonic stem cell research has been a hotly debated topic.

Then the first main point in the body of the speech would present the advantages, or pros, of this research (see figure 14.9).

The second main point would present the disadvantages, or cons (see figure 14.10). This format allows your audience to consider both sides of the issue.

The third main point in the body of the speech is where you present your position in light of the evidence you reviewed. Your third main point could be expressed, as outlined in figure 14.11.

In this point, you would then make your claims that even though embryonic stem cell research could potentially cure diseases, the embryos' right to life supersedes the possibility of curing diseases. You would also need to provide evidence that adult stem cell research could be a feasible way to achieve the same results as embryonic stem cell research.

You can see that the moral implications of this topic make it a subject for much controversy. However, by providing evidence for both sides of the issue, you stand a better chance of influencing your audience, particularly those listeners who don't agree with you but who are open to hearing your position.

The "Pros"	A. Embryonic stem cell research has several advantages.
	1. Embryonic stem cell research could result in cures for many diseases.
	2. Embryonic stem cell research offers potential to reduce human suffering.
	3. Embryonic stem cell research is based on evidence that human life doesn't begin until 14 days after fertilization.

FIGURE 14.9 ■ The Pros

The "Cons"	B. Embryonic stem cell research has several disadvantages.
	1. Embryonic stem cell research destroys living embryos.
	2. Embryonic stem cell research violates living beings who have the right to dignity and respect.
	3. Embryonic stem cell research could lead to further violations of individual rights.

FIGURE 14.10 ■ The Cons

| Your Position | C. Embryonic stem cell research should be replaced by adult stem cell research. |

FIGURE 14.11 ■ Your Position

CAUSE–EFFECT

Cause–effect is another pattern of organization that works well for persuasion because it establishes connections between variables. Using this pattern, persuasive speakers can take one of two approaches: a) identifying significant causes and their respective effects, b) pinpointing important effects and suggesting their possible causes.

Although this pattern addresses existing concerns, resolutions are generally implied rather than specifically stated. In addition, you need to avoid fallacies involving faulty causation. For example, it may be tempting to attribute global warming (an effect) solely to carbon emissions (a cause). Although carbon emissions may contribute to this environmental problem, other causes might be equally, if not more, significant. As a skillful persuader, you must avoid oversimplifying cause–effect relationships in order to maintain credibility with your audience.

Take a look at the two examples of this pattern described in figures 14.12 and 14.13.

If you make sound connections in a cause–effect speech, you make it easier for your audience to determine what steps they might need to take in order to find resolutions to the concerns being addressed.

As you conclude this chapter, you are likely to be more aware of the complexity of the persuasion process. You have had an opportunity to read about the importance of persuasive messages, whether you are the sender or the receiver. In both instances, you may encounter topics of fact, value, and policy. In addition, successful persuasion is dependent upon logical, emotional, and ethical appeals and an avoidance of reasoning fallacies. Finally, the strategies and organizational patterns for persuasion can make you more effective in influencing your target audiences at school, work, or home.

Cause	A. Several causes can contribute to workplace injuries.
	1. Repetitive motion
	2. Improper lifting
	3. Faulty equipment design
Effect	B. Several effects result from workplace injuries.
	1. Loss of productivity
	2. Financial costs
	3. Short- and long-term disabilities

FIGURE 14.12 ■
Cause–Effect

Effect–Cause

Effect	A. Several health problems plague Americans.
	1. Obesity
	2. High cholesterol
	3. Type II diabetes
Cause	B. Several causes can be responsible for these problems.
	1. High fat diets
	2. Lack of exercise
	3. Genetic predisposition

FIGURE 14.13 ■
Effect–Cause

Review Questions

1. List several benefits that result from your ability to use persuasion effectively.

2. This chapter lists three types of persuasive presentations: Fact, Value, and Policy. Identify the following topics as F, V, or P.

   a. _____ Students achieve higher grades with individualized instruction.

   b. _____ We need to curb violence in our city's schools.

   c. _____ Capital punishment is inhumane.

   d. _____ Vitamin C cuts the rate of colds in half.

   e. _____ We must find a way to reduce alcohol-induced traffic fatalities.

   f. _____ Child abuse is a problem that needs to be solved.

   g. _____ Hybrid cars are the best way to protect our environment.

   h. _____ Professional athletes are paid too much money.

   i. _____ A majority of community college students finds jobs after graduation.

   j. _____ Parking availability on campus needs to be improved.

3. You can be a more effective persuader by using logical (logos), ethical (ethos), and emotional (pathos) appeals in your presentation.

List two suggestions that you can use to create each of these appeals.

   a. Logical Appeal
      1.
      2.
   b. Ethical Appeal
      1.
      2.
   c. Emotional Appeal
      1.
      2.

4. Describe some information you read or heard about that motivated you to do something. For example, maybe you heard a speaker talk about the benefits of exercising regularly, and you began a more consistent exercise program yourself. Then for your example, tell which of the needs on Maslow's hierarchy motivated you in this instance. Increased self-esteem could have been the motivator in the exercise example.

5. Briefly describe what the persuasive speaker tries to accomplish in each of the five steps of Monroe's Motivated Sequence.

6. When does the Advantages–Disadvantages pattern of organization work best for a persuasive speaker and why?

7. Explain the two approaches you can use in the Cause–Effect pattern of organization.

Key Terms and Concepts

Abraham Maslow's Hierarchy of Needs   282

Action/Approval Step   286

Advantages–Disadvantages   288

Attention Step   284

Cause–Effect   289

Common Ground   283

Delayed Thesis   283

Either/or Thinking   280

Elements of Persuasion   280

Ethos   282

Faulty Causation   280

Faulty Comparison   281

Hasty Generalization   280

Hypothetical Story   286

Logos   280

Monroe's Motivated Sequence   284

Pathos   281

Problem Step   285

Ramifications   285

Slippery Slope   281

Solution Step   285

Target Audience   284

Topics of Fact   279

Topics of Policy   279

Topics of Value   279

Visualization Step   286

Web Activities

- For a detailed discussion of Monroe's Motivated Sequence and sample speeches refer to Steven H. Kaminski's website: http://www.shkaminski.com/Classes/Handouts/Motivated%20Sequence.htm.

- Another sample speech, "A Friend in Need" by Sandy Hefty, can be found at http://www.myrafritzius.com/per-fin.htm.

- Stephen's Logical Fallacies Index will help you develop a mind like a steel trap. Check it out at http://onegoodmove.org/fallacy/toc.htm.

- Can You Spot the Fallacy? will help you identify common logical fallacies in a fun short quiz at http://www.funtrivia.com/playquiz/quiz2814762039ae8.html.

- The following websites that will help you come up with a topic for your persuasive presentation:

  - http://www.speech-topics-help.com/persuasive-speech-ideas.html
  - http://www.goodpersuasivespeechtopics.com/persuasive.htm
  - http://www.uttyler.edu/meidenmuller/rhetoricand westernculture/speechtopics.htm
  - http://www.nvcc.edu/home/npeck/spd100/units/perstopics.htm
  - http://www.presentationhelper.co.uk/persuasive_ speech_topic.htm

Assignments

ASSIGNMENT 14.1: AD ANALYSIS

Find at least two advertisements from print media or online images or videos. Analyze each ad to determine the logical (logos), emotional (pathos), and ethical (ethos) appeals being used. Bring your ads to class and share your analysis with others.

ASSIGNMENT 14.2: LOGICAL FALLACY IDENTIFICATION

Match the logical fallacies in Column A with the example in Column B.

Column A	Column B
A. Hasty Generalization	_____. I passed my Communication Skills test on Monday. That was right after I went to church on Sunday. I can see the power of prayer.
B. Either/or Thinking	_____. Emotions are like an onion. As you peel away the outer layers, you become more tearful.

Column A	Column B
C. Faulty Comparison	_____. If I make an exception for you and let you turn in your assignments late, I will have to make an exception for everyone.
D. Slippery Slope	_____. Three of my friends say they are going to vote for Senator Smith. I guess Senator Smith is a very popular candidate.
E. Faulty Causation	_____. In our class, students either study and pass, or they don't study and fail.

ASSIGNMENT 14.3: PRACTICE OUTLINES

Directions: Your instructor will divide the class into several small groups and assign a pattern of organization to each group (Motivated Sequence, Advantages–Disadvantages, Cause–Effect).

Work with your group to create an outline for a persuasive presentation using the assigned pattern of organization.

Follow these steps to prepare your outlines:

1. Select a topic appropriate for your group's pattern of organization.
2. Construct an outline for your presentation.
3. Copy your outline onto poster paper.
4. Present your outline to the class.
5. Observe how others used different patterns to develop their persuasive presentations.

Here are some topics to get you started:

Health Care

Smoking

Volunteering

Hybrid Cars

Immunizations

Organ Donation

Gun Control

Recycling

Gay Marriage

Euthanasia

You may expand your topic selection choices by consulting http://www.valencia.cc.fl.us/lrcwest/kaysmith.html.

ASSIGNMENT 14.4: PERSUASIVE SPEECH ANALYSIS

Directions: Listen to a live persuasive presentation, a televised persuasive presentation, or obtain a video such as "Great Speeches Volume 1–12" from your local library. Analyze the persuasive effectiveness in terms of its logos, pathos, and ethos. Determine what elements of persuasion were particularly effective and what elements could be strengthened in the presentation. Prepare a written summary of your findings and present them to the class in an oral report.

Presentation Title: _____

Date Reviewed: _____

Elements of persuasion included in presentation
Logos
Pathos
Ethos

ASSIGNMENT 14.5: THE PERSUASIVE SPEECH

Directions: The goal of this assignment is to prepare and present a **five- to seven-minute** persuasive speech in which you will choose a topic of fact, value, or policy. Make sure the topic you select is of interest and concern to you as well as to your listeners.

Here are some examples of topics that might be appropriate:

Topics of Fact: Open-door policies encourage workplace communication. Rising health care costs increase employee insurance premiums. Time management skills can reduce workplace stress.

Topics of Value: Attitudes are the most important factors in job performance. Good customer service is critical to company success. Flextime has many advantages for single-parent families.

Topics of Policy: Get involved in a Big Brother/Big Sister program. Practice on-the-job safety to reduce work-related injuries. Sign up for "Lunch & Learn" to upgrade your computer skills.

In order to complete this assignment, you must meet the following objectives:

1. **Analyze** your audience.
2. **Select** a persuasive topic of fact, value, or policy.
3. **Gather** supporting material from at least three authoritative sources. No more than two of your sources may come from the Internet.
4. **Construct** a typed outline that organizes your presentation using one of the patterns discussed in this chapter.
5. **Prepare** a reference page that lists your sources in APA format. Consult the following website for documenting your sources: https://www.baker.edu/library/handouts/apa.pdf.
6. **Include** at least four different kinds of verbal supports in your speech.
7. **Prepare** a visual aid that enhances your speech.
8. **Practice** your speech by videotaping it or rehearsing in front of a live audience.
9. **Present** your speech using effective verbal and nonverbal strategies.

ASSIGNMENT 14.6: CASE STUDY: PERSUASIVE POSTING

Is conceal-carry the answer to violence on campuses?

GREEN BAY—Eric Thompson, the owner of the Internet-based sporting goods and firearms retailer that has sold products to the shooters involved with the Virginia Tech and Northern Illinois University tragedies, says his unfortunate twist of fate is spurring him to take a more active role in protecting the public—especially young people—from future attacks.

Thompson is lending his voice to those who support giving the public the right to protect themselves from mass murderers like Cho and Kazmierczak. Specifically, Thompson believes that college students and university faculty members who are properly licensed and trained to carry a firearm should be allowed to do so. Thompson also wants his home state of Wisconsin to join the 48 states who already allow private citizens to carry a firearm for protection. (Thompson, 2008, p. 1)

Eric Thompson has started gundebate.com, a newly formed site dedicated to an unbiased and open discussion of the gun debate in the United States. He says, "We invite both sides of the issue to come to this site to get involved in coming up with a real solution that works for America. We would like to extend specific invitations to gun rights organizations, gun regulation organizations, politicians, journalists, writers and anyone that is currently involved in the gun debate. Please contact us to inform us of your interest in becoming a part of this solution based web site" (Thompson, 2008, p. 1).

Research your position on this question, and prepare a persuasive posting for gundebate.com.

References

Harrison, K. (2005–2007). Four steps in persuasive communication at work. *Cutting edge PR*. Retrieved June 21, 2007, from http://www.cuttingedgepr.com/articles/empcomm_foursteps.asp

NPR. (2007). Diving bell celebrates life of the mind. Retrieved December 7, 2007, from http://www.npr.org/templates/story/.php?storyId=16780118

Thompson, E. (2008). Owner of web-based firearms company that sold to Virginia Tech and NIU shooters looks to turn tragedy into platform to improve public safety. Retrieved February 29, 2008, from http://www.gundebate.com/, p. 2.

Violent song lyrics may lead to violent behavior. (2003, July/August). *Journal of Personality and Social Psychology, 34*(7), 1–3. Retrieved February 29, 2008, from http://www.apa.org/monitor/julaug03/violent.html

Chapter **15**

Interviewing Skills

Learning **Objectives**

At the end of this chapter, you should be able to meet the following objectives:

1. Identify the importance of interviewing.
2. Describe three main types of interview questions.
3. Respond appropriately to illegal questions.
4. Participate effectively in the interview.
5. Follow up effectively after the interview.

"A good way to think about the process of getting a job is that a resume gets you in the door, and an interview is where you close the deal."

Penelope Trunk

Interviewing Is Important

You're nearing completion of your degree at the local community college. Before long, you'll be getting resumes out to prospective employers and hoping to receive a call that invites you for an interview. With the availability of online resources for job hunters, many will begin their job search with the click of a computer mouse. In July of 2008, an estimated 3,864,100 job vacancies were posted on the Internet alone (ConsumerAffairs.com Inc., 2008).

The prospects you will have for securing employment interviews are dependent upon a variety of factors ranging from your qualifications to the state of the economy. For example, the economic downturn of 2008 resulted in the greatest loss of jobs since the Great Depression. Highly-skilled individuals with years of experience lost their jobs. Employees working in retail, hospitality, finance, and manufacturing (particularly in the automotive industry) suffered some of the greatest losses in employment. Even with a 6.5 percent unemployment rate, 93.5 percent were still employed, and despite what many perceived as a dismal economy, certain occupational areas remained relatively stable. Occupations such as nursing, police and fire protection, and education, for example, offered security for individuals. Regardless, however, of whether you are seeking employment in a field with multiple opportunities or few, the interviewing skills you need to be successful remain essentially the same.

Chances are, too, that you will face a variety of employment interviews throughout your professional life. Jane M. Lommel, Ph.D., president of Workforce Associates, states:

> "During the last two months, I've conducted several focus groups with very bright graduating seniors at high schools and community colleges in several areas of the country. The world looks sunny to them, and I'm sure that they'll do well. But I can't suppress my worry that although they may be prepared academically for what will be thrown their way, their skills in finding and keeping multiple careers throughout their lifetimes are pretty weak. For example, when asked about how many careers they thought they might have, the consensus was two, or at most, three. Meanwhile, we who are over the age of 40 know full well that there are many twists and turns in life that will greet them, and they should really be told to expect at least 7–10 major career shifts during their working lifetimes." (Lommel, 2003, p. 1)

Lommel is pointing to the likelihood that you will have occasions for many employment interviews during your career. However, you are also likely to encounter special types of employment interviews, including those conducted online and those designed to secure job advancement.

Taken from an interviewer's perspective, your ticket to getting a job, as well as advancing on the job, is being the most desirable candidate in the field of applicants. Interviewers are trying to match qualified applicants with the company's needs. They try to recognize potential leaders

Top 10 Interview Blunders

1. Don't Prepare
2. Dress Inappropriately
3. Poor Communication Skills
4. Too Much Communication
5. Talk Too Much
6. Don't Talk Enough
7. Fuzzy Facts
8. Give the Wrong Answer
9. Badmouthing Past Employers
10. Forget to Follow Up

FIGURE 15.1 ■ Interview Blunders
Source: Doyle, 2008, p. 1.

for their company. They seek people they "like" and trust. Interviewers want to feel that they know you and know what to expect from you. All interviews provide you with an opportunity to show employers that you are the perfect fit for the job.

As important as the interview process is in securing and maintaining employment, you may also have experienced the discouragement that comes from an interview that didn't go as smoothly as you had hoped. Once the interview is over, you may find it easy to think of what you could have said or should have done differently. Interviews can be less than successful for a variety of reasons. Figure 15.1 lists some of those reasons.

In this chapter, you will learn more about what it takes to prepare for, participate in, and follow up after the various interviews you are likely to encounter. With this information in hand, you'll avoid common interviewing mistakes and feel more confident about your ability to market your skills to an employer.

"He came in for an interview 3 hours ago, and I made the mistake of telling him to make himself comfortable."

Source: www.CartoonStock.com.

Prepare for the Employment Interview

Preparation for the interview begins long before the initial contact with the employer. In fact, four major steps are involved in the preparation process: researching the company, updating your paperwork, rehearsing your responses, and ensuring a positive first impression.

According to *The 25 Worst Job Interview Mistakes,* "It isn't necessary to memorize the company's annual sale and profit figures, but you should know something about their products or services. One candidate lost out in an AT&T interview by mentioning their involvement in a news story that had been about ITT, and there was no way for the candidate to regain credibility after such a glaring error. Check out information about large companies in business magazines or corporate directories at your public library, or call the company to ask for a copy of the annual report. For smaller organizations, you may have to rely on the grapevine: some of the best information can come from people who used to work there" (Employment Resource Center, n.d., pp. 1–2). Other ways to find out about a company include accessing online resources such as company webpages, checking out company advertisements, and visiting the actual company facility to observe its layout. Company directories such as www.thomasregister.com provide information about the size, location, products and activities, and assets of the company.

You may ask yourself why doing this research is so important before the interview. First, if you can show an employer you made the extra effort to learn about the company, you will increase your chances of making a positive first impression and avoid the embarrassment of the candidate mentioned previously who confused AT&T with ITT. In addition, the information you gain from your research can help you determine if, in fact, this is a company that would be a good match for your skills, interests, and goals.

Your preparation would not be complete without determining what information you need from the prospective employer in order to decide whether or not to accept a job. Prepare yourself for that point in the interview when the employer asks, "Do you have any questions?" by listing several questions that will give you insight into the position, the company, and your future there. Questions you might consider asking are shown in figure 15.2.

In general, avoid questions about salary or benefits until you have been offered a position.

Along with researching the company and preparing questions to ask the interviewer, you need to update your paperwork. Be certain that your resume includes your most recent employment, education, and related experience. Also, make sure you have a copy of the resume to take to the interview. In addition, you may be asked to complete an application form

To Find Out About:	Consider Asking:
Job Responsibilities	What are your expectations of a successful long-term employee in this position?
Work Environment	What uniforms or protective equipment are provided?
	How would you characterize the climate between workers and managers?
Education and Training	What opportunities might I have for professional growth?
Company Philosophy	What is the mission or vision of your company?
	To what extent does your company empower workers to share in decision making?
Work Performance	How frequently do worker evaluations occur?
	On what competencies should I focus my attention during the first six months?

FIGURE 15.2 ■ Interview Questions

prior to the interview. Sometimes these forms require you to supply information that is not on your resume, such as your Social Security number, and specific addresses and phone numbers of schools or employers. It is a good idea to have this information on a separate sheet of paper that you can readily transfer to the application form. Such a form is available on a Job Service form: Make the Most of a Job Interview. Finally, if you intend to send a letter of application prior to the interview, be sure to personalize this letter so that it speaks directly to the employer about the specific position rather than sending a generic letter suitable for a variety of jobs.

Interview Questions

One of the most important steps in preparing for an interview is anticipating the questions you will likely be asked. A good place to start is by accessing the numerous websites that list the questions most frequently asked. One such site comes from the University of Maryland Career Center at http://www .careercenter.umd.edu/STUDENT/STEP5/QUESTION.htm. Another excellent site is http://www.quintcareers.com/interview_question_collections.html, where you will find traditional interview questions, sample behavioral questions, job interview questions for college seniors or recent graduates, and a job interview question database.

Two types of questions will challenge you during your interviews. The first type includes traditional questions that are broad-based and designed to elicit information about your skills and abilities. For example, you may be asked, "What kind of equipment can you operate?" "Did you hold any leadership positions while you were in school?" "What computer skills can you bring to this position?" The following list shows some commonly asked interview questions.

COMMONLY ASKED JOB INTERVIEW QUESTIONS

1. Why do you want to work for our company?
2. Tell me something about your last job.
3. How do you feel about your last employer?
4. Why did you leave your last job?
5. Do you feel that you are mature enough to handle the responsibilities of this job?
6. What salary do you expect to be getting here?
7. What are your future career plans?
8. How do you spend your spare time?

9. Are you taking any courses right now?

10. Tell me something about yourself.

11. At school, what courses did you like best? Least? Why?

12. What one person had the greatest influence on your life and why?

13. Why did you choose this particular field of work?

14. How did you finance your way through school?

15. How did you rate scholastically in your senior year in high school?

16. Where do you hope to be five years from now? Ten years from now?

17. What prompted you to apply for our company?

18. How does your family feel about your career choice and its requirements?

19. What, in your estimation, is the key to success, particularly in this job?

20. Are you looking for temporary or permanent work?

BEHAVIOR-BASED QUESTIONS

The second category of interview questions includes behavior-based questions. These questions are based on the theory that your past performance is the best indicator of your future behavior. In order to give an employer evidence of past performance, applicants should describe a situation that they encountered in the past, the actions that they took, and the results that they achieved as a result of that action. Interviewers may use behavior-based questions such as these:

> "Describe an instance on your last job when you had to get yourself out of a difficult situation by thinking on your feet."

> "Tell me about a time on your last job when you went 'above and beyond' the call of duty."

> "Describe a day when you had multiple tasks to handle at work."

Figure 15.3 shows a recruiting ad from the Kohler Company, a company that uses a behavioral interview format.

If you would like to learn more about behavior-based interviews, you may find the following websites helpful:

http://www.uwec.edu/Career/online_library/behavioral_int.htm

http://www.mrichampions.com/behaviorbsd.html

http://mu-sp.missouri.edu/sites/umhchr/Resources/Interviewing%20-%20 Behavior%20Based%20Interviewing%20Questions.doc

http://www.spherion.com/careers/resources/interviewing/PAR.jsp.

As an applicant, you should be prepared to share five qualifications you want the employer to remember. List these five qualifications and provide

How We Recruit

How We Interview

Kohler Co. utilizes a behavioral interviewing format.

Behavioral interviewing is based on the foundation that the best predictor of your future behavior is your past behavior in similar situations. Behavioral interviews generally last 60 to 90 minutes.

Hiring managers prepare for behavioral interviews by identifying the necessary areas of competency required for the job. They then ask questions designed to elicit specific examples of how you've used these skills.

In preparing for a behavioral interview, research the position tasks required and write down specific, job-related examples of past experiences.

Be prepared to communicate your strengths and developmental needs and to provide examples of each.

The following are some examples of behavioral-based interview questions:

- Tell me about a time when you were resistant to change even though you knew that it was necessary. What did you do? What was the outcome?
- Tell me about a time you openly accepted accountability regarding a mistake that was made. How do you drive this same level of accountability in your organization?
- Describe a time when you had to go more than halfway to communicate with a "problem person."
- Give me an example of a time in which you had to be persuasive in getting your idea across, even when the odds were against you. What did you do? What was the outcome?
- Give me an example of how you identify your own personal developmental areas. Be specific.

FIGURE 15.3 ■ Kohler Advertisement
Source: Kohler Co.

PAR stories (Problem–Action–Results) to give specific examples that will show the interviewer that you have the qualities you claim to have. See figure 15.4.

For instance, if you tell the interviewer you have great customer service skills, you could describe a time when you encountered a difficult customer (Problem). Perhaps you listened patiently to the customer's complaint and took steps to get the complaint resolved (Action). Your initiative solved the customer's problem and resulted in that disgruntled customer becoming a "regular" (Results). Providing an example like this gives the interviewer a "picture" of your past successes, unlike applicants who respond to the interviewer's questions with incomplete, brief, or vague replies. Specific replies with examples are especially important during a behavior-based interview.

Maximize Impact & Credibility with "PAR" Stories

One approach to creating the work history/accomplishments section of your resume is to communicate your experience in terms of Problem–Action–Results ("PAR") stories.

Throughout your career, you have seen problems, taken actions to solve them and created results—and this is an effective and compelling way to describe your career history.

The PAR structure

- Problem/Purpose you encountered
- Action(s) you took (alone or with others) to overcome that problem or purpose
- Result(s) you achieved, in as concrete terms as possible

FIGURE 15.4 ▪ PAR Stories
Source: Spherion Atlantic Enterprises, LLC, 2008.

Remember: This type of interview looks at job experiences of the past as predictors of future performance.

ILLEGAL QUESTIONS

Despite laws designed to protect applicants from discrimination in the hiring process, some illegal practices continue to plague interviews. According to an article in *USA Today,* "Various federal, state, and local laws regulate the questions a prospective employer can ask you. An employer's questions—on the job application, in the interview, or during the testing process—must be related to the job for which you are applying. For the employer, the focus must be: 'What do I need to know to decide whether or not this personcan perform the functions of this job?'" (Illegal Interview Questions 2001, p.1).

Although most application forms have been cleansed of illegal questions, these questions may come up during the course of an interview. Whether knowingly or just by accident, employers may ask questions that legally you are not bound to answer. Let us examine the types of illegal questions you might be asked and the various choices you have for responding to these questions.

Questions about national origin, disabilities, arrest record, marital/family status, age, race, religion, physical attributes, military background, and affiliations have the potential to be illegal if they are asked in a way that discriminates. For example, although it is illegal for an employer to ask you about your height and weight, an employer may ask if you are able to lift seventy-five-pound packages as a part of the job. Likewise, if the job requires a

Factor	Illegal Questions	Legal Questions
National Origin	Are you a U.S. citizen?	What languages do you speak fluently?
Disabilities	Do you have any handicaps?	Can you perform this job with reasonable accommodations?
Arrest Record	Have you ever been arrested?	Have you ever been convicted of auto theft?
Marital Status/ Family	Are you married? Do you have any children?	Are you able to work overtime?
Age	How old are you?	Are you over 18 years of age?
Race	What is your race?	None!
Religion	What church do you belong to?	Are you able to work Saturday and/or Sunday shifts?
Physical Attributes	How tall are you?	Are you able to stand for eight hours?
Military Background	Were you honorably discharged?	What type of training did you receive in the military?
Affiliation	To what organizations do you belong?	What professional organizations do you belong to that would enhance your job performance?

FIGURE 15.5 ■ Illegal and Legal Questions
Source: http://www.careerone.com.au/webdav/site/jobs/shared/Intrusive_large.gif.

security clearance, you may be asked about your arrest record. See figure 15.5 for examples of illegal and legal questions.

When confronted with illegal questions, you can respond in a variety of ways. One way you can respond is simply to answer the question you have been asked. Be aware, however, that your response may lead to discrimination on the part of the employer. A second way you can respond is to refuse to answer the question. This choice may preserve your legal rights, but you may be perceived as uncooperative. A third way to respond is to consider why the employer might be asking the question and respond to your perception of the employer's intent. For example, when the interviewer asks if you have any children, you may respond by saying, "I have adequate child care that will not prevent me from working overtime." Another way to respond is by asking a question. For instance, you might say, "Could you explain how you think my having children would affect my job performance?"

Once you have determined possible interview questions, you need to review your own responses to them. The best practice for this review is to video record your mock interview. The playback of these recordings gives you the added benefit of being able to review and revise your responses, along with observing your nonverbal behavior.

Participate in Your Interview

TIME FOR SUCCESS

When scheduling the interview with the employer, you should note the time, place, and name of the person that you will meet. Write these down to be sure they are correct. Prior to the interview, consider traveling to the employer's address to know where it is and how long it takes to get there. Check for parking areas and entrances. Be sure that you arrive in plenty of time before the scheduled interview. You do not want to be late or lost.

Creating a positive impression begins the moment you enter the company, and as the saying goes, "You never get a second chance to make a good first impression." You will want to be on time, ideally ten to fifteen minutes early. If you did a travel-time dry run as a part of your preparation, you are likely to arrive in plenty of time. Even before you meet the interviewer, other employees may be observing you. Sometimes their feedback influences the employer's decision of who will be hired. Therefore, "put your best foot forward" by being pleasant and courteous to those you meet.

In addition, if you brought along your updated resume, you will be prepared to complete an application form. You may also want to bring along a portfolio as evidence of your past accomplishments: auto body technicians may keep a photo album of projects they have completed; interior design graduates may bring a sample board that shows design choices for a room they are redecorating; administrative assistants may bring samples of correspondences that they have prepared. Finally, knowing the interviewer's name and title ahead of time can be a plus when you are finally introduced.

"First off, there's no 'y' in resume..."

Source: www.CartoonStock .com.

DRESS FOR SUCCESS

Your appearance is a very important consideration as you prepare for an interview. In fact, the first impression you make as you walk through the interviewer's door could determine whether or not you get the job. In one study, researchers "rated 40% of all applicants as having grooming problems that created a negative first impression" (First Impressions On Job Interviews, 2002, p.1). In order to avoid being among these 40 percent, you need to dress and groom appropriately. In part, your choice of attire is determined by the job for which you are applying. Showing up in a three-piece suit for a technical job is just as inappropriate as wearing jeans and a T-shirt to an interview for an executive position. The best rule of thumb is to be well groomed and dress conservatively. You could also pay a visit to the company as part of your research and observe how others are dressed. Follow their lead, and dress like you belong there too. You might also find some of the following suggestions helpful:

- Clothes must be clean and well pressed.

- Men should be clean-shaven or have facial hair neatly trimmed.

- Remove body piercings and conceal tattoos.

- Use fragrances with caution. Subtle scents are generally okay.

- Make sure nails are manicured.

- Avoid smoking cigarettes just before the interview (the smell lingers).

- Do not chew gum.

- Be sure to turn off your cell phone.

Once you are called into the interviewer's office, let the interviewer take the lead. If a hand is extended to you, extend yours. If you are asked to have a seat, do so. Sit up straight with feet flat on the floor and hands resting comfortably in your lap. Wait to see which direction the interview goes. The interviewer may engage you in small talk or may provide you with valuable information about the company. Regardless of how the meeting proceeds, listen and respond accordingly.

RESPOND FOR SUCCESS

During the interview, you will be asked a variety of questions. Respond with honesty and completeness. Also, a favorable first impression is achieved by being positive about yourself and your previous experiences at work and at school. Avoid any temptation to "bad mouth" former employers or teachers. Keep your previous complaints to yourself.

When answering the interviewer's questions, avoid one- or two-word responses. Rather, explain what qualifications you have and give concrete

An Interview Setting

examples of those qualifications, as in the behavior-based formula discussed earlier. Use your responses to convince the interviewer that your previous accomplishments are accurate predictors of your future performance. If you're unsure of what the interviewer is asking, paraphrase the question to clarify any misunderstanding. Consider beginning such paraphrases with statements like these: "Let me make sure I understand what you're asking me . . ." or "In other words, you're wondering if I ever encountered a situation like this before." Regardless of the questions, however, limit your responses to about thirty seconds, and certainly no longer than two minutes to avoid rambling. In all of your answers, emphasize what you have to offer the company.

Even if an employer asks questions about your weaknesses, respond positively. Consider how you might respond to this question: "Tell me about a time when you had difficulty satisfying a disgruntled customer." Rather than saying, "I've never had any trouble satisfying customers," say, "I wasn't able to give a customer a refund because the customer didn't have a sales slip, which our store policy requires. I know that the customer was very unhappy. So after checking with my manager, I was able to offer the customer two discount coupons to apply to future purchases."

Your nonverbal communication also conveys much in the interview process. To show that you are confident, energetic, and enthusiastic about the prospects of employment, sit up in your chair and lean slightly forward. Make eye contact, smile, and keep an "open" body posture by avoiding crossed arms and legs. Use head nods and facial expressions that signal attentiveness and interest.

At the close of the interview, employers will give you a chance to ask questions. Use this opportunity to show interest in the company. Prior research you did on the company will allow you to ask appropriate questions such as, "In what direction do you think the company is heading during the next five to ten years?" or "What recent innovations have affected the electronics department here?" Avoid questions about salary, vacation time, sick days, etc. These are important questions that should be asked only after being offered the job.

End the interview on a positive note. Look the interviewer in the eye, express your sincere interest in the job, and reinforce your strongest qualifications for the position. Express thanks for the interviewer's time and attention, and find out when a decision will be made and how you will be contacted. Ask the interviewer for a business card, and use it for writing your follow-up letter. You should also consider having a briefly prepared closing statement that makes you a memorable candidate in the eyes of the interviewer. One of our students ended an interview in this way: "I may not have the highest grades among the other candidates you interview, but you won't find a candidate who will work harder than I. Throughout college, I had to work in order to support a family and couldn't devote as much time to my studies as some of my other classmates. What I mean to say is that you may find a better student, but you won't find a better worker."

Follow Up After Your Interview

After the interview, you may think you have finished selling yourself to an employer. In fact, many applicants share this same belief. Unfortunately, you might be overlooking a very important opportunity to follow up on all the prior work you have done. The "thanks-for-the-interview" letter may be the most important one you ever write; yet fewer than 10 percent of applicants send one. The follow-up letter says a lot about you. It says, "I care"; "I am responsible"; "I'm better qualified than the other applicants for these specific reasons." It also says, "I appreciate the time you spent with me, and I would like to work for your company."

This follow-up or thanks-for-the-interview letter provides another contact with the employer. It sets you apart from the countless applicants who don't take the time or initiative to write one. This extra effort on your part will certainly affect your standing in the eyes of the employer.

Immediately after the interview, write a thank-you letter. "The follow-up is the way to turn interviews into jobs," says Kate Wendelton (1998) in her article, "Following Up After a Job Interview: The *Only* Job Hunting Technique" (p. 1). The follow-up should take place within twenty-four hours of the interview.

FOLLOW-UP LETTER FORMAT

Several types of follow-up letters can be used. Some will simply thank the employer for the interview; others will express acceptance or rejection of a job offer. The content of these short letters should state your appreciation, explain what you liked about the position, and sound enthusiastic about working for the firm. See a suggested format for follow-up letters in figure 15.6.

These brief, to-the-point letters need not fill the page, but they should let the employer know you are grateful, regardless of the outcome of the interview. Notice in the samples (figure 15.7) how the applicants express their thanks and interest in just a few short words. Finally, the follow-up letter provides another contact with your potential employer. Each contact you make offers an opportunity to present your skills and should bring you closer to the job you are seeking.

Follow-up Letter Format

Street Address City, State, Zip Date (Phone optional)	HEADING
Mr./Ms. Name, Title Company Name Street Address City, State, Zip	INSIDE ADDRESS
Dear Mr./Ms. Name:	SALUTATION/ GREETING
Thank you for . . .	
I really liked your . . .	BODY
My training in . . .	
Sincerely,	COMPLIMENTARY CLOSE
Stew Dent	SIGNATURE
Stew Dent	TYPED NAME

FIGURE 15.6 ■ Follow-up Letter Format

SAMPLE FOLLOW-UP LETTERS

Sample Follow-up Letters   Sample # 1

387 Apple Lane
Newtown, Illinois 61433
April 9, 2009

Mr. Bob Marks
Director of Personnel
ABC Travel, Incorporated
3287 Westgate Avenue
Chicago, Illinois 60619

Dear Mr. Marks:

It was a pleasure to meet you yesterday and discuss with you my application for the position of Travel Agent with ABC Travel, Incorporated. I especially appreciated the opportunity to meet the other agents.

With my diploma in Travel Marketing and my strong organizational skills, I believe I would be an asset to your firm.

I appreciate your consideration and look forward to hearing from you.

Sincerely,

Jo Morgan

FIGURE 15.7 ■ Three Sample Follow-up Letters

(Continued)

Sample Follow-up Letters   Sample # 2

903 Palm Drive
Miami, Florida 23984
June 28, 2009

Ms. Sandra Melendez
Director of Employment
Ace Corporation
11274 Orange Grove Road
Fort Lauderdale, Florida 24321

Dear Ms. Melendez:

Thank you for offering me the position of material handling technician at the Ace
Corporation. I was impressed with the organization of your department and its
commitment to quality robotic repair.

While my schedule at school does not permit me to accept the position at this time, I
look forward to a future opportunity.

As you suggested, I will contact you when I finish my robotics training. If another
position should occur that you think would fit my schedule before completion of my
training, please feel free to contact me at (305) 783-9730.

Sincerely,

Carroll Rowe

Sample Follow-up Letters   Sample # 3

3207 Birch Drive
Jefferson, WI 53549
April 9, 2009

Ms. Roberta Long
Director of Personnel
XYZ Manufacturing Company
1800 Main Street
West Allis, WI 53029

Dear Ms. Long:

It was a pleasure to meet you yesterday and discuss with you my application for the
position of fabricator with your company. I especially appreciated the opportunity to
meet the supervisor and other fabricators.

Although you said that you preferred to hire someone with more experience, I hope
that you will consider my application in the future as I gain more familiarity with your
processes and equipment.

I appreciate your consideration and look forward to hearing from you.

Sincerely,

Chris Morgan

FIGURE 15.7 ■ Three
Sample Follow-up
Letters (*Continued*)

Review Your Interview

After your interview, you will probably think of ways you could have been more effective. However, remember that you are very often your own harshest critic. No applicant ever has a perfect interview. What is important though is that you learn to improve your interviewing skills with each interview experience you have. You also need to have a balanced perspective of your performance, acknowledging both strengths and weaknesses.

Take some time after you leave the interview to jot down what you feel good about, and be very specific. For example, you might write that you used five PAR stories to highlight your skills. You also had a carefully prepared closing statement that you shared with the interviewer. Then take stock of what you could have handled better. Perhaps the interviewer asked for your opinion about union participation. Although you knew the workers at this company are unionized, you had never given any thought to being a union member. Consequently, you stumbled for words and seemed hesitant about how to respond. This question took you by surprise. You realize this question may come up again and that you need to think about an honest and thoughtful reply.

If you feel you could use some professional support to improve your interviewing skills, consider paying a visit to your college career center or placement office. These resources give you the opportunity to speak to a staff member who can address questions and concerns you have about your performance. Generally, community colleges offer plenty of opportunities for students to polish their interview skills with one-on-one counseling and interview workshops, both of which are typically free.

Phone Interviews

In today's busy business world, some employers are screening candidates with phone interviews. You may think that being interviewed on the phone is easier than being interviewed in person. After all, you don't have to dress up or travel to an unfamiliar location, right? However, phone interviews pose some challenges of their own that you need to take into consideration. Phone interviews can be every bit as important to landing a job as face-to-face interviews. "Career-management experts estimate that more than 80% of job interviews are won or lost during the first five minutes of conversation. This includes telephone screening interviews" (Anderson, 2007, p. 1). Following are some tips to keep in mind in anticipation of a phone interview.

1. **Select an appropriate voice mail message.** Remember that an employer may contact you when you are not available. Consequently, you need to have a message that sounds professional on your home phone or cell phone. A message that you leave for friends and family may not be suitable for a prospective employer.

2. **Call back.** If you miss an employer's call and retrieve your phone messages later in the day, return the call immediately, even if you call after

business hours. Leave a message, indicating the time you called, and offer another convenient time you can be reached. Responding promptly indicates that you are serious about the position.

3. **Choose the right environment.** When you do finally connect with the employer, make sure that you have access to quiet surroundings. If you are at home, let family members or roommates know ahead of time that you are expecting an important call and need some privacy. Move to a spot where you will not be distracted or interrupted. If you receive a call on your cell phone away from home, make the same effort to find some space free from distraction. If you take the call while you are in your car, don't continue the conversation while you are driving. Pull over!

4. **Stay focused and listen.** Sometimes it takes extra effort to be attentive when you are on the phone. In part, this difficulty occurs because you do not have the advantage of seeing your receiver's body language. When an employer calls, give him or her your complete attention and listen carefully to the questions you are being asked. If you don't understand something the employer says, use paraphrases or clarifying questions to ensure understanding.

5. **Practice for the interview.** Just like you practice for face-to-face interviews, do the same for telephone interviews. Have a friend or family member call you with a list of sample interview questions you have provided. Your mock interviewers can even throw in some questions of their own to give you practice in responding on the spot.

6. **Pay attention to both speech and body language.** Speak slowly, clearly, and distinctly when answering an employer's questions. Also, don't be afraid to request a few moments to think about your reply if you need some extra time. Make sure you don't eat, drink, smoke, or chew gum while you are speaking. Even though the employer cannot see you, let your body language communicate strength and poise. Sit or even stand tall and avoid nervous mannerisms. Nonverbal behavior that signals self-assurance will make you feel more confident and at ease.

7. **End on a positive note.** When the employer indicates that the interview is over, be sure to thank him or her for the opportunity to discuss your qualifications. Make sure you also ask when you might receive notification about the company's hiring decision.

8. **Send thanks.** Finally, send a thank-you letter just as you would for a "live" interview. Taking this additional step can even be the deciding factor for who gets the job.

As you can see, preparing for an employment interview is a challenging task that takes lots of careful thought. You need to plan responses for the questions you are likely to be asked, whether those questions are traditional, behavior-based, or illegal. Remember too that the first impression you make can be the deciding factor in being offered a job. In addition, don't forget the follow-up after the interview. Sending a word of thanks shows your appreciation and keeps your name fresh in the employer's mind.

Review Questions

1. Describe the importance of interviewing in today's business world.

2. List three of the most common mistakes made during an interview.

3. Name the four major steps to prepare for an interview.

4. Give three examples each of the three main types of interview questions.

5. Write a PAR story for each of the following two questions:

   Describe a time when you had to go more than halfway to deal with a co-worker in a difficult situation.

Tell me about a time when you had to make an important decision with limited facts.

6. Describe how you would respond to two of the illegal questions mentioned in this chapter.

7. List three guidelines to help you participate effectively in the interview.

8. Describe the essential information to be included in an effective follow-up letter.

Key Terms and Concepts

Behavior-Based Question   299

Closing Statement   305

Complimentary Close   307

Greeting   307

Heading   307

Illegal Questions   301

Inside Address   307

Interview   295

Signature   307

Web Activities

- How to Respond—Ronald L. Krannich, Ph.D., offers specific advice on How to Respond to 38 Illegal, Sensitive, and Stupid Interview Questions at http://www.washing tonpost.com/wp-dyn/articles/A8963-2003Apr11.html.

- Interview Questions—This wonderful site discusses the type of question, specific job questions, behavioral interview questions, illegal questions, disability questions, sample interview questions, and much more. It's a must see!

  http://images.google.com/imgres?imgurl=http://www.jobinterviewquestions.org/questions/images/illegal-uestions.jpg&imgrefurl=http://www.jobinterviewquestions.org/questions/interview-questions.asp&h=69&w=100&sz= 12&hl=en&start=20&tbnid=twqwwACKw3zFPM:&tbnh=57& tbnw=82&prev=/images%3Fq%3Dillegal%2Bquestions%26gbv%3D2%26svnum%3D10%26hl%3Den%26sa%3DG

- Twelve Job Interview Mistakes—A clever presentation of the most common mistakes applicants can make in job interviews. You don't want to be unprepared or too rehearsed, or oversharing or be labeled an HR stalker.

  http://images.businessweek.com/ss/06/08/hiring_mistakes/index_01.htm

- Behavior-Based Questions—Check out the advice offered for how to behave in behavior-based interviews at the following three sites:

  http://www.jobweb.com/Resources/Library/Interviews/How_to_Behave_in_a_59_01.htm

  http://www.baseops.net/transition/behavior.html

  http://jobsearch.about.com/cs/interviews/a/behavioral.htm

- Illegal Questions—Discover what others have to say about illegal interview questions by checking out the following sites:

  http://jobsearch.about.com/od/interviewsnetworking/a/illegalinterv.htm

  http://www.usatoday.com/careers/resources/interviewillegal.htm

  http://www.jobweb.com/Resources/Library/Interviews/Handling_Illegal_46_01.htm

Assignments

ASSIGNMENT 15.1: EMPLOYMENT INTERVIEW ASSIGNMENT

You will be preparing for mock interviews in which you will be both an interviewer and an applicant. You will be paired with another student to role-play these interviews. During one interview, you will be the interviewer and ask twenty questions of another student. Note his or her answers, and provide feedback on his or her Interview Report Form.

During the second interview, you will be the applicant responding to interview questions by sharing your qualifications and making a closing statement. Your goal is to present your qualifications to the interviewer in such a clear fashion that the interviewer can list all five of your qualifications on your Interview Report Form.

To prepare for these interviews, you will complete the Interviewer's Question Sheet and the Applicant's Response Sheet that follow. When these are completed, you will be assigned a partner and conduct two mock interviews. After both interviews are finished, complete the Interview Report Forms and discuss the information on these with one another.

Interviewer's Question Sheet

Use the list of frequently asked interview questions and behavior-based questions in your text, or use any of the following websites to select a total of twenty (20) interview questions that you will ask during your mock interview. Five (5) questions should be **behavior-based interview questions,** two (2) questions should be **illegal questions,** and the other questions may be your choice. On the **Interviewer's Question Sheet** list the interview questions that you will ask when you conduct an interview with another student. During the interview, jot down notes on the answers you receive. These notes will help you complete the **Interview Report Form.**

For more questions check out the following websites:

http://dept.fvtc.edu/ses/Documents/
InterviewQues.htm

http://www.quintcareers.com/interview_
question_database/

http://www.msj.edu/career/manual/bbi.htm

http://little.nhlink.net/nhlink/employme/
frequent.htm

Applicant's Response Sheet

Prepare to answer interview questions by deciding which qualifications you wish to emphasize in the interview. Be specific about the qualification you are presenting to the interviewer. Support your claims by sharing a **PAR story** that discusses the **problem** you faced, the **action** that you took, and the **results** that you achieved. Identify at least five specific qualifications and prepare **five PAR stories** to support your claims. Also, prepare a short **closing statement** to share with the interviewer at the end of your meeting. In a sentence or two, summarize why you are the best candidate for this position, why you merit further consideration, or why you should be hired for this opening. Try to make a positive impression and be a memorable applicant.

When you have completed both interviews and have discussed the information recorded on the interview report forms, turn in these forms and your plan sheets to your instructor.

Interviewer's Question Sheet for Assignment #15.1

Name _____

On the lines that follow, list the questions that you will ask when you conduct an interview with another student. Include at least five behavior-based interview questions and two illegal questions. The other questions may be whatever type question you think is most appropriate. During the interview, jot down notes for the answers you receive. These notes will help you complete the Interview Report Form.

1. _____?
2. _____?
3. _____?
4. _____?
5. _____?
6. _____?
7. _____?
8. _____?
9. _____?
10. _____?
11. _____?

12. _____?
13. _____?
14. _____?
15. _____?
16. _____?
17. _____?
18. _____?
19. _____?
20. _____?

Include five behavior-based questions and two illegal questions.

Applicant's Response Sheet for Assignment 15.1

Name _____

Note the five dominant qualifications that you intend to emphasize in your responses to the interviewer's questions. Add **PAR stories,** including specific **problem, action,** and **results** that provide examples to support each qualification.

1. _____ (PAR Story)

2. _____ (PAR Story)

3. _____ (PAR Story)

4. _____ (PAR Story)

5. _____ (PAR Story)

Write your short closing statement that you will use at the end of your interview.

Interview Report Form for Assignment 15.1

Applicant _____ Interviewer _____

List two things that you liked about your applicant's interviewing style.

1.

2.

List two changes that would improve your applicant's interviewing style.

1.

2.

Note the five dominant qualifications that were supported by PAR stories in your applicant's responses to your questions.

1.

2.

3.

4.

5.

Comment on how well you thought your applicant responded to the illegal questions in the interview.

Comment on how well you thought your applicant presented a closing statement in the interview.

How well did this candidate use the PAR story techniques of behavior-based interviewing?

ASSIGNMENT 15.2: FOLLOW-UP LETTER ASSIGNMENT

Write a letter that would be appropriate to send to a prospective employer after a job interview. Include the following elements:

A thank-you-for-the-interview message

Some positive comment about the interview, the company, or the people

A reminder of a strong qualification of yours

A restatement of your interest in the company

ASSIGNMENT 15.3: CASE STUDY: JOBHUNTERSBIBLE.COM

Go to Richard Bolles' website: www.jobhuntersbible .com; select any article from the Article Archive. Read the article, prepare a typed summary of its key points, and present your summary to the class.

References

Anderson, H. (2007). Phone interview tips for savvy candidates. *Career Journal.com The Wall Street Journal*. Retrieved September 14, 2007, from http://www.careerjournal.com/jobhunting/interviewing/19990310-anderson.html

Bolles, D. (1996). Two-minute crash course on interviews. *Jobhuntersbible.com*. Retrieved September 6, 2002, from http://www.jobhuntersbible.com/library/hunters/crashcourse.shtml.

Brown-Glaser, C. & Steinberg-Smalley, B. (1993, August). Four minutes that get you hired. *Reader's Digest*, 129–132.

Consumeraffairs.com. (2008, August 15). Proliferation of online job sites overwhelms job seekers. Retrieved November 7, 2008, from http://www.consumeraffairs.com/new04/2008/08/job_search_internet.html

Doyle, A. (2008). Top 10 interview blunders. Retrieved February 10, 2008, from http://jobsearch.about.com/od/interviewsnetworking/a/interviewblund.htm

Employment Resource Center. (n.d.). The 25 worst job interview mistakes. Retrieved November 7, 2008, from http://www.jobs.fresnocitycollege.edu/Cmx_Content.aspx?cpId=38

First impressions on job interviews. (2002, July 1). Career Services Office, Fort Hays State University. Retrieved August 23, 2007, from www.fhsu.edu/career/readyresourcespdf/Firstimpressionsonjobinterviews.pdf

Goyer, B. (1999, November). What are employers looking for? *The Job Market*. Retrieved August 13, 2002, from http://www.mariononline.com/columnists/goyer/1999/nov99.htm

Illegal interview questions. (2001, January 29). *USA Today*. Retrieved August 26, 2001, from http://www.usatoday.com/careers/resources/interviewillegal.htm

Job Service form. *Make the most of a job interview*.

Kohler Company. (2007). How we interview. *Kohler careers*. Retrieved August 16, 2007, from http://www.kohler.jobs/about/howweinterview.html

Lommel, J. M. (2003). Job hunting advice to the brand new graduate. Retrieved August 16, 2007, from http://www.newwork.com/Pages/Networking/2003/Advice%20to%20grads.html

Saint Louis University School of Law. (n.d.). Reasons for rejection. Retrieved September 11, 2002, from http://law.slu.edu/careersvcs/student/rejection.html

Spherion Atlantic Enterprises, LLC. (2008). Maximum impact & credibility with "PAR" stories. Retrieved May 9, 2008, from http://www.spherion.com/careers/resources/interviewing/PAR.jsp

Thomas Publishing Company. (2008). ThomasNet. Retrieved November 7, 2008, from http://www.thomasnet.com/

University of Maryland Career Center at http://www.careercenter.umd.edu/STUDENT/STEP5/QUESTION.htm

Wendelton, K. (1998). Following up after a job interview: The *only* job hunting technique. Retrieved August 13, 2002, from http://www.fiveoclockclub.com/careerCoach/10followingUp.htm

Index